GREAT THEATRE

The American Congress in the 1990s

The 104th Congress, the first in four decades to be Republican-controlled, may prove to have ushered in an era of party dominance by congressional Republicans or to be a transitory aberration. Either way, the 104th is a watershed in congressional history. Using the theatre metaphor to characterize the actions of Congress and to help make the institution more understandable, congressional life and behavior are dissected and placed in the broader context of changes in Congress in the 1990s. The contributors evaluate the way members of Congress play to the media and the larger audience, the electorate; analyze leadership roles in a cast of 535 "leading players"; evaluate the committee systems as "little theatre"; and analyze relations among the various branches of government. Coeditors Herbert Weisberg and Samuel Patterson conclude the unique presentation by reminding us that in Congress, "the play's the thing."

GREAT THEATRE

The American Congress in the 1990s

EDITED BY

HERBERT F. WEISBERG
Ohio State University
SAMUEL C. PATTERSON
Ohio State University

CAMBRIDGE
UNIVERSITY PRESS

PUBLISHED BY THE PRESS SYNDICATE OF THE UNIVERSITY OF CAMBRIDGE
The Pitt Building, Trumpington Street, Cambridge CB2 1RP, United Kingdom

CAMBRIDGE UNIVERSITY PRESS
The Edinburgh Building, Cambridge CB2 2RU, United Kingdom
40 West 20th Street, New York, NY 10011-4211, USA
10 Stamford Road, Oakleigh, Melbourne 3166, Australia

First published 1998

Printed in the United States of America

Typeset in Sabon

Library of Congress Cataloging-in-Publication Data
Great theatre : the American Congress in the 1990s / edited by Herbert
F. Weisberg, Samuel C. Patterson.
p.   cm.
Includes bibliographical references and index.
ISBN 0-521-58518-X (hb). – ISBN 0-521-58525-2 (pb)
1. United States. Congress.   2. United States – Politics and
government – 1993–   I. Weisberg, Herbert F.   II. Patterson, Samuel
Charles, 1931–   .
JK1021.G74   1998
328.73'072 – dc21   97–36637
CIP

*A catalog record for this book is available from
the British Library*

ISBN 0 521 58518 X hardback
ISBN 0 521 58525 2 paperback

Congress is the great commanding theatre of
this nation. . . .
 —President Thomas Jefferson

Congress is the highest theater that anyone plays in upon
this earth today.
 —Speaker Sam Rayburn (D-TX)

Contents

Contents

Figures and Tables

Figures and Tables

Figures and Tables

Preface

This book has three major objectives. First and foremost, we intend it as a report on the 104th Congress, the first in forty years to be controlled by the Republican party. Like many of our students, colleagues, and fellow citizens, we have marveled at the historic congressional party change that transpired with the 1994 midterm election. We have sought to account for that change and assay its consequences for the present Congress and for the future. Confirmed by the 1996 congressional elections, the Republican majority and its House and Senate leaders consolidated their dominion, hoping to enjoy an era of congressional hegemony akin to that enjoyed by the Democratic Party for four post–World War II decades.

Congress is the keystone of the American democratic system. In the United States, the legislature truly makes the laws of the land. It is not a rubber stamp for the executive branch. Congress actually is remarkably representative of the American people. It displays their diversity, their strengths and weaknesses, their foibles and indiscretions, and their intelligence and decency. Understanding Congress is an important undertaking in the classrooms, among intellectuals, and within the American citizenry. Where Congress needs to be reformed, effective institutional change requires careful knowledge about how things now work. Knowledge about Congress helps to dispel excessive, myopic, ignorant, and vitriolic negativism about the congressional institution, its members, and its politics.

Our second objective is to set the 104th Congress, meeting in 1995–6, within the perspective of change in Congress in the 1990s more generally. Some of the changes in the 104th Congress had their beginnings in earlier developments. We aim to inspire better appreciation of the processes of political change themselves by thinking of the Congress we are studying as part of a web of change going back (almost immediately) to the 1970s and extending forward to the Congress meeting in Washington today. In thinking about congressional change, you would best conclude that such a democratic body transforms itself continuously, responding to changes in the environment, frequent elections, alteration of political forces, the impact of major world events, and the shift of generations that the passage of time inevitably engenders.

Third, our intention is to show that Congress can readily be understood as theatre. Everybody knows how scripts are written, how sets are built, and how roles are played by actors on the stage. As we argue in various ways, Congress is great theatre and the theatre metaphor applies cogently, providing a perspective for thinking about the institution and how it works. Thinking of Congress as theatre has helped us as authors and, we think, will help readers to make better sense of Congress. But we stress that the theatre metaphor is merely a perspective, a way of looking at things, and we have tried diligently not to overwork it or to claim for it exalted theoretical guidance.

We have accumulated many debts of gratitude in editing this book. Not the least of these is to each other; we have enjoyed our collaboration. Moreover, we owe considerable appreciation and respect to our colleagues in the Ohio State University Department of Political Science, who are the authors of most of the book's chapters. Even profounder thanks go to colleagues from other universities who joined our project – Kenny Whitby, University of South Carolina; Frank Gilliam, University of California at Los Angeles (UCLA); Paul Herrnson, University of Maryland; David King, Harvard University; Barbara Sinclair, UCLA; and Shelly Goldman, University of Massachusetts. Also, we appreciate the insightful and helpful review of our manuscript provided by James Pfiffner, George Mason University, Andy Tomlinson and April Kelly for their fine work in helping prepare this manuscript, and of course, we are indebted to Alex Holzman, Cambridge University Press, for encouraging us along the way and for shepherding this project through to completion.

More generally, we would like to use this opportunity to acknowledge long-standing intellectual and scholarly debts. We are thinking of our special mentors over the years gone by – Warren E. Miller and Donald E. Stokes, for Herb Weisberg, and Ralph K. Huitt and Charles O. Jones, for Pat Patterson. Also, we are thinking of our longtime colleague and friend, John Kessel. Finally, we appreciate the support and consideration of Judy Weisberg and Sue Patterson.

And now, on with the show!

Contributors

Lawrence Baum is Professor of Political Science at The Ohio State University. One of his research interests is relationships between courts and other public policy makers. He is the author of *The Puzzle of Judicial Behavior*, *The Supreme Court*, and *American Courts*.

Barry C. Burden is a Ph.D. candidate in political science at The Ohio State University. His research has appeared in the *American Journal of Political Science* and the *American Political Science Review*. He is currently co-authoring a book manuscript with David C. Kimball on split-ticket voting in American elections.

Aage R. Clausen is Professor Emeritus of Political Science at The Ohio State University. He is the author of *How Congressmen Decide*. His studies of Congress have focused on floor voting within a conceptual framework in which policy decisions are the foci of the analysis. Work in progress assays the scope and depth of the partisan influence in roll-call voting in the House and Senate.

Franklin D. Gilliam, Jr. is Associate Director of the Center for American Politics and Public Policy and Associate Professor of Political Science at the University of California, Los Angeles. His research focuses on the nexus between race and politics, including African-American political empowerment, the impact of race on congressional behavior, and the effect of television news on racial attitudes. His research has appeared in such journals as the *American Political Science Review*, *American Journal of Political Science*, and *Journal of Politics*.

Sheldon Goldman is Professor of Political Science at the University of Massachusetts at Amherst. He is the author of *Picking Federal Judges: Lower Court Selection from Roosevelt through Reagan* and numerous other books and articles dealing with constitutional law and judicial politics.

Tim Groseclose is Assistant Professor of Political Science at The Ohio State University. He has had faculty appointments at Harvard University, Massachusetts Institute of Technology, Carnegie Mellon University, and George Mason University. He has published articles on the U.S. Congress and mathematical models of politics in such journals as the *American Political Science Review, American Journal of Political Science, Journal of Politics,* and *Economic Inquiry.*

Lori Hausegger is a Ph.D. candidate in political science at The Ohio State University. Her research interests include political litigation and comparative judicial behavior; those interests are reflected in her dissertation project on the impact of interest groups on women's rights policies of the U.S. and Canadian supreme courts.

Paul S. Herrnson is Professor of Government and Politics at the University of Maryland, College Park. He is the author of *Congressional Elections: Campaigning at Home and in Washington* and *Party Campaigning in the 1980s* and numerous articles on Congress, campaign finance, political parties, and elections. He is co-editor of several volumes, including *The Interest Group Connection: Electioneering, Lobbying, and Policy Making in Washington* and *After the Revolution: PACs and Lobbies in the Republican Congress* (forthcoming).

David C. Kimball received his Ph.D. in political science from The Ohio State University in 1997 and will be an Assistant Professor of Political Science at Southern Illinois University in the fall of 1998. His research interests include American electoral politics, public opinion, representation in Congress, and interest group lobbying. He has published articles on split-ticket voting and public support for Congress.

David C. King is Associate Professor of Public Policy at Harvard University's JFK School of Government, where he teaches about legislatures, interest groups, and political strategy. He is the author of *Turf Wars: How Congressional Committees Claim Jurisdiction* and co-editor (with Joseph Nye and Philip Zelikow) of *Why People Don't Trust Government.*

Dean Lacy is Assistant Professor of Political Science at The Ohio State University, where he specializes in campaigns and elections, voting behavior, and democratic institutions. His research has appeared in the *American Journal of Political Science, Journal of Theoretical Politics, Public Choice,* and other journals. He is currently completing a project on nonseparable preferences in public opinion and elections.

Samuel C. Patterson is Professor of Political Science at The Ohio State University. His research has focused on legislative and parliamentary politics. He has been a Guggenheim Fellow, a Fellow at the Center for Advanced Study in the Behavioral Sciences, and a Fulbright Distinguished Lecturer at the University of Bologna, Italy. He was editor of the *American Journal of Political Science, Legislative Studies Quarterly,* and the *American Political Science Review.* He has written and edited several books, including most recently *Parliaments in the Modern World: Changing Institutions.*

Randall B. Ripley is Professor of Political Science and Dean of the College of Social and Behavioral Sciences at The Ohio State University. He has written extensively on congressional behavior, bureaucratic behavior, and the making and implementation of national public policy, both domestic and foreign. He has recently co-edited (with James Lindsay) *Congress Resurgent: Foreign and Defense Policy on Capitol Hill* and *U.S. Foreign Policy after the Cold War.*

Barbara Sinclair is Marvin Hoffenberg Professor of American Politics at the University of California, Los Angeles. She has written several books on the U.S. Congress, including most recently *Legislators, Leaders and Lawmaking: The U.S. House of Representatives in the Post-Reform Era* and *Unorthodox Lawmaking: New Legislative Processes in the U.S. Congress.*

Elliot E. Slotnick is Associate Dean of the Graduate School and Associate Professor of Political Science at The Ohio State University. He is the editor of *Judicial Politics,* co-editor of *Readings in American Government and Politics,* and co-author of *Television News and the Supreme Court: All the News That's Fit to Air?* (forthcoming). He has published numerous articles in the area of judicial politics generally and, in particular, on federal judicial selection processes.

Herbert F. Weisberg is Professor of Political Science at The Ohio State University. He enjoys politics, theatre, metaphors, and books of quotations. His research interests include voting behavior, Congress, and research methods. He has been co-editor of the *American Journal of*

Political Science, edited *Democracy's Feast* on the 1992 presidential election, and is co-editing (with Eric Heberlig and Lisa Campoli) a book on *Classics in Congressional Politics* (forthcoming).

Kenny J. Whitby is Associate Professor of Political Science at the University of South Carolina. His research focuses on the politics of race, and he has written research articles on the impact of race on political attitudes, racial representation, and the responsiveness of members of Congress to African-Americans' interests. He is the author of *The Color of Representation: Congressional Behavior and Black Interests*.

Introduction

I

Theatre in the Round: Congress in Action

HERBERT F. WEISBERG AND SAMUEL C. PATTERSON

From across the nation come the representatives of the people – from cities great and small, from towns and hamlets, a few from farms – to gather in the halls of the U.S. Congress. In the House of Representatives, the sergeant at arms installs the mace, a symbol of authority, and the Speaker of the House strikes the gavel to bring the House to order. The chaplain offers the morning prayer, the House approves the journal of the previous day's business, and a member solemnly delivers the Pledge of Allegiance. In the Senate, in a starker, simpler ceremony, the president pro tempore normally calls the assembly to order. On extraordinary occasions, the Senate may be convened by the vice president of the United States. The chaplain prays, the majority leader is recognized to announce the day's legislative business, and then the leader calls for "morning business" so that senators can make prepared remarks on any subject. Thus, the congressional drama begins.

Congress as theatre? That is not how either the public or political scientists usually think of it. Yet the idea of Congress as theatre resonates with people very naturally. Citizens' political socialization may embrace the drama of presidential campaigns more fully than the theatre of congressional politics (Starobin 1996). Nevertheless, both inside and outside the beltway around Washington, D.C., Congress provides plenty of drama for aficionados and the mass audience alike. The media, especially television, more often than not convey negatives about Congress – spawning "a kind of naive cynicism about the theatre – the ancient and necessary conceits – of politics." As with the quadrennial presidential contest, media critics of Congress "trained to watch the drama focus obsessively on the backstage ropes and pulleys, . . . and seem to think they have discovered a radically new practice of politics in the age of video, but 'twas ever thus" (Starobin 1996: 2107).

Congress certainly was theatre on January 4, 1995. After forty years of Democratic control, in the 1994 midterm election the Republicans

3

Great Theatre

had regained power in the House of Representatives. Republican leaders had promised to push through a series of rules changes on the first day of the new, 104th Congress. To forestall Democratic obstruction, the Republican leadership scripted its actions for the first day of the Congress and carefully rehearsed a couple of days in advance. Then, on January 4, with the full attention of the media, the Republicans showed that they were able to change House rules in a single day, in vivid contrast with the deadlock that had characterized much of the Democratic 103rd Congress. This made great theatre, particularly when Newt Gingrich (R-GA) became Speaker and adopted a more public and combative persona than that of the previous Speaker, Democrat Tom Foley (WA). Speaker Gingrich, it is said, "wanted to see guerrilla theatre on the floor" (Duncan and Lawrence 1995: v).[1]

However, Congress was theatre long before Newt Gingrich took the Speaker's gavel in his hand. Congress has been theatre even before its proceedings began to be televised by C-SPAN. Indeed, Congress was theatre long before the invention of modern electronic media. Moments of drama, high and low, define the historical development of the institution. For its first meeting, held in temporary quarters in New York City, great impatience surrounded the House of Representatives as members waited for enough of their colleagues to arrive in the city to comprise a quorum sufficient to conduct the first business of the new nation. The House first officially convened in Federal Hall on Wednesday, April 1, 1789, when, at last, Representative Thomas Scott arrived from western Pennsylvania, completing the quorum. After much waiting and suspense, the House elected its first Speaker, Frederick A. C. Muhlenberg of Pennsylvania. On the evening of April 5, Richard Henry Lee of Virginia reached New York, completing the quorum in the U.S. Senate. Shortly thereafter, Speaker Muhlenberg led House members into the Senate chamber to count the electoral votes that made George Washington the first president of the United States.

Congress was theatre back when the American public followed congressional debates in the mid-nineteenth century, which pitted great orators like Henry Clay, John C. Calhoun, and Daniel Webster against one another. Perhaps the most dramatic moments before the Civil War came as Congress, spurred by Clay's leadership, adopted the provisions of the Compromise of 1850 that permitted California to enter the federal union free of the taint of slavery. After the midpoint of the nineteenth

---

1 Congress was also theatre when the House met in early January 1997 to reelect Newt Gingrich as Speaker (after he had admitted to ethics violations) and again later that month to reprimand him, episodes that will be described in detail in Chapter 12.

4

century, the defining moment of congressional drama took place the day the Senate voted on the impeachment of President Andrew Johnson. On May 16, 1868, Senator Edmund G. Ross of Kansas cast the vote preventing adoption of the resolution that would have deposed the president. Ross himself described the scene:

The galleries were packed. Tickets of admission were at an enormous premium. The House had adjourned and all of its members were in the Senate chamber. Every chair on the Senate floor was filled with a Senator, a Cabinet Officer, a member of the President's counsel or a member of the House. (quoted in Kennedy 1956: 137).

Dramatic congressional moments have produced the great theatre of more recent memory. On December 8, 1941, the day after the infamous surprise attack by Japanese air and naval forces on the American naval base at Pearl Harbor, Hawaii, members of Congress assembled to adopt a declaration of war against Japan. One House member, Jeannette Rankin of Montana, provided the lone vote against war; she had also voted against a declaration of war against Germany in 1917. On August 30, 1957, Senator Strom Thurmond of South Carolina, then a Democrat, provided yet another dramatic moment in the Senate's history when he single-handedly filibustered in the Senate for a record 24 hours, 27 minutes, to try to kill a civil rights bill.

In 1974, the Watergate hearings and the impeachment proceedings against President Richard M. Nixon captivated Americans watching their television screens. The Senate Select Committee on Presidential Campaign Activities, chaired by Sam J. Ervin (D-NC), began the Watergate hearings in May 1973, investigating a presidential cover-up of a burglary of the Democratic Party campaign offices in the Watergate Building in Washington, D.C. The televised Watergate hearings provided Congress with the highest approval ratings it had received in a long time. On July 30, 1974, the House Judiciary Committee voted articles of impeachment against President Nixon, and on August 8, Nixon resigned.

The description of Congress as theatre goes far back in the history of the United States – to 1808, when President Thomas Jefferson wrote to William Wirt that "Congress is the great commanding theatre of this nation, and the threshold to whatever department of office a man is qualified to enter" (Lipscomb and Bergh 1903: 423–4). Wirt had just gained fame the previous year as prosecutor in the treason trial of Aaron Burr, and Jefferson was recommending to Wirt that if he wanted a political career, he should run for a seat in Congress. Instead, Wirt served as attorney general under Presidents James Monroe and John Quincy Adams and then, in 1832, ran against Andrew Jackson as the presidential candidate of the Antimasonic Party. But when he corresponded with

5

his friend and political supporter in 1808, Jefferson recognized that Congress was to be the theatre of democracy, the stage on which policy and political debates are played out before the public.

We argue in this chapter that viewing Congress as theatre provides a useful perspective on what happens there that extends beyond the usual approaches to understanding. Congress is theatre because it plays to an audience, because it seeks to provide enlightenment just as theatre does, and because of the symbolic meaning of what happens on its stage. Congress is theatre in many respects, and viewing the institution in this way leads to insights that would otherwise be missed.

THE THEATRE METAPHOR

In arguing that Congress may be viewed as theatre, it is useful to make sure that there are some shared understandings of the nature of theatre. This is not a body of knowledge that is generally studied by political scientists in their professional lives, though we would expect and hope that most readers have more than a passing acquaintance with theatre in their nonprofessional lives. Therefore, this section will describe the history of theatre and its relationship to politics generally, as well as how we see this metaphor as useful in studying Congress more specifically.

The History of Theatre

According to Aristotle's treatise, *Poetics* (circa 330 B.C.), theatre can be traced back to the ceremonial worship of the god Dionysus in ancient Greece. The death and rebirth of the god were celebrated in a communal fashion, with a choral leader, Thespis (sixth century B.C.), assuming the part of the leading character in a choral hymn. Greek theatre was mainly religious, but it evolved over the following centuries, with comedy eventually supplanting tragedy as the main form and with individual actors becoming more important at the expense of the chorus.

Roman theatre picked up where Greek theatre left off. Some early Roman plays were meant to be read rather than acted, but by the second century A.D., Roman theatre emphasized spectacle. The Christian church attacked the Roman theatre as licentious, so the classical theatre came to an end with the fall of the Roman Empire in A.D. 476. Theatre developed anew in the medieval period in the religious milieu of the Catholic church, with mystery plays recounting Bible stories, miracle plays portraying the lives of saints, and morality plays imparting moral lessons. It was not until the Renaissance that nonreligious plays became prevalent.

Congress in Action

Politics has long been part of the theatre. Early Greek dramas, such as *Antigone*, were politically relevant. Shakespeare's histories used drama to retell stories from political history, whereas his tragedies often offered warnings about weaknesses of the state. Political intrigue provided the plot for many of the Shakespearean plays, most notably *Macbeth* and *Hamlet*.

This brief recital of the history of theatre is useful in reminding us that theatre serves several functions. It can provide religious ritual and moral teaching as well as offer entertainment and artistic expression. It can serve as an occasion for emotional catharsis while, at a more directly political level, it can bind a community together, provide direct political persuasion, and explore current political events and problems. On the other side of the coin, politicians have always recognized that they, too, must play to an audience.

Politics and Theatre

Of course, politics can be regarded as theatre whenever it is played out publicly. Congress does not provide the only theatrical stage in Washington. Presidential actions are theatre, too; even Supreme Court arguments and decisions can be regarded in this way. Campaign politics are also theatre. Politics can be viewed as theatre because it is readily interpreted symbolically and its symbolic aspects are theatre. However, it is also the case that politics is played out on a public stage in an attempt by politicians to elicit particular reactions from the watching populace, and that makes politics into theatre. Consider Samuel Johnson's (1747) statement about the theatre: "The stage but echoes back the public voice. The drama's laws the drama's patrons give, for we that live to please, must please to live." The concern with pleasing an audience to live is a common thread for politicians and actors. Politicians generally, and members of Congress in particular, are as concerned with the need to satisfy their audience as are actors, whether on- or off-Broadway.

The extent to which politics and theatre share common elements is visible in the definitions of each. Compare Harold Lasswell's classic definition of politics with Kenneth Burke's equally classic definition of the elements of drama. To Lasswell (1936), politics is a matter of "Who Gets What, When, How?" To Kenneth Burke (1945: xv), the elements of the "dramatistic pentad" are the act (what took place), the scene (the situation in which the act occurred), the agent (who performed the act), the agency (the means used to perform the act), and the purpose (why the act occurred). These two definitions are virtually identical. Both emphasize the actor (the "who" who serves as agent), the action (the "what" that constitutes that act) and the means (the "how" that pro-

7

vides the agency for the act). The main difference between these schemes is that Lasswell focused on the time frame – the when – whereas Burke emphasized the purpose – the why – and the setting of the scene, the "where." Yet we would expect that drama is also interested in the "when" (which Burke probably meant to include as part of the scene), while politics also must be concerned with the "why" and the "where"; thus, these two didactic schemes are even more similar than they may seem at first.

Congress as Theatre

The term *theatre* has several meanings. Theatre is variously defined as drama, the theatrical world, theatrical technique, a playhouse (the auditorium in which plays are performed), or, more generally, the place where events take place (e.g., a battlefield, as in the Pacific "theatre of operations" during World War II). At "an evening at a theatre," said longtime *New Republic* drama critic Stark Young, "the dramatist's share takes its place with the other elements that go to make up the art. Along with the acting, the decor and the directing goes the drama itself – all make up . . . the theatre art" (Young 1986: 12; see also Cameron and Hoffman 1969: 1–25).

Congress can be viewed as theatre in all of these senses. It is a playhouse in which drama occurs. Like the august chambers of the U.S. Supreme Court or the impressiveness of the White House's Oval Office, the halls of Congress confer all of the dignity, authority, and independence that their public architecture can muster (see Goodsell 1988). Such massive, ornate, imposing public spaces, which are the stages for political discourse and decision making, help to mold and shape the behavior of political actors and potentially influence the citizenry, who provide the audience for government (see Edelman 1964: 108–10). Accordingly, "people are taught to see legislative halls, courtrooms, executive mansions, and even administrative offices as symbols of government by the people and equality before the law" (Edelman 1995: 77). Again, Congress can be viewed in the light of the social, political, cultural, or economic conflicts that are taken there to be resolved. It is viewed, thereby, as the battlefield on which important events take place, as "combat on the legislative terrain" (Gross 1953: 151). But more than anything else, Congress is theatre in the sense of providing drama.

Of course, televised congressional hearings can provide drama. Congressional debates can also provide drama, though most watchers of Congress on television's C-SPAN probably also find them to be a good substitute for sleeping pills. Similarly, congressional debates in the 1800s

8

were well covered by newspapers, when many of the main issues of the day were fought out in floor debates.

But Congress is not only theatre when it holds hearings or debates. Congress is always theatre and, as Jefferson maintained, it is great theatre. Congress provides the arena in which political issues can be fought out, and it provides the battlefield on which the leading political personalities of the day can make their marks and attract public attention. Whether the politicians are Newt Gingrich, Bob Dole, Ted Kennedy, and John Kasich in the 104th Congress or James Madison, Samuel Adams, Frederick Muhlenberg, and Patrick Henry in the very first, Congress has always provided the theatre in which the great scenes of American politics are played out.

While we are arguing that Congress is always theatre, during the 104th Congress, it was certainly great theatre, and the participants understood that they were playing to an audience. The Republicans gained control of the House largely through the strategizing of their new leader, Newt Gingrich. From the time he was first elected to the House in 1978, Gingrich consciously took steps to make the Republicans fight to become the majority party. Having succeeded, he wanted his majority to enact a series of laws that would change the course of government policy and would lead to a new conservative era in the United States. This required showing the nation that the new Republican majority in the House could make a difference, but that it had to be accompanied by a Republican president in order for its program to triumph. Thus, winning control of Congress was only to be the first step of gaining conservative ascendancy. Accomplishing this agenda required playing successfully to the watching public (see Gimpel 1996).

Theatre as a Metaphor for Studying Congress

The term "theatre" is originally derived from the Greek word *theatron*, ("a seeing place"), emphasizing that theatre is something that is seen in a special location. *Drama* comes from the Greek *drama*, for "action." By contrast, *Congress* is derived from the Latin word *congressus*, for "a coming together." Thus, the original usage implied that Congress involved a coming together of representatives, while theatre was a place for seeing action. In viewing Congress as theatre, then, our attention is subtly shifted from viewing the actions as real and important in their own right to viewing them as occurring for the viewing of others.

The biggest difference between theatre and Congress may seem to be that in the theatre, the playwright usually gives the actors a full script in advance, whereas there is usually no literal script in Congress. Of course, there is also "improvisational" theatre, in which actors are not given scripts but are just told the basic scene and are expected to work out the script as they proceed. In a real sense, that is very similar to Congress – the legislators know the situation when a new session of Congress begins, but after that, all must be improvised.

However, we would rather emphasize three similarities between theatre and Congress. First, and foremost, is the emphasis on the audience. The successful playwright knows what will sell to the audience in the theatre, while the successful member of Congress has learned what will sell to the political audience. The member of Congress plays to the public just as the actor plays to the audience.[2] Second, both institutions are intended to provide enlightenment to the audience. From the earliest days of Greek theatre, drama was intended to help educate the public. Congress similarly provides enlightenment to its audience, as its debates clarify the issues underlying legislation. Third, actions may not always mean what they seem. There can be a symbolic meaning to the plot of a play just as there is usually a symbolic element to actions in a legislature.

Another commonality between theatre and Congress involves the importance of the concept of representation. The distinction in drama is between "presentational theatre," in which the theatricality is emphasized (as by making stage machinery visible) so that the audience always remembers that it is watching a play, and "representational theatre," with realistic plots, characters, and scenery so that the audience is temporarily caught up in the illusion that what transpires on the stage is real. Representation in Congress also involves one thing being considered equivalent to another – here, not the play equivalent to reality, but, in some sense, the legislator equivalent to the constituent.

As we have suggested, each of the elements of theatre – the story, the audience, the director, the theatre building and stage, the actors, and the staging – is present in Congress as well. The Capitol building is the theatre building, with the Senate and House chambers providing two separate stages for action, where the rituals and symbols of politics and policy making unfold in civic space (see Goodsell 1988). The legislators are the actors, playing their roles as delegates, trustees, and politicos – interest-group advocates, president's men and women, and clarion callers for a cause (see Davidson 1969; Wahlke et al. 1962). The committee meeting rooms are the rehearsal chambers in which behind-the-scenes actions shape what will happen when bills reach center stage (as described in Fenno 1973). The party leaders can serve as directors, though

2 Also, both actors and members of Congress can wear out their welcomes with their respective audiences, though no one has yet proposed term limits for actors.

sometimes action in Congress seems more like free theatre, in which every actor can take uncoordinated action – reminiscent of Edmund Burke's description of plays as a republic in which anything goes.

To describe Congress as theatre suggests that it provides drama. The idea of drama implies a story with action and human melodrama. The action in Congress is a matter of attempting to pass legislation, while the human melodrama involves the interplay of powerful leaders and rank-and-file members in the consideration of that legislation. Thus, books on the passage of particular bills emphasize both the steps involved in passing the bills and the roles of particular members of Congress in getting them passed.

Because we have characterized congressional life as much like theatre does not mean that it is drama that always receives, or always deserves, rave reviews. Sometimes congressional theatre is bad theatre, being engaged in what Barbara Sinclair (in Chapter 8) calls "governing ugly." Occasionally Congress "gives off" negative symbols, engages in farcical actions, or provides low comedy. Its performance has been malodorous – as when, in the aftermath of the Cold War, the House Un-American Activities Committee, led by a xenophobic, bullying chairman, Martin Dies, Jr. (D-TX), conducted witch hunts, whereby individuals were charged with disloyalty, with being Communist sympathizers, or with working as spies. By the same token, Congress gave off negative symbols in 1952, when Senator Joseph R. McCarthy (R-WI), chairman of the Senate's Permanent Investigations Subcommittee, launched an anti-Communist crusade. By the end of the subcommittee hearings, the label "McCarthyism" denoted using congressional committee hearings as a platform for character assassination, sullying of reputations, baseless defamation, unsubstantiated charges of disloyalty or other offenses, and, ultimately, disgrace to the Senate itself. The McCarthyism of the early 1950s gave new meaning to James Fenimore Cooper's admonition, in *The American Democrat*, that "the true theatre of a demagogue is a democracy."

Alternative Metaphors for Studying Congress

In proposing to study Congress through the theatre metaphor, we are clearly viewing much of what transpires there as symbolic (see Wilshire 1982: 30–7). By contrast, when Bertram Gross (1953) wrote his book, *The Legislative Struggle* (using a military metaphor borrowed from Clausewitz's *On War*), he clearly took everything that happens in Congress at face value. Gross depicted great floor fights in Congress as the equivalent of great battles between opposing armies whose generals engaged in careful strategic thinking. On the other hand, the theatre motif instead suggests that what happens on stage may not be very indicative of what transpires behind the scenes. The battles shown to the public are mere theatrical devices to amuse, bemuse, or becalm the public audience. The maneuvering behind the scenes may be more significant.

This leads to the important question of whether Congress has changed so much over a half-century that what used to be seen as a military engagement can now be viewed as just theatre or whether Congress has always been appropriately viewed as theatre. With due respect to alternative interpretations, we would maintain that the theatre metaphor has always provided an appropriate lens through which to understand Congress. It was as true in Jefferson's days as Gingrich's, let alone the period that Gross described. It is just that we, as political scientists, have not looked sufficiently beyond the obvious to see that much of what transpires in Congress is a matter of playing to an audience.

Note that we are not arguing that the theatre metaphor is the only way in which Congress should be viewed. Congress is a complex organization, and many different perspectives are useful in understanding it. We are arguing that theatre is a useful and insightful metaphor that has not previously been employed in the study of Congress, but we would not expect this to supplant other approaches. For instance, our use of the theatre metaphor certainly does not require a rejection of the formal models of Congress that have been developed in recent years. We view the emphasis on the reelection goal in formal analysis as compatible with the emphasis on Congress as theatre playing to an audience. Power goals for members of Congress remind us of egoistic actors and actresses who are more concerned with their careers than with the plays in which they act. The policy goals of members of Congress parallel the ideological grounding that underlies the work of some playwrights, whose work is intended as much to proselytize as to entertain.

The newer, formal theory approach to congressional life interprets Congress from various economic perspectives, viewing congressional parties as cartels and congressional committees as information systems. These are potentially powerful perspectives, with perhaps more explanatory power than we would claim for the theatre metaphor. But we believe it is worth underscoring that formal theorists must acknowledge the theatrical element in Congress. There are multiple levels of action in Congress, just as there are multiple levels of action in a play. To focus on one set of actions is to miss some of the underlying complexity of the congressional institution. By the same token, economic perspectives, although useful analogies for understanding Congress, have their limitations as well.

Congress in Action

CONGRESS IN THE 1990S

If we continue with the theatre metaphor, we can see each new Congress as a new play. The directors do not give the actors their full scripts at the beginning of each session; instead, the plot develops as the Congress proceeds. The metaphor may seem a little clumsy at this point, but it is useful to consider recent Congresses in terms of their play structure.

Consider the first three Congresses of the 1990s. First, however, the stage must be set. The last period of unified government when the same party controlled the presidency and both houses of Congress was during the Jimmy Carter administration (1977–80). The 1980 election not only brought Ronald Reagan into the White House, it gave the Republicans control of the Senate for the first time since 1953–4. The House of Representatives remained under Democratic control, as it had been since the 1954 election. This pattern of divided control of Congress remained in effect from 1981 through 1986, yet much of the Reagan program was successfully enacted because the president could use his personal popularity to go over the heads of Congress and appeal directly to the American public. Democrats regained control of the Senate in the 1986 election, and the last two years of the Reagan administration were marked by partisan sparring on such issues as the Iran-contra affair. The presidency remained in Republican (GOP) hands when George Bush won the 1988 election, but the Democrats retained their majorities in both chambers of Congress. Public dissatisfaction with Congress began to climb by this point, but the Democrats were again successful in the 1990 congressional elections.

The 102nd Congress (1991–2) was to become known for serious scandals, particularly the House Bank scandal, in which it was revealed that several members of Congress had cashed checks from their accounts with the House Bank even though their accounts had insufficient funds to back the checks. As the scandal exploded, a record number of House members decided not to run for reelection in 1992.

The presidency returned to Democratic control when Bill Clinton won the 1992 election, but Clinton received only a muted mandate. George Bush was held to a weak 37 percent of the popular vote, but the presence of H. Ross Perot's independent candidacy limited Clinton to 43 percent, one of the weakest showings of any winning president over the years. There had been some expectation that the redistricting in the 1992 election would hurt Democratic chances for Congress, but the Democrats succeeded in maintaining control of the House as well as the Senate.

The record of the 103rd Congress (1993–4) was mixed (Pfiffner 1996). This was ironic given that unified government prevailed. The Republicans were strong enough in Congress to block several Clinton

13

initiatives, while Democratic support for Clinton-sponsored reforms was often lukewarm. Actually, President Clinton had one of the best records in recent history in terms of the number of his legislative proposals that were enacted by Congress (86.4 percent according to *Congressional Quarterly Weekly Report*, December 21, 1996, pp. 3427–30), but some of the most visible proposals failed. Thus, attempts to pass campaign reform legislation proved futile, as did the Clinton health insurance reform, which was the centerpiece of the administration's legislative program for its first two years. At the same time, Clinton was able to get Congress to pass his deficit reduction proposal, albeit without any GOP votes. Furthermore, the Clinton administration had pushed a tax increase through Congress, despite campaign promises of a middle-class tax cut. Also, the administration won passage of the North American Free Trade Agreement (NAFTA), but this resulted in decreased labor union support for Democrats who voted for it.

Republican House leaders decided to try to nationalize the 1994 congressional election. Using polling and focus-group data, they developed a series of legislative proposals that had substantial support among the public and packaged them in a document they called the "Contract with America" (see the end of this chapter). Republican candidates campaigned on the Contract, and the 1994 election turned into a one-sided result as Republicans won control of both the House and the Senate in an election that was widely described as the political equivalent of an earthquake. The national vote totals were actually relatively close, and the Republican margin in the new House was relatively narrow. However, many Democratic incumbents were swept aside, while Republicans won the vast majority of the open seats. The result was the first Republican Congress since 1953–4.

Interpretations of the 1994 election differ only in degree. Clearly it was a repudiation of recent Democratic Congresses, along with a vote of nonconfidence in the Clinton administration. For example, Brady and colleagues (Brady et al. 1996) show that Democratic members from conservative and moderate districts who supported President Clinton on key votes in the 103rd Congress were most likely to be defeated in 1994. The disagreement only extends to whether the election signified a major move toward the Republicans. Weisberg (1995) provides the counterargument that the margin of the Republican victory was actually narrow and that Republicans did not gain a majority in party identification prior to the election. In any case, divided government had returned, but with an unusual twist – an apparent legislative mandate for House Republicans to enact their contract.

This provides the setting for the 104th Congress. The new House leaders had promised to bring all planks of the contract to a vote in the first one hundred days of the new session, and that proved to be the first act of this play. The new Republican Speaker, Newt Gingrich (GA), was the director, being ably assisted by the new majority leader, Dick Armey (TX).

It is vital to note two aspects of this Republican theatre: the role of timing and the importance of cast changes. Just as the director of a play must work to keep the action moving in a sufficiently lively fashion that it keeps the attention of its audience, so the House leadership must skillfully plan the timing of floor consideration of legislation. Much of the preliminary work is behind the scenes in committees, but careful coordination occurs before bills reach the floor. Newt Gingrich masterminded the timing at the beginning of the 104th Congress. The artificial, hundred-day deadline focused media attention on the House and forced it to deal quickly with the reform agenda before momentum could be lost. The result was very high levels of Republican support for each part of the Contract.

Another important aspect involved the cast changes. In early 1997 the Broadway producers of the musical *Les Miserables* assembled a new cast for the start of its second decade because they felt that their play could be reinvigorated only through replacing virtually everyone in the production. Cast changes can also be important in a legislature, providing new momentum for policy change. The cast change in the instance of the 104th Congress was the election of seventy-three Republican freshmen in the 1994 election. These new members were part of a continuing conservative revolution in Washington (see Chapter 7). In the end, they had to accept compromises, for which they sometimes blamed the House Republican leadership; however, these freshmen provided the votes needed to push the Contract with America through the House and to try to cut government spending.

What proved to be missing from the script was the Senate, which has often proved to be the saucer that cools the legislative tea brewed by the House. Senate Republicans decided to moderate the House actions, and as a result, the contract bills made it through the Senate much more slowly, if at all. Indeed, even the House defeated some parts of the contract, most notably the constitutional amendment for term limits on members of Congress. (A full account of congressional actions on the contract is given in the Appendix to this chapter.)

In the heady days after the contract was pushed through the House like clockwork, Republican leaders envisioned two more acts to their play. The second act was to be the budget process, in which the bills to fund the government are to be enacted by September 30. In 1995 the Republicans tried using those bills to push back the size and scope of the federal government. After forcing fiscal responsibility, the Republicans planned a third act in which conservative social legislation would reach center stage. However, congressional Democrats and President Clinton did not accept this script.

The funding bills proceeded through Congress very slowly, with Democrats arguing over several specific Republican proposals. Clinton eventually accepted Republican demands for a budget that would be balanced in seven years, but he drew a line in the sand against achieving balance through limiting the growth of the Medicare program. Partisan stalemate resulted as Republican leaders stood firm. The result was two federal government shutdowns, one in November and a second in December 1995. The media personalized this shutdown with many stories of individual hard-working federal workers who were losing their pre-Christmas paychecks because the Republicans were playing Scrooge. Public opinion polls soon began to record increased popularity for President Clinton and decreased popularity for Speaker Gingrich. By early January 1996, Republicans conceded defeat and continuing resolutions were passed to reopen the government. As in a Greek tragedy, Gingrich had fallen while Clinton had been reborn. The Democrats had been better able to play to the audience, while the Republicans had overplayed their hand when they went ahead with the government shutdowns.

With the presidential race capturing public attention in the early months of 1996, the Congress received less attention. By the time Senate Majority Leader Bob Dole (KS) had won enough primaries to capture the Republican nomination, legislative gridlock had set in. When the Republicans refused to allow voting on the Democratic proposal to increase the minimum wage, Democrats created legislative chaos by trying to attach the proposal as an amendment to one bill after another. When it finally passed, Republicans blocked the appointment of a conference committee to resolve differences between the versions passed by the two congressional houses in retaliation for the Democratic block of the appointment of a conference committee on a health insurance reform bill. President Clinton remained high in the polls while Republican presidential candidate-to-be Robert Dole was being associated with congressional gridlock. Finally, Dole resigned his Senate seat, and the gridlock was ended with compromises leading to August presidential signing ceremonies for both bills plus a bill making historic reforms in the welfare system – to the dismay of the Dole campaign, which did not support the GOP compromises. The original Republican script had been scrapped, while the Democrats were able to take advantage of the situation and appear successful.

The writers of the Greek tragedies would have appreciated being given this material for their plays. There was President Clinton, who had been humbled by the electorate's repudiation of the Democratic Congress in

1994, achieving wide popularity by 1996. Meanwhile, Speaker Gingrich, who had appeared so confident after the Republican victory in 1994, had overstretched and became one of the least popular political personalities by 1996.

This provides the setting for the 1996 elections. In Klinkner's (1996) edited book focusing on the 1994 midterm elections, several authors repeated the conventional wisdom of the time when the book was written (in early 1995) – that the Republicans were likely to retain control of both houses of Congress for the foreseeable future. This forecast by itself shows how the 1994 election changed the long-standing view that the Democrats had a lock on Congress, and especially on the House of Representatives. Yet, like most political prognostications taken too soon after an important news development, this turns out to have been too facile a forecast. Events during 1995 and 1996 made the outcome of the 1996 election more a toss-up than seemed to be the case in early 1995. In the end, the Republicans maintained their control of both chambers, as will be described in more detail in Chapter 12.

THE CHAPTERS

The chapters in this book seek to describe many aspects of the congressional theatre. The first part of the book focuses on the relationships between Congress and its audience. Kenny Whitby and Franklin Gilliam describe how minority districting affects representation in Congress. Samuel Patterson and David Kimball look at evolving public views of Congress. Finally, Dean Lacy examines the underpinnings of divided government in the 1994 election. In these chapters there is a focus on how its audience views Congress as well as on how it can play to that audience.

Part II focuses on Congress in action. Paul Herrnson provides a comprehensive look at the role of party leadership. Tim Groseclose and David King examine congressional committees and reassess the changes the Republicans made in House committees for the 104th Congress. Last, Barry Burden and Aage Clausen focus on the role of partisanship and ideology in roll call voting in Congress, with a comparison between the Republican Congress of 1995–6 with the Reagan Congress of 1981–2. These chapters each remind us of the complexity of the modern Congress, as well as showing us how the radical changes in the 104th Congress have worked out.

Part III turns to the relationships between Congress and the other branches of government. Barbara Sinclair analyzes the role of the President vis-à-vis Congress. Elliot Slotnick and Sheldon Goldman turn to one specific aspect of this relationship – Senate confirmation of the president's judicial nominations. Lori Hausegger and Lawrence Baum study how Congress reacts to statutory interpretation by the Supreme Court. Finally, Randall Ripley dissects the role of Congress relative to the President in foreign policy. Together, these chapters remind us that the policy realm involves the interplay between different actors who often work from different scripts.

Our concluding chapter reviews the 1996 election results. It also pulls together several of the themes of this book while turning to some comments on how Congress may change in the future.

APPENDIX: SOME HIGHLIGHTS OF THE 101ST THROUGH 105TH CONGRESSES

101st Congress

1989

Jan. 3: 101st Congress began. George Mitchell (ME) began his first year as majority leader of the Senate, with Bob Dole as minority leader.

Feb.: Congress blocked a pay raise for itself, one day before it was to take effect.

March: House Republicans chose Newt Gingrich to be the party's whip, by an 87–85 vote over Edward Madigan (IL).

March 9: The Senate rejected President Bush's nomination of John Tower to be defense secretary.

April 13: Congress ratified an agreement to continue nonmilitary aid to the contra rebels until after Nicaragua's elections.

June 6: Jim Wright (TX) stepped down as Speaker after the ethics committee announced he might have broken House rules as many as sixty-nine times, and Tom Foley (WA) was elected to replace him. Tony Coelho (CA), the House majority whip, also stepped down due to ethics issues. Dick Gephardt (MO) was elected majority leader, and William Gray (PA) was named to be the new whip.

Oct. 19: Senate rejected a constitutional amendment to overturn a June Supreme Court opinion permitting flag burning.

Oct. 25: House failed to override a Bush veto of an appropriations bill that permitted federal funding of abortion in cases of rape and incest.

Nov. 17: Bush signed a bill raising the minimum wage after successfully vetoing an earlier version of the bill.

Nov. 22: Congress adjourned for the year after enacting thirteen separate appropriations bills. Major bills passed included restructuring the savings and loans deposit insurance system, repealing a catastrophic health insurance law, and changing the way Medicare pays its doctors.

Dec. 22: Senate Ethics Committee voted to begin a preliminary inquiry into five Senators (the "Keating five") (Cranston [D-CA], DeConcini [R-AZ], Glenn [D-OH], McCain [R-AZ], and Riegle [D-MI]) who had contacted regulators on behalf of savings and loan magnate Charles Keating, who was later convicted of security fraud.

1990

Jan. 23: Congress convened.

Jan. 25: Senate failed to override a Bush veto of a bill, which had passed Congress unanimously in 1989, to permit Chinese students to remain in the United States in the aftermath of the June 1989 Tiananmen Square massacre.

June: President Bush abandoned his "no new taxes" pledge as part of deficit reduction negotiations with Congress.

June 26: The Senate defeated a constitutional amendment to protect the flag.

July 25: The House failed to override a Bush veto of a Family and Medical Leave bill.

July 26: President Bush signed the Americans with Disabilities Act.

Oct. 5: The House rejected the budget package, with the opposition led by Republican Whip Newt Gingrich. Eventually, Bush vetoed a stopgap spending bill and the government shut down for three days; however, a larger group hammered out a budget agreement, which was adopted Oct. 27. The agreement set up budget "walls" that put defense, domestic, and international appropriations into separate categories.

Oct. 24: By one vote, the Senate failed to override a Bush veto of a civil rights bill overturning Supreme Court decisions on filing job discrimination suits.

Oct. 28: Congress adjourned, just nine days before the midterm election. In its final month, Congress passed a plan to reduce the budget substantially, overhauled the Clean Air Act, and passed a child care assistance bill. An immigration reform bill was also passed. However, Congress was not able to pass campaign finance bills, and U.S. actions in the Persian Gulf were not considered.

Nov. 6: Midterm election. Only one Senate incumbent and fifteen House members lost. Altogether, the Republicans lost one Senate and eight House seats.

102nd Congress

1990

Nov.: Senate Republican Conference ousted moderate John Chafee (RI) as its chair and replaced him with conservative Thad Cochran (MS).

Dec.: House Democrats ousted two committee heads: Frank Annunzio (IL) (House Administration Committee) and Glenn Anderson (CA) (Public Works).

1991

Jan. 3: Congress convened.

Jan. 12: After three days of debate, Congress gave President Bush authorization for war against Iraq.

May 8: The Brady gun-control bill passed the House.

July 17: The Senate voted to ban lawmakers from accepting honoraria for speeches to interest groups.

Oct. 2: Senate backers failed to invoke cloture on an anticrime package that included the Brady bill.

Oct. 3: The House instructed its Ethics Committee to start investigating House members who had written checks on the House Bank without sufficient funds in their accounts to cover them.

Oct. 11: Televised Senate hearings over allegations that Supreme Court nominee Clarence Thomas had sexually harassed Anita Hill; Thomas was confirmed to the Court on Oct. 15.

Oct. 23: The House passed a highway and mass transit bill that had been the source of controversy all year.

Nov.: The Senate Ethics Committee reprimanded Alan Cranston (CA) for his actions on behalf of savings and loan chief Charles Keating having criticized the other four senators involved in the scandal. Cranston gave up his whip position.

Nov. 15: Bush signed a bill extending unemployment benefits, after much partisan wrangling over the issue through the fall.

Nov. 21: Bush signed a civil rights bill overturning Supreme Court decisions on job discrimination.

Nov. 27: Congress finished work on a bill that allowed aid to the former Soviet Union. It then completed its business, but did not formally adjourn until Jan. 3, 1992.

1992

Jan. 3: Congress convened.

Feb. 5: The House voted to order the House Administration Committee to continue its investigation into charges that some members had converted public funds into cash at the House Post Office.

March 13: The House voted to make public the names of its members who had overdrawn their accounts at the House Bank. On April 1, the Ethics Committee cited seventeen members and a few past members for abusing their privileges. The full list of names was revealed on April 16.

May 13: The Senate failed to override a Bush veto of a campaign finance reform bill.

June 11: Balanced budget amendment failed in the House.

July 3: Bush signed a bill extending unemployment compensation with permanent changes in the system, after initially opposing it.

Aug. 6: The House completed congressional action on a bill giving aid to the ex–Soviet Union.

Sept. 30: The House sustained the president's veto of the family and medical leave bill.

Oct. 5: For the first time Congress overrode a Bush veto (on a bill re-regulating the cable TV industry).

Oct. 9: Congress adjourned after enacting a major energy policy bill but failing to override President Bush's vetoes of the "motor voter" bill, intended to permit voter registration at driver license bureaus.

Nov. 3: Election Day. Bill Clinton defeated President Bush, winning 43 percent of the popular vote (versus 38 percent for Bush and 19 percent for Ross Perot). Record numbers of women, blacks, and Hispanics were elected to Congress. The partisan composition of the Senate was unchanged, but Republicans added ten seats in the House.

103rd Congress

1993

Jan.: Congress convened. A quarter of the House members were freshmen.

Jan. 21: President Clinton withdrew the nomination of Zoe Baird as attorney general.

Feb. 5: Passage of the family and medical leave bill.

March 18 and 25: Clinton budget passed Congress by near party-line votes.

April 21: Clinton's economic stimulus package failed in the Senate when the fourth cloture attempt to stop a GOP filibuster proved unsuccessful.

May 20: Clinton signed the motor voter bill.

Aug. 3: Senate approved Clinton's nomination of Ruth Bader Ginsburg to replace Byron White on the Supreme Court.

Aug. 5–6: Congress passed Clinton's $500 billion budget deficit reduction plan, cutting spending and raising income taxes on the wealthy, without any votes from Republicans.

Sept.: Senate and House voted on homosexuals in the military; although not accepting the lenient Clinton policy, they allowed the secretary of defense some discretion. The same month, Clinton's National Service bill establishing the AmeriCorps program passed Congress.

Sept. 9: Senate adopted an amendment cutting funds for antimissile defense.

Sept. 20: Senate voted against rejecting military base closing recommendations made by a special commission.

Sept. 22: First Lady Hillary Rodham Clinton's universal health care reform proposals were unveiled.

Sept. 30: Congress cleared, and the president signed, a foreign appropriations bill that included funds for the ex–Soviet Union.

Oct. 3: Eighteen U.S. soldiers were killed in Somalia. Within a couple of weeks, Congress adopted an amendment to cut off funds for troops in Somalia after Clinton's March 31 pullout date.

Oct. 6: President signed Hatch Act revision, permitting off-duty federal workers to participate in campaign activity.

Oct. 19: House killed superconducting supercollider project.

Nov. 17 and 20: Congress passed implementation legislation for the North American Free Trade Agreement (NAFTA), in a vote with more support from Republicans than from Democratic party leaders.

Nov. 22: Clinton won in the House, defeating an attempt to cut the budget further.

Nov. 30: President signed Brady bill for handgun control.

Congressional Quarterly (CQ) presidential success rate in the first session: 86.4 percent. (*Congressional Quarterly Weekly Report*, Dec. 21, 1996, p. 3427).

1994

Feb. 2: House defeated the rule for a bill giving the Environmental Protection Agency cabinet status, effectively killing the Clinton proposal.

March 1 and 17: Senate and House rejected the balanced budget amendment to the Constitution.

April 14: House rejected a motion to instruct budget conferees to increase budget cuts.

May 5: House approved conference report on abortion clinic access bill.

May 31: Ways and Means Chair Dan Rostenkowski (IL) was indicted.

June 29: Product liability limitation bill failed when Senate cloture motion was defeated.

June 30: President signed bill renewing the independent counsel statute.

Aug.: Congress passed assault weapons ban as part of an omnibus anticrime bill.

Aug. 26: Health care reform declared dead for the year by White House and congressional leaders.

Sept. 7: Democrats file first ethics complaint against Newt Gingrich.

Sept. 13: Clinton signs $30.2 billion anticrime bill, including provisions for 100,000 new police officers and a ban on the sale of certain assault weapons.

Sept. 19: Troops sent to Haiti. Subsequently, in late October, the president signed a bill calling for the troops' prompt and orderly withdrawal.

Sept. 27: Contract with America signed on Capitol steps by Republican House candidates.

Sept. 30: President signed final spending bills for the new fiscal year. The same day, the campaign finance bill failed when the Senate was unable to stop a GOP-led filibuster against considering the conference committee report.

Oct. 6: Lobbying reform bill died in the Senate when a GOP-led filibuster on the conference report could not be stopped.

Oct. 8: Congress adjourned for the election.

Nov. 8: Midterm election. The Republicans won control of both congressional chambers as Democrats lost fifty-two House and eight Senate seats.

Nov. 29–Dec. 1: Lame duck session of Congress to pass a bill implementing the General Agreement on Tariffs and Trade (GATT).

CQ presidential success rate in the second session: 86.4 percent (*Congressional Quarterly Weekly Report*, December 21, 1996, p. 3427).

104th Congress

1994

Nov. 30: House Democrats voted to keep Richard Gephardt (MO) and David Bonior (MI) as their leaders.

Dec. 2: Senate Democrats chose Daschle (SD) over Christopher Dodd (CT) as their minority leader by a 24–23 vote. Senate Republicans chose Trent Lott (MS) over Alan Simpson (WY) as their new assistant majority leader by a 27–26 vote.

Dec. 5–7: House Republicans met to organize the new House. They chose Newt Gingrich (GA) as their nominee for Speaker, Armey (TX) for majority leader, and Tom DeLay (TX) as whip. They also made decisions about rules and committee changes and selected committee chairs.

Dec. 30: Newt Gingrich renounced a $4.5 million advance for a book deal with HarperCollins Publishing Company, whose owner, media mogul Rupert Murdoch, had substantial interest in issues currently before Congress. Gingrich signed a new contract for a $1 advance and a share of royalties on sales.

1995

Jan. 4: House of Representatives changed its rules in the first day of its session, adjourning at 2:24 A.M. Jan. 5 after a marathon, 14½ hour opening day.

March 2: Balanced budget amendment defeated in the Senate by one vote, with all Republicans voting yes except for Mark Hatfield (OR).

March 29: House defeated constitutional amendment for congressional term limits.

April 7: House passed Republican tax-cut bill.

April 13: First one hundred days of Republican Congress ended; most parts of the Republican Contract with America had passed the House in this period.

April 18: Clinton declared that he was "not irrelevant" in the face of a the new Republican majority in Congress.

June 29: Congress passed a compromise, seven-year budget plan, cutting spending and taxes and holding down increases in Medicare and other social programs.

July 27: Clinton signed a package of spending cuts, after vetoing an earlier version of this bill.

Sept. 7: Bob Packwood (R-OR) announced he would resign from the Senate because of sexual misconduct charges.

Sept. 8: House defeated an attempt to disapprove of military base closings recommended by a commission.

Oct. 19: Clinton came out in favor of a seven-year balanced budget provided it did not harm education, health, or environmental programs.

Nov. 14: Six-day shutdown of nonessential federal government services as part of budget stalemate.

Dec. 6: Clinton vetoed balanced budget bill, including welfare reforms and changes in Medicare and Medicaid. The same day, the House Ethics Committee found Gingrich guilty of violating House rules in three cases but imposed no punishment; two other complaints were dismissed, and a final complaint, regarding the funding of a college course he taught, was turned over to independent counsel James M. Cole.

Dec. 12: Senate rejected, by three votes, a constitutional amendment banning flag desecration.

Dec. 16: Second government shutdown due to the budget impasse between the president and Congress, with government employees being furloughed over the Christmas season.

CQ presidential success rate in the third year of Clinton's presidency: a record low 36.2 percent (*Congressional Quarterly Weekly Report*, December 21, 1996, p. 3427).

1996

Jan. 3: House sustained Clinton veto of defense authorization bill that would have accelerated the deployment of a defense against ballistic missiles.

Jan. 5: House passed a modified version of the Senate budget bill, after Republican leaders conceded. The longest-ever U.S. government shutdown would now be ended.

Jan. 9: Clinton vetoed second welfare reform bill.

Jan. 24: Congressional Republicans abandoned their attempt to get a seven-year balanced budget and worked with the administration on a stopgap funding bill so the government would not shut down again on January 27.

Feb. 7: The "Freedom to Farm" bill passed the Senate over the opposition of Democratic leader Tom Daschle. Final version passed the House Feb. 29 and was signed by the president on April 4.

Feb. 8: President Clinton signed a telecommunications bill after Dole agreed to let the bill clear with free allocation of a new broadcast spectrum.

March 12: The president signed a Cuba sanctions bill, which Congress had passed after Cuba shot down a U.S.-registered plane.

March 29: The House Ethics Committee criticized Speaker Gingrich for allowing a telecommunications businessperson to volunteer in his office, but it recommended no punishment.

April 4: Clinton signed the "Freedom to Farm" bill, revamping federal farm programs.

April 9: President Clinton signed a bill giving the president a modified line-item veto.

April 23: Constitutional amendment for term limits on members of Congress failed in the Senate when the vote to stop a filibuster lost.

April 25: Congress approved a five-bill omnibus spending measure for the current fiscal year (a record six months late).

May 9: House failed to override the Clinton veto of a product liability bill.

May 23: Ninety-three House Republicans helped pass an increase in the federal minimum wage.

June 11: Senate Majority Leader Bob Dole resigned from the Senate to campaign full time as the Republican presidential nominee.

June 25: Campaign finance reform legislation failed in the Senate when the vote to stop a filibuster was defeated.

July 17: TWA flight 800 crashed, with terrorism suspected as a possible cause.

Aug. 5: Clinton signed a bill increasing sanctions on Iran and Libya.

Aug. 20: Clinton signed a minimum wage increase.

Aug. 21: Clinton signed the Kennedy–Kassebaum health insurance portability bill.

Aug. 22: Clinton signed a welfare reform bill.

Sept. 21: Clinton signed the Defense of Marriage Act, ensuring that states do not have to recognize same sex marriages performed in other states.

Sept. 26: By nine votes, the Senate failed to override Clinton's April 10 veto of a bill to ban "partial-birth" abortions. The same day, the House Ethics Committee announced it would investigate whether Speaker Gingrich had provided it with accurate and complete information.

Sept. 30: The Senate passed an omnibus spending bill. All spending bills were enacted in time, without a continuing resolution. Six bills had been put into the omnibus package. Reforms affecting illegal immigrants and antiterrorism precautions were incorporated as part of this bill.

Oct. 4: Congress adjourned. CQ presidential success rate of 55.1 percent (*Congressional Quarterly Weekly Report*, December 21, 1996, p. 3427)

Nov. 5: Election Day. Only one Senate incumbent lost. The net gain for the Republicans was two seats in the Senate, while the net gain for the Democrats was nine in the House.

105th Congress

1996

Nov. 20: By acclamation, Republicans renominated Gingrich as Speaker.

Dec. 21: The subcommittee investigating the ethics charges against Speaker Gingrich announced an admission by Gingrich that he had violated House rules by providing inaccurate and incomplete information but had not intended to mislead the committee.

1997

Jan. 7: House reconvened and reelected Newt Gingrich Speaker by a vote of 216–205, with four Republicans voting for other candidates and five Republicans and one Democrat voting only, "present."

Jan. 21: House accepted, by a 395–28 vote, the ethics committee report recommending that Speaker Gingrich receive a reprimand and a $300,000 fine.

Feb. 12: House voted down a constitutional amendment for term limits on members of Congress, 217–211.

March 4: Senate failed by one vote to pass a balanced-budget constitutional amendment, 66–34.

March 20: Eleven Republican conservatives disaffected with Gingrich's leadership join Democrats in defeating rule on House committee funding.

April 17: Gingrich announced former Senator Bob Dole (KS) will lend him $300,000 to pay his ethics penalty.

May 2: Congressional leaders reached agreement with the White House on a plan to balance the budget in five years.

May 14: Majority Whip Tom DeLay (TX) led more than 40 GOP defectors in defeating a rule on a supplemental appropriations bill.

May 15: The Ethics Committee leadership approved a plan for Gingrich to pay half of his $300,000 penalty out of his own funds and the rest with a loan from Dole.

May 20–23: House and Senate passed bipartisan budget agreement negotiated between Republican congressional leaders and the White House, with some dissatisfaction from Democratic liberals and Republican conservatives.

June 12: Republicans yielded to the President Clinton on a disaster relief bill, removing GOP-sponsored riders on unrelated matters.

July 10: Majority Whip DeLay met with GOP rebels to discuss ousting the Speaker. Armey (TX) and Boehner (OH) later denied their participation in this coup. Bill Paxon (NY) resigned as leadership chairman because of his role in the coup attempt, though the dissidents say that he was less involved than Armey, Boehner, and DeLay.

July 23: Late night GOP conference in which Gingrich, Armey, DeLay, and Boehner all retained their leadership positions and Republicans agreed to communicate better with one another.

Aug. 5: President Clinton signed budget reconciliation and tax-cut bills, and on August 11 he used the line-item veto for the first time on three provisions in these bills.

Nov. 10: Major Clinton defeat in the House when he could not round up enough Democratic votes to pass fast-track trade negotiating authority; House Minority Leader Richard Gephardt (MO) led the opposition, while House Republican leaders backed the president.

Nov. 13: Congress adjourned for the year after passing the last of the thirteen separate annual appropriations bills. CQ presidential success rate in the first session: 53.6 percent (*Congressional Quarterly Weekly Report*, January 3, 1998, p. 14).

CONTRACT WITH AMERICA OUTCOMES

Passed and Signed by President

Preface (Congressional process): End exemptions for Congress from safety and workplace issues.

3. (Welfare): Welfare reform.

4. (Families and children): Tax benefits for adoptions and home care for elderly, increased penalties for sex crimes against children, and stronger enforcement of child support orders.

Congress in Action

8. (Capital gains and regulations): Reduce unfunded federal mandates; reduce federal paperwork.
9. (Civil law and product liability): Make it harder for investors to sue companies.

Parts Passed and Signed by President

2. (Crime): Restitution to crime victims, limit death row appeals.

Parts Passed and Signed by President, after Earlier Version Vetoed

5. (Middle-class tax cut): $500–per-child tax credit, eased "marriage penalty" for joint filers, and other, similar features.
7. (Social security): Repeal 1993 increase in income taxes on social security benefits, give tax incentive for long-term health care, and other, similar features.
8. (Capital gains and regulations): Cut capital gains taxes; increase depreciation rates.

Passed and Signed by President, but under Court Challenge

1. (Balanced budget amendment and line-item veto): Line-item veto for the president on appropriations and tax breaks.

Passed by House and Did Not Require Senate or Presidential Action

Preface (Congressional process): Revise House rules to cut number of committees, put term limits on committee chairs, and require a three-fifths majority vote for tax increases.

Passed by Congress, but Vetoed by President

9. (Civil law and product liability): National product liability law with limits on punitive damages.

Passed by House, Partially Passed Senate, but Did Not Get Through Conference Committee

8. (Capital gains and regulations): Require federal agencies to use cost-benefit analysis for regulations.

29

Great Theatre

Passed by House, but Failed in Senate

1. (Balanced budget amendment and line-item veto): Constitutional amendment to balance the budget; failed the Senate by a one–vote margin

9. (Civil law and product liability): "Loser pays" rule in certain federal legal cases.

Passed by House, but Did Not Reach Senate Floor

6. (National security): Prohibit putting U.S. troops under foreign command, defense missile defense system, and other, similar features.

Defeated in Floor Votes by Both House and Senate

10. (Term limits): Constitutional amendment to limit congressional terms.

Source: Adapted from *Congressional Quarterly Weekly Report*, October 5, 1996, p. 2838. The numbers refer to the relevant plank numbers in the Contract with America.

Congress and Its Audience

2

Representation in Congress: Line Drawing and Minorities

KENNY J. WHITBY AND
FRANKLIN D. GILLIAM, JR.

The process of drawing congressional district boundary lines is crucial to representation in Congress. To a very large extent, districting defines who the actors can be in congressional politics. The ideal of "one person, one vote" was defined initially in the famous U.S. Supreme Court case of *Baker v. Carr* (1962), and thereby "the reapportionment revolution was born" (Dixon 1968: 3). Three decades after the *Baker* decision, important issues of congressional representation remain alive, above all, the issue of the representation of African Americans.

The current maelstrom over racial redistricting revisits an old theme in American politics: the inclusionary rules for racial minorities in representative government. These rules define important features of the stage on which the drama of congressional elections unfolds. Ralph J. Bunche once observed that "minority populations, and particularly racial minorities, striving to exist in any theoretically democratic modern society, are compelled to struggle strenuously for even a moderate participation in the democratic game" (quoted in Meier, Rudwick, & Broderick 1965: 184). Bunche knew that representation is intrinsically valuable but not equally attainable by all people in American society. From the debate over slavery at the Constitutional Convention (1787) to recent court decisions such as the 1995 decision in *Miller v. Johnson* (a case involving racial redistricting in Georgia) and the 1996 *Bush v. Vera* ruling (a racial-redistricting case in Texas), the United States has struggled to find the appropriate remedy for proven exclusion of racial minorities from the representational process.

Race-conscious districting is the latest remedy for the diminution of minority-vote influence, but it is not without its critics. The case against creating "majority–minority" districts is largely based on three points. First, people such as Justices Antonin Scalia and Clarence Thomas argue that representation should be defined solely in formal terms, that is, as the right of individuals to vote for the candidate of their choice. Put

33

differently, they argue that a democratic society's obligation is to provide only for universal suffrage, not to promote the political rights of particular groups.

A second criticism is that race-conscious districting violates the principles of "color-blindness." Proponents of this view highlight the divisiveness of race in American society. Conservatives and liberals converge on the point that all race-based policy making is suspicious on its face because it recognizes skin color as the defining factor. In *Shaw v. Reno* (1993), Justice Sandra Day O'Connor echoes this sentiment when she notes that:

A reapportionment plan that includes in one district individuals who belong to the same race, but who are otherwise widely separated by geographical and political boundaries, and who may have little in common with one another but the color of their skin, bears an uncomfortable resemblance to political apartheid. (p. 2827)

The third attack on racial redistricting concerns substantive policy outcomes reflected by the roll call votes of members of Congress. This position is based on two related arguments. Some observers challenge the notion that racial minorities are better served by legislators from their group. Carol Swain (1993) is often cited as proof that there are few differences in the voting records of liberal white and African-American legislators. Similarly, many believe that the increase in African Americans in Congress after the 1990 round of redistricting was largely responsible for dramatic gains by Republicans in the South (Hill 1995; Lublin 1995). Thus, if Republicans *generally* do not share black political interests, then it is optimal to prefer an increase in liberal white legislators at the expense of a decrease in the number of majority–minority districts.

In this chapter we examine the case against racial redistricting. The first section studies the historical case to determine if individual rights are the sole basis for inclusion. Here we briefly remind readers of the group nature of African-American exclusion prior to the 1965 Voting Rights Act.

Next, we consider the notion that contemporary American society can, and does, proceed on the basis of color-blindness. Our analysis elevates two important mechanisms of color consciousness – minority-vote dilution schemes devised by public officials and racially polarized voting behavior among the electorate. The long-term consequences of these variables seriously call into question the principle of color-blindness. The irony is that the very failure to adhere to the principle of color-blindness produced the impetus toward districting to promote minority representation. In this discussion, we highlight the exogenous impact of the U.S. Supreme Court.

The last section of the chapter concerns substantive representation. Our argument on this issue unpacks two interconnected points. First, we present evidence that constrains the argument about the ability of nonblacks to represent black policy interests. There are differences – black legislators do more often vote the common policy interests of African Americans than do nonblacks. We make the case that most analysts conceive of substantive representation far too narrowly. We advocate a broader view of the concept that takes into account the context of the times (i.e., the nature of the legislative proposal lawmakers are asked to vote on in any given Congress), a more nuanced understanding of the legislative process (i.e., indicators other than floor votes), the power of symbolic politics, and the value of long-term institutional representation. Second, we study the question of whether increasing minority representation actually harms black policy interests by increasing the number of Republicans. Our review of the evidence suggests a more tempered version of that claim. It is still debatable whether racial redistricting was the sole, or most important, determinant of Republican seat gain. We conclude the chapter by considering the prospects of racial redistricting and the likely consequences for electoral politics, congressional behavior, and representative democracy. We end by calling for refined racial-redistricting strategies.

HISTORICAL CONTEXT: GROUP BASIS OF RACIAL POLITICS

The modern mechanisms for racial representation in American political life are historically rooted in a complex weave of economic, social, and political factors. It is widely known that the issue of black inclusion posed a dilemma for America's Founding Fathers at the Constitutional Convention of 1787. Whether best understood as compromising politicians or self-interested elites, the Framers forged an uneasy consensus regarding the status of blacks. The Three-Fifths Compromise, the slavery commerce clause, and, later, the fugitive slave law triggered a pattern of political exclusion that extended from the national level down to the states and localities. These constitutional provisions provided a basis for a pattern of exclusion best characterized as the "slave codes." The codes were a method of social control to maintain the advantages of cheap, black labor (Franklin 1964; Jarvis 1992; Quarles 1964). Although conditions varied across the colonies, the imposition of the codes meant that enslaved blacks could not own property, vote, make contracts, have standing in court, or control the lives of their children. As James McGregor Burns (1982: 143) notes, "In general, the life of the enslaved Afro-American was nasty, poor, brutish, and often short." The effect

35

was to deny blacks, en masse, basic citizenship rights and institutionalize their marginal status in the society.

It is beyond the scope of this chapter to devote the necessary space to the significance of the Civil War, Radical Reconstruction, and Jim Crow. It is enough to say that before passage of the Voting Rights Act of 1965, blacks were routinely prevented from voting by such practices as physical intimidation, literacy tests, and poll taxes (Foner 1988; Jarvis 1992; Lawson 1976; Matthews and Prothro 1967). To illustrate the effectiveness of disenfranchising practices in 1947, only 20 percent of eligible blacks were registered to vote, and only 25 percent were registered in 1956 and 1958 (Matthews and Prothro 1967: 184). While there were a few nonsouthern states where blacks could fully participate in electoral politics, the fact remained that as a group, blacks were unable to impact governmental decisions through the electoral system.

The Voting Rights Act (VRA) of 1965 is generally regarded as the most effective federal voting-rights law enacted since Reconstruction. The VRA targeted those states (Alabama, Georgia, Louisiana, Mississippi, South Carolina, Virginia, and parts of North Carolina and Arizona) where white conservative politicians had succeeded in systematically disenfranchising a large segment of the black voting-age population through voter registration barriers, intimidation, and outright violence.

There are three key provisions in the VRA. The first (Section 2) bars the adoption of any electoral devices that would result in the denial of the vote to any person because of race and color. Second, the Section 4 "triggering formula" suspends the use of literacy tests in any political subdivision or state where less than 50 percent of the voting-age population was registered to vote in 1964, and so authorizes federal registrars to register voters and monitor elections in these areas. The third major provision (Section 5) is designed to prevent the dilution of minority-voter strength. This provision states that political units in areas covered by the act may make no change in their voting practices without preclearance by the U.S. attorney general or the Federal District Court for the District of Columbia.

It is barely contestable that the VRA was a major policy instrument for dismantling the "first generation" of overt barriers (e.g., literacy tests, poll taxes) to minority voter participation. As a result of this act, along with the large-scale voter registration drives of the Voter Education Project under the Southern Regional Council, the proportion of blacks registered to vote rose from an estimated 29 percent in 1960 to 62 percent in 1970 (U.S. Bureau of the Census 1972: 374).

To date, the VRA has been extended and strengthened on three occasions, in 1970, 1975, and most recently, in 1982. The extension of the act in 1970, along with passage of the Twenty-sixth Amendment, lowered the minimum age for voting from twenty-one to eighteen in all elections. It also banned the use of literacy tests. The 1975 extension boosted the number of Hispanic and Asian voters by requiring bilingual ballots. The 1982 amendments to the Voting Rights Act were especially noteworthy because they were designed to encourage a more benign form of racial gerrymandering to promote minority representation. Section 2 of the law has been revised to stipulate that a violation could be proven by the existence of an election procedure that "results in the denial or abridgement" of the right to vote. The revision is significant because it replaces the "intent" standard of proof applied in the *Mobile* case (discussed in the next section). In short, the 1982 extension is a significant attempt to more clearly define the rules of inclusion for American racial and ethnic minorities.

In this section we have argued for a rejection of the idea that representative government only recognizes individual rights. In an ideal world, this might be the case. But the history of America is such that race is much more than a biological category. It is a political category born of a system that systematically excluded certain groups. Moreover, it is a form of government more plural than democratic in nature. That is, it has, and does, recognize the political interests of groups. The fact that blacks were excluded as a group and that the system is group based surely undermines the notion that remedies such as racial redistricting violate a principled commitment to individualism.

COLOR-BLINDNESS VERSUS COLOR-CONSCIOUSNESS

Shortly after the passage of the VRA, state and local officials attempted to continue the pattern of representational exclusion by configuring district boundaries to frustrate the electoral opportunities of minority-supported candidates. *Negative gerrymandering* was the most common vote dilution practice. Officials typically employed two strategies: packing – the overconcentration of minorities in one district to prevent them from having much influence in another – and cracking – the dispersion of concentrated minorities across districts to prevent them from having much influence in any one district. The Court's response to these tactics ultimately created pressures for group-based remedies such as majority–minority districts.

In *White v. Regester* (1973), a Texas legislative reapportionment case involving the claim by minority plaintiffs of vote dilution, the Supreme Court held that although the Texas plan was not invidiously discriminatory, and thus was not automatically unconstitutional, it could be rejected on the grounds that it appeared to decrease minority-voting strength. In *Beer v. United States* (1976), the Supreme Court continued to refine its views on what the VRA required. In this case, the issue was whether a New Orleans redistricting plan providing for two black majority districts was acceptable even though a different redistricting plan could have provided the chance for the election of black city council members in addition to more black representatives. Although the Court ruled in favor of the New Orleans plan, it noted that an electoral plan was only acceptable as long as there was no electoral scheme devised to dilute minority voting power.

In *United Jewish Organizations v. Carey* (1977), the Supreme Court took another step in the direction of redistricting to achieve a specific electoral outcome. The case involved a redistricting plan that divided the Hasidic Jewish community in Brooklyn, New York, to create an additional black-majority district. The Supreme Court rejected the claim by the affected Hasidic community that the redistricting plan was unconstitutional. In effect, the Court ruled that the VRA could be used as a device for improving the lot of protected groups, most notably, black voters.

The movement toward redistricting to improve minority electoral prospects was soon curtailed as a result of the Supreme Court's decision in *City of Mobile v. Bolden* (1980). The case focused on whether the at-large election system in Mobile, Alabama, provided black voters with a realistic chance of electing black commissioners to the three-person governing body. The Supreme Court ruled that the Voting Rights Act required that voting rights plaintiffs show "intent" to discriminate before there could be a violation under Section 2 of the act. In effect, the Court rejected the ruling in *White v. Regester*, which stated that plaintiffs could provide circumstantial evidence (e.g., past history of discrimination) as proof of discriminatory intent. In sum, by the early 1980s there was considerable judicial tension between a focus on "expected outcome" and a focus on "discriminatory intent" as the central interpretative tool for the VRA.

In 1982, Congress overturned the *Mobile* decision by revising Section 2 of the VRA. The 1982 amendments replace the intent test with the results test. The revised law opened the way for another important Supreme Court ruling that would soon bring the issue of minority-controlled districts to center stage in the decennial battles over fair representation. In essence, the 1982 amendments sought to rectify the continuing problem of racial-bloc voting and vote dilution practices in America. It was an effort to tie the voting practices of the white electorate to the vote dilution schemes of public officials. In *Thornburg v. Gingles* (1986), a case involving whether or not redistricting of North

Carolina's multimember legislative districts violated the VRA by diluting black-voter strength, the high court accepted the new results test in the revised Section 2 provision of the VRA.

In the *Thornburg* case, the Court set out three criteria for determining what constitutes a violation of Section 2 of the VRA: polarization, compactness, and cohesiveness. Polarization refers to the relationship between votes for minority candidates and the racial composition of voting precincts. Polarization is said to exist when the majority votes as a bloc to defeat the minority's preferred candidate.[1] Compactness considers whether or not minority voters can constitute a majority in a compact enough geographic area. Given America's peculiar racial differences in residential patterns (Massey and Denton 1993), the Court was concerned about the ability of proposed plans to draw reasonable district lines to create black majorities. Finally, the issue of cohesiveness asks for evidence that the minority group solidly votes for its preferred candidate. Creating black-majority districts would obviously be irrelevant if the community did not vote as a bloc for a single candidate of choice.

The combination of the 1982 amendments and the *Thornburg* decision paved the way for the "color-conscious" creation of majority-minority districts. Following the 1990 census, a record number of congressional districts were consciously created to give minority voters numerical majorities. A total of thirty-two African-American districts (up from seventeen in 1990), and twenty Hispanic districts (compared to nine in 1990) were created for the 1992 elections. These districts were initially supported by Democrats, who assumed that minority-controlled districts would enhance the electoral fortunes of Democratic representatives. Republicans, however, have become increasingly supportive of redistricting plans that would produce more minority-controlled districts, reasoning that concentrating minority voters in a few districts would make adjoining districts whiter, more conservative, and more likely to elect Republican representatives.

Table 2.1 shows the proportion of African Americans and Hispanics serving in the House before and after district lines were redrawn following the 1990 census.[2] The proportion of African Americans rose from

---

1 Evidence for racially polarized voting is well documented in the social science literature. For some research on the topic, see Grofman, Migalski, and Noviello (1985); Wildgen (1988); Engstrom and McDonald (1988); Loewen (1990); Ards and Lewis (1992); Grofman, Handley, and Niemi (1992); Firebaugh (1993).

2 Because the focus of this chapter is on line drawing and minorities, we do not directly address the issue of minority underrepresentation in the U.S. Senate. We should note, however, that racial minorities remain underrepresented in the upper chamber of Congress as well. For example, in 1992 Carol Moseley-Braun was

Table 2.1. *Proportions of African Americans and Hispanics Serving in the House of Representatives (99th–104th Congresses)*[a]

	African-Americans[b]	Hispanics[c]
1985-1986 99th Congress	4.6 (20)	2.8 (12)
1987-1988 100th Congress	5.3 (23)	3.2 (14)
1989-1990 101st Congress	5.5 (24)	2.8 (12)
1991-1992 102d Congress	6.0 (26)	2.8 (12)
1993-1994 103rd Congress	9.0 (39)	4.4 (19)
1995-1996 104th Congress	9.0 (39)	4.1 (18)

[a]Numbers in parentheses are the members of the House, including nonvoting delegates.
[b]The proportion of African Americans in the United States was 11.8 percent in 1980, 12.3 percent in 1990, and 12.5 in 1994.
[c]The proportion of Hispanics in the United States was 6.4 percent in 1980, 9.0 percent in 1990, and 10.0 percent in 1994. Note: "Hispanic origin" may mean any race. *Sources*: Data for the number of African-American and Hispanic members in each House were derived from *Congressional Quarterly Weekly Report*, November 10, 1984; November 8, 1986; November 12, 1988; November 10, 1990; November 7, 1992; November 12, 1994. Data for the proportion of African Americans and Hispanics in the United States were taken from Table 13 of the *Statistical Abstract of the United States* (U.S. Bureau of the Census 1995: 1).

6.0 percent (totaling twenty-six) in the 102nd Congress (1991–2) to 9.0 percent (a total of thirty-nine) in the 104th Congress (1995–6), or a 33 percent increase between 1991 and 1996. The Hispanic delegation in the House rose from about 3.0 percent (totaling twelve) in the 102nd Congress to approximately 4.0 percent (for a total of eighteen nationwide) in the 104th Congress. This represents about a 25 percent increase during this period. Despite these gains, both groups remain underrepresented compared to their relative share of the population (see footnotes *b* and *c* in Table 2.1).

elected to serve in the U.S. Senate, becoming only the fourth African American to hold this position in the nation's history. The other three African Americans were Hiram R. Revels (1870–1), Mississippi; Blanche K. Bruce (1875–81), Mississippi; and Edward W. Brooke (1967–79), Massachusetts.

Figure 2.1. *Gerrymandering in North Carolina (1993)*

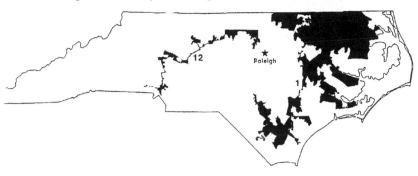

The issue of whether minorities should be elected in numbers equal to their proportion in the general population is a debatable one and is beyond the scope of this chapter. The point here is that there is a relationship between the number of minority representatives in Congress and the size of the minority population in congressional districts. That is, the size of the minority delegation in Congress is related to the creation of majority–minority districts. For example, of the thirty-two black-majority districts created after 1990, all but one (Pennsylvania's first, which elected Thomas Foglietta) elected a black representative to serve in the 103rd and 104th Congresses. After the 1994 elections (104th Congress), Republicans Gary Franks (CT) and J. C. Watts (OK) were the only black representatives to come from districts with a majority of non-Hispanic white voters.

The post-1990 redistricting to promote minority electoral prospects has been controversial. White voters have filed federal court lawsuits in several states claiming a violation of their rights to equal protection under the Fourteenth Amendment. One of the first lawsuits to reach the Supreme Court was *Shaw v. Reno* (1993). In this case, white voters claimed that North Carolina's redrawn Twelfth District (majority-black) violated their constitutional rights (see Figure 2.1). The *Shaw* case turned on the compactness test. Because of asymmetrical residential patterns, blacks do not always live in a compact configuration (particularly in the South). To get around this problem of geographical dispersion, some state legislatures abandoned traditional redistricting standards of compactness and contiguity and drew oddly shaped district boundaries. Justice Sandra Day O'Connor, writing for the Court majority in this 5–4 decision, asserted that if district boundaries were so "bizarre" as to be indefensible on any grounds other than an effort to elect minorities to political office, white voters would have legal justification for claiming that they had been the victims of unconstitutional racial gerrymandering. Although the Supreme Court had never previously held that compactness was an independent federal constitutional requirement, the Court gave legal standing to challenges to any congressional redistricting plans with an oddly shaped majority–minority district.

In *Shaw*, the Court sidestepped the general question of what actually constitutes racial gerrymandering. The vagueness of the ruling has opened the way for challenges by white voters to the drawing of these districts. A number of states, mostly in the South, have challenged the constitutionality of majority–minority districts. In *Miller v. Johnson* (1995), the Court began to address the extent to which race could be used as a factor in drawing district boundaries. In its ruling, the Court declared that Georgia's 1992 congressional map was unconstitutional because race played a dominant role in the configuration of the Eleventh District. Writing for the majority in the 5–4 opinion, Justice Anthony M. Kennedy attempted to clarify the compactness ruling rendered in *Shaw*. He also attempted to define more clearly the Court's position on racial gerrymandering. According to Kennedy, a constitutional violation may exist in any case in which race was the "predominant" factor in determining the configuration of district lines. While the Court struck down the "race-based" redistricting plan in Georgia, it provided little direction on how redistricting authorities in Georgia or other states should draw new maps.

In *Bush v. Vera* (1996), which was decided by another 5–4 vote, the Court once again left many questions unanswered about the proper role of race in the districting process. In this Texas ruling involving one majority-Hispanic district (Twenty-ninth District) and two major-ity-black districts (Eighteenth and Thirtieth Districts), the high court decided that the state had relied too heavily on race and thus moved too far from traditional districting principles. Despite the Court's in-tentions, neither *Miller* nor *Bush* spell out when race is the "predom-inant" factor in district line drawing. Consequently, it is still unclear which race-based redistricting plans will be acceptable to the federal courts in the future.

In sum, we contend that vote dilution schemes and racially polarized voting present a severe challenge to notions of color-blindness. Seem-ingly, the majority of justices on the Supreme Court are willing to concede that the color-blind argument is not totally defensible on con-stitutional grounds. In effect, the high court has stopped short of saying that there is no room for color-consciousness in configuring district boundaries.

SUBSTANTIVE REPRESENTATION

From a policy perspective, does it matter if Congress is not a racially or ethnically representative assembly? To a large degree, the use of the VRA as a tool to elect more racial minorities to public office is based on the putative assumption that the race of the member does affect the quality of substantive representation for minorities. Put somewhat differently, racial minorities will, on average, receive better policy representation from minority lawmakers than they will from white legislators.

Theoretical tradition in the literature on congressional representation holds that the need to face the electorate forces lawmakers to be responsive to all significant groups in their constituencies. So, for instance, a representative from a blue-collar district will be responsive to blue-collar constituents even if he or she is not a blue-collar worker. From this perspective, legislators should be judged in terms of how well they perform their legislative duties and not in terms of whether they mirror the social characteristics of their constituents (Eulau and Karps 1977; Pitkin 1967). However, many who feel that they are not well represented in Congress (e.g. women, African Americans, Native Americans) believe that the quality of representation is directly related to the number of congressional representatives from their group.

One simple way of testing for racial differences in congressional voting is to examine the mean scores of representatives. Relying on roll call votes in the post-redistricting Congresses (103rd Congress, 1993–4; 104th Congress, 1995–6) for which complete data were available, we use this testing procedure to learn more about who in Congress best represents the policy interests of racial minorities. First, it should be established that racial minorities generally favor liberal policies. That is, they prefer greater governmental intervention on behalf of the federal government in eliminating racial discrimination and assisting the economically disadvantaged. Public opinion research reveals that the black community as a whole holds markedly more liberal views than whites (Gilliam and Whitby 1989; Jaynes and Williams 1989; Schuman, Steeh, and Bobo 1985; Wood 1990). Previous studies also reveal that Hispanic citizens on average tend to be more liberal than whites (de la Garza et al. 1992; Hero and Tolbert 1995; Welch and Hibbing, 1984).

Interest group ratings compiled by the Americans for Democratic Action (ADA), the Committee on Political Education (COPE), and the Leadership Conference on Civil Rights (LCCR) are used as measures of liberal voting. These indices are standard measures of ideology and are often used by researchers to study congressional behavior. The ADA index is a general measure of ideology, the COPE index tends to focus on a broad range of domestic issues, and the LCCR scale focuses exclu-

43

Table 2.2. *Mean Liberal Roll-Call Voting Scores of U.S. Representatives by Race*

	ADA	COPE	LCCR[a]
103rd Congress (1993-94)			
Black (38)[b]	90	93	93
Hispanic (17)	68	79	82
White (375)	44	52	54
104th Congress[c]			
Black (38)	86	94	90
Hispanic (17)	70	80	84
White (375)	34	38	42

[a]ADA = Americans for Democratic Action, COPE = Committee on Political Education, LCCR = Leadership Conference on Civil Rights.
[b]Total number of representatives (in parentheses).
[c]Due to the timing of this investigation, mean ADA and COPE scores for the full session of the 104th Congress were unavailable for analysis. Mean scores reported are for the first session of the 104th Congress (1995).

sively on issues of primary interest to racial minorities. For each representative the index varies from zero (most conservative) to 100 (most liberal). These alternative measures present a clear, stable picture of liberal voting, even though we are only examining two Congresses. If race matters, distinct patterns of voting behavior should emerge from the data. That is, minority representatives will be more liberal than white members of the House.

We first examine the mean scores of the representatives by race (Table 2.2). As expected, minority legislators are more liberal than their white colleagues in the House. African-American representatives are the most liberal of the three racial groups, with mean scores consistently in the high-liberal voting range. Average scores of Hispanic legislators generally are in the upper-middle range of liberal voting, and those of white lawmakers vary widely throughout the middle range of liberal voting. Each racial group performs better on the COPE and LCCR scales than on the more general, ADA scale.

Taking party into account produces some interesting distinctions (Table 2.3). While the discrepancy between white Democrats and white Republicans is expected, there is also about a 17 point average difference between white Democrats and black Democrats in the 103rd Congress, and the mean difference is about 14 percentage points in the 104th. The findings also reveal that both white and Hispanic Democratic legislators

Table 2.3. *Mean Liberal Roll-Call Voting Scores of U.S. Representatives by Race and Party*

	ADA	COPE	LCCR
103rd Congress (1993-94)			
Democrats			
Black (37)[a]	92	94	95
Hispanic (14)	79	86	90
White (204)	70	79	80
Republicans			
Black (1)[b]	15	22	21
Hispanic (3)	20	51	45
White (171)	14	20	22
104th Congress[c]			
Democrats			
Black (36)	90	99	94
Hispanic (14)	83	95	90
White (146)	75	88	78
Republicans			
Black (2)[d]	13	4	18
Hispanic (3)	12	14	55
White (229)	7	6	19

[a]Total number of representatives (in parentheses).
[b]Scores of Gary Franks, Connecticut.
[c]First session (1995) mean ADA and COPE scores.
[d]Average scores of Gary Franks and J. C. Watts of Oklahoma.

vote considerably more liberally than their aggregate group averages. Finally, because of the very small number of black and Hispanic Republicans in both Congresses, we do not generalize too much about their roll call voting scores.

Table 2.4 breaks down the data more discretely by including region. The analysis is restricted to House Democrats so that we can present a clearer picture of the role of race in legislative voting behavior. Not surprisingly, nonsouthern Democrats, on average, are more liberal than southern Democrats. While it is true that the voting behavior of southern Democrats is less conservative than it was two decades ago, it is some distance away from the more liberal voting of nonsouthern Democrats.

Table 2.4. *Mean Liberal Scores of Democratic U.S. Representatives by Race and Region*

	ADA	COPE	LCCR
103rd Congress (1993-1994)			
Non-southern Democrats			
Black (20)[a]	95	96	97
Hispanic (10)	89	88	96
White (149)	77	84	87
Southern Democrats			
Black (17)	90	92	92
Hispanic (4)	53	79	73
White (55)	49	65	63
104th Congress[b]			
Non-southern Democrats			
Black (19)	89	100	95
Hispanic (10)	92	99	95
White (111)	80	93	83
Southern Democrats			
Black (17)	92	95	94
Hispanic (4)	60	85	80
White (35)	61	73	62

[a]Total number of representatives in parentheses.
[b]First session (1995) mean ADA and COPE scores.

The table conveys three additional findings of note. First, there is significant regional variation in voting scores for white members, but not for black members. Across our three measures (103rd Congress), white Democrats not from the South score an average of 24 points higher than their southern partisan colleagues. The magnitude of difference is 20 points across the three measures in the 104th Congress. Conversely, the mean scores of black Democrats in both regions are 90 percent or better on each interest-group scale.

This finding is noteworthy because redistricting after the 1990 census was a major factor in the election of twelve first-term black representatives in the South (it is significant that this new cohort had mean voting scores on a par with the other members of the Congressional Black Caucus). Second, while interracial differences (103rd Congress) in voting scores between black and white Democrats average about 13 points out-side the South, the average difference in the South is 32 points across the three voting scales. Similarly, in the 104th Congress, interracial differences constitute, on average, 9 percentage points in the North and approximately 28 points in the South. Third, the small number of Hispanic legislators (particularly in the South) makes it difficult to interpret their voting scores. It is intriguing, however, that the scores of nonsouthern Hispanic legislators are more similar to those of blacks than whites.

The findings here are suggestive, and more rigorous testing is clearly required before one can comment with greater certainty that race is a significant factor in congressional voting. Only recently have researchers begun to conduct systematic investigations in this area. Carol Swain's multivariate analysis of the roll call voting behavior of House members in the 100th Congress reveals that race does not impact a member's substantive representation once the effects of party and region are held constant (1993: 215). Swain's findings really raise questions about the meaning of representation and minorities. An enlarged notion of representation, however, calls the Swain interpretation into question. First, the political context certainly conditions the extent of interracial differences in roll call votes. While Swain's findings apply to the one Congress she examined, the accuracy of the description for other sessions is still open to question. Kenny Whitby (1997) examines roll call votes in multiple legislative sessions (93rd–103rd Congresses), concluding that the impact of race is a function of the particular bills voted on by representatives in any given Congress. When a Congress considers racially salient legislation, the race of the member matters. Second, Whitby extends the concept of substantive representation by calling attention to the fact that the floor vote is the end result of a multifaceted process. In particular, he examines such things as amendment votes and finds continued racial differences in legislative behavior.

There are two additional ways that the conception of substantive representation might be expanded. Although early researchers (Eulau and Karps 1977; Pitkin 1967) recognized the importance of symbolic representation, very little attention has been paid to this component of majority–minority districts. Race is a powerful cognitive cue, which goes beyond the notion of, "My representative looks like me." One cannot underestimate the power of symbolic representation to groups long excluded from the political system. The fact that members of the group noticeably participate in public decisions produces a wide array of pyschic benefits such as higher political efficacy (see Bobo and Gilliam 1990). Visible and numerous African-American members of Congress represent a "black voice" in the public decision-making process. Members such as Charles Rangel and Kweisi Mfume (before his resignation to become head of the National Association for the Advancement of Colored People) became "regulars" on the most important public forums – television news programs. In the broadest sense, then, the high visibility of African-American legislators evokes group pride and symbolizes the fact that the community's interests are being conveyed (Edelman 1964; Gilliam 1996; Sears 1993).

Another, more tangible way that majority–minority districts serve black interests is by providing the opportunity for long-term black empowerment. The tenure that incumbency affords, we believe, means that black representatives are included in the queue for leadership positions in Congress. Provided the Democrats can manage to win back a majority of the seats in the House, several black members are poised to ascend to important committee positions.[3] In sum, these are positive results for pluralist and democratic theorists because the involvement of previously disenfranchised groups supports the legitimacy, and hence stability, of the political system.

Before we conclude this section, we should point out the potential policy trade-offs of racial redistricting. In some instances, the creation of majority–minority districts might undermine substantive representation of minorities. Going to great lengths to create majority–minority districts necessitates draining off the black population in some adjoining districts, leaving the voters whiter and more conservative. This increases the possibility of eviscerating the biracial power bases of many Democrats. Republicans were quite happy to support minority group efforts to form their own districts after the 1990 census, reasoning that "packing" black and Hispanic voters into minority-controlled districts would result in the election of more Republicans in adjacent districts. If this scenario occurs, then the quality of representation for racial minorities will decline because Republicans are generally less supportive of minority-preferred legislation. The problem appears to be more acute in the South because of the geographical dispersion of the black population in most southern states.

Does racial redistricting affect the partisan composition of Congress? Republican gains in the House have led to widespread speculation that the creation of majority–minority districts mightily contributed to the demise of Democratic candidates. Kevin Hill (1995), in his analysis of the partisan consequences of racial redistricting for the 1992 elections, reports that the Democrats lost at least four seats in the South as a result.

3 Two African Americans served as chairs of important committees in the 103rd Congress. They were Ron Dellums of California (chair of the Armed Services Committee) and John Conyers of Michigan (chair of the Government and Operations Committee). Several other African-American members served as chairs of subcommittees.

David Lublin (1995), responding to the Legal Defense Fund's analysis of the role of redistricting in the 1994 elections (which argues that Democratic losses were the result of white voter defection), presents evidence indicating that racial redistricting cost the Democrats thirteen seats. Swain (1995) echoes Lublin's sentiments when she argues that racial redistricting was largely responsible for the Republican takeover of the House after the 1994 elections.

This line of research, however, generally suffers from a rather limited view of the 1992 and 1994 House elections. John Petrocik and Scott Desposato (1995) argue for a more complex effect on electoral outcomes. They contend that neither the loss of African-American constituents in southern districts nor the shifts in the white population to accommodate majority–minority districts can, alone, account for the Democratic demise. Rather, Democratic losses are best understood as a combination of the twin forces of racial redistricting (the loss of black voters and the addition of white voters unfamiliar with the Democratic incumbent) plus a dramatic anti-Democratic national tide in 1994.

In conclusion, researchers must be careful not to overinterpret election results. While the creation of majority–minority districts hurt the Democrats in some areas, this was not the sole story of the 1992 or 1994 House elections. A more complex understanding of majority–minority districts is needed, suggesting that the issue merits further, systematic investigation.[4]

CONCLUSION AND IMPLICATIONS

The creation of a record number of majority–minority districts after the 1990 census reopened an old wound in American politics: what constitutes fair and equal treatment for minorities under the current system of electing members to legislative assemblies? Our review leads us to the conclusion that the critics of racial redistricting have failed to make their case on three grounds. First, American politics is fundamentally about groups. While the notion of individual rights is a lofty ideal, the reality of daily political life is that groups matter. The history of African-American exclusion is testimony to the fact that race is not simply a

---

4 Another potential harmful effect of racial redistricting is that representatives might become less responsive to minority constituents as a result of losing significant numbers of minority voters in their districts. Charles Bullock's analysis of the voting behavior of southern representatives in 1993 reveals that white representatives did not modify their voting behavior as a result of constituency changes. More research is needed in this area because the behavioral consequences of racial redistricting may be a long-term phenomenon (see Bullock 1995). For the impact of racial redistricting on House incumbents' behavior, see Overby and Cosgrove (1996).

biological construct, but rather a social and racial category. Second, vote dilution techniques employed by public officials and racially polarized voting indicate that we are far from the ideal of a color-blind society. Race matters, and does so in a big way. While we do not believe this outcome is inevitable, and we surely wish the reality were different, we must acknowledge this fact if we are to have productive dialogue and constructive remedies. Third, there is great psychic and institutional value to increasing black office holding. A "seat at the table" is important. Furthermore, having an opportunity to occasionally sit at the head of the table is immeasurably significant at this point in history.

We recognize that our view comes with consequences. It is a mathematical fact that only a finite number of these districts can be drawn. This is hardly troubling to us because nowhere in our position is the argument that African-Americans could not seek coalition partners. We also do not denigrate the notion that nonblacks cannot represent black interests. We must, however, point out the fact that there are still significant racial differences in legislative behavior when the issues of the day are racially charged (i.e., affirmative action) and at other stages of the legislative process (e.g., bill sponsorship, committee work, amendment votes). Additionally, the viability of the Congressional Black Caucus is an issue of concern. The caucus played a major role early in the Clinton administration on such issues as the North American Free Trade Agreement, the ban on assault weapons, and the crime bill. Setbacks on welfare reform and the treatment of Haitian refugees and the reduction of committee sizes by the new Republican majority have pointed out that the number of members is not the only issue. African-American politicians and their constituencies must recognize the subtleties of power politics. We are optimistic that this will come about with time.

A final comment concerns the linkage of recent Republican gains to the increase in majority–minority districts. From our view, this calls for a "fine-tuning" of line drawing rather than a rejection of principle. Providing underrepresented groups with a fair chance to elect candidates of their choice should not fall hostage to a mechanistic application of the 65 percent rule, which holds that the black population should not fall below this threshold level. Advocates should carefully study given jurisdictions for voting patterns, political climate, partisan balance, and geography. In some instances, given a particular weave of cultural, social, and economic factors, extraordinary districts may have to be drawn. On the other hand, some districts may need fewer than a 50 percent African-American threshold to effectively run and elect candidates of their choosing. The 1996 elections for membership in the 105th Congress are interesting from this point of view.[5] On the one hand, four black congressional candidates (Georgia's Sanford Bishop and Cynthia McKinney, Oklahoma's J. C. Watts, and Indiana's Julia Carson) won in districts with white majorities. On the other hand, Gary Franks (R-CT) lost in a majority-white district. The rub is that four of the candidates (Bishop, McKinney, Franks, and Watts) were incumbents, making it difficult to disentangle the effects of incumbency from race. The election results are an optimistic sign that large numbers of white voters voted for black candidates who won. But because race and incumbency are conflated, it is premature to conclude that there has been a significant decline in racially polarized voting.

The mechanistic application of any strategy, we believe, decreases the possibility of a successful remedy. The best recommendation is for malleability, because this debate will surely continue in the future. Only with a more sophisticated understanding of race and representation should hard policy decisions be made in the future.

5 The number of African-American and Hispanic members of the 105th Congress will closely resemble those in the 103rd and 104th Congresses. A total of forty African Americans (including Senator Carol Moseley-Braun of Illinois and non-voting delegates Eleanor Holmes Norton from the District of Columbia and Donna Christian Green from the Virgin Islands, both of whom are Democrats) will serve. Also, nineteen Hispanics were elected to serve in the 105th Congress (including nonvoting Democratic representative Carlos Romero-Barcelo from Puerto-Rico) (*Congressional Quarterly Weekly Report*, January 4, 1997, p. 28).

3

Unsympathetic Audience: Citizens' Evaluations of Congress

SAMUEL C. PATTERSON AND
DAVID C. KIMBALL

Today, many Americans think of "Congress as public enemy" – they are the notably unsympathetic audience for congressional politics (Hibbing and Theiss-Morse 1995). Much of the time, Americans' evaluations of Congress and its members are negative. Perhaps this is merely part and parcel of a more general suspicion about, and negativism toward, politics and politicians. But this is not the whole story. Americans are not simply negative about politics and government, or hostile toward Congress. In fact, citizens' attitudes about public affairs are ambivalent. On the one hand, Americans hold the constitutional system and governing institutions in high regard. They revere the Constitution, show patriotism and loyalty, and express admiration for the nation's basic institutional framework. On the other hand, though, Americans can express highly negative sentiments about "politicians," about the governmental agencies of the moment, and about members of Congress in general. What factors help to account for the relative hostility of Americans toward members of Congress? In this chapter, we address this question by taking an approach rather different from that of previous students of the matter. We want to see whether or not evaluations of Congress are shaped by gaps between the expectations Americans have about members of Congress and their perceptions of the real-world representatives.

PUBLIC ATTITUDES TOWARD CONGRESS

This audience of citizens is interesting for various reasons. First, it has probably always been a relatively hostile audience and a difficult crowd to play before. In recent decades, public esteem for Congress, as it was denoted in citizens' evaluations of congressional job performance, had its ups and downs, reaching fairly high levels in the 1960s and then rapidly declining (Patterson and Caldeira 1990). The 1980s came to an end with a tremendous cacophony of "Congress bashing," rising to crescendo in media commentary and in the political diatribe emanating from the cascading scandals and peccadilloes involving Congress and its members (Patterson and Barr 1995). The leading scholars of congressional unpopularity think that "the public's negativity toward . . . Congress has reached the saturation point" (Hibbing and Theiss-Morse 1995: 1; 1997).

In the mid-1990s, the congressional approval ratings have waxed and waned, as Figure 3.1 demonstrates. Like calm ocean waves, the public's approval and disapproval of Congress, read evermore frequently by the leading public opinion pollsters, ripples around an average of about 31 percent, far from even a modest endorsement. Recently, from autumn 1994 until early in 1996, congressional approval only rarely rose above 40 percent and public disapproval of Congress was well above 50 percent most of the time, occasionally climbing into the 60 percent range of negativity. Public support was notably unfavorable in the weeks leading up to the November 1994 congressional election. After the Republican victory in that contest, congressional approval rates climbed modesty, only to shrink below average on several occasions during the winter of 1995–6.

Second, Americans can feel a very strong sense of favorableness, and even affection, for Congress as a political institution and an integral part of the constitutional system. Public negativity lies in citizens' appraisal of the present-day members of Congress; citizens are a pretty unforgiving audience for the Congress meeting in Washington, D.C., today. A national survey conducted in 1992 showed that 88 percent of Americans approved of Congress as an institution, while only 24 percent approved of the members of Congress (Hibbing and Theiss-Morse 1995: 44–5). Paradoxically, Americans love the historic Congress that is part of our constitutional constellation but dislike what its members are doing now.

Third, Americans, interestingly enough, evaluate members of Congress in the aggregate much differently than they assay the representative from their own community. Typically, citizens appraise their own representative much more favorably than they rate the performance of Congress as a whole. Figure 3.2 depicts the difference between the percentages of respondents in the surveys conducted by the American National Election Studies (NES) who said they "approve" and those who said they "disapprove" of members of Congress or their own representative. For instance, in the 1994 NES survey, only 30 percent approved of Congress's work whereas 62 percent disapproved, a difference of −32 percent. By the same token, in 1994, 59 percent approved of the performance of their own representative whereas only 14 percent disapproved, a difference of +46 percent. Such differences are plotted in Figure 3.2 for 1980

Figure 3.1. *Congressional Fever Chart, 1994–6*

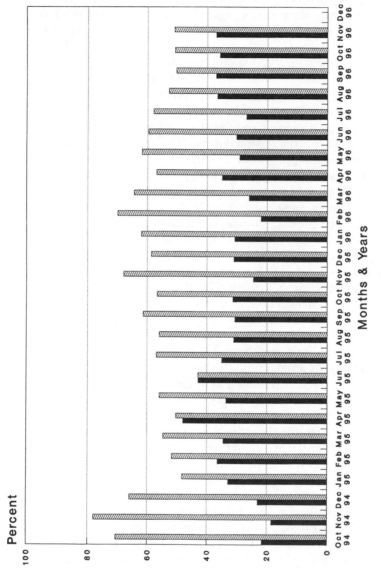

Note: Based upon eighty-four surveys conducted in various months. Where multiple surveys were conducted in a single month, the graph presents the mean percentages of approval or disapproval.
Sources: From surveys conducted by the following organizations: Gallup Organization; Yankelovich Partners, Inc.; Hart and Teeter Research Companies; ABC News/*Washington Post*; Tarrance Group and Mellman, Lazarus & Lake; CBS News/*New York Times*; Princeton Survey Research Associates; NBC News; *Wall Street Journal*/NBC News; Voter News Service.

Figure 3.2. *Citizens' Support for Congress and for Representatives, 1980–94*

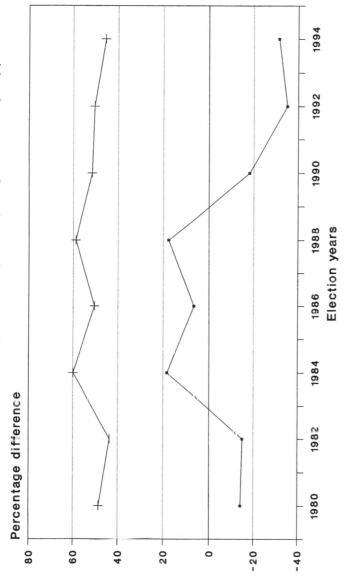

Percentage difference

Election years

— Congress   + Representative

Note: The entries in the figure are the differences between the percent of respondents who "approved" minus the percent who "disapproved" for each year. The questions were: "In general, do you approve or disapprove of the way the U.S. Congress has been handling its job?" and "In general, do you approve or disapprove of the way Representative _____ has been handling his/her job?"
Source: National Election Studies surveys, 1980–1994.

to 1994. The difference between congressional approval and disapproval plunged dramatically in the 1990s, while citizens continued to accord their own representatives pretty high marks for their performance. It appears that Americans dislike members of Congress in general but love their own representative. Accordingly, incumbent return rates in congressional elections are high. Even the 1994 election, which produced the first Republican Party majorities in Congress in four decades, was an election in which incumbents who sought reelection were overwhelmingly returned by the voters in their districts.

AMERICANS' EXPECTATIONS AND PERCEPTIONS OF CONGRESS

Citizens carry with them expectations, however rudimentary, about political institutions like Congress, about processes such as those taking place within Congress and about the people who serve as its members. Such expectations may develop in the form of fuzzy images of the institution as a whole; arise from very partisan or ideological perspectives, biases, and distortions; focus on particular institutional actions or events; or concern the characteristics or attributes of the institution's members. Citizens' expectations about Congress may develop from specific socialization, perhaps in early life experience, about what Congress should be like. Civics textbook expectations about Congress's constitutional function, its members and their conduct, its representativeness, its accessibility, or its reliability in passing legislation may shape citizens' expectations, forming an image, or "prototype," of the congressional ideal.

Citizens' perceptions of the congressional reality – what they think Congress is actually like – may emerge from first-hand contact with members, exposure to media coverage of congressional activities and events, or the reinforcement of personal interactions. For some citizens, Congress lives up to expectations, but for many, there is a discrepancy, or gap, between what they think Congress ought to be like and how they believe it really is. This relative mismatch between the prototype and perceived reality contributes to citizens' beliefs that Congress is doing a poor job, cannot be trusted, is run by the wrong kinds of people, or passes misguided laws resulting in bad public policies.

We seek to draw attention to the importance of expectation–perception differentials in endeavors to explain public satisfaction – or, most often, dissatisfaction – with Congress. Congress is, after all, a popularly and freely elected, quite representative, constituency-oriented, national legislative institution exercising major law-making powers. Americans deeply support its institutional part in the constitutional constellation and believe in the importance of the institution in the abstract. But the everyday, real-world Congress is held to pretty high standards and often found wanting. Our investigation establishes the unmistakable effect of expectation–perception discrepancies on public support for Congress, even when the familiar and conventional predictors are taken into the explanatory family.

A variety of scholarly undertakings have sought to discover why public distrust of political institutions is so pervasive in America. One important grounding for distrust is broadly politicocultural. It develops from the postulate of a "disharmonic" American polity in which political appraisals historically have shown a gap between the kind of constitutional system Americans believed the Founders had established, on the one hand, and the imperfectly working political processes, on the other hand (see Huntington 1981). More specifically, an interpretation of political distrust in America can rest on the widespread view that politicians are, as Mark Twain once said, "the only native American criminal class" – that politicians are scoundrels lacking in honesty, integrity, and civic-mindedness (see Kerbel 1995; Lipset and Schneider 1987). Disparagement of politics and politicians may stem both from politicocultural values and populist sentiments and from more concrete reactions to malfeasance in office, conflict of interest, or other criminality or scandal. Whatever its source, public distrust of government reflects dissatisfactions with politicians and the political processes they manipulate (Miller 1974).

A second component of political distrust is largely partisan. Citizens respond much more favorably to politicians of their own partisan persuasion and more positively evaluate governmental bodies when they are controlled by those who share the citizens' political party affiliation (Citrin 1974; Patterson, Ripley, and Quinlan 1992). Citizens' partisan attachments deeply influence whether or not they perceive Congress as woefully gridlocked, overly beholden to the president, or overly professionalized. Our own focus upon both the expectations citizens have for congressional behavior and their perceptions of actual performance will shed light on both of these components – politicocultural and partisan – of public support for one major political institution, the U.S. Congress.

Some inquiries have demonstrated that diffuse support for Congress is higher among citizens with high socioeconomic status (see Hibbing and Theiss-Morse 1995: 119–21; Patterson, Hedlund, and Boynton 1975). Other research has suggested that public sentiments about congressional performance owe primarily to fluctuations in presidential popularity, to negative media coverage of the institution, and to news reporting about unethical conduct (Patterson and Caldeira 1990; see also Asher and Barr 1994). Another study showed the effects of partisan

57

attachment, presidential support, and political efficacy on variations in citizens' evaluations of Congress (Patterson et al. 1992; see also Ripley et al. 1992). More recent investigations underscore the importance of political process–related concerns about inefficiency, inequities in interest-group influence, and overprofessionalization (Hibbing and Theiss-Morse 1995); the impact of political information (Kimball 1995), and the effects of negative campaigning and reporting in the media, especially television (see Center for Responsive Politics 1990; Mann and Ornstein 1994; but compare Theiss-Morse and Hibbing 1995).

A 1994 postelection survey conducted in Ohio by the Polimetrics Laboratory for Social and Political Research of Ohio State University provided us the opportunity to measure the discrepancies, or distances, between citizens' expectations about Congress and their perceptions of its actual properties. Our theory about the impact of expectation–perception discrepancies led us to anticipate a strong relationship between the expectation–perception measure and the degree of favorableness toward Congress. Indeed, we demonstrate a very weighty effect, after controlling for other, well-known predictors of congressional approval. Our findings present important implications for the legitimacy of Congress and for its capacity for effective performance in a milieu of negativism and distrust.

DISCREPANCY THEORY AND CONGRESSIONAL EVALUATION

We have said that our analysis is an exploration of the effects of the gap between expectations and perceptions of Congress on citizens' favorableness or affect toward the institution (see Klaaren, Hodges and Wilson 1994). We are not the first to think that evaluations of individual, social, or political objects are partly grounded in disparities between expectations and perceptions. Social psychologists studying self-esteem have argued that high self-esteem results when individuals believe that their actions or performances equal their ideal level of achievement. According to discrepancy theory, low self-esteem occurs when achievement fails to reach ideal expectations (Higgins 1987; Moretti and Higgins 1990). Inasmuch as citizens appear to evaluate Congress based primarily on the members of Congress rather than other characteristics of the institution, it is plausible to argue that individuals are exerting the same cognitive processes to evaluate other people or groups that they invoke to evaluate themselves.

A similar argument has been advanced regarding other cognitive evaluation processes (Bem and McConnell 1970; Markus 1986). Other work in social psychology suggests that people use "prototypes," or ideal images of a group, to form expectations about the characteristics of the group and make inferences about its members. It is possible that citizens acquire a prototypical image of Congress (whose members are dedicated, hard-working, honest, respected public servants in touch with the public) as part of their upbringing or in civics classes in school (see, e.g., Andrain 1971; Easton and Dennis 1969). Then, people compare the way members of Congress actually behave to this prototype (Fiske and Taylor 1991: 96–141).

Political scientists have found this concept of discrepancy, differential, or gap useful in various ways. Spatial theories of voting invoke the differential between voter and candidate positions on political issues (see, for example, Enelow and Hinich 1984). One scholar has argued that citizens become cynical about government when political institutions fail to produce policies that match their own policy prescriptions (Miller 1974; see also Citrin 1974). In a study of citizens' diffuse support for the state legislature, a group of investigators directly assayed discrepancies between public expectations and perceptions concerning influences on, and membership in, the legislature (Patterson, Boynton, and Hedlund 1969).

In 1973 the U.S. Senate Committee on Government Operations contracted with Louis Harris and Associates to conduct a national survey of citizens' perceptions of the responsiveness of government. This survey uncovered a series of discrepancies between public expectations and perceptions, leading to the conclusion that "Americans expect more integrity and energy of the men and women in government than the public thinks elected and career officials are now delivering" (U.S. Senate 1973: 132). Finally, an analysis of the parliaments of the world generally concluded that "people constantly confront their expectations of the legislature with their perceptions of how the legislature and its members are operating," and that it is the mismatch of the two that promotes diminished support for the legislature as an institution (Mezey 1979: 32; see also Hibbing and Patterson 1994).

We aim to demonstrate the empirical validity of this general line of theorizing. We show that gaps or discrepancies between citizens' expectations about the congressional membership and their perceptions of that membership help importantly to drive disapproval of Congress. Our data for this purpose derive from telephone interviews with citizens in a household probability sample of Ohioans ($N = 808$) conducted in November and December 1994. In the course of these interviews, respondents were asked to (1) evaluate members of Congress using a "feeling thermometer"; and (2) declare their expectations of members and their perceptions of them concerning eight discrete attributes – legal training, presidential support, party loyalty, congressional experience, reelection interest, personal gain or profit, community leadership, and attention to the district.[1]

CITIZENS' EVALUATIONS OF CONGRESS

A survey of Ohio residents demonstrates that most people do not much like Congress. We asked Ohioans to evaluate members of Congress in two ways. First, we invoked the feeling thermometer measure, asking respondents to declare their feelings of warmth or favorableness toward members of Congress on a thermometer scale running from zero to 100 degrees. Respondents were cued to the thermometer by being instructed that ratings between 50 and 100 degrees denoted feeling "favorable and warm," while ratings between 0 and 50 degrees denoted unfavorableness, or that they did not "care too much" for members. The distribution of the congressional thermometer ratings for our sample is laid out in Figure 3.3. On the average, Ohioans leaned to the unfavorable side, accruing a mean thermometer rating of 44.4 degrees. For the sake of comparison, we can report that the average thermometer rating for the Ohio state legislature was higher ($\overline{X}$ = 52.0) than for Congress, and even higher for the Ohio State Supreme Court ($\overline{X}$ = 56.3). As usual, citizens rated their own incumbent House member much higher ($\overline{X}$ = 61.1) than they rated members of Congress generally, although three Ohio House incumbents were, in fact, defeated in 1994.

In addition, we asked our respondents a standard approval-rating question – "Generally speaking, how would you evaluate the job the United States Congress has been doing in the last few months? Has it been doing an excellent job, a good job, a fair job, or a poor job?" Only one person in our sample thought congressional performance was "excellent"; about 12 percent rated Congress "good"; 57 percent said Congress was "fair"; and 31 percent gave Congress a "poor" evaluation. This is roughly equivalent to the results from national surveys and indicates a historical nadir in public satisfaction with Congress (see Patterson and Barr 1995; Patterson and Caldeira 1990; Patterson et al. 1992).

We chose the thermometer ratings as our dependent variable. This approach appears to capture citizens' satisfaction with, and approval of, members of Congress somewhat better than the standard approval-disapproval survey question. The feeling thermometer affords respondents far greater latitude for appraisal – fully 100 options – compared to the limited response categories provided by the approval–disapproval

1 A thorough and detailed description of the variable measurements, sampling, and survey work upon which this chapter is based can be found in Kimball and Patterson (1997).

Figure 3.3. *Ohioans' Feelings toward Congress*

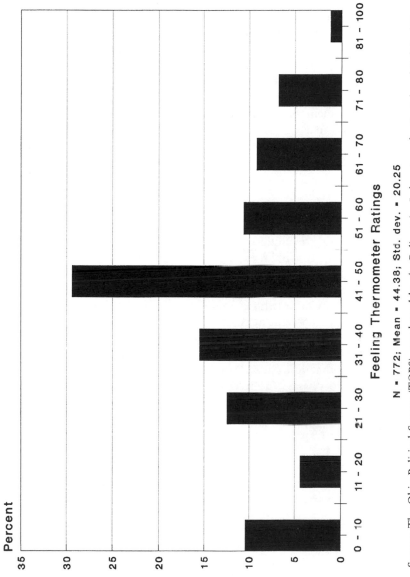

Percent

Feeling Thermometer Ratings

N = 772; Mean = 44.38; Std. dev. = 20.25

Source: The Ohio Political Survey (TOPS), conducted by the Polimetrics Laboratory for Social and Political Research, Department of Political Science, Ohio State University, November 1994.

item (see Hibbing and Theiss-Morse 1995: 42–6). Clearly, respondents rate Congress, whether on the feeling thermometer or in response to the performance evaluation question, with its members in mind (see Markus 1986: 39). Our thermometer item refers specifically to the members of Congress, and not broadly or diffusely to Congress as a political institution. It has been demonstrated that, while only a minority of Americans are satisfied with the members of Congress (other than their own representative), respondents are strongly positive about Congress as an institutional part of the constitutional system (Hibbing and Theiss-Morse 1995: 45). More pertinently, in our own data, ratings of the congressional membership on the feeling thermometer and evaluations of the performance of Congress run together; the correlation between them is $r = .47$. Fortunately, our multivariate results and substantive conclusions are very similar using either measure of the dependent variable.

CITIZENS' EXPECTATIONS AND PERCEPTIONS

Not surprisingly, our Ohio survey found that members of Congress failed to live up to public expectations on several counts. We tapped respondents' expectations and perceptions about Congress by asking them to indicate what characteristics or attributes members ought to have and, then, what attributes they thought members actually have. We offered respondents eight attributes for their appraisal. These are listed in Table 3.1, along with mean responses. For each expectation item, respondents were asked whether they thought it was "extremely important," "somewhat important," or "not at all important" for members of Congress to possess the relevant characteristic (scored, respectively, 1, 2, and 3). A lower mean score for the expectation items shown in Table 3.1 indicates greater importance attached to that attribute. For the perception items, respondents indicated whether each attribute was "extremely accurate," "somewhat accurate," or "not at all accurate" as a description of members of Congress (again, respectively scored 1, 2, and 3). The lower the mean score on the perceptions items in Table 3.1, the more accurately the particular attribute described members of Congress.[2]

2 We know that expectations and perceptions about political objects can go in a variety of directions. We might have included representatives' gender or race, their socioeconomic status, their ideological leanings, their campaign spending, or their stands on various issues of the day. We might have asked respondents to channel their expectations away from members toward congressional processes, policy outputs, or agencies influencing the legislative process (see Patterson et al. 1969). Surely we would have enlarged our roster of attributes and objects of appraisal had we enjoyed the luxury of unlimited interview time, but we had to shape our interview items to fit a limited time budget. Because citizens tend to have members

Table 3.1. *Mean Congressional Expectation–Perception Differentials of Ohioans, 1994*

Items	Expectations			Perceptions			Differential (E - P)
	Mean	S.D.	Rank	Mean	S.D.	Rank	
Trained in legal work	1.88	.71	4	1.88	.59	5	.00
Support the president	1.84	.69	3	2.07	.51	6.5	-.23*
Loyal to party	1.93	.77	5	1.68	.61	2	.25*
Have prior experience in Congress	2.39	.68	6	1.84	.59	4	.55*
Interested in re-election	2.67	.56	7	1.69	.54	3	.98*
Seek personal gain or profit	2.81	.47	8	1.62	.69	1	1.19*
Are community leaders	1.38	.60	2	2.07	.60	6.5	-.69*
Keep in touch with the district	1.10	.31	1	2.14	.63	8	-1.04*

*Means significantly different, $p \leq .001$.
Source: The Ohio Political Survey (TOPS), conducted by the Polimetrics Laboratory for Social and Political Research, Department of Political Science, Ohio State University, November 1994.

Great Theatre

The comparisons shown in Table 3.1 establish that there are, indeed, substantial differences between what citizens expect of members of Congress and what they perceive to be the reality of the situation. Although Ohioans tend to think members of Congress have legal training in about the right measure, many also think members are deficient in their support for the president, excessively loyal to their political party, long of tooth in office experience and overly interested in getting reelected, and inclined to dishonesty and personal aggrandizement. In addition, representatives are viewed as lacking in community leadership and insufficient at keeping in touch with their constituents. Notice particularly that the attributes ranking highest in importance tend to rank lowest in accuracy, a further indication of low public esteem for Congress.

The Expectation–Perception Gap

We anticipated that citizens' expectations and perceptions of Congress would cluster around both populist and partisan considerations, so we selected survey questions that would appropriately tap these dimensions. Populist orientations will tend to reflect basic qualities of integrity and responsiveness which should apply to any public official, unaffected by partisan debate. For example, are members of Congress honest leaders who keep in contact with the people they represent? Partisan orientations will tend to reflect overtly political aspects of the representative's job and be highly sensitive to partisan or ideological disputation. Should a member of Congress support the president? Should legislators be loyal partisans? Should representatives have had legislative or legal experience?

These comparisons of expectations and perceptions targeted to eight discrete attributes of representatives underscore the gaps, or discrepancies, at play. When we examine our calculations of the general magnitude of these discrepancies across the eight attributes, determining the proportion of respondents whose perceptions of Congress surpass, match, or fall short of their expectations, it is apparent that the expectation–perception discrepancy is considerably wider for some attributes than for others. Table 3.2 shows that there is greatest variation in the direction of the expectation–perception gap on partisan items (especially party loyalty, support for the president, and legal training), reflecting lack of public consensus on these attributes. The discrepancy is narrowest – congruency is more evident – for legal training and presidential support than for the other attributes.

of Congress in mind when they assay congressional performance, it is desirable to focus particularly upon member attributes.

Table 3.2. *Congruent and Differential Expectations and Perceptions of Congressional Membership* (*in percentages*)

Items	Congruent	Expectations > Perceptions	Perceptions > Expectations	Number of Cases
Trained in legal work	55.2	23.6	21.2	364
Support the president	49.5	34.4	16.2	390
Loyal to party	39.2	21.0	39.7	385
Have prior experience in Congress	40.1	9.8	50.1	387
Interested in re-election	21.7	3.6	74.7	392
Seek personal gain or profit	20.9	2.0	77.0	392
Are community leaders	30.9	62.7	6.4	391
Keep in touch with the district	15.2	82.0	2.8	394

Source: The Ohio Political Survey (TOPS), conducted by the Polimetrics Laboratory for Social and Political Research, Department of Political Science, Ohio State University, November 1994.

In contrast, there is considerably less variation on the populist items. For about three-fourths of our respondents, members of Congress are thought to be far more preoccupied with their reelection and personal gain than they should be. And for very large majorities of our respondents, expectations greatly exceed perceptions – representatives are thought to lead their communities far less frequently than they should and are deemed out of touch with their constituencies. Members of Congress clearly are not serving their constituencies well, as measured by these politicocultural standards.

Dimensions of Expectation–Perception Differentials

Our analysis uncovered two discrete dimensions of congressional failure to live up to expectations. We might simply have used the absolute gaps between expectations and perceptions as our measure of discrepancy. But our theoretical inclinations, and the comparisons in Tables 3.2, suggest that investigation is warranted of a latent structure in two major dimensions embedded in the eight member attributes. Accordingly, we subjected our expectations and perceptions data to factor analysis, using principal components extraction with varimax rotation (for technical details, see Kim and Mueller 1978; Long 1983). The factor analysis uncovered two underlying dimensions among these eight attributes. Table 3.3 presents "factor loadings" for these attributes. Large numbers (close to ± 1) indicate that the attribute belongs to the underlying dimension; numbers near zero indicate that the attribute does not belong. The discrepancies between expectations and perceptions provide a clear expression of the dichotomy between candidacy and experience, as linked by the reelection motive. Two discrepancy factors are sharply defined: a candidacy factor, embracing such candidate qualities as personal motivations and constituency connections, and an experience factor, including training, experience, loyalty, and reelection interest.

These two factors properly reflect our theoretical expectations. The candidacy factor grows out of items reflecting populist, and largely bipartisan, distrust of politicians; the experience factor develops from items powerfully subject to partisan debate. The two factors suggest distinct aspects of the lawmaker's representative role. The candidacy factor reflects universal or diffuse conceptions of proper representation – are members conducting themselves in an honest and upstanding fashion? The experience factor reflects the partisan and political facets of representation – do members have adequate training and experience and are they in harmony with other organizational units?

We put these factor loadings to work to derive a pair of factor scores for each survey respondent. The two resulting scales indicate distinctive

66

Table 3.3. *Factor Analyses of Expectations, Perceptions, and Expectation–Perception Differentials for Congress*

Items	Expectations		Perceptions		Expectation-Perception Differentials	
	Attributes: Factor I	Constituency: Factor II	Candidacy: Factor I	Experience: Factor II	Candidacy: Factor I	Experience: Factor II
Trained in legal work	.6506	.2931	.0694	.7558	.0634	.7006
Support the president	.5146	.3106	.4462	.2925	.3680	.4565
Loyal to party	.6209	.1313	.2084	.5891	.0175	.6586
Have congressional experience	.7157	.0025	-.3197	.6943	-.2842	.6530
Interested in re-election	.6654	-.1218	-.5932	.1663	-.4903	.5010
Seek personal gain or profit	.5944	-.2297	-.7051	.3034	-.6867	.3571
Are community leaders	.3041	.7390	.6669	.2620	.7184	.2377
Keep in touch with the district	-.2752	.7181	.7712	.1642	.7791	-.0159
Percent of variance	32.6	16.0	28.1	21.1	29.0	21.6

Source: The Ohio Political Survey (TOPS), conducted by the Polimetrics Laboratory for Social and Political Research, Department of Political Science, Ohio State University, November 1994.

dimensions of public expectations about members of Congress. Those scoring low on the candidacy factor feel that members are not meeting public standards on the items loading on that factor (e.g., members are not adequately keeping in touch with the district or are overly concerned about personal gain or profit). In contrast, respondents scoring high on the candidacy factor do not perceive legislators as falling short on these kinds of standards, and a handful actually feel that Congress exceeds expectations on these attributes. By the same token, those scoring low on the experience scale feel that lawmakers fall short of expectations (e.g., they do not have enough prior experience in Congress, do not support the president sufficiently, or are not very loyal to their political party). Respondents at the high end of the experience scale hold the opposite mix of expectations and perceptions – they feel that members support the president excessively, that they are overly loyal to their party, and that they have spent too much time serving in Congress.

We investigated the factor scores for our candidacy and experience factors to test the viability of our conceptualization of separable populist (or nonpartisan) and partisan components of citizens' evaluations, and we found our predictions to be well supported. The experience factor is moderately correlated with citizens' partisan identification ($r = -.23$, $p < .001$) and with approval of President Clinton ($r = -.26$, $p < .001$). Neither approval of Clinton ($r = .05$, n.s.) nor partisanship ($r = -.07$, n. s.) is importantly related to the candidacy factor.

IMPACT ON EVALUATIONS OF CONGRESS

The two expectation–perception discrepancy factors, *candidacy* and *experience*, have an apparent impact on citizens' favorableness toward, or approval of, Congress. The linear bivariate correlation between the candidacy factor and congressional support is positive ($r = .23$), while the correlation between the experience factor and congressional support is negative ($r = -.21$). This cross-correlation suggests that members of Congress can alienate the public through perceived sins of omission and commission. Citizens who have a strong sense that Congress falls short on standards of integrity and keeping in touch with the district score low on the candidacy factor and exhibit negative evaluations of Congress, while those who feel that members of Congress meet these standards are at the top of the candidacy factor and generate high congressional ratings.

In contrast, as respondents' scores on the experience attributes climb, congressional approval diminishes, reflecting citizens' rejection of "politics as usual" in 1994. To harbor a belief that perceptions exceed expectations about experience attributes – legal training, presidential support, party loyalty, congressional experience, and reelection interest – fosters declining favorableness toward Congress. Indeed, a fair number of our respondents feel that Congress needs more partisan, legally trained legislators who support the president. In fact, the negative sign for the experience factor suggests that these respondents generated some of the most positive ratings that Congress received. In Table 3.4, we show mean congressional support levels by the direction of expectation–perception differentials for the attributes which load on the experience factor. These comparisons indicate that, for the most part, the group producing the highest mean evaluations of Congress is the one feeling that members of Congress fall short of expectations on each trait included in the experience factor. This monotonic relationship does not hold for the candidacy factor, where the group of citizens with congruent expectations and perceptions and the group of those who think members exceed their standards were equally supportive of Congress.

In querying Ohioans about their attitudes toward the legislature, we included a question asking them to express their level of support or opposition to proposals to place a constitutional limit on the number of terms of office legislators could hold. In 1992, Ohioans had overwhelmingly approved a constitutional initiative that extended to legislators the very same term limitations applying to Ohio governors (adopted in 1954). Now neither the governor nor the state legislators could serve more than eight consecutive years in office. In our survey, Ohioans supported legislative term limits, again by lopsided margins. More interesting, both of our expectation–perception factors are significantly correlated with support for term limits (for the candidacy factor: $r = .22$, $p < .01$; for the experience factor: $r = -.17$, $p < .01$). When we control these correlations for other factors – partisanship, ideology, knowledge, and approval of Congress – the associations between the two expectation–perception factors and attitudes toward term limits remain statistically significant. In a nutshell, public attitudes toward term limits for legislators reflect the partisan and politicocultural dimensions that we describe in this chapter.

The Model

How does this nexus between expectation–perception discrepancies and congressional approval fare in the context of a multivariate model in which fairly standard predictors are included? We have estimated the effects of the independent variables in our analysis on the dependent variable of congressional approval (using the thermometer measure). Except for the expectation–perception factors, this panoply of independent variables has appeared in all recent modeling efforts and needs little

Table 3.4. *Mean Congressional Thermometer Ratings by Experience Factor Discrepancies between Expectations and Perceptions*

Experience Factor Items	Congruent	Expectations > Perceptions	Perceptions > Expectations
Trained in legal work	47.5 (n = 196)	45.4 (n = 81)	40.6 (n = 77)
Support the president	44.5 (n = 183)	47.2 (n = 130)	41.5 (n = 63)
Loyal to party	45.0 (n = 147)	51.5 (n = 77)	40.9 (n = 149)
Have prior experience in Congress	48.4 (n = 148)	48.7 (n = 36)	41.4 (n = 191)
Interested in re-election	47.1 (n = 82)	65.0 (n = 14)	42.9 (n = 284)

Source: The Ohio Political Survey (TOPS), conducted by the Polimetrics Laboratory for Social and Political Research, Department of Political Science, Ohio State University, November 1994.

elaboration here (see Hibbing and Theiss-Morse 1995; Patterson et al. 1992). The independent variables in the congressional approval model include, in addition to the two expectation–perception scales, standard measures of socioeconomic status, race, and gender; partisanship; ideology; media exposure; political knowledge and participation; incumbent evaluations; and presidential support.

The components of our analytical model embrace a dependent variable and eight sets of independent variables. A brief elaboration of these variables is in order here. Of course, the dependent variable – congressional approval – is measured using the feeling thermometer. The model includes eight sets of explanatory variables, with the independent variable of major interest being expectation–perception discrepancies.[3] Because we suspected that the relationship between the discrepancy factors and congressional approval would be nonmonotonic, we tested several alternatives to the monotonic assumption. A simple linear relationship between these measures may be distorting in the sense that the direction of the discrepancy between expectations and perceptions may influence the relationship between these differential variables and congressional approval. For instance, it may be that citizens who feel that lawyer-legislators are in excess in Congress harbor greater negativity toward the institution than those who feel an insufficient number of representatives have legal training. Alternatively, those who think legislators need more legal training may, hypothetically, generate the same evaluations of Congress as people who believe representatives have about the right level of legal skills.

In order to accommodate these concerns, we anticipated a quadratic relationship between the discrepancy factors and congressional approval. Because, conveniently, the discrepancy factor scales have means of zero, a quadratic equation means that the effect of the factor scales is condi-

3 Respondents' expectations of Congress on eight attributes were measured with the following question: "People often talk about what members of Congress ought to be like – what kind of people they should be. I'm going to read you a series of characteristics members of Congress might have. Please tell me how important it is for the representative to have each of these characteristics." Respondents' perceptions of Congress on the same eight attributes were measured with the following request: "Now we would like to know what you think members of Congress are actually like. For each of the characteristics I will mention, please tell me how well you think they describe members of Congress." The differences, or gaps, between respondents' expectations and perceptions were calculated by subtracting the perception scores from the expectation scores on each of the eight items. The other independent variables in this analysis were measured in conventional fashion (see Kimball and Patterson 1997). The sampling and interviewing were conducted in November and December 1994 as part of the Ohio Political Survey (TOPS) by the Polimetrics Laboratory for Political and Social Research, Ohio State University.

tioned by whether respondents are above or below the mean on these scales. Accordingly, a quadratic form suggests a diminishing return in congressional disapproval from widening gaps between expectations and perceptions, and vice versa.[4]

The other sets of independent variables include socioeconomic status, personal attributes, political party identification, political ideology, political involvement, incumbent evaluations, and presidential performance appraisal. Except for presidential support, these explanatory variables are measured in the model in more than one mode. We measured three socioeconomic indicators – age, income level, and educational attainment – to control for hypothetical circumstances in which high-status individuals systematically support political institutions more than low-status persons. Two personal attributes, race and gender (both of which are genetic and not subject to short-run change by individuals), are included in the model to control for the possibility that blacks and women (who may feel discriminated against) may be less supportive of political institutions.

Because the rose-colored glasses of partisan identification may bias citizens' favorableness or unfavorableness toward Congress – with Democrats more favorable toward a Democratic-majority Congress and Republicans more favorable to a Republican-majority Congress – we naturally include the conventional seven-point party identification measure in our model, which allows us to incorporate in the model the dual indicators of party affiliation and strength of party loyalty. Although party and ideology are correlated, so that Democrats tend to be liberal and Republicans tend to be conservative, the two indicators are not the same; we include measures of ideological orientation to recognize the possibility that congressional support might have an ideological basis independent of other (even related) effects. The model includes three indicators of citizens' political involvement – media exposure, participation, and knowledge – in order to assay the distinct possibility that those who are familiar with political affairs and more directly exposed to political figures and events are more prone to strong feelings, one way or another, about the congressional institution. Finally, our model embraces two categories of evaluations of incumbent politicians: appraisal of incumbent members of the House of Representatives and Senate and evaluation of the president. There is good reason to believe that positive or negative feelings about individual representatives and the chief exec-

4 We tried recoding or transforming the discrepancy variables so as to test other nonmonotonic relationships. For instance, we tested whether the absolute value of the discrepancy was a better predictor of congressional approval than the alternatives. The quadratic form survived the competition with the alternatives because it best fit the data.

utive affect the public's assessment of Congress as a whole (see Patterson et al. 1992: 329–31).

The Findings

The results of the multivariate estimation presented in Table 3.5 are most interesting. The two expectation–perception factors, along with party identification and appraisals of President Clinton and the respondent's own member of Congress, directly influence congressional evaluations.

First and foremost, the analysis indicates the powerful effect of expectation–perception discrepancies on attitudes toward members of Congress. Both candidacy and experience factors are significantly related to congressional approval, and the signs are correct even when all the other variables in the model are controlled. More specifically, the positive coefficient for the candidacy factor means that an increase in the candidacy factor scale improves the warmth of congressional approval. Similarly, the negative sign for the experience factor means that an increase along the experience factor scale should reduce congressional approval.

Additionally, the quadratic term is negative and significant for the candidacy factor. This suggests that as the candidacy factor grows more positive, the translation into more positive ratings of Congress becomes weaker. It is also the case that the quadratic term for the experience factor is not statistically significant. This underscores the simple linear relationship between the experience factor and congressional approval, supporting the bivariate results we reported in Table 3.4.

In Figure 3.4, we show the curvilinear, bivariate effects of both discrepancy factors on congressional approval. The figure presents the expected contribution to congressional approval or disapproval for different values of each factor scale. There is, indeed, some symmetry here. Scoring above zero on the candidacy factor or below zero on the experience factor generates for respondents a small positive contribution to their overall evaluation of Congress. On the whole, however, the candidacy factor produces a substantial contribution to negative evaluations of Congress. The more citizens score below zero on the candidacy factor (which a majority of our respondents did), the more support for Congress drops, and this decline grows increasingly large for those falling farther and farther below zero on the candidacy scale. In our analysis, populist sentiments that are embedded in American political culture greatly contribute to disapproval of Congress.[5]

---

5 Important support for our argument requires comparing the explanatory power of

Table 3.5. *A Model of Public Approval of Congress*

Independent Variables	Coefficient	Standard Error
Intercept	21.971**	8.79
Expectation-Perception Differential		
Candidacy factor	4.838***	1.23
Candidacy factor squared	-1.658*	.84
Experience factor	-2.801**	1.25
Experience factor squared	- .172	.81
Socioeconomic Status		
Age	- .072	.07
Income level	- .114	.58
Educational attainment	- .088	1.24
Personal Attributes		
Race	2.499	3.99
Gender	3.385	2.38
Partisanship		
Party identification	-1.306*	.77
Strength of party loyalty	.658	1.28
Ideological Orientation		
Ideological self-placement	- .202	.81
Strength of ideological attachment	1.794	1.39
Political Involvement		
Media exposure	- .109	.17
Political participation	-1.000	1.68
Political knowledge	.533	.68
Evaluation of Incumbents		
Incumbent representative	.111**	.05
Sen. John Glenn	.171**	.07
Sen. Howard Metzenbaum	.062	.06
Presidential Support		
Presidential approval	1.399**	.63

Adjusted R^2 = .20; N_{max} = 807, N_{min} = 261[a]

[a]Numbers of cases vary by variable; pairwise deletion was used.
*$p <$ .10, two-tailed test.
**$p <$ .05, two-tailed test.
***$p <$ .01, two-tailed test.
Source: The Ohio Political Survey (TOPS), conducted by the Polimetrics Laboratory for Social and Political Research, Department of Political Science, Ohio State University, November 1994.

Figure 3.4. *Expectation–Perception Factors and Support for Congress*

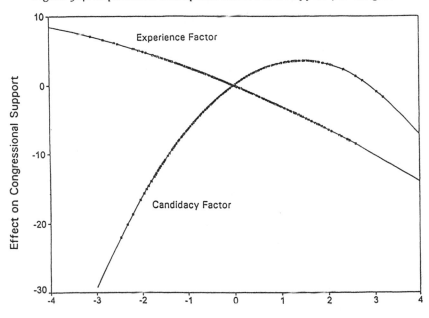

Expectation-Perception Scale

Source: The Ohio Political Survey (TOPS), conducted by the Polimetrics Laboratory for Social and Political Research, Department of Political Science, Ohio State University, November 1994.

Our estimates verify the substantial influence of appraisals of respondents' own members of Congress upon their favorableness or unfavorableness toward members of Congress as a group, with one exception. As previous research has shown, Ohioans' approval of the performance of their two U.S. senators – John Glenn and Howard Metzenbaum – and the respondents' own U.S. representative powerfully influence their approval of Congress (Patterson et al. 1992: 324). Of course, the payoff in congressional approval for favorableness toward respondents' own incumbent members of Congress cannot be expected to be one-for-one. But we did anticipate some return in approval of Congress for favorableness toward citizens' own representatives, and indeed there is some such payoff. As the estimates in Table 3.5 indicate, a 10-unit increase in the thermometer ratings of Senator Glenn is associated with a 1.7-

the discrepancy indicators against the expectation and perception measures standing by themselves. In fact, the expectation–perception differential items do perform better than either the expectation or the perception measures by themselves (see Kimball and Patterson 1997: 718 n. 5).

unit increase in the thermometer for Congress. And, equally interesting, a 10-unit increase in the aggregate thermometer rating for incumbent House members elevates congressional approval by 1.1 units.

Research on congressional approval drawing upon national sample survey data underscores this twist on the "incumbency effect" on a broader canvas (Hibbing and Theiss-Morse 1995: 118). Interestingly, Senator Metzenbaum was an ex-senator by the time our 1994 interviews were conducted; he did not run for reelection, so by the time of the postelection interviewing he was no longer an incumbent senator. Also, interesting was the fact that Ohioans were hardly affected by their evaluation of his performance when appraising Congress.

Again, whether measured over the long haul, in aggregate presidential popularity levels, or cross-sectionally, in presidential approval ratings, citizens' esteem for the president profoundly and independently influences their attitudes toward Congress (Patterson and Caldeira 1990; Patterson et al. 1992). In our data, approval of President Bill Clinton's performance is powerfully linked to favorableness toward Congress. A 1-unit jump in presidential approval (on a scale ranging from 1 to 10) generates a 1.4-unit increase in congressional approval. This trend was evident despite the president's low national performance ratings at the time and the fact that voters had, only a few days before our interviewing, endured months of Congress bashing, culminating in a remarkable feeding frenzy against incumbents and the election of a Republican congressional majority in 1994 (a result also shown in Hibbing and Theiss-Morse 1995: 118).

Political party identification plays a modest role in our model. Partisanship has been a significant predictor in some other work on congressional approval (Patterson et al. 1992), where Democrats are found to approve of Congress, and Republicans to disapprove, when it houses a Democratic party majority. Our data were collected just after the election of the first Republican Congress in four decades, during what must have been a transition period for our respondents. The party identification variable carries the appropriate negative sign: Democratic party identifiers tended to rate the new Republican Congress lower and Republicans tended to rate it higher. This result suggests an interesting degree of citizen sensitivity to partisan change in Congress.

Moreover, the multivariate model is interesting for the elements that are not statistically significant. Our results confirm the findings of other recent multivariate analyses that sociodemographic variables like income, education, race and gender are not major influences on congressional approval. As related modeling (Patterson et al. 1992) has demonstrated, ideological orientation is not significant in our model, nor does it bear a significant bivariate correlation with congressional approval, despite the theoretical possibility that approval or disapproval of the congressional membership might carry ideological overtones. Finally, the political involvement measures in our model did not bear fruit. Thus, measures of media exposure, political interest, and political knowledge are not significant correlates of congressional approval.

Because a number of the variables in our explanatory model, (depicted in Table 3.5), are not significant direct predictors of congressional approval, we naturally suspected the presence of indirect effects – that these predictors were, in fact, influencing congressional approval through their relationship with the two expectation–perception measures. Such indirect effects are, indeed, plausible. It is reasonable to think, for instance, that higher levels of education, media exposure, political knowledge, or income may provide sustenance for an awareness of congressional shortcomings. Educated citizens may be more inclined than the less educated to see wide discrepancies between what they expect members of Congress to be like and their perceptions of the real-world membership, and thereby to be more strongly disapproving of Congress.

By the same token, citizens exposed to the admittedly negative political news emanating from the media, and particularly exposed to the drumbeat of Congress bashing, may thereby experience larger expectation–perception discrepancies and, accordingly, be less supportive of Congress than those who are underexposed to the media. The same might be argued for the politically knowledgeable and aware and for those enjoying the resources of high economic status. We might expect these variables to be negatively associated with the candidacy factor and to indirectly fuel lower evaluations of Congress.

At the same time, age, strength of partisanship, and participation may have a positive influence on the candidacy factor. The political experience of those who have strong ties to the political system through firm partisan attachments or regular political participation or who have the longevity that allows for perspective and balance leads them to take a less jaundiced view of politicians. For these kinds of citizens, there may, indeed, be greater congruence between their expectations and perceptions about the responsiveness of members of Congress.

In contrast, we envision the experience factor in congressional approval as one much influenced by partisan predispositions, inclinations that include presidential support, and party and ideological orientations. Democrats, liberals, and people who support President Clinton will tend toward lower scores on the experience factor, indirectly producing more congenial evaluations of Congress. Finally, partisanship and ideology may indirectly shape congressional evaluations through their influence on citizens' ratings of President Clinton and Senator Glenn, such that

Figure 3.5. *Path Analysis of Congressional Approval*

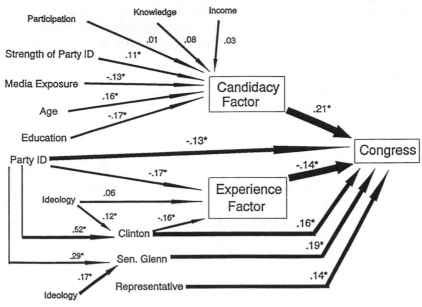

Note: Numerical entries in the graph are path coefficients.
*Statistically significant, $p < .10$.

liberals and Democrats appear more favorable toward them, and thereby harbor higher ratings of Congress.

A path analysis uncovered several variables with measurable indirect effects on ratings of Congress (results are portrayed in Figure 3.5). Six of the ten indirect effects assayed here are statistically significant and in the predicted direction. On the one hand, strength of partisanship and age have notable indirect effects on congressional approval through their positive relationship with the candidacy factor, which is, in turn, correlated with congressional approval. On the other hand, educated respondents and those substantially exposed to the media exhibit lower ratings of Congress because their appraisals flow through candidate discrepancies. Also, participation, income, and political knowledge do not significantly affect the candidacy factor scores. Both partisanship and support for Clinton bear positive indirect effects on congressional approval on account of the significant negative relationship between these variables and the experience dimension (the experience factor scale is negatively associated with congressional approval). The relationship between ideology and the experience factor is statistically insignificant and carries the wrong sign. Moreover, the positive indirect effects of partisanship on congressional approval are strong enough to counteract the negative direct effect of party identification.

While the indirect effects upon which we have been commenting are statistically significant, their substantive impact is, regrettably, rather weak. This disturbing fact of life is underscored by saying, for instance, that a standard deviation increase in education (roughly 1.4 units on the 5-point education scale) should reduce congressional approval approximately 0.8 units on the feeling thermometer on account of the indirect influence of education on the candidacy factor.

CONCLUSION

Citizens appear to make comparisons between what they expect their elected representatives in Congress to be like and how they perceive them to actually be. If there is a discrepancy, citizens are likely to take a dim view of Congress. We have been able to demonstrate the effects of this mismatch on congressional approval in a striking and unequivocal way. Public attitudes toward Congress hinge very much upon public expectations, citizens' perceptions of congressional performance, and, presumably, the actual performance of the institution. In fact, our discrepancy variables suggest two distinctive forces driving public sentiments toward Congress. For the candidacy factor, citizens disapprove of Congress because they are not getting the Congress they want (with honest, community-minded members); for the experience factor, many citizens similarly disapprove of Congress because they feel they are getting a Congress they do not want (comprised of partisan, career-oriented, lawyer-legislators).

The analysis has sharpened our understanding of the interplay of expectation–perception discrepancies and evaluations of Congress by suggesting that the absolute discrepancy between expectations and perceptions is not sufficient to explain support for Congress. The direction of the gap matters, particularly for attributes associated with congressional experience and behavior in office. A sizable minority of our survey respondents feels that members of Congress do not have sufficient legal training, and should exhibit stronger loyalty to their party and their president. As it turns out, these interesting members of the body politic are more approving of Congress than others and, often, more approving than citizens whose perceptions match their expectations. Perhaps these folks sense that they are rooting against the roar of majority public opinion.

Of course, Americans may misperceive what Congress and its members are really like. Surely there is room for better public understanding. But the problem of congressional support lies heavily in the domain of member behavior and performance. Public attitudes are greatly infected by a sense that Congress is scandal ridden, that it is inefficient and laggard, and that it is unresponsive and has lost touch with the public (Hibbing and Theiss-Morse 1995: 96–100; Patterson and Barr 1995).

It is not merely the process that is at work, but also how well citizens believe the members of the institution are living up to expectations. Americans' expectations about political institutions may be too high or idealistic; and their perceptions may be too negative and unyielding. Perhaps Congress can perform so as to make expectations more realistic and perceptions more in accord with actual performance. Moreover, perhaps other amelioration, such as civic education programs, can help to close the expectancy gap that so profoundly drives congressional approval. Surely it is on the right track to exclaim that "it's the process, stupid," that is souring public attitudes toward Congress. But we suggest that this is not enough – that to explain how process and performance affect public attitudes, we must focus analysis directly upon public expectations and perceptions and the discrepancy between them.

The successes of the Republican congressional candidates in the 1994 election, bringing forth the first Republican Congress in more than four decades, was, to some degree, a ramification of the low public esteem to which members of Congress had fallen. The Republican 104th Congress sought to recapture public support through concerted leadership, especially by Representative Newt Gingrich (R-GA), Speaker of the House of Representatives. Republican leaders, pressing a definitive legislative agenda in the so-called Contract with America, and capitalizing on the extraordinary cohesiveness of rank-and-file Republican members, endeavored to present a congressional image of responsibility and effectiveness. This proved difficult, partly because of notable differences between the House and Senate in policy predispositions and partly because a Democrat in the White House, President Bill Clinton, frustrated the exertions of congressional Republican leaders. Congress temporarily recovered some support in the polls, but the president proved to have the most to gain in public sentiment from the challenge of divided government.

The American people tend to expect Congress to pass laws addressing important public problems (see Edelman 1965; Sinclair 1989a). The congressional Republicans tapped into such expectations after their 1994 election victory by featuring a coherent program of action – the Contract with America, and the party theme of "promises made, promises kept" (Gimpel 1996). While the contract, with its unifying focus on national issues, may have helped elect Republicans to Congress, it probably also created high public expectations for the newly elected Congress. For a time, Republicans in the House of Representatives succeeded in meeting widely held expectations of congressional productivity and change by adopting most of the contract's planks.

As Figure 3.1 shows, Congress did enjoy a short-lived boost in its public approval ratings, but public supportiveness soon diminished when the contract provisions stalled in the Senate and found rejection at the president's desk. As retiring Senator Alan K. Simpson (R-WY) deduced, House Republicans may have erred by "building up expectations too high" without creating a bipartisan coalition to adopt their legislative innovations (Federal News Service 1996). A Republican voter in 1994 offered a parallel diagnosis, concluding that congressional Republicans "had a lot of good ideas, but they didn't live up to expectations" (Morin and Brossard 1996). In short, the "Republican revolution," gravitating mainly around the House of Representatives and cascading from the provocative leadership of Speaker Newt Gingrich, has been able to do little to revive public support for Congress or narrow the discrepancy between public expectations about congressional performance and their perceptions of congressional action.

Democratic candidates running for Congress in 1996 tried to capitalize on the low popularity of both Congress and Speaker Newt Gingrich. For a time it looked as if many Republicans incumbents were in some political trouble. Figure 3.1 indicates that public approval of Congress dropped to very low levels in the early months of 1996, nearly matching the low scores posted by the Democratic Congress in late 1994. However, with the passage of legislation raising the minimum wage, making health insurance portable, and reforming the welfare system, Congress helped to repair its public image in the months leading up to the 1996 election. By election day, approval of Congress had rebounded to nearly 40 percent, slightly above its average for the last decade and certainly a more comfortable level for incumbents seeking reelection. Congressional incumbents usually campaign on local issues and their own personal appeal so as to insulate themselves from an unpopular Congress and national political tides. Moreover, the fact that a Democratic president was running for reelection hampered the efforts of other Democrats to wage an effective antigovernment, Congress-bashing campaign. As a result, Republicans maintained control of both the House of Representatives and Senate after the 1996 results had been counted.

Repairing Congress's public image and restoring the public trust will require serious attention to both sides of the expectation–perception coin. Improving public perceptions of congressional integrity will depend upon changes in both Congress and the mass media so that citizens receive more positive information about members of Congress. An adversarial press no doubt focuses public attention on congressional scandal and on politicians' motivations for pursuing power, status, and wealth (Kerbel 1995; Patterson 1993a). But the chances for improvement do not seem very good; if anything, press coverage of Congress has tended to be more, not less, negative in recent years (Mann and Ornstein 1994).

Moreover, changing citizens' expectations of congressional experience and partisanship may be quite difficult without a change in administration. It is conceivable that the public could be educated to the benefits of electing representatives who have considerable professional experience, ultimately enhancing congressional support. But the results of this analysis suggest that public expectations and perceptions about experience attributes are driven largely by partisan attachments and citizens' affinity for the president. A regular alternation in the political party in power might help cement citizens' attachment to the political system, insofar as partisans could thereby enjoy a real-world experience with their own political party in control of government.

ACKNOWLEDGMENTS

Some of the analysis in this chapter derives from Kimball and Patterson (1997). For various types of methodological and conceptual advice, we thank William Bianco, Pennsylvania State University, and our Ohio State University colleagues, Gregory A. Caldeira, Janet Box-Steffensmeier, and Laura W. Arnold. For the development of the survey instrument and the conduct of the Ohio Political Survey (TOPS), we especially owe thanks to Herbert F. Weisberg and Kathleen Carr, Polimetrics Laboratory for Social and Political Research. The TOPS survey was conducted with the support of the Ohio State University Department of Political Science, College of Social and Behavioral Sciences, and Vice-President for Research. Patterson's initial work on this project took place while he was a Fellow at the Center for Advanced Study in the Behavioral Sciences, Stanford, CA. He is, thereby, indebted to National Science Foundation grant #SES-9022192.

4

Back from Intermission: The 1994 Elections and the Return to Divided Government

DEAN LACY

More than a cast change occurred on November 8, 1994 – it was more like a simultaneous revolution and retrenchment. The revolution: Republicans seized control of both houses of Congress for the first time since the elections of 1952. The retrenchment: voters split control of the presidency and Congress between the two major political parties for the thirteenth time in the twenty-five post–World War II Congress and for the seventh time in the eight post-1980 Congress. Just when the 1992 presidential elections provided Americans a respite from divided government, the 1994 midterm elections brought it back in force, though with a twist that reversed a decades-old pattern. The 1994 and 1996 versions of divided government have a Democratic president and a Republican Congress.

The return to divided government raises the possibility that American voters like to split control of Congress and the presidency between the two parties. But the reversal in control – a Democrat in the White House and a Republican majority on Capitol Hill – undermines several prevailing theories of the causes of divided government (Jacobson 1990b; Petrocik 1991; Wattenberg 1991). The conventional wisdom on divided government, expressed in Gary Jacobson's book, *The Electoral Origins of Divided Government* (1990b), holds that Americans like a Republican president and a Democratic Congress. Jacobson argues that many voters believe Republicans perform best at managing the economy, keeping taxes low, and defending U.S. interests abroad while Democrats fare better at directing domestic programs and allocating tax dollars. Jacobson's theory became the conventional wisdom on divided government since the theory explained the only form of divided government Americans had witnessed since 1948: a Democratic Congress and a Republican president.

When George Bush lost the Republican hold on the presidency in 1992, political scientists blamed the economy and Bush's poor campaign

83

for reversing Republican dominance in presidential elections (Abramson, Aldrich, and Rohde 1994; Alvarez and Nagler 1995). But when the Republicans gained control of both houses of Congress two years later, the return to divided government raised the possibility that Americans intentionally divide control of national institutions. Voters may like divided government either because they want policy outcomes somewhere between Democratic and Republican positions or because they fear unified control of the White House and Congress (Fiorina 1988, 1992). Other possible explanations of the surge in the Republican congressional vote in 1994 include a swing in national and local forces that favored Republican candidates over Democrats.

This chapter assesses whether Republican victories in 1994 resulted from voters' desire to divide the government. While I focus on voter preferences for divided government, I also test other theories of voter choice in congressional elections and other explanations of why Republicans captured Congress in 1994. Alternative explanations of voter choice in congressional elections include the incumbency advantage, campaign spending, turnout, party identification, ideology, the economy, and national issues such as welfare, social security, and health care. I test the competing explanations of voter behavior in the 1994 congressional elections using data from the 1994 Ohio Political Survey and from the American National Election Studies 1992–4 panel survey.

The results demonstrate that the 1994 Republican victories had little to do with voter preferences for divided government or changes in turnout from previous elections. National issues such as welfare and social security carry little explanatory power, but voter opinion on health care spending is closely related to the congressional vote. Voter assessments of the economy are marginally related to the Senate vote and unrelated to the House vote. What, then, does explain voter behavior in 1994? The answer is the same things that have explained voter behavior in the past: congressional incumbency, campaign spending, partisanship, ideology, and presidential approval.

NATIONAL AND LOCAL FORCES IN CONGRESSIONAL ELECTIONS

Students of congressional elections debate the extent to which elections are driven by national or local forces. Incumbency, challenger quality, campaign spending, and district issues are among the most important local forces in congressional elections. National forces include changes in voter turnout between presidential and midterm elections, presidential popularity, national swings in partisanship and ideology, national issues, and the national economy.

The Return to Divided Government

All Politics Is Local

The dictum of Former House Speaker Tip O'Neill (D-MA) that "all politics is local" suggests that Republican success in the 1994 congressional elections is best explained by focusing, not on national swings in voter sentiment, but on differences between the candidates in each House or Senate election. Incumbency is the most important local factor in elections. Incumbents usually win reelection, although how and why they win is open to dispute (Hinckley 1980; Jacobson 1981, 1987a, 1987b; Mann 1978). Suffice it to say that the value of incumbency varies over time and across parties. Incumbency itself does little to sway voters, but the tools of incumbency – "the favorable public images that members of Congress acquire" (Jacobson 1981: 237) – combined with poor-quality opponents, tend to provide incumbents with an electoral advantage.

As an explanation of divided government, incumbency holds some appeal. The Democrats have controlled the House of Representatives in every Congress in the television age, and they have controlled the Senate in most Congresses. One explanation for divided government may be that the Democrats happened to hold Congress at the advent of television, that they used the powers of the majority party to further their electoral strategy, and that defeating enough Democratic incumbents to tilt the partisan balance in the House has been nearly impossible. Republicans have won most of the presidential elections in the television age since presidential elections tend to be more "wide open." Had congressional elections been as open, Republicans would have captured Congress long ago. This explanation of divided government ignores two facts: (1) the Republicans did win both houses of Congress in 1994, and (2) the partisan composition of the electorate has not changed appreciably in a Republican direction (Weisberg 1995).

Incumbency alone cannot explain the 1994 Republican victories. No Republican incumbent lost a House or Senate race, yet several well-liked and high-profile Democratic incumbents were defeated by challengers with little, if any, prior political experience. Speaker Tom Foley (D-WA) and David Price (D-NC) are good examples.

Campaign spending is another critical local factor in congressional elections. It is possible that the Republicans took control of Congress by outspending Democrats. At first glance, the claim appears false in House elections: Democrats spent a combined $134.4 million in 1994 while Republican candidates spent $107.9 million (Federal Election Commission 1996).[1] Democratic incumbents outspent Republican incumbents,

1 Figures are for spending through twenty days before the election.

85

$100.5 million to $54.5 million. However, Republican challengers out-spent Democratic challengers, $33.7 million to $14.1 million. Republicans and Democrats were nearly even in spending in open-seat races, with totals of $19.7 million and $19.6 million, respectively.

Aggregate spending figures fail to tell the whole story. Spending levels often reflect the competitiveness of the race (Green and Krasno 1988), which in turn may be due to the quality of the candidates and to national conditions. Democratic incumbents may have spent more than Republicans in 1994 in part because they faced stiffer challenges. Aggregate spending levels also fail to reveal the impact of candidate spending on an individual voter's decision after controlling for other variables such as party identification, presidential approval, and incumbency. Spending may be part of the story, but it does not appear to be the whole story.

The quality of the candidates – particularly challengers – is a final local factor in congressional elections. Fiorina (1992) surmises that divided government results from the poor quality of Republican challengers in congressional elections. Democrats have dominated state legislatures, particularly in the South, for decades. Since state legislative candidates often move up the political career ladder to Congress, Democrats have a deeper pool of candidates than Republicans. Jacobson (1990b) offers a similar explanation for Republicans' lack of success in congressional elections: they have failed to field high-quality challengers in many congressional districts, especially districts with strong Democratic incumbents. Democrats, on the other hand, typically contest more congressional races, even when facing strong Republican incumbents.

A rise in Republican challenger quality does not clearly explain the 1994 Republican victories. According to Jacobson, 15 percent of Republican challengers in 1994 had prior political experience, which is average for the party in recent elections (1996: 11). Jacobson conducted a statistical analysis by regressing the Democratic House incumbents' share of the two-party vote on challenger experience, challenger spending, incumbent spending, and measures of the incumbents' support for President Clinton. Challenger quality is not statistically significant, though higher spending by Republican challengers clearly reduces the share of the vote earned by Democratic incumbents. The quality of Republican challengers appears to be defined by the money they spend, not their prior political experience.

For a party to run a challenger in a House election may be more important than the quality of the challenger. Jacobson shows that in 1994, the number of House elections uncontested by Democrats exceeded the number uncontested by Republicans for the first time since 1946 (1996: 12). This fact is remarkable and may explain Republican successes, but the explanation is incomplete. To begin with, in 1994 Republicans earned more votes than Democrats in *contested* midterm elections for the first time since 1950. Second, the new Republican competitiveness raises more questions than it answers: Why did so many Republicans run against Democratic incumbents in 1994, and why did the Democrats forfeit more races than in the previous five decades?

Quality challengers like to enter races when the probability of success is high. Since many Republicans decided to take the next step in their political careers in 1994, something about the election must have foretold a rising Republican tide.

But Sometimes Politics Is National

Political scientists, pundits, and politicians often speak of national moods, sea changes, and realignments in congressional elections. Substantial evidence suggests that the national economy, national issues, the partisan balance in the electorate, and even presidential approval can influence the congressional vote.

One regularity of congressional elections is impossible to overlook: the president's party has suffered a net loss of seats in the House of Representatives in all but one of the midterm elections since 1862.[2] The Democrats' loss of fifty-two seats in 1994 was not the worst loss of seats by a president's party in the past century, but it does mark one of the worst losses for a first-term president.[3] Many theories of congressional elections seek to account for presidential midterm losses. Tufte (1975) suggests that presidents lose popularity during the first half of their term. Coupled with the economic downturns brought on after the stimulus of presidential election years, the president's party suffers at the polls during midterm elections. Erikson (1990) argues that the economic effect is much less than Tufte estimated. He also suggests that voters like to balance the policies of a president whose popularity is waning by electing more opposition members to Congress (Erikson 1988). Alesina and colleagues (Alesina and Rosenthal 1994; Alesina, Rosenthal, and Londregan 1993) argue that voters "correct" the economic strategy of in-

2 In 1934 the Democrats gained nine seats in the House during Franklin Roosevelt's first term in office. In 1902 the Republicans gained nine seats during Theodore Roosevelt's term in office, but the Democrats gained twenty-five seats due to an increase in the size of the House. Thus, the Republicans suffered a net loss of seats in 1902.

3 In 1938, 1942, and 1946, the Democrats lost seventy-one, fifty-five, and fifty-five seats, respectively. The Republicans' worst loss in a midterm election this century was in 1922, with a loss of seventy-five seats (Ornstein, Mann, and Malbin 1992: 53).

cumbent presidents by electing members of Congress from the opposition party. All of these theories imply that a president's midterm loss is an intentional act of (some) voters.

The "surge and decline" thesis ascribes midterm losses to changes in the electorate (A. Campbell 1960; J. Campbell 1985, 1993). Presidential elections tend to stimulate turnout, bringing to the polls many independents, who vote for the most popular candidate. Advantaged partisans (those identifying with the winner's party) tend to turn out in high numbers in presidential elections, but their turnout falls to normal levels by the midterm election. Disadvantaged partisans (identifying with the presidential loser's party) exhibit low turnout during presidential years and normal levels turnout during the midterm. The surge and decline thesis relies heavily on the idea of a "normal vote," or partisan balance in the electorate, which has favored Democrats over the past several decades. As an explanation of Republican victories in 1994, the surge and decline thesis begs the question: Why did the normal vote change to favor Republicans?

The 1992–4 American National Election Studies panel survey provides a test of the surge and decline thesis. If it is correct, then most of the voters who voted in 1992 but failed to vote in 1994 should have voted Democratic in 1992. In fact, however, of the 1992 presidential voters who did not vote in the 1994 House elections, 37 percent voted for Bush in 1992, 34 percent voted for Clinton, and 29 percent voted for Perot. Of the 1992 House voters who did not vote in the 1994 House elections, 50 percent voted Democratic in 1992 and 50 percent voted Republican (Kimball 1997). The Democrats' loss of votes in 1994 was not due to a disproportionate decline in turnout.

Another turnout-based account of the 1994 Republican victories is the "nine million new voters" thesis. Between 1990 and 1994, the number of voters in congressional elections increased by 7.25 million (Federal Election Commission 1996). Some accounts of the Republican landslide suggest that between 1990 and 1994, conservative groups such as the Christian Coalition and the National Rifle Association registered nine million new voters.[4] According to the story, these voters turned the tables on the Democrats and will continue to provide Republican victories in congressional elections now that they are in the voting pool. The explanation is appealing, but the 1992–4 NES survey demonstrates that the legend of nine million new voters is false. The voters in the 1994 survey who did not vote in 1992 split their vote evenly between Dem-

---

4 Ralph Reed and William Kristol made this claim on several political talk shows after the 1994 election.

ocratic and Republican House candidates, making them slightly more Democratic than other 1994 voters.

National economic conditions also influence congressional elections. Kramer (1971, 1983) demonstrates that economic conditions are related to the congressional vote. Economic downturns appear to hurt the president's party in congressional elections. Tufte (1975) shows that changes in presidential popularity and economic conditions closely fit changes in the congressional vote. Kinder and Kiewiet (1980) find that national economic conditions better explain the congressional vote than personal economic conditions. Applying the economic voting hypothesis to 1994, one should expect that voters are more likely to vote Republican if they believe that the national economy worsened in the past year. Even though national economic conditions were generally better in 1994 than in 1990, there may have been enough voter disapproval of the economy to hurt Democrats at the polls.

Given the prevalence of divided government in recent decades, one should include voter preference for divided government in the list of national factors affecting congressional elections. At least since the work of Fiorina (1988) and Jacobson (1990b), political scientists have entertained the idea that voters intentionally divide the federal government between the two political parties. Fiorina (1988) first advanced the theory that moderate voters like to divide the government between Republicans and Democrats. If the Democratic and Republican parties adopt different positions on a single-dimensional policy space, then voters between the two parties may prefer split control of the government as a way to get their ideal policies realized, assuming that public policies are a compromise between the positions of the party holding Congress and the party in the White House. Moderate voters closer to the Republican Party should vote for Republican presidents and Democratic members of Congress; moderate voters closer to the Democratic Party should do the reverse, assuming that voters believe the president carries more weight than Congress in national policy making. Fiorina's spatial model has undergone a series of empirical tests that impugn its validity (Alvarez and Schousen 1993; Born 1994). These tests rely on voter placements and candidate placements on an ideological scale to determine which voters should, under Fiorina's theory, split their ballots in presidential elections.

Fiorina's theory of divided government does not require a spatial model, however. Tests of Fiorina's theory based on the spatial model may find no support for the theory because the spatial analogy introduces errors in measuring voter and candidate placements, not necessarily because Fiorina's theory is wrong. Fiorina's theory requires only that some voters, probably moderates, prefer to elect a president of one party and a member of Congress from the other party. The critical assumption behind Fiorina's theory is that some voters prefer a Democratic Congress under a Republican president but a Republican Congress under a Democratic president. In other words, the preferences of some voters in congressional elections depend on who holds the White House.[5]

If voters' desire for a return to divided government is to succeed as an explanation of the 1994 elections, one should expect significant numbers of voters to prefer divided government. The 1992 NES asked respondents, "Do you think it is better when one party controls both the presidency and Congress; better when control is split between the Democrats and Republicans; or doesn't it matter?" Of the respondents, 22 percent prefer one-party control; 28 percent prefer split control; and 19 percent do not believe it matters whether the federal government is unified or divided. A plurality of Americans appear to like divided government in principle, which lends credence to Fiorina's theory of intentional ticket-splitting.

The Ohio Political Survey (TOPS), which was conducted in 1994 and confined to respondents in Ohio, presented a similar set of questions to voters during the 1994 congressional elections. Respondents were first asked, "If the president is a Democrat, would you prefer that the Democrats or the Republicans control Congress?" Respondents were then asked, "If the president is a Republican, would you prefer that the Democrats or the Republicans control Congress?" Answers to these two questions provide a better sense of public preferences for unified and divided government than the NES questions since one can sort out voters who prefer unified control of the president and Congress only when their preferred party is the one in control. From these two questions, it appears that 40 percent of Ohioans strictly prefer a Republican Congress regardless of who is president, 23 percent strictly prefer a Democratic Congress, and 18 percent prefer divided government: if the president is a Democrat, they want a Republican Congress, but if the president is Republican, they want a Democratic Congress. The remaining 19 percent of respondents prefer unified government: they want Congress under the control of the same party that holds the White House. The evidence from the Ohio Political Survey reveals that over one-third of voters actually change their preference for control of Congress depending on who controls the White House. Roughly equal numbers of Ohioans prefer unified government and divided government.

Fiorina's theory of divided government implies that ideological mod-

5 Voters' preferences are then nonseparable in presidential and congressional elections (Lacy 1994; Lacy and Niou 1997).

Table 4.1. *Preference for Divided Government and Ideological Self-placement*

Preference for Divided Gov't	Liberal	Moderate	Conservative
Unified gov't best	43%	32%	31%
Divided gov't best	32%	44%	45%
Doesn't matter	25%	24%	24%
Number of cases	150	177	278

Note: Entries are column percentages.
χ^2 significant at the .001 level.
Source: 1994 American National Election Study.

erates should prefer divided government more than ideologues on either end of the ideological spectrum. Table 4.1, based on data from the 1992 NES, shows the percentage of self-proclaimed moderates who prefer divided government.[6] Thirty-two percent of liberals favor divided government, compared to 44 percent of moderates and 45 percent of conservatives. Liberals are more likely than moderates or conservatives to favor unified government. Perhaps voters view the Democratic Party as centrist and the Republican Party as very conservative, leaving both moderate and conservative voters between the two parties and in favor of divided government. Another possibility is that both moderates and conservatives are Madisonians, who prefer a system of partisan checks and balances in the federal government. Liberals, who tend to approve of government more than conservatives, may like a strong, unified central government. It is also possible that conservatives and moderates like divided government only because Bill Clinton is president. However, the divided government question appeared in the 1992 NES survey, after the election but before Clinton assumed office.[7]

Fiorina's theory of divided government implies that voters who prefer divided government should have voted Republican in 1994 since they

6 Ideological placement is based on voters' self-placement on the seven-point liberal–conservative scale in the 1994 wave of the 1992–4 panel survey. Respondents who place themselves as 1–3 are liberals, 4 indicates moderates, and 5–7 are conservatives.

7 Differences also emerge between Republicans (strong and weak identifiers, excluding independents leaning Republican) and Democrats (strong and weak identifiers, excluding independents leaning Democrat) in preference for divided government. Based on the NES data, 35 percent of Republicans prefer unified government and 46 percent prefer divided government. Among Democrats, 37 percent prefer unified government and 34 percent prefer divided government.

Table 4.2. *House Vote by Preference for Divided Government, 1994*

House Vote	Unified Gov't Best	Divided Gov't Best	Doesn't Matter
Democrat	48%	42%	54%
Republican	52%	58%	46%
Number of cases	145	162	110

Note: Entries are column percentages.
χ^2 significant at the .05 level.
Source: 1994 American National Election Study.

Table 4.3. *Senate Vote by Preference for Divided Government, 1994*

Senate Vote	Unified Gov't Best	Divided Gov't Best	Doesn't Matter
Democrat	52%	37%	50%
Republican	48%	63%	50%
Number of cases	119	134	94

Note: Entries are column percentages.
χ^2 significant at the .001 level.
Source: 1994 American National Election Study.

knew the president was a Democrat. Alesina and Rosenthal (1994) also suggest that midterm voters may like to balance the position of the president by electing an opposition Congress. Tables 4.2 and 4.3 show the vote in House and Senate races among voters who prefer divided government. Voters who prefer divided government are slightly more likely to vote Republican in 1994 than voters who prefer unified government or who think it does not matter whether the government is unified or divided.[8] Fifty-eight percent of voters who prefer divided government voted Republican for the House, while 63 percent voted Republican for the Senate. Conversely, only 52 percent of voters who prefer unified government voted Republican for the House, while 48 percent voted Republican for the Senate. People who believe that it does not matter whether government is unified or divided roughly split their vote in both House and Senate races (46 percent Republican in House races, 50 per-

8 Since the divided government question appears in the 1992 wave, I do not believe that preference for divided government is a rationalization of a respondent's 1994 congressional vote.

cent Republican in Senate races). The evidence suggests that even though the people who prefer divided government may not be ideological moderates, their preference for divided government may influence their congressional vote.

Jacobson offers a different explanation of divided government. He provides evidence that most voters prefer the Democratic party's position on issues that are usually decided by Congress and the Republican party's position on issues under the control of the president (1990b). Such voters should have voted for Democrats in 1994 since they favor the Democratic party in congressional elections regardless of which party controls the White House.

Several other theories of divided government ring similar to Jacobson's. Wattenberg (1991) believes that divided government during the post–World War II era has resulted from the Republicans' reputation as good executives who are decisive in crises, committed to law and order and public safety, and fiscally conservative. Voters tend to perceive Democrats as better legislators, who are deliberative, committed to fairness, and inclined to protect popular public spending programs. Petrocik (1991) offers a similar "issue-ownership" theory of divided government. Voters believe that the Republican Party provides a strong national defense, cuts taxes, prevents inflation, polices the streets, and provides moral guidance. The Democrats protect the elderly and the poor, provide public education, clean up the environment, and protect civil liberties. The voters' choice of candidates in an election depends on which of these issues they believe is most important at the time. Jacobson argues that the primary cause of divided government is the Democrats' stronghold on congressional elections; Wattenberg believes it is the Republicans' grip on presidential elections. Jacobson and Petrocik both suggest that the issues voters care about in congressional elections differ from the issues they care about in presidential elections.

The outcome of the 1994 congressional elections undermines Jacobson's issue-oriented theory of divided government. That Republicans captured both houses of Congress, no Republican incumbent lost, and many high-quality Democratic House incumbents lost to relatively poor-quality challengers all suggest that divided government can result from something other than voters preferring Democratic policies in congressional elections. It may be that voters changed their minds in 1994, preferring the Republican congressional agenda to the Democratic agenda.

Welfare reform, social security, and health care were among the prominent issues in the 1994 House and Senate campaigns. Jacobson's theory of divided government suggests that voters evaluate congressional candidates on issues such as these, while they evaluate presidential candidates on the economy, foreign affairs, and taxation (1990b: 112). If significant numbers of voters turned against welfare, social security, and health care reform in 1994 and if voters' opinions on these issues are closely related to the vote, then Republican victories would be explained. I test this hypothesis in the next section.

While the 1994 election result undermines the conventional wisdom on divided government, it appears to strengthen Fiorina's theory of intentional ticket splitting, since Fiorina's is the only theory to predict that Republicans would seize Congress if a Democrat held the White House.

Voter disapproval of Congress may provide another explanation of the Republican victories in 1994. Voters who disapprove of Congress may have inflicted their disdain on its majority party. This would explain why Republican incumbents retained their seats and why several high-profile Democrats lost. Public disdain of Congress reached a fevered pitch after the House Bank scandal, the Keating Five scandal, and Newt Gingrich's strategy of discrediting the institution to bring about a turnover in its membership. If disdain for Congress is the cause of the Democrats' losses in 1994, then we should expect to see a close relationship between vote choice and approval of Congress among voters.

Current evidence on the relative impact of national and local forces in the 1994 congressional elections is mixed. Abramowitz (1995) demonstrates that voter choice in 1994 House elections is best predicted by party identification, ideology, evaluations of President Clinton, and incumbency. Voter evaluations of Congress and of national and personal economic conditions appear unrelated to whether voters voted for Democratic or Republican candidates. Abramowitz's model does not include voter preferences for divided or unified government, national issues, or campaign spending.

THE 1994 CONGRESSIONAL ELECTIONS:
A MODEL AND TEST

The 1994 NES and TOPS surveys provide an opportunity to assess the impact of local and national forces, including divided government, on voter behavior. I focus on individual-level behavior, aggregated across congressional districts. In addition to providing an important test case for divided government, the 1994 congressional election also generated a new source of data to test theories of divided government. The 1994 NES includes a panel study of voters in 1992 and 1994, which allows an examination of voter choice across a presidential election and a midterm congressional election.

To present a more complete picture of voter behavior in the 1994 congressional elections, I estimate a model that accounts for incum-

Table 4.4. *A Model of the 1994 Congressional Vote*

Independent Variable	House Vote Model 1	House Vote Model 2	Senate Vote Model 1	Senate Vote Model 2
Constant	-2.35 (2.37)	-0.32 (3.15)	1.56 (3.21)	1.58 (4.14)***
Democrat incumbent	-0.23 (0.44)	-0.87 (0.59)**	-0.13 (0.42)	-0.35 (0.53)
Republican incumbent	0.91 (0.64)*	1.39 (0.81)***	0.85 (0.45)**	1.01 (0.56)***
Ln (Democrat spending)	-0.44 (0.18)***	-0.57 (0.22)***	-0.41 (0.27)*	-0.50 (0.34)*
Ln (Republican spending)	0.30 (0.13)***	0.17 (0.17)	0.03 (0.20)	0.07 (0.24)
Approve of Clinton	0.98 (0.16)***	0.38 (0.22)**	1.08 (0.16)***	0.57 (0.22)***
Approve of Congress	-0.15 (0.17)	-0.13 (0.23)	-0.22 (0.17)	-0.30 (0.23)*
Divided gov't best	0.35 (0.36)	0.22 (0.46)	0.26 (0.37)	0.34 (0.46)
Unified gov't best	-0.06 (0.37)	0.75 (0.49)*	-0.30 (0.38)	0.25 (0.47)
Health care spending	0.92 (0.25)***	0.49 (0.32)*	0.67 (0.25)***	0.40 (0.31)*
Welfare spending	0.05 (0.24)	-0.31 (0.32)	0.51 (0.26)***	0.40 (0.32)
Social Sec. spending	0.16 (0.29)	0.18 (0.39)	-0.03 (0.30)	-0.30 (0.38)
National economy	0.08 (0.10)	0.10 (0.12)	-0.09 (0.11)	-0.20 (0.13)*
Party identification	--	0.74 (0.13)***	--	0.57 (0.12)***
Ideology	--	0.47 (0.19)***	--	0.43 (0.17)***
Number of cases	376	341	311	284
-2 x LL(df)	992 (12)	1106 (14)	784 (12)	878 (14)
Pseudo-R^2	0.40	0.58	0.33	0.50

Note: Entries are logit estimates with standard errors in parentheses.
*Statistical significance at the .10 level, one-tailed test.
**Statistical significance at the .05 level, one-tailed test.
***Statistical significance at the .025 level, one-tailed test.
Source: 1994 American National Election Study.

bency, campaign spending, the national economy, issues, approval of Clinton and Congress, and voter preference for divided or unified government. Table 4.4 presents the results of a logistic regression where the dependent variable is congressional vote coded as (1) if the voter voted Republican and (0) if the voter voted Democratic. The independent variables include dummy variables indicating that the race had either a Republican incumbent or a Democratic incumbent. Open-seat races constitute the base category. I operationalize campaign spending as the log of the amount of money spent by the Democratic and Republican candidates in each respondent's congressional district (or state for Senate races).[9] Approval of Bill Clinton and Congress are each coded on a 1–4 scale where 1 indicates strong approval, 2 indicates approval, 3 indicates disapproval, and 4 indicates strong disapproval. Two dummy variables capture whether a voter likes divided government or unified government; the base category of response is, "it doesn't matter." I also include voter preferences on three issues – welfare, social security, and health care – coded as (1) if the voter believes that spending on these programs should increase, (2) the voter believes spending on these programs should stay at current levels, and (3) the voter believes spending on each program should be cut. I include these issue positions since Republican candidates campaigned on welfare reform and on blocking the Clinton health care plan, which would increase federal spending on health care. Similarly, many Democratic candidates campaigned on social security protection, claiming that Republicans would cut social security programs if they gained control of Congress. Each of these issues is the kind of issue that voters evaluate more in congressional elections than in presidential elections according to Jacobson's theory of divided government. A final variable describes the voter's evaluation of the change in the national economy over the past year, ranging from 1, much worse, to 5, much better.

I also estimate the model with a voter's party identification and ideology included as independent variables (Model 2). Each of these variables is coded as a seven-point scale. Party identification ranges from strong Democrat to strong Republican; ideology ranges from very liberal to very conservative. I do not include these variables in Model 1 since partisanship and ideology may be endogenous: voters who vote Republican will claim to be Republican and conservative. Including these variables in the model will likely wash out the effects of other variables, especially the issues.

Table 4.4 presents the results from both House and Senate elections. In both types of elections, a voter is much more likely to vote Republican if the race includes a Republican incumbent. Voters in a House district with a Democratic incumbent are more likely to vote Democratic in Model 2, but not in Model 1. Democratic incumbents appear no more likely than challengers to earn votes in 1994. But once the model controls for voter party identification, the value of incumbency rises for

9 By using the log of spending rather than the raw dollar amount, I am assuming that the impact of spending exhibits diminishing marginal returns or, in other words, that the first $10,000 a candidate spends has a greater effect on voters than the last $10,000. I code spending as $5,000 for any candidate who reported less than $5,000 in expenditures (see Jacobson 1990a).

Democrats. This may reflect the fact that many Democratic incumbents represent Republican-leaning districts. When the model accounts for voter partisanship, the incumbency effect appears stronger for Democrats. In states with a Democratic Senate incumbent, voters are no more likely to vote Democratic than voters in states without an incumbent. The value of incumbency for Republicans in both House and Senate races is larger than the value of incumbency for Democrats, as indicated by comparing the coefficients for the two variables in each race. The difference in coefficients may represent a national tide unexplained by the model.

Candidate spending produces surprising results. In House contests, spending by Republicans appears closely related to voter choice in Model 1, but not in Model 2. Voters appear more likely to vote Republican in districts where Republicans spend more, but not after controlling for a voter's party identification. Spending by Democrats, however, is closely related to the vote: a voter is more likely to vote Democratic when Democrats spend more in his or her district. The effect of spending in Senate contests is lower than in House contests, both statistically and substantively. In both models, Democratic spending is barely statistically significant and Republican spending is not significant. Senate races are more visible affairs, in which money has a smaller marginal impact on candidate visibility and voter choice than in House races. These results suggest that the swing in the 1994 congressional vote toward Republicans is not a product of Republicans spending more money than in previous years. Money spent by Republicans had little effect on voter choice.

Approval of President Clinton is closely associated with voter choice in both House and Senate races. Voters who disapprove of Clinton's performance as president are much more likely to vote Republican than voters who approve of Clinton's performance. This result confirms earlier work by Tufte (1975) and Erikson (1988) that voters express their disapproval of a president by voting against the president's party in midterm elections.

Approval of Congress bears a statistically significant relationship to voter choice only in Senate Model 2, but the sign is in the wrong direction. Voters who disapprove of Congress appear more likely to vote Democratic in Senate races. One explanation of the relationship may be that people who voted Democratic in Senate races disapproved of Congress for its unwillingness to pass Clinton's initiatives, particularly on health care. Alternatively, since the congressional approval question was asked after the election, voters who voted for Senate Republicans may have expressed approval of the Republican victories even before the new Congress assumed office. For present purposes, the apparent insignificance of congressional approval in House races is the more interesting result. Voters' impressions of Congress appear unrelated to their choice of candidates in specific congressional races.

Voter preference for divided or unified government is not statistically significant in either House or Senate races. Though voters may have expressed a preference for divided or unified government, this preference appears unrelated to their choice of candidates in congressional elections. I also estimated a model (results not reported) that includes incumbency, candidate spending, and voter preference for unified or divided government as the only independent variables. The divided government variable is statistically significant in the expected direction: Voters who prefer divided government are more likely to vote Republican. Once I included approval of Clinton in the model, the effect of divided government disappeared. Voters may vote for the opposition party in congressional elections to counteract a president whom they dislike, but they do not appear to vote based on the principle of divided government.

Among the issues, health care spending appears statistically significant as an explanation of voter choice. People who want health care spending to increase vote Democratic; voters who want spending cut, vote Republican. Since Clinton had campaigned vigorously in 1992 on his proposal to reform health care while Republicans in the Senate, particularly Bob Dole (R-KS), opposed much of his program, health care became a high-profile issue. Republican strategist William Kristol convinced many Republicans to claim that there was no health care crisis. Given the importance of voter preferences on health care spending in congressional elections, one might presume that Kristol's strategy worked and that Republicans gained votes due to voter opposition to increases in health care spending. However, voter support for increases in health care spending is overwhelming in the NES sample: 56 percent of House voters favored increases in health care spending, 30 percent favored spending at current levels, and only 14 percent opposed increases. Apparently, Democrats could have lost more votes in 1994 had it not been for the health care issue.

Voter opinion on social security is not statistically significant as a predictor of voter choice in either House or Senate races. Welfare spending is not statistically significant in the House vote model, but it is significant in the Senate vote model. Senate voters overwhelmingly opposed increases in welfare spending: 9 percent favored an increase in welfare spending, 31 percent believed spending should remain at current levels, and 60 percent favored cuts in welfare. Republican Senate candidates appear to have gained votes from antiwelfare sentiment. Overall, the results do not lend much support to Jacobson's claim that Republicans won in 1994 because they took the right side on issues about which

Table 4.5. *Partisanship of the Congressional Electorate*

Party Identification	1990 House Voters	1994 House Voters	1990 Senate Voters	1994 Senate Voters
Strong Dem.	27.9%	19.8%	28.7%	18.5%
Weak Dem.	18.5	16.2	15.0	16.1
Ind. lean Dem.	10.2	9.7	11.0	9.5
Independent	5.4	6.0	5.4	5.5
Ind. lean Rep.	10.6	13.4	12.1	13.0
Weak Rep.	13.9	13.2	14.6	14.9
Strong Rep.	13.5	21.9	13.3	22.6
Number of cases	813	941	481	779

Source: 1990 and 1994 American National Election Studies.

voters were concerned. Aside from the high-profile issue of health care, it appears that traditional legislative issues played little role in voter behavior, particularly in House races.

A voter's perception of the national economy is significant as a predictor of the vote only in Senate elections (Model 2). Voters who believe the economy improved over the past year are more likely to vote Democratic, as expected. Perhaps in years with strong economic declines, the economy may appear more significant to voter choice. But in 1994 the economy was in good shape and voters based their choice of candidates on other things.

In Model 2, party identification and ideology are statistically significant as explanations of voter choice in both House and Senate races. The importance of partisanship as a predictor of vote choice is well documented in the literature on congressional elections (Jacobson 1985; Jacobson and Kernell 1983). Abramowitz (1995) demonstrates that across several recent congressional elections, the impact of partisanship on vote choice, after controlling for evaluations of the economy and the president, remains stable. This raises the possibility that the change in the electoral fortunes of Democrats from 1990 to 1994 may have been due to changes in aggregate levels of partisanship. Table 4.5 presents the partisan composition of the House and Senate electorates in 1990 and in 1994. Aggregate levels of partisanship shifted between the two elections, with the model category of voter moving from strong Democrat in 1990 to strong Republican in 1994. In 1990 a majority of House voters identified themselves as strong, weak, or leaning Democrat. In

Great Theatre

Table 4.6. *Breakdown of 1994 House Vote by 1992 Presidential Vote*

1994 House Vote	Clinton	Bush	Perot	Did Not Vote
Democrat	75%	22%	38%	50%
Republican	25%	78%	62%	50%
Number of cases	384	375	141	42

Source: 1994 American National Election Study.

1994 a plurality of voters identified themselves as Republican. The shift in partisanship may be endogenous: as more voters vote Republican, more voters claim to be Republican. Surprisingly, the greatest change in partisanship levels occurs among strong partisans. The percentage of independents, independent leaners, and weak partisans remains relatively stable between the two elections.

By the 1996 election, however, the rise in Republican support appears to have waned. Strong Democrats once again made up more than 20 percent of the House and Senate electorates, while strong Republicans dropped below 20 percent of both electorates. In 1996 a majority of House voters once again identified themselves as Democrats. Whether the 1998 midterm election pulls the partisanship of the electorate back toward the Republicans remains to be seen. But based on the 1996 numbers, there appears to be little evidence of an enduring Republican realignment.

The results confirm that presidential approval, incumbency, and partisanship explain the congressional vote. Voter preferences for divided and unified government, the economy, and national issues – except for health care – are not significant. Voters appear not to have divided the government intentionally; instead, they disapproved of Clinton and voted against his party's candidates in both House and Senate elections.

VOTER BEHAVIOR FROM 1992 TO 1994

The fall in Democratic fortunes from 1992 to 1994 hints that many voters who voted for Clinton in 1992 may have abandoned his party in 1994. Tables 4.6 and 4.7 show how the 1992 voters and nonvoters voted in the 1994 House and Senate elections. Bush and Clinton supporters abandoned their presidential party at roughly equal rates: 22 percent of Bush's voters voted Democrat for the House in 1994, while 25 percent of Clinton's supporters voted Republican for the House in 1994. The rates of party switching from the presidential election to the

Table 4.7. *Breakdown of 1994 Senate Vote by 1992 Presidential Vote*

1994 Senate Vote	Clinton	Bush	Perot	Did Not Vote
Democrat	78%	18%	32%	50%
Republican	22%	82%	68%	50%
Number of cases	304	316	124	37

Source: 1994 American National Election Study.

Senate election are slightly lower, at 18 percent and 22 percent, respectively, for Bush and Clinton supporters. Perot voters voted 2-to-1 in favor of Republican candidates in 1994. This does not necessarily mean that in 1992 Perot drew votes from Bush (Alvarez and Nagler 1995; Asher 1995; Nichols and Beck 1995). Instead, it may be that Perot voters are anti-incumbent or antiestablishment and would have voted Democratic had Republicans controlled Congress. People who did not vote in 1992 split their vote equally between the two parties in House races, but they voted 2-to-1 for Republicans in Senate races.

Many American voters vote for a presidential candidate of one party and a congressional candidate of another party. Since divided government is most often a product of midterm elections (Fiorina 1992), the tendency of midterm voters to abandon their earlier presidential candidate may be one cause of divided government. To assess why voters would abandon the party of their presidential choice during midterm congressional elections, I estimated a model of the 1992 presidential vote and 1994 House vote using respondents' self-reported vote in the 1992–4 NES panel study. A voter across these two elections could cast a vote in one of six ways, excluding abstention: Clinton in 1992–Democrat for House in 1994, Clinton–Republican, Bush–Democrat, Bush–Republican, Perot–Democrat, and Perot–Republican. Each of these vote combinations is a different value of the dependent variable.

Independent variables in the model include dummy variables representing a Republican House incumbent in 1994 and a Democratic House incumbent in 1994, with open-seat races as the base category. I also include candidate-spending measures, which were operationalized as the log of spending above $5,000. Preference for divided government, preference for unified government, 1994 approval of Clinton, and 1994 approval of Congress are the same as in the 1994 vote model in Table 4.4. I also include measures of partisanship and ideology, though these were operationalized to allow for nonlinear effects across the scale since Perot supporters tend to be independents and ideological moderates. Two dummy variables capture whether the voter is a Democrat or a Republican and whether the voter is a liberal or a conservative.[10] I estimated the model using multinomial logit, with a 1992 vote for Clinton and a 1994 House vote for a Democrat as the base category. Table 4.8 presents the results.

All coefficients in Table 4.8 represent the impact of the independent variable relative to its impact on voters who voted for Clinton in 1992 and for a Democratic House candidate in 1994. Congressional incumbency has mixed effects across different groups of voters. Voters who voted Republican in 1994 are more likely to live in districts that had a Republican incumbent running for reelection in 1994, regardless of how they voted in the 1992 presidential election. The effect of having a Democratic House incumbent is weaker, both statistically and substantively.

Candidate spending also exhibits mixed effects. Democratic spending in 1994 reduces the probability that a voter chose Clinton in 1992 and a Republican in 1994. Democratic spending also increases the probability that a voter chose Perot in 1992 and a Democrat in 1994. Spending thus appears to have swayed some Perot supporters to vote Democratic in 1994. Republican spending has a statistically significant effect only for voters who supported Bush in 1992 and a Republican House candidate in 1994.

Approval of Clinton is statistically significant for all of the vote combinations, and the sign is in the expected direction, as low values on the variable indicate approval of Clinton and high values indicate disapproval. It is not surprising that voters who voted for Bush in 1992 are less likely to approve of Clinton's performance, but it is surprising that approval for Clinton does not have a larger effect on voters who chose Clinton in 1992 and then chose Republicans in the 1994 House races. If the 1994 Republican victories were due to defections by Clinton voters, then the coefficient on Clinton approval should be high for Clinton–Republican voters. Instead, the coefficient is moderate and barely statistically significant.

Approval of Congress exhibits a surprising effect. For Clinton–Republican voters, approval of Congress is statistically significant in an unexpected direction: Clinton voters who voted Republican in the House elections are more likely to approve of Congress than Clinton voters who voted Democratic in the House elections. I can only speculate about the relationship. First, since the NES question about congressional approval appeared in the postelection survey, voters who elected Republican candidates may have expressed approval of Congress due to the

10 The party identification dummy variables include strong partisans and weak partisans. I code liberals as 1–3 on the left–right scale and conservatives as 5–7.

Table 4.8. *A Model of the 1992 Presidential and 1994 House Votes*

Independent Variable	Bush 1992 Rep. 1994	Bush 1992 Dem. 1994	Clinton 92 Rep. 1994	Perot 1992 Rep. 1994	Perot 1992 Dem. 1994
Constant	-7.01 (4.30)*	-13.56 (5.58)***	4.54 (4.22)	-7.83 (4.72)**	-9.99 (6.45)*
Democratic incumbent	0.36 (.85)	1.94 (1.23)*	-0.75 (0.98)*	-1.28 (0.95)*	-1.36 (1.01)*
Republican incumbent	2.37 (1.17)***	3.37 (1.57)***	1.65 (1.06)*	2.99 (1.18)***	2.05 (1.31)*
Ln (Democrat spending)	-0.39 (.31)	0.42 (0.44)	-0.68 (0.27)***	0.05 (0.31)	0.69 (0.50)*
Ln (Republican spending)	0.47 (.21)***	0.11 (0.21)	0.34 (0.29)	0.14 (0.26)	-0.08 (0.27)
Approval of Clinton	1.38 (0.30)***	0.94 (0.29)***	0.42 (0.30)*	0.95 (0.31)***	0.48 (0.36)*
Approval of Congress	0.31 (0.32)	0.35 (0.32)	-0.49 (0.31)*	0.77 (0.39)***	0.06 (0.39)
Divided gov't best	0.72 (0.64)	0.71 (0.70)	0.75 (0.66)	0.13 (0.71)	0.12 (0.84)
Unified gov't best	1.59 (0.68)***	1.52 (0.74)**	0.62 (0.67)	1.50 (0.72)***	1.09 (0.83)*
Democrat	-3.36 (0.93)***	-0.93 (0.65)*	-1.84 (0.65)***	-3.50 (0.95)***	-2.08 (0.82)***
Republican	3.32 (0.81)***	1.89 (0.89)***	0.98 (0.92)	1.65 (0.87)**	0.45 (1.08)
Liberal	-1.88 (0.84)***	-1.81 (0.82)***	-1.47 (0.73)***	-2.40 (1.01)***	-1.59 (1.02)*
Conservative	0.89 (0.65)*	0.55 (0.65)	-0.24 (0.71)	0.84 (0.72)	0.85 (0.81)
% of cases	32.7%	9%	10.6%	9.8%	5.9%

Note: Entries are multinomial logit estimates with standard errors in parentheses. Number of cases = 347; percentage of cases in base category = 32%; pseudo R^2 = .38 $-2 \times$ LL = 1,126.
*Statistical significance at the .10 level, one-tailed test; except for constant.
**Statistical significance at the .05 level, one-tailed test.
***Statistical significance at the .025 level, one-tailed test.
Source: 1994 American National Election Study.

Republican victories, even though the interviews occurred before the new Republican majority took their seats. Second, voters who supported Clinton in 1992 and Democrats in 1994 may have expressed disapproval of Congress for its failure to pass Clinton's program. Many voters may associate Congress with Senator Bob Dole (R-KS) and his opposition to health care reform. The effect of congressional approval is greatest for voters who voted for Perot in 1992 and Republicans in 1994. Perot supporters, the classic "angry" voters, appear more likely to vote Republican in 1994 if they disapproved of Congress. Approval of Congress is unrelated to the vote choice of Perot supporters who voted Democratic in 1994.

Voter preference for divided government is not statistically significant for any vote combination. However, preference for unified government is statistically significant. Voters who expressed a preference for unified government in 1992 are more likely to vote straight Republican, for Bush and a Democrat, for Perot and a Republican, or for Perot and a Democrat, even though the baseline category is a unified vote. The preference for unified government is particularly strong for Bush–Republican and Perot–Republican voters, who likely desire unified Republican government.

Partisanship and ideology are significant in the expected direction. Democrats were more likely to vote for Clinton in 1992 and a Democrat in 1994. Republicans were more likely to vote for Bush in 1992, even though some of them also voted Democratic in 1994. Voters who supported Clinton in 1992 but voted Republican in 1994 were no more likely to be Republicans than voters who cast a Clinton–Democrat vote. Taken together, these two results confirm that a voter's party identification has a stronger influence on the presidential vote than on the congressional vote. Liberals were more likely to vote for Clinton and a Democrat than for any other vote combination. Compared to the baseline moderates, conservatives were only slightly more likely to cast a Bush vote in 1992 and a Republican vote in 1994 than they were to vote Clinton–Democrat. Conservatives and moderates appear to have behaved similarly across the two elections, while liberals supported Clinton and a Democrat.

The results from the 1992–4 vote model support two conclusions. First, voter preferences for divided government are not closely associated with voting behavior. Voters who split their ballots from 1992 to 1994 did so for other reasons. Second, disapproval of Clinton is closely associated with the vote of Bush and Perot supporters, and it is weakly related to voter defection to Republicans in 1994. Although results from the previous section (Table 4.4) suggest that approval of Clinton is closely associated with the House vote, that was based on a simple binary model of Republican or Democratic House vote. The results in Table 4.8 differentiate voters by their previous presidential vote, showing a much weaker effect for approval of Clinton. Table 4.8 also reveals that disapproval of Congress as well as disapproval of Clinton turned many of Perot's 1992 supporters into Republican voters in the 1994 elections. The nature of the congressional contest – incumbency and spending – also influences voter defection from Clinton and his party.

The story that emerges from these results is not too far from conventional wisdom. In 1992 Bill Clinton won a three-way race with less than a majority of the popular vote. Some of his supporters in 1992 may have abandoned him, primarily because they lived in districts with Republican incumbents. Of the remaining voters – those who voted for Bush or Perot in 1992 – disapproval of Clinton and Congress appears to have driven many away from Democratic House candidates. These results confirm the continued value of incumbency in congressional elections, the impact of presidential approval on voters who did not support the president initially, and the insignificance of intentional ticket splitting to produce divided government.

CONCLUSION

The 1994 election was not an intentional return to divided government. Although voters may voice a preference for divided or unified government, such a preference did not influence their vote in the 1994 congressional elections. However much voters may like divided or unified government, their approval of the incumbent president appears to carry more weight as an explanation of voter behavior. Even voters who like divided government are willing to have Congress and the White House under control of one party if they like the president. Voters who prefer unified government appear willing to divide the government if the president does not meet their approval.

The impact of presidential evaluations on the congressional vote is still partly a mystery, however. Though we know that voters' evaluations of the president influence their choice of candidates in midterm elections, we do not know if those evaluations are based on policy or personality. If voters who disagree with the president's policy positions then vote against his party in congressional elections, Fiorina's theory of divided government may still be correct. If, however, voters' evaluations of the president are driven primarily by evaluations of his character and job performance, then the policy-balancing explanation of divided government does little to explain the midterm vote.

Regardless of the impact of voter preferences for divided government and of how the 1994 election may bolster claims that Americans like divided government, these congressional elections do not mark a break with earlier patterns of voter behavior. The same factors that determined the congressional vote in earlier years – partisanship, incumbency, campaign spending, and presidential approval – still determine the vote. But in 1994, all of these factors leaned Republican for the first time in decades. Many quality Democratic incumbents had retired from Congress during the previous years, due in part to scandals (Dimock and Jacobson 1995; Stewart 1994). With fewer long-time Democratic incumbents, Republicans were able to field well-funded challengers in races that they had, up to then, long forgotten. The president was a Democrat for the first time in seven congressional elections. Not since Jimmy Carter's term could the traditional post-honeymoon drop in presidential popularity help Republican congressional candidates. The division of Democrats and Republicans in the electorate appears more equal now than in previous decades. Republican pundits like to claim that 1994 marked a realignment. The evidence shows a small change in aggregate partisanship, but it is not significant or enduring enough to call a realignment, at least not until a few more elections show the same trend.

ACKNOWLEDGMENT

The 1992–4 National Election Studies survey data were collected with the support of the National Science Foundation. The 1994 TOPS survey was conducted by the Polimetrics Lab with the support of the Ohio State University Department of Political Science, College of Social and Behavioral Sciences, and Vice-President for Research.

Congress at Play

5

Directing 535 Leading Men and Leading Ladies: Party Leadership in the Modern Congress

PAUL S. HERRNSON

Successful movie, television, and theatre productions all require compelling scripts, gifted actors, talented set builders, and above all, expert directors. Directors provide the coordination and sense of purpose needed to transform a diverse group of individuals who work on different aspects of a project into a unified team in pursuit of a common goal. Congress is no different in its need for strong direction. In this era of independent-minded politicians, hyperactive lobbying groups, gavel-to-gavel media coverage, and hyperbolic and often rancorous debate, good direction is more important then ever for Congress to perform its duties. Good direction is also needed for congressional parties to mobilize public support for their policies and the reelection of their members. Most of this direction is provided by congressional party leaders. This chapter focuses on the challenges, strategies, and tactics that congressional party leaders use to try to direct their troupes and obtain favorable reviews from the press and the general public.

THE CAST OF CHARACTERS: MEMBERS OF CONGRESS

Members of the House of Representatives are locally elected officials who make national policy. Members of the Senate have a similar job description even though they are elected in statewide elections and serve six-year instead of two-year terms. Candidate-centered elections have a major impact on the behavior of both legislators and leaders in Congress. They result in legislators being highly responsive to constituents and generally temper leaders' expectations that party members will toe the party line on major issues. Institutional arrangements that allow congressional leaders to lose on a major policy vote without having to issue an immediate call for elections also leave members of Congress less inclined to follow party directives than are legislators in parliamentary democracies.

The independent style of representation that is rooted in American political institutions is reinforced by the diverse constituencies, interests, and values that different members of Congress represent. Congressional committees, subcommittees, state delegations, and other groups provide information, support, and decision-making cues that further support legislators' individualism. The more heterogeneous their party's membership and the more autonomy afforded to congressional committees and other groups, the more difficult it is for party leaders to get their members to support core policy objectives or coordinate the comments they make to the mass media.

Backbench members of Congress may be denied leading roles on Capitol Hill, but as popularly elected officials, most enjoy celebrity status back home. They cultivate this status by holding town meetings, attending ceremonial events, and using their press aides to build good relations with journalists and voters (Cook 1989: ch. 4; Fenno 1978). Leaders recognize that they must accommodate their members' electoral concerns, policy preferences, and egos when they formulate their legislative and media strategies. Political institutions, a diverse membership, and the home styles of individual members work to decentralize Congress.

THE DIRECTORS: CONGRESSIONAL PARTY LEADERS

Political parties have been the chief organizing agents of Congress since 1793. Party leaders, in consultation with their members, make committee assignments, schedule floor and other activities, and distribute many of the resources Congress needs to do its work. Party leaders also endeavor to develop and advance their party's vision for the nation's future, publicize their party's accomplishments, and assist their members with reelection. The modern Congress has developed extensive leadership structures and norms of operation to help congressional leaders overcome the legislative branch's tendency toward decentralization.

Bicameralism and the two-party system result in Congress having four independent leadership structures. The majority-party leadership organization in the House is headed by the Speaker, who is assisted by the majority leader; the assistant majority leader, or "whip"; and the caucus (or conference) chair. Below these officials is a network of deputy, regional, and assistant whips and other officials, including those who serve on party policy and research committees and task forces.

The minority party in the House is headed by the minority leader rather than the Speaker, but its structure is similar to that of the majority party. It has its own whip system, policy and research committees, and caucus officials. In addition, each congressional party has a campaign committee that works to reelect the party's incumbents and elect new party members to the House. These committees are not officially part of Congress, but their chairs are congressional party leaders, and members view them as a part of the party's extragovernmental leadership apparatus.

Senate leadership organizations are less extensive than those in the House, reflecting the upper chamber's smaller membership. Each Senate party organization is headed by a leader and has a whip, a conference chair, other whips, a policy committee, and other officials. Like their House counterparts, Senate Democrats and Republicans have party campaign committees to assist them and nonincumbent candidates with their elections.

The organizational structures of all four congressional parties have grown in recent years to allow leaders to better serve the individual and collective needs of party members. These include helping members campaign for reelection, conducting policy research, building legislative coalitions, and carrying out public relations activities. The whip systems in the House, in particular, have experienced tremendous growth. During the 1970s, House Democrats had a majority whip, a deputy whip, and roughly eighteen regionally elected zone whips. By 1993 this force of twenty had expanded to ninety-four (Sinclair 1995: 119). The House GOP's whip system experienced a similar expansion. By the 104th Congress, House Republicans had 55 legislators in their formal whip system.[1] Different leadership offices have also chartered numerous ad hoc task forces to help formulate and carry out legislative and public relations activities. These enlarged leadership organizations have helped party leaders incorporate their members' views when crafting legislative proposals and public relations campaigns. They have also helped the leaders mobilize their members on important roll call votes.

The number of participants involved in Senate leadership activities also expanded in 1989, when then-Senate majority leader George Mitchell (D-ME) dispersed power by appointing Senator Daniel Inouye (D-HI) to chair the Democrats' Steering Committee and Senator Tom Daschle (D-SD) to cochair the Democratic Policy Committee. As minority leader, Daschle increased this decentralization, appointing Jay Rockefeller (D-WV) to head the party's Steering Committee, John Kerry (D-MA) to lead the Technology and Communications Committee, and Harry Reid (D-NV) to cochair the Policy Committee. Under Senator Robert Dole (R-KS), Senate Republicans increased the number of legislators involved in their leadership efforts, but not as much as the Democrats. The initial activities of Dole's successor, Senate Majority Leader Trent Lott (R-MS), suggested that he will not change the Senate Repub-

1 Information provided by the office of Representative Tom DeLay, majority whip.

lican leadership structure but rather will try to centralize power through rules changes and by clamping down on Senate procedures (Stiehm 1996). Decisions by party leaders to increase the size of the leadership structures are informed by a strategy of inclusion premised on the belief that the more members involved in drafting or implementing a legislative program, the easier it is to build a coalition behind it and the more likely it is to succeed (Sinclair 1981).

Congressional leaders are selected privately in party caucuses, but the majority party's choice for Speaker of the House is formally ratified on the House floor. Party leaders have traditionally been senior members of Congress who have displayed high levels of party loyalty, helped colleagues with their electoral needs, and assisted in building policy coalitions (e.g., Davidson and Oleszek 1994: 172). Besides seniority, Senate Democrats usually consider region and ideology when selecting their leaders. House Democrats often consider race and gender, reserving some lower-level leadership posts, including a few deputy whip slots, for women and minorities. Given their greater homogeneity, Republicans have been somewhat less concerned with race, but they, too, have assigned women to lower leadership posts. During the 104th Congress, House Republicans downgraded the importance of regional balance in favor of conservatism, party loyalty, and aggressive leadership styles. Three of the top four GOP leaders are southern conservatives, and two – majority leader Dick Armey and majority whip Tom DeLay – are from Texas.

Both parties have emphasized telegenic skills in recent years. Former Senate majority leader George Mitchell was chosen as the replacement for Senator Robert Byrd (D-WV) because he had more media savvy and television appeal than Byrd. House minority leader Richard Gephardt (D-MO) and House minority whip David Bonior (D-MI) were, in large part, selected by their Democratic colleagues because of their media presence. Telegenic skills also played a role in the selection of Senator Trent Lott as Senate majority leader, Representative Newt Gingrich (R-GA) as Speaker of the House, and Representative Armey as House majority leader.

The selection of more telegenic leaders is not the result of mere accident. The proportion of candidates for leadership posts who established a media presence in order to advance their leadership campaigns grew between the 1970s and 1990s. These media-oriented strategies have had a significant effect on the outcome of races for caucus chair and the other lower-level leadership offices that serve as stepping stones to higher posts (Hardt 1993: ch. 6).

Even though legislators seem to agree about the importance of a leader's ability to appeal to the media, there is some disagreement about the other qualities that are desirable in a leader. In recent years, House Democrats have preferred leaders who have collegial styles that emphasize bargaining, negotiation, and cooperation (Davidson and Oleszek 1994: 172–3). Former Democratic Speakers "Tip" (Thomas P.) O'Neill (D-MA) and Thomas Foley (D-WA) utilized these styles of leadership. Former Democratic Speaker Jim Wright (D-TX) was an exception to the norm. His forceful style of leadership made him unpopular with some House Democrats and led many to desert him after he was brought up on ethics charges. The lack of fealty that some House Democrats showed to Wright hints at the fact that leaders are responsible to their members. Congressional leaders who forget this fact run the risk of being stripped of some of their powers (Jones 1968).

For much of the forty-year period when they were in the minority, House Republicans also selected consensus-oriented, collegial leaders such as former Minority Leader Bob Michel (R-IL). Michel often deferred to the GOP's ranking committee members and worked with the Democratic majority in order to enhance GOP input into the legislative process. The coming of age of the conservative, southern wing of the party; the decline of its moderate northeastern wing; and frustrations and indignities associated with being in the minority, encouraged House Republicans to turn to some more combative leaders, many of whom are members of the Conservative Opportunity Society (COS), a group of obstructionists who worked to overthrow the former Democratic establishment through confrontational tactics (Connelly and Pitney 1994: 27). The election of COS member Newt Gingrich as minority whip and three other COS members to leadership posts in 1989 marked a turning point in the Republican party. From that point forward, House Republicans have been led by a team that is more forceful, more partisan, and more conservative (Connelly and Pitney 1994: 27).

Once in the majority, the Gingrich regime transformed House procedures, centralizing power under the Speaker. During the 104th Congress, Gingrich gave less free rein to committee and subcommittee chairs than recent Republican and Democratic leaders, often expecting them to subsume their own goals to those of the leadership. Chairs who expressed an unwillingness or inability to follow the Speaker's directives were threatened with replacement. When one committee chairman informed Gingrich that he thought he would be unable to meet a deadline for one of the elements of the Republicans' Contract with America, Gingrich told him "If you can't do it . . . I will find someone who will" (Rosenstiel 1995).

Gingrich also centralized power by using task forces to bypass the committee system when developing legislation. This is not without precedent, but the degree to which Gingrich used task forces to draft major bills comprises an important institutional change in the legislative process in the House. During the 104th Congress, the GOP leadership used task forces to develop some major legislation, including most contract-related and politically sensitive bills. The Republican Medicare proposal, for example, was developed by a task force that was handpicked by the Speaker rather than by the Commerce and Ways and Means committees. Commerce Committee Chairman Thomas Bliley (R-VA), and Ways and Means Committee Chairman Bill Archer (R-TX), the American Medical Association, and other pro-Republican groups had input into the bill, but the legislation was written outside the committee system, beyond the public purview, and without the input of the minority party and groups that generally do not support the GOP.

Republican House leaders centralized power in order to encourage party discipline, minimize opportunities for Democratic opposition, and enable the Speaker to tightly control the GOP's public relations activities. The seventy-three House Republican freshmen elected during the 1994 election and other GOP House members who credited Gingrich with the Republican takeover supported giving the Speaker more power. Many of these individuals had little, if any, interest in supporting the existing legislative procedures and believed that empowering the leadership was the best way to promote the major change that they considered to be their mandate. Committee and subcommittee chairmen and rank-and-file GOP House members initially acquiesced for many reasons, including agreement with the leadership's broader policy goals, a desire to pass decades' worth of legislation that had been bottled up under successive Democratic-controlled Congresses, and a recognition that supporting leadership bills would be necessary to keep or obtain desirable committee assignments and other posts. The belief that the GOP's prospects for maintaining control of Congress after the next election would be tied to the party's success in implementing its agenda was also critical (Czwartacki 1995). However, as the debate over the federal budget became prolonged, moderate and conservative House and Senate Republicans, including some freshmen and committee leaders, began to feud with each other, showing the limits to this centralization.

WRITING THE SCRIPT: PARTIES AND ELECTION AGENDAS

One of the most important things that contemporary congressional leaders do to help unify party members is to encourage them to campaign on similar issues and themes. Traditionally, party manifestos were written by the party's national committees and oriented toward the presidential election. Party briefing materials expounded on a party's platform, presented biographical information on its candidates, criticized the opposing party and its standard-bearers, and presented speeches, statistics, and other information for the use of candidates, campaign workers, and journalists (Sait 1927: 494). Most of the central direction that was given to the campaign was provided by the parties' national committee.

During the late 1970s and early 1980s, congressional party leaders stepped up their campaign activities in several important ways. They strengthened the Democratic and Republican national, congressional, and senatorial campaign committees, enabling the committees to air party-focused campaign ads on television and provide many congressional candidates with money and services in campaign management, fundraising, polling, issue and opposition research, and communications (Herrnson 1988: chs. 2–4; 1995: ch. 4). Since the early 1980s House Democrats also produced issues handbooks from which they and other Democrats could draw talking points and statistics for use in their campaigns. The first issues handbook, which was titled *Rebuilding the Road to Opportunity*, was published in time for the 1982 election (Democratic Caucus 1982). It was followed by a series of other handbooks and lengthy election memoranda that were published in every election cycle through 1992, when the Democrats won control of the presidency and both chambers of Congress (Herrnson and Patterson 1995; 617, 625; Patterson 1992: 81). During the 1996 elections, the House Democratic Caucus once again decided not to produce an issues handbook. Democratic leaders in the House and Senate did, however, collaborate in producing the Families First Agenda, a campaign manifesto that articulated a series of moderate, incremental policy changes to help working families.

House Republicans have also published a variety of election-oriented documents, including issues handbooks, talking points, and other campaign memoranda. In November 1993, then–House Republican Conference Chairman Dick Armey published *Under the Clinton Big Top*, a detailed critique of the president's performance on domestic policy, defense policy, foreign affairs, ethics, and leadership (Armey 1993). In August 1994, Armey and Representatives Jennifer Dunn (R-WA) and Christopher Shays (R-CT) published *It's Long Enough: The Decline of Popular Government under Forty Years of Single Party Control of the U.S. House of Representatives*, a "populist/progressive" critique of the special interest culture they assert developed in the House under forty years of Democratic control (Armey, Dunn, and Shays 1994). These publications laid the groundwork for the negative, anti-Clinton/anti-Congress campaigns waged by many GOP congressional candidates.

Then–Minority Whip Gingrich supplied the positive message that was used by many Republican candidates when he and other GOP leaders distilled some popular ideas into a ten-point program that eventually became known as the Contract with America (e.g., Gimpel 1996). Elements of the contract were tested in polls and focus groups to help package it in a way that Perot voters, ticket splitters, and conservative Democrats would find appealing (Koopman 1994). In late September, the contract was unveiled and signed by 367 Republican House members and candidates at a formal ceremony that took place on the Capitol steps. The signing of the contract was an unprecedented event in the history of congressional elections because the document would later be treated as a binding platform by most Republican House members. Previous attempts to publicize a binding campaign agenda, such as the manifesto that Republican House members had hoped to present to voters on Governing Team Day (September 27, 1980), had failed because some Republican candidates were reticent to make specific policy pledges and would only agree to the presentation of election documents that consisted of a statement of party principles (see Herrnson, Patterson, and Pitney 1995). House Republican leaders did not produce a new campaign manifesto in 1996, opting instead to give their members talking points to highlight the high points of the 1994 contract and defend their legislative performance against Democratic attacks.

Senate candidates tend to be more independent of their party than are House candidates. Senate campaigns have larger staffs, enabling them to be more independent of their party for policy and political research. The greater visibility of the office also means that the Senate candidates' issue positions tend to be better known by voters. Nevertheless, in recent years Senate leadership organizations, including the parties' senatorial campaign committees, have disseminated more issue-oriented campaign materials (Herrnson et al. 1995; Langdon 1995; Smith 1993: 259). These materials have promoted greater issue consistency in the campaigns that party members wage for the Senate.

The contract, *It's Long Enough,* and other partisan communications do not guarantee that congressional candidates of the same party will campaign on the same issues. Candidates for Congress exercise their freedom to choose the themes and issues around which their campaigns are based. What these publications and the research and communications assistance distributed by the parties' congressional and senatorial campaign committees do, however, is provide candidates with useful information from which they can develop their issue positions and stump speeches. Increased party activity in elections has helped to promote similarities in the congressional campaigns waged by members of the same party and to sharpen the differences between the campaigns waged by members of different parties. However, because party recommendations are largely advisory, the parties' increased campaign role has not transformed the candidate-centered U.S. election system into a party-focused system similar to those in most other modern democracies.

CASTING THE ROLES: MAKING COMMITTEE ASSIGNMENTS

One of the most important powers that congressional party leaders possess is concerned with the distribution of committee assignments. Each congressional party has a special committee to consider members' assignment requests. These panels are chaired and largely dominated by the party's leader in the chamber.[2] They weigh a number of factors when considering member requests for committee assignments. Seniority, electoral security, substantive expertise, ideology, party loyalty, region, district characteristics, gender, and the role played by the member who has vacated the seat have traditionally been important (see Davidson and Oleszek 1994: 218–19; Rieselbach 1995: 88–90).

The number and variety of criteria utilized in the assignment process give party leaders tremendous leeway in submitting recommendations for committee assignments to their members for approval. Majority-party leaders can also increase the size of a committee or change its partisan balance to accommodate member requests. This gives party leaders a large measure of control over committee appointments, which they can use to reward or build loyalty and to punish disloyalty or limit the power of rivals. During the 104th Congress, Speaker Gingrich shored up his goodwill with House freshmen by enabling several from their ranks to leapfrog more senior colleagues and gain assignments to such prestigious committees as Ways and Means, Appropriations, Budget, and Rules. He also used his influence over the House Republicans' Committee on Committees to reassign freshman Representative Mark Neumann (R-WI) from the powerful National Security Subcommittee of the House Appropriations Committee to the less influential Subcommittee on Military Construction after Neumann failed to support the Republican leadership's position on the Security Committee's appropriations

2 Control over most of the appointments to the assignment panel (or, in the case of House Republicans, weighted voting procedures) give congressional party leaders the ability to dominate the assignment process (see Davidson and Oleszek 1994: 218–19; Jacoby 1994a, 1994b).

bill.[3] By bypassing senior members when making committee assignments and by removing, and implicitly threatening to remove, others, the Speaker established his influence over committee activities.

The influence that party members and leaders have over the selection of committee and subcommittee chairs has also grown since the 1970s, largely at the expense of seniority (Rohde 1991: 74–6). House Democrats weakened the seniority norm when they ousted several longtime committee chairs whose age, health, or dispositions served to undermine their leadership abilities. Other chairs, most notably Representative Les Aspin (D-WI), have faced challenges because of policy disagreements between themselves and the majority of their congressional party (see Davidson and Oleszek 1994: 220).

The seniority system came under what has been perhaps its biggest assault immediately following the 1994 election. Within a week of the GOP takeover of the House, Gingrich announced that Representative Robert Livingston (R-LA), who was the fifth in seniority on the Appropriations Committee, would vault over other GOP committee members to become committee chairman (Kahn and Burger 1994). Others who would be promoted to chairmanships over more senior members include Representative Thomas Bliley (R-VA), on Commerce, and Representative Henry Hyde (R-IL), on Judiciary.[4] Moreover, Representative David McIntosh (R-IN), a House freshman, was selected to chair the National Economic Growth, Natural Resources, and Regulatory Affairs Subcommittee of the Government Reform and Oversight Committee. These chairmen were chosen because of their support for the contract, activist credentials, loyalty to the Speaker, and ability to serve as strong, articulate party spokesmen (Kahn and Burger 1994; Karmin 1994). House Republicans have gone much further in emphasizing party loyalty than their Democratic counterparts. Prior to receiving their assignment, all Republican members of the Appropriations Committee were required to sign a "letter of fidelity" to the Speaker's program for cutting the budget (Ornstein 1995).

GOP House leaders also changed some of the rules governing committee activities to reinforce the message that Republican members serve on committees at the leadership's pleasure and will be expected to promote the party's legislative agenda. GOP leaders enhanced the power of full committees vis-à-vis subcommittees, while at the same time reducing the overall power of committee chairmen. New rules were passed to

3 After GOP freshmen expressed outrage, Neumann was compensated with an appointment to the much sought-after House Budget Committee (Cassata 1995b).
4 Both were chosen over Representative Carlos Moorhead (R-CA), who was ranking member on the Energy Committee and second in seniority on the Judiciary Committee (Karmin 1994).

allow full committee rather than subcommittee members to elect sub-committee chairs and to authorize full committee chairs to hire all majority-party committee and subcommittee staff. The new rules also imposed six-year term limits on committee and subcommittee chairs and banned proxy voting (Cloud 1995a). Under the new rules it is more difficult, if not impossible, for committee chairs to create "mini-empires," such as the one that former chairman Representative John Dingel (D-MI) had built at the Energy and Commerce Committee when the Democrats controlled the House.

Senate party leaders have less ability to dominate the committee assignment process because the upper chamber more strongly embraces the seniority system. However, the Senate Republican Conference also sought to encourage greater party discipline by passing term limits for committee chairs and ranking members (Dewar 1995). The six-year limits, which went into effect at the beginning of the 105th Congress, were in part a response to the decisive vote of Senate Appropriations Committee Chairman Mark Hatfield (R-OR) against the balanced budget amendment to the Constitution.

Changes in the procedures that the congressional parties use to make committee assignments substantially increased House and Senate leaders' influence over the legislative process, but as Neumann's and Hatfield's dissenting votes demonstrate, the assignment process remains too blunt an instrument to guarantee party discipline, even on key party votes. Some members of Congress will vote their conscience or with their district on major issues despite possessing the knowledge that doing so could cost them a desirable committee assignment and may result in their party's failure to enact one of its core programs.

SETTING THE STAGE: DEFINING THE LEGISLATIVE AGENDA

Presidents normally dominate the political agenda in contemporary American politics. The very nature of their office enables them to draw attention to major issues, identify critical problems, and build pressure for resolving them. Presidents also usually have a tremendous impact on the issues that are debated in Congress, particularly when their party controls both chambers. Congressional leaders who belong to the president's party work closely with the White House in setting the legislative agenda and negotiating the substance of major bills.

This is not to imply that congressional leaders have no influence over the legislative branch's agenda. The agenda-setting activities of congressional party leaders have grown significantly since the 1970s (Sinclair 1993; 237–58). They enable leaders to exercise a great deal of control over which bills will be sent to committee, how they will be debated on the floor, and whether they ultimately have a chance to become law. Although the leaders set the legislative agenda, they do so with the input of their party's membership.

During the early 1980s, party organizations in the House formalized opportunities for their members to influence the congressional agenda. They began to use their annual winter retreats as vehicles to identify critical issues, discuss potential solutions to national problems, and develop a consensus around those solutions (Herrnson and Patterson 1995: 619–22; Sinclair 1994: 308–10). These retreats and the closed-door party meetings that follow them allow party members and leaders to set legislative priorities and lay the foundations for building legislative coalitions. They also help party leaders develop public relations strategies to influence the national political agenda.

Since the early 1980s, members of the Senate have also increased the number of retreats, closed-door meetings, and other opportunities to influence their chamber's agenda (Patterson 1992: 82; Smith 1993: 259). In July 1995, following Senator Hatfield's refusal to support the balanced budget amendment, the Senate Republican Conference decided to adopt a nonbinding legislative agenda every two years (Dewar 1995). These changes strengthen the roles of congressional parties in setting the Senate's agenda.

Following the 1994 elections and the GOP takeover of Congress, Speaker Gingrich and the House Republicans set some new standards for congressional agenda setting. Armed with the Contract with America, Gingrich proclaimed that the American people had voted for Republican policies and conservative principles. They then proceeded to reshape the national political agenda. What is perhaps most significant about Gingrich's proclamation and the "Republican Revolution" that flowed from it is that the Clinton White House at first offered relatively little resistance to Republican congressional leaders. The 104th Congress was exceptional in that, for most of its duration, the Speaker of the House, not the president, dominated both the national political agenda and the legislative agenda. It was not until the battle over the federal budget and the beginning of the presidential nomination season that President Clinton reclaimed control over the political agenda.

Their power to set the legislative agenda enhances congressional leaders' prospects of passing their policy priorities. It also allows them to use the legislative process for purely political purposes. House and Senate leaders often use their chambers to stage debates over bills that they know cannot pass – and may not even want to have pass – in order to score points with the public or the media. Congressional term limits are an example of legislation that was used primarily for political purposes.

Even though some Republican House leaders were unenthusiastic about term limits and knew they could not muster the 290 votes needed to amend the Constitution, they scheduled the topic for seven hours of debate.[5] This enabled the Republicans to associate themselves with an overwhelmingly popular issue, demonstrate that they were keeping their word to hold a vote on it, and blame the Democrats for the amendment's failure, all the while running little risk that term limits would actually be enacted (Gimpel 1996: 95–8).

The efforts that congressional party leaders have taken to strengthen their influence over the legislative agenda have had a significant impact on the political process. They have enabled Speaker Gingrich and other Republican House leaders to capitalize on their stunning election victory and reshape the nation's political dialogue. Nevertheless, the House Republicans' temporary success in dominating the political agenda is more a result of their takeover of the House after having been in the minority for forty years than a product of their agenda-setting efforts. It is likely that presidents, not congressional leaders, will dominate the national agenda under normal political circumstances.

ACT ONE: THE COMMITTEE STAGE

Committees and subcommittees have been described as the workhorses of Congress. During the 1990s, party leaders have used their power to refer bills to specific committees to better coordinate their "troupes." They have used the assignment process strategically to ensure that their preferred legislation gets a favorable and expeditious hearing and that other bills are pigeonholed or written in language that is unacceptable to a majority of their chamber. Moreover, in situations where congressional leaders believe that their party will be unable to craft the legislation they desire in committee or wish to shield the bill-writing process from public scrutiny, they have increasingly sidestepped the normal committee process by employing task forces to do what is usually considered committee work (e.g., Sinclair 1981).

For much of our nation's history, congressional committees have worked largely behind closed doors.[6] The "sunshine reforms" that were passed in the 1970s opened committee meetings to television, radio, and newspaper photographers. These changes led committee hearings to be-

---

5 The rule governing term limits allowed for three hours of general debate and one hour of debate for each of four bills (*Congressional Record*, 1995).

6 Hearings that dealt with highly salient issues, such as Senator Joseph R. McCarthy's (R-WI) crusade to expose American communists in 1954 and the Senate Select Committee on Presidential Activities investigations of Watergate in 1973, were exceptional in that they received tremendous media coverage.

come public relations as well as policy-making forums. Members now routinely use committee hearings to advertise their Washington activities to constituents, and parties use them to disseminate their views through the national media (Mayhew 1974: 87–97).

The ability to choose the number and location of committee hearings and control their proceedings gives the majority party a tremendous advantage in getting out its message. Following a tradition that had been practiced by their Democratic predecessors, Republican leaders have used their control of Congress to hold hearings for partisan gain. In 1995, for example, House Republicans held dozens of highly publicized committee hearings on a questionable land deal that involved the president and the First Lady, frequently referred to as the Whitewater scandal, which had the potential to help them score political points. Yet they held only one committee hearing on a controversial proposal to downsize Medicare – a popular program that provides health care coverage to the elderly. Their Democratic counterparts, finding themselves unable to schedule committee hearings, had to resort to other means for generating publicity about congressional investigations and pending legislation. Taking a page out of the GOP's old playbook, House Democrats walked out of the Medicare hearing complaining that the GOP had cut the Medicare program without adequate discussion (Rich 1995; Rich and Pianin 1995). The Democrats later held a hearing on the Capitol lawn to publicize their support for the program.

The importance that congressional leaders place on the publicity aspects of committee hearings was revealed in a memorandum from the GOP House leadership that voiced dissatisfaction with the hearings its members held on Whitewater and the fatal confrontation in Waco, Texas, which involved agents from the Bureau of Alcohol, Tobacco, and Firearms. The two-page memo indicated that "The leadership has been concerned with the ability of the Democrats to upstage hearings, place the Republicans on the defensive, and capitalize on media events" (Kamen 1995: A21). It listed a variety of strategies to promote success. In a section called "Getting Your Message Out," the memo suggests that members:

Define the goals of the hearings. Focus on humanizing the story. Bring out a theatrical theme to illuminate the facts to make your story more appealing to the press. . . . Schedule your witnesses in the morning to meet press deadlines . . . [and] schedule Democratic witnesses later. (Kamen 1995: A21; italics in original)

Under "Ways to Accomplish Getting Your Message Out," the memo instructs Republicans to

Heighten the hypocrisy of the other side when they don't follow the facts. Make them try to defend their left liberal side . . . Beware of the media cycle. What

else is happening in the world and how are we going to compete against it? For example, Watergate and Iran–contra hearings were held in August, when it was the only real game on which the media could focus. (Kamen 1995: A21; italics in original)

Woodrow Wilson's observation in the 1880s that "Congress in session is Congress on public exhibition, whilst Congress in its committee-rooms is Congress at work" (Wilson [1885] 1973: 69) is still useful over a century later, despite the fact that committee work has changed somewhat. Party leaders increased their abilities to coordinate committee activities, yet committee chairs continue to enjoy much power and autonomy in most areas of legislation. In the 104th Congress, for example, committees held hearings on campaign finance reform and other issues for which Gingrich and other Republican House leaders possessed little enthusiasm.

ACT TWO: THE FLOOR DEBATE

By far the most dramatic part of the legislative process takes place on the floors of the House and the Senate. Great historical moments have been marked by spirited debates and close roll call votes. The decisions made by the House in 1979 and the Senate in 1986 to allow congressional floor activities to be televised brought these debates into the homes of many Americans (e.g., Davidson and Oleszek 1994). C-SPAN, a cable television network, features continuous coverage of the House and Senate floors when Congress is in session.

The Speaker and other majority-party House leaders exercise tremendous control over floor debates. Through the Rules Committee, the House majority-party leadership dictates the amount of time that is devoted to debating each section of a bill and which, if any, sections will be subject to amendment. Restrictive rules have routinely been used to minimize the time of debate, keep a bill intact from unwanted amendments, and limit the number of politically difficult votes that members of the majority party must cast. House Democratic leaders made greater use of restrictive rules for partisan purposes over the last few decades. The proportion of bills that were debated under such rules increased from 15 percent to 71 percent between the 95th Congress (1977–8) and the 103rd Congress (1993–4) (Davidson and Oleszek 1994: 333).

House GOP leaders employed fewer restrictive rules on amendments during the 104th Congress, instead using restrictive time allocations to limit Democratic input into the legislative process. By subtracting the seventeen minutes reserved for voting on each amendment from the total time allotted for debating entire bills, GOP leaders drastically reduced the number of amendments that Democrats (or Republicans) could offer to Republican legislation. This strategy enabled the Republicans to consider bills more rapidly and helped them avoid having to cast difficult votes on popular Democratic amendments.

Senate leaders have less power over floor proceedings than their House counterparts because the Senate's rules allow for more freewheeling debate. Senators can propose amendments that are not germane to a bill, and they can delay Senate action through the filibuster and other dilatory tactics. Nevertheless, the Senate majority leader's ability to schedule legislation is an important leadership tool because it enables the majority party to take up legislation at the time when it is most likely to win (Sinclair 1989a: 148–52).

The power that the leadership has over legislation is perhaps most visible when leaders reschedule a second vote on an amendment that has already been defeated or resuscitate a piece of legislation that has failed either in committee or on the chamber floor by inserting it into a bill that has better prospects for passage. Examples of both kinds of tactics can be found in the 104th Congress. When 155 Democrats and 51 Republicans defeated (by a 212-to-206 vote) a series of deregulatory measures to the Environmental Protection Agency's budgetary appropriation, the House Republican leadership brought the issue back for a second vote at a time when the opposition was unable to mobilize its forces. The result was that a second motion to remove the measures from the bill failed in a 210-to-210 vote tie (Katz 1995). When the House Agriculture Committee failed to win approval of cuts in farm subsidies, the Republican leadership won their passage by placing them in a "must-pass" budget reconciliation bill (Hosansky 1995).

In addition to their scheduling authority, the leaders of the majority and minority parties receive priority recognition on the chamber floor. Party leaders' power to appoint floor managers for specific bills enables them to strategically select members to take the lead on various pieces of legislation. During the 104th Congress, for example, Senate Majority Leader Dole selected Senator Bill Frist (R-TN), a medical doctor, to lead GOP Senators in the fight over Medicare reform. House Democratic leaders learned that their prospects for amending GOP-sponsored legislation were improved when conservative and moderate southern Democrats played a major role in floor debates and the proposal of amendments. The amendments that these members offered were typically not as liberal as those that would have been offered by northeastern or midwestern Democrats, but the conservative Democrats' amendments had a better chance of having a moderating impact on GOP legislation. For example, by allowing Representative John Spratt (D-SC) to take the lead in opposing House Resolution (HR) 7 – the National Defense Revitalization Act – the Democrats were able to entice a sufficient number of GOP members to cross party lines to accept a Democratic amendment that modified one of the core elements of the Contract with America (Gimpel 1996: 77). Of course, party leaders' enhanced ability to structure floor debates has still not given them the power to determine policy outcomes. Strategic maneuvers cannot substitute for the support of a majority of legislators.

THE GRAND FINALE: ROLL CALL VOTES

Setting the agenda, distributing committee assignments, arranging committee hearings, and holding floor debates are all important aspects of the legislative process, but they are only precursors to the final act of the congressional drama – the floor vote. Passing legislation is Congress's major mission, and it is of critical importance to members of the majority party. Majority-party members expect their leaders to deliver enough votes to pass their legislation. They believe that passing laws that fulfill their campaign promises has a major impact on their prospects for reelection. Nationalized election campaigns, like the one waged by House Republicans in 1994, have not been the norm in American politics, but even in other years, congressional party members have considered their electoral fortunes to be tied to their party's ability to keep its campaign promises.

Members of the minority party need not be as concerned with enacting legislation as do members of the majority, but they, too, expect their leaders to offer popular policy alternatives. By providing contrasting viewpoints on major issues, the minority party can influence how voters cast their ballots in the next election. On a few occasions, minority amendments and bills have won enough opposition support to become law.

Although it is harder to build a coalition in support of legislation than in opposition to it, majority and minority leaders face similar obstacles and use similar tactics to influence their members' roll call votes. The biggest challenge that both sets of leaders must meet is to devise ways to get independent-minded members who represent different constituencies and values to act in concert on legislation that addresses national issues. The decentralizing features of Congress do not make meeting this challenge an easy task.

Congressional leaders use both "inside" and "outside" strategies to promote their legislative goals. Inside strategies involve substantive and logistical issues, such as scheduling, structuring the alternatives that will be voted on, and framing the rules for debate. Omnibus bills are often used as vehicles for unpopular pieces of legislation that could not pass on their own. Restrictive rules and time limits help leaders hold their policy coalitions together by minimizing opponents' opportunities to attack legislation. Scheduling is used to maximize a piece of legislation's prospects for success. House GOP leaders, for example, established a deadline of 100 days for voting on legislation informed by the contract in order to capitalize on the momentum from their party's electoral landslide.

Inside strategies also involve using the party leadership apparatus to mobilize the vote. Party leaders often distribute policy research, talking points, polling figures, and suggestions for media events to convince members to vote with their party position and to influence the news spin that accompanies major votes. Special whip task forces are used to enlarge the leadership circle on controversial legislation (Price 1992: 83–5). It takes numerous whip polls, task force meetings, and caucuses to monitor members' level of commitment to specific bills. The information the leaders collect is sometimes used in order to make legislation more palatable to a majority of members.

Inside strategies also involve the distribution of specific benefits. Sometimes leaders help members with their reelection campaigns, grant them desirable committee assignments, or invite them to offer an amendment or play some other visible role in the legislative process. Leaders also occasionally threaten to take sanctions, such as removing a member from a desirable committee or blocking his or her advancement toward a committee chairmanship or other leadership post. Because the Senate's rules give majority-party leaders fewer institutional resources, providing individual senators with personal favors and services is much more important than it is in the House (Sinclair 1989a: 148–52).

Outside strategies bring the pressure of public opinion to bear on wavering lawmakers. Party leaders appear on television and radio, are quoted in newspapers, and give speeches in order to sway public opinion. Interest-group leaders are recruited to mobilize their members at the grass roots. Letters, postcards, and telephone calls from concerned constituents can have a significant impact on legislators' decisions (Fowler and Shaiko 1987). Mass media campaigns that mobilize group members and others are also important. During the 104th Congress, Citizen Action, a liberal public interest group, aired television commercials attacking the Republicans' Medicare reform bill for raising costs and cutting services in order to create a tax cut for the wealthy. The Seniors Coalition, a conservative group, defended the bill, spending $2 million on TV ads touting it as a necessary measure to save Medicare from bankruptcy (Maraniss and Weisskopf 1995). These public relations campaigns helped both parties hold together their legislative coalitions.

Party unity has grown significantly in the House and Senate since the

Party Leadership in the Modern Congress

Figure 5.1. *Party Unity in the U.S. House, 1971–96*

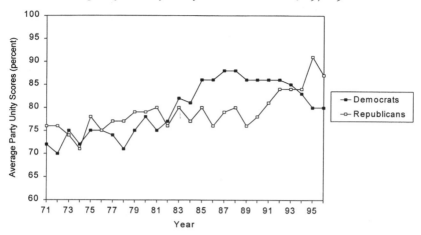

Figure 5.2. *Party Unity in the U.S. Senate, 1971–96*

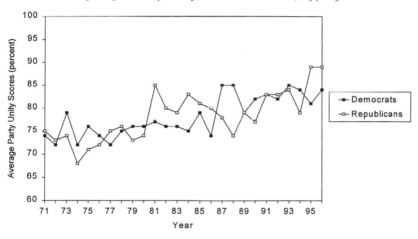

1970s (see Figures 5.1 and 5.2). The increased resources that party leaders had at their disposal and the skills with which they deployed them contributed to this trend (Herrnson and Patterson 1995). The ideological sorting out of the parties' congressional delegations, which resulted in fewer moderate Democrats and moderate Republicans serving in both houses, contributed to the increase in party unity (Rohde 1991: 46). The GOP takeover of Congress acted as a catalyst that propelled Republicans in both chambers to display record-setting levels of party unity.[7] House

7 According to Hurley and Kerr (1997), should the second session the 104th Con-

Republicans were strongly united in their support for the Contract with America. This is especially true of the seventy-three Republican House freshmen, many of whom credited their election victories to Newt Gingrich and were willing to support legislation that met with his approval. Moreover, GOP members of both chambers recognized that their continued control of Congress would rest largely on their ability to pass legislation.

It is difficult to underestimate the importance of Republican congressional leaders, especially Speaker Gingrich, in fostering the record levels of unity displayed by House Republicans. General conditions may have been ripe for House Republicans to pass much of their political agenda, but Gingrich's leadership was a necessary ingredient to the juggernaut that originated in the House Republican Conference. The strength of the Speaker's vision and political skills was on display during the campaign and in the new rules, procedures, strategies, and tactics that Republican House leaders used to rally their troops behind the contract. Similarly, shortcomings in the Speaker's political acumen, which led him to overreach on the GOP's mandate and underestimate the influence of the White House and the Senate, may have prevented some of the House Republicans' legislative goals from becoming law. Public discontent with Gingrich, anger over the shutdown of the federal government, and uneasiness with the GOP's rhetoric of "revolution" made some Republican House members feel vulnerable. Many Republicans chose to abandon some of their conservative goals in favor of compromise after their Democratic opponents began to label them as "extremists" during the 1996 elections, resulting in a small drop-off in party unity during the second session of the 104th Congress.

Their unfamiliarity with life in the minority and a leadership vacuum that emerged during the early days of the 104th Congress were responsible for the decline in party unity among Democrats in both chambers. However, through helping their members recognize the strategic importance of voting as a bloc in opposition to the GOP, Senate Minority Leader Daschle, House Minority Leader Gephardt, and President Clinton were able to later bolster the Democrats' unity. The levels of Democratic party unity for the 104th Congress are lower than those for the 103rd, but they did not sink to the levels that existed during the 1970s.

The ideological sorting out of the parties and the strengthening of the leadership apparatuses laid the groundwork for more cohesive congressional parties. The Republican takeover of Congress had a catalytic effect on GOP unity during the early days of the 104th Congress.

gress continue to show these levels of party unity, Congress will set a record that goes back to the 61st Congress in the House (1909–11) and the 67th Congress in the Senate (1921–3).

However, as demonstrated by divisions within the Democratic ranks, which emerged immediately after the 1994 election, and splits among House GOP members, which became evident during the budget battle, constituency pressures, ideological disagreements, bicameralism, and other decentralizing features of Congress continue to limit party cohesion on major issues. The strengthening of the congressional parties' leadership apparatuses may have helped increase legislators' party unity, but its is doubtful that members of Congress will come close to exhibiting the levels of sustained solidarity associated with legislative parties in most other democracies.

MEETING THE CRITICS: THE LEADERSHIP AND THE PRESS

Major events in Congress are usually preceded, accompanied, and followed by public relations campaigns. Each congressional party tries to put a spin on the news in order to present itself in a favorable light and cast a negative shadow on its opponent. All four congressional parties have developed specialized techniques for delivering their messages. Political communications have become an important part of a congressional leader's job.

Newt Gingrich's ability to dominate the news during the 104th Congress was due to more than his party's overwhelming election victory. Gingrich took deliberate steps to more effectively manage the news than did his predecessors. By delegating much of the daily management of the legislative process to Majority Leader Armey, he gave himself more time to make speeches, lecture in college classrooms, and appear on television and radio talk shows (Babson 1995; Cloud 1995b). During the early months of his speakership, Gingrich even arranged to have his daily news conference broadcast nationwide on C-SPAN.[8]

Gingrich and the other members of the House Republican leadership used a three-tiered system to develop and disseminate their messages before and during the 104th Congress. The Planning and Learning Team, which helped formulate the idea behind the Contract with America, was in charge of developing long-term party strategy. It has focused on developing ideas and messages that will be disseminated between six months to three years in the future. The Speaker's Advisory Group took a more short-term view, meeting twice per week to create a communi-

---

8 Gingrich stopped holding daily news briefings for the press in early May after he found that reporters' inquiries about the ethics charges brought against him made it difficult for him to control the message he wanted to project. Gingrich's decision ends a custom that was begun by Speaker Sam Rayburn (D-TX) circa the 1940s and 1950s (Cassata 1995a).

cations strategy for upcoming legislation. Finally, the communications and strategy team ("CommStrat") met three times per week and held teleconferences early each morning to plan the party's daily communications. The three groups included some of the House GOP's most creative and articulate members and staff and drew on the research and expertise of the Republican national and congressional campaign committees and prominent Republican consultants. CommStrat also drew on Republican expertise in the Senate and coordinated its message with Republican National Committee Chairman Haley Barbour and his staff. The GOP's message operation enabled the party to develop support for its policies and articulate those policies in appealing themes and phrases, which it then persuaded GOP legislators to repeat to the press (Czwartacki 1995; Weisskopf and Maraniss 1995).

Republican House leaders relied on a number of vehicles to deliver their message. They published two fact sheets, the "Leg Digest" and "Floor Prep," to familiarize members with what was taking place on the House floor. Issue briefs containing factual statements, talking points, and party rhetoric were distributed to GOP House members in order to coordinate their one-minute speeches and interviews with journalists. "Blast faxes" were disseminated to thousands of traditional newspaper, television, and radio outlets to put a Republican spin on the events of the day and counter communications distributed by the Clinton White House and congressional Democrats. Additional blast faxes were disseminated to 1,200 radio talk show hosts daily (Czwartacki 1995). House and Senate Republican leaders held joint press conferences, issued joint press releases, and held special events to get out the GOP message. In addition, they used the Internet to post information about congressional Republicans and their legislative activities.

Republican leaders also disseminated their messages through briefings held for sympathetic Washington lobbyists and trade association representatives who, in turn, repackaged the messages and disseminated them to their clients and members. Leaders of pro-Republican interest groups frequently urged their members to attend Republican legislators' town meetings and write letters to the editor of their local newspaper in support of individual GOP House members and congressional Republicans more generally. These techniques enabled the Republicans to raise issues, rally public support for their policies, and claim credit for their legislative successes (Czwartacki 1995; Maraniss and Weisskopf 1995).

Other leadership communications provide members with political cover for difficult votes. During the Medicare debate, for example, GOP leaders instructed House members on how to defend their votes to change the program. The leadership provided members with talking points and sample quotes and faxed tactical updates to them daily. They encouraged members to use the words "preserve," "protect," and "strengthen" in lieu of "cut," "cap," "freeze," or "change" when discussing Medicare in order to calm the fears of program recipients and win them over to the Republican position (Weisskopf and Maraniss 1995).

GOP leadership staff also helped individual members defend themselves against events organized by opponents. When Project '95, a coalition of labor and consumer groups planned to drive a steamroller bearing a poster-sized photograph of freshman Representative Phil English (R-PA) over six gray-wigged mannequins on a major street in English's district, GOP leadership aides counseled the congressman to prepare a counterattack ahead of time. English appeared on a conservative radio talk show and denounced the event as the work of outsiders. The Coalition to Save Medicare, a broad-based alliance of health industry and conservative senior groups organized by House Republican Conference Chairman John Boehner (R-OH), arranged for interest-group members to speak from GOP-scripted talking points at English's town meetings and to distribute "fact" sheets supporting the Republican program. The Seniors Coalition was drafted to air TV ads in English's district praising the Republican initiative. The Republicans' counterattack was highly successful in deflecting the offensive of Project '95. English was defended in a local newspaper editorial, and he used the episode as the centerpiece of a successful direct-mail fundraising appeal. Interest groups normally mobilize in response to major policy initiatives, but the degree to which the Republican House leaders coordinated the groups' response in this instance is unusual.

The House Democrats' message group consists of their party leadership and roughly fifteen to twenty other members and their staffs. It has been advised by representatives from the Democratic National Committee and the Democratic Congressional Campaign Committee and by the president (Herrnson and Patterson 1995; Moss 1995; Sinclair 1995: 269–70). House Democratic leaders have relied on communications techniques similar to those used by their GOP counterparts, but the Democrats had more difficulty calling attention to their message because the minority party in Congress gets less press attention than the majority party or the President. Moreover, the need to coordinate messages with the Clinton White House as well as Democrats in the Senate made House Democrats' task more difficult, especially when the president's vision on some issues changed.

Senate leaders face a more difficult task in getting their members to work in unison. Although there are fewer of them, rank-and-file members of the Senate tend to be more independent than members of the House. With the opening of the 104th Congress, Majority Leader Dole and Minority Leader Daschle revived the practice of holding "dugout" sessions to brief the press just before the Senate convened to conduct its daily business (Sammon 1995). They used these sessions to put a partisan spin on the news coverage of the Senate. In addition, the leaders worked to develop core party messages on major issues and provide members with talking points and briefings to build message discipline. Like their House counterparts, Senate leadership staff distributed blast faxes, arranged press events, and used other methods to disseminate their message, including mobilizing coalitions for these same purposes. The congressional party leaders' increased focus on message development and dissemination improved their ability to influence the news but did not enable them to exercise full control over it.

CONCLUSION

Party leaders work in a congressional system that makes leadership difficult under most circumstances. The institutional structures, electoral arrangements, and diverse constituencies that define the modern Congress are better suited to local representation and policy entrepreneurship than the development of cohesive majority-party government. Rather than assume that members will support their party or command them to do so, congressional party leaders must work to persuade legislators to cooperate in passing and publicizing party programs.

Congressional party leaders have used a number of resources and techniques for orchestrating the support of their members in recent years. Party leaders set the stage for more cooperative and productive relations with their members by becoming more involved in election campaigns, increasing the number of individuals who participate in leadership activities, making party loyalty a more important criterion for major committee assignments and leadership posts, and creating more opportunities for membership input into the legislative agenda. They enhanced their ability to direct the legislative process by strategically referring bills to sympathetic committees or task forces, becoming heavily involved in committee hearings, employing restrictive measures to control floor debates, and using combinations of inside and outside strategies to build coalitions. The leaders also improved their capacities to project a favorable image for their party by developing sophisticated message-delivery systems.

Several developments worked to strengthen the hands of party leaders in Congress. The ideological sorting out of the parties reduced the tensions that existed within each party's congressional caucuses. Gridlock and the electorate's increasing hostility toward what was perceived as a series of "out of touch," "do-nothing" Congresses led rank-and-file legislators to accept leadership-strengthening reforms with the hope that they would have positive results. The GOP takeover of Congress acted as a catalyst for institutional change, especially in the House. Legislators acquiesced to the movement toward a more centralized leadership because they recognized that this trend enabled their leaders to better serve their individual and collective needs. Many of the changes introduced by individual leaders lasted beyond their tenure in office.

The efforts of party leaders contributed to the growth in party unity that occurred during the latter part of the twentieth century. Yet they also give insights into the fundamental limits on the leadership's power. The institutional context within which members of Congress legislate and the diverse preferences, goals, and political styles of each party's congressional membership prevent its leaders from enjoying as much power as their counterparts in parliamentary democracies. These same centrifugal forces can be expected to continue to prevent American congressional parties from becoming as cohesive as legislative parties in other democracies.

Congress occasionally resembles a three-ring circus, and its leaders, ring masters. Some of Congress's most entertaining acts have featured members who gave speeches to empty chambers, grabbed each others' ties, or slogged through the mud to an area of the Capitol grounds known as the "swamp" in an attempt to secure ten seconds on the nightly news. Yet some of its more memorable performances have also been marked by eloquent debate in which party members presented clear and opposing viewpoints on fundamental issues and their leaders acted like statesmen. On these occasions, Congress has more closely resembled a Shakespearean drama than a circus performance.

Congress's performance largely depends on how well party leaders coordinate their members' activities. The leaders have a variety of resources at their disposal, but these resources provide them with only limited influence over rank-and-file legislators. Like directors in the theatre, congressional party leaders must allow for the differing talents, goals, opinions, and egos of those whose efforts they strive to coordinate. Moreover, congressional party leaders and directors can both suffer unpleasant consequences if they fail to perform up to the expectations of their colleagues or the public. Leaders and directors, and the legislators or actors whose efforts they seek to coordinate, often search for ways to improve their performances in order to stave off negative reviews. Leaders, directors, and many in their troupes understand that a failure to address public dissatisfaction can cost them influence or result in their being ushered off the stage.

Public acclaim for Congress will probably never come close to the rave reviews won by the show *1776*. Yet Congress has enjoyed a longer continuous run than any show on Broadway. When it comes to appraising democratic institutions, longevity is more important than a second curtain call.

ACKNOWLEDGMENT

I wish to thank Jim Gimpel, Mark Graber, Forrest Maltzman, and Ric Uslaner for their helpful comments and suggestions.

6

Little Theatre: Committees in Congress

TIM GROSECLOSE AND DAVID C. KING

Committees are "the little legislatures" of Congress (Goodwin 1970), for in these small arenas much of the law-making work happens, and committee deliberation sets the stage for legislating on the House or Senate floors. Yet just as the dramas on a theatrical stage are more illusory than real, the same is true when Congress appears to institute radical reforms in committee structures. Congressional committees are marked much more by stability than by change – recent Republican reforms notwithstanding.

In 1890 a cartoon appeared in the *Judge*, a national political magazine that survived into the early 1900s. The cartoon shows congressmen bringing "goodies" back to their districts and cutting deals among themselves to support each others' bills. The date on the cartoon could just as well have been 1998. Despite all that has changed – the dramatic growth of the federal government, the growth of Capitol Hill staff, the explosion in the number of Washington lobbyists, the modernization of media outlets, the gradually developing presence of women and racial minorities, and so on – despite all this, Congress of the 1890s seems entirely familiar. So, too, the committees of the early 1880s, which preoccupied and frustrated Woodrow Wilson as he wrote *Congressional Government* ([1885] 1973). If we could put today's committee entrepreneurs in a time machine bound for the 1880s, they could navigate the policy process safely and with alacrity.

As the curtain rose on the House of Representatives in early 1995, Speaker Newt Gingrich and a legion of Republican freshmen promised sweeping changes in the committee system. It was not the first time political reformers had railed against committee structures. Indeed, long before Wilson called them "dim dungeons of silence," committees were the persistent targets of critics (Wilson [1885] 1973: 63). Among political cognoscenti, committees have received the brunt of blame for gridlock, graft, pork, turf wars, stifling control by the majority party, and other purported evils of the First Branch. Yet while political observers (right or wrong) widely believe those indictments, legislators were loath to alter the recipe that made committees work: (1) relatively autonomous jurisdictions, (2) leadership determined by seniority, (3) general freedom from caucus or party pressure, and (4) respect, and often deference, to the committee's expertise and positions. By the mid-1990s, however, reformers were questioning the necessity of each of these (and other, less critical) ingredients. Newt Gingrich promised to give the committees in his House a whole new look.

Gingrich made changes indeed, and they had all the appearances of being important and dramatic: Three House committees disappeared; the number of subcommittees was slashed from 115 to 84; staffs were cut by a third; rules about committee voting changed; task forces – which short-cut the committee system – gained great (though short-lived) powers; and committee chairs were subjected to term limits.

We argue, however, that in most respects the "new" committee system hardly changed at all. Once the 104th Congress got past the dizzying haze of its first one hundred days, committees operated much as they have for one hundred years. It would be a mistake to generalize much beyond what happened in those first hundred days, when legislation was rushed to the floor, leadership-led task forces were active, and party discipline was high. Republican committee chairs, after waiting years to gain control over their panels, were not eager to cede authority to the gentleman from Georgia. Rather, the chairs rode out the storm and the committee system returned to the rough equilibrium it had long known. The widespread sense on Capitol Hill today is that the committees, for better or worse, are "back to normal."

Furthermore, some truly revolutionary changes that could have occurred, did not. For instance, Congress did not decide to follow some state legislatures and make more committees joint between the House and Senate. Committee chairs are still drawn exclusively from the majority party. Party caucuses still elect the chairs (still subject to a ratification vote by the floor). A seniority system (albeit somewhat weakened) remains in place. Minority-party members retain participation rights virtually equal to majority-members' rights, and the minority still receives proportional representation on committees. Bills can still be discharged from committees if enough members sign a petition. Legislators still spend far more time legislating in committees than they do on the House or Senate floors. Committee members still provide the most potent voting cues for noncommittee members; and so on. Indeed, we warrant that almost all of the aspects that distinguish the congressional committee system from other committee systems did not change at all in Speaker Gingrich's new little theatre.[1]

Of course, it should be noted, change is a matter of degree, and where we see little, others see lots (Aldrich and Rohde 1995), but the fundamental motivations driving political actors are as old as Aeschylus. We suspect that many of the great political actors, like House Appropriations Chairman Clarence Cannon (D-MO, 1922–64) and Naval Affairs Chairman Carl Vinson (D-GA, 1914–65), would feel right at home on today's congressional stage (see Patterson 1978: 130–4).

PLAYBILL: NOTES ON CONGRESSIONAL COMMITTEES

Every theatre provides a playbill sketching a production's plot and players. This section does the same for congressional committees. It sketches the primary functions of committees and the institutions surrounding them. We have already mentioned four basic ingredients of the committee system: relatively autonomous jurisdictions; leadership determined by seniority; general freedom from caucus or party pressure; respect, and often deference, to the committee's expertise and positions. Those are absolutely critical – and found in most state legislatures – but there are several more aspects of U.S. committee systems with which one should be familiar.

First, committees directly shape the overwhelming majority of legislation. For example, in a typical two-year Congress, about ten thousand bills and resolutions are introduced in the House and Senate. More than 99 percent of these are referred to a committee within twenty-four hours, yet only 14 percent emerge from these committees and just 6 percent become law (Oleszek 1996: 93). Put differently, 86 percent of the bills and resolutions die in committee. These are dim dungeons of silence, indeed. Some state legislatures require that all bills referred to committees receive hearings and get reported back to the legislature, but in the U.S. Congress, committees are significant gates for preventing bills from becoming law.[2]

---

1 In the 105th Congress (1997–9), House committees changed even less. The most important changes were (1) the Committee on Economic and Educational Opportunities was renamed the Committee on Education and the Workforce, and (2) nongovernmental agencies testifying before committees were required to provide a list of the federal grants and contracts they had received. One can argue, however, that even these changes were trivial.

2 Committees from the following state legislative bodies must report all bills: Arkansas House, California Assembly, Colorado Senate and House, Idaho Senate, Illinois Senate, Indiana House, Maine Senate and House, Maryland Senate, Massachusetts Senate and House, New Hampshire Senate and House, North Carolina House, North Dakota Senate and House, South Dakota Senate and House, Utah Senate and House (American Society of Legislative Clerks and Secretaries 1991:

Second, administrative control of committees rests almost entirely with members of the majority party. One aspect of this is that chairs of committees and subcommittees are always members of the majority. Although observers of Congress often think of this norm as existing since time immemorial (and almost decreed by God) it is not written on stone tablets. In early Congresses some chairs were members of the minority party (Stewart et al. 1995), and presently, a few state legislatures, including the California and Minnesota assemblies, allow minority-party members to chair committees.

Third, committee chairs have traditionally had great leeway in setting agendas, selecting staff, and deciding which bills to kill. In fact, it is argued that part of the reason the majority has a disproportionate staffing advantage is because the majority sets the agenda. As the minority party for forty years in the House of Representatives (until 1995), Republicans complained bitterly about a growing gap between the committee powers of the two parties, arguing that deliberation was being severely undermined (Solomon and Wolfensberger 1994).

Fourth, another aspect of administrative control involves the staffs of committees. Here again, power rests largely with the majority party. For instance, in the House, even though the majority may have only slightly more than half the members of committees, it hires approximately two-thirds of the staff. Thus, while minority members receive their fair share of seats on the committee, they do not receive their fair share of staff.[3]

Fifth, a relatively stable characteristic of congressional committees is their autonomy from the party leadership. This is, of course, a matter of degree – but in contrast with the party leadership exercised over committees in European parliaments, the U.S. Congress seems a partyless anarchy. While committee chairs are elected by party caucuses, which, one should expect, should make them beholden to the caucus, in practice it tends not to work that way, thanks largely to the seniority system, which remains the norm in selecting chairs. Since chairs depend on seniority within their committees for selection, they show little fear when bucking the caucus. A second check on the majority-party caucus is that the entire chamber must ratify the slate of chairs. Thus, if a liberal Republican is denied reelection to a chair, he or she can appeal to the Democrats on the floor. Anticipating this, the majority party has a less viable threat to punish chairs who do not toe the party line.

29). Political scientists know very little about whether (and how) this variance in gatekeeping powers makes a difference, although a natural experiment could be conducted to examine this. For information on state committees generally, see Francis (1989).

3 In the Senate, however, the majority and minority members hire staff in proportion to the party ratio of the committee (Smith and Deering 1990: 149).

A sixth element of the committee system is the route a bill takes before it reaches the floor of the full House or Senate. Bills sent to a committee are assigned to a subcommittee, whose chair determines whether to hold public hearings. Most receive none, and they quickly disappear. Committees vary widely, based on how much deference is accorded subcommittees, but few bills ever emerge over the objections of subcommittee chairs (Smith 1994: 659).[4] Traditionally, public hearings have been dominated by witnesses selected by a committee's majority party. If a bill advances after public hearings, "markup" sessions are scheduled, during which a series of votes can amend the original bill. In theory, these markup sessions are very democratic and are intended to improve the legislation based on civic-minded deliberations in public hearings. In practice, however, committee and subcommittee chairs have had disproportionate influence through the use of proxy votes (now greatly restricted in the House), and sometimes they have used this to further their own personal ideologies. With these proxies the majority party has been virtually assured of winning markup fights even when few members of the majority were physically present.

Bills surviving this gauntlet next have to be scheduled on the House and Senate floors. On the House side this involves securing a temporary "rule" from the Rules Committee governing the terms of debate and the number of amendments permissible. In the early 1970s, more than 80 percent of these rules allowed for open debate and unrestricted amendments; thus, if minority party members had weak voices in the committees, at least they could be heard in the full chamber. By the early 1990s, the number of "open" rules dropped to less than 25 percent, greatly frustrating Newt Gingrich and his fellow House Republicans (Towell 1994).

Seventh, committees are "gatekeepers," a term of art in political science meaning that the committees generally get to decide what issues get past them and out to the whole legislature. The phrase "die in committee" applies to 86 percent of all bills introduced and, for a generation of us, evokes images of a "School House Rock" cartoon in which bills literally die in committee. But does a committee (with perhaps no more than 35 members of the House) really have the power to kill a bill it does not like (thereby keeping the other 400 members from passing judg-

---

4 This does not necessarily mean that subcommittee chairs have the power to kill legislation and, de jure, they have no such power. That is, a committee always has the power to overturn a subcommittee chair's decision. Do subcommittee chairs have de facto power to kill legislation? It may be that they do not. Although subcommittee chair's objections are rarely overturned, this may be because of a fear of looking foolish should the committee overturn a decision. Because of this, chairs only object to legislation that they are sure the committee does not favor.

ment)? Strictly speaking, it does not. If a committee attempts to keep the gates in this fashion, any member can request a discharge petition. To do so, 218 signatures requesting that the bill come out of committee must be collected to force it to the floor. However, this procedure is costly (in terms of time and political capital), so members are often reluctant to sponsor discharge petitions, thereby granting a committee de facto gatekeeping power. Indeed, there is evidence that the costs to sponsoring a discharge petition are very large (Beth 1994). For instance, Ripley (1983) reports that it is very rare for a member to sponsor a discharge petition and even rarer for him or her to gather the required 218 signatures. Out of 396 total petitions filed between 1923 and 1975, only 25 reached the required number.[5]

Finally, besides the negative power of a committee to keep the gates and thus block legislation, they also sometimes have the positive power to set the agenda. This comes from special rules it may receive for legislation it reports. For instance, the Rules Committee in the House (with concurrence from the floor) and the Senate (through a unanimous consent agreement) can grant a closed rule to the committee's bill. This means that the bill cannot be amended on the floor. Accordingly, when the status quo is strongly disfavored on the floor, this allows the committee great power. It can write a bill that reflects its own desires, while ignoring the floor's. Since the floor cannot amend it, this allows the committee to get what it wants, possibly in spite of the floor's wishes.

If all of these powers seem somehow undemocratic, there is little new in that complaint. Over a century ago, the House's legendary Speaker Thomas Brackett (Czar) Reed allegedly responded to critics who complained of his autocratic style. "Democracy," he warned his foes, "stops at the door of the U.S. Congress." The quote may be apocryphal, but the sentiment is not. The list of seemingly undemocratic rules and procedures governing legislatures around the world is long. Of course, there are lasting reasons why legislatures, which lie at the core of democracies, are run with only a modicum of democracy. To do otherwise invites institutional chaos. As politicians vie for the public eye, minority parties play blame-game politics in hopes of winning the next elections (Groseclose 1996), and vote coalitions can cycle among incompatible alternatives (McKelvey 1976; Plott 1967). Undemocratic rules and procedures can – indeed, sometimes must – be tolerated. But do they sometimes go to far? Do they fail to serve the preferences of the members

5 The reason some of the petitions never reach 218 signatures is because the committee concedes on account of the petition. That is, rather than being embarrassed by being "rolled" through the petition, the committee releases the gates and reports the bill to the floor.

of Congress? It is concerns such as these that have prompted reformers, such as Speaker Gingrich, to try to improve the committee system.

WHAT'S NEW IN THE "NEW" COMMITTEE SYSTEM?

Even before the Republican takeover of 1995, a growing faction in both parties was working toward overhauling the committee system. A special Joint Committee on the Organization of Congress (JCOC) was active in the 103rd Congress (1993–4). Members testifying before the JCOC overwhelmingly supported reducing jurisdictional fragmentation, cutting the number of committees and subcommittees, and decreasing committee sizes (JCOC 1993). Most of the JCOC's recommendations went unheeded, notably those directed toward the Senate and especially those regarding committee turf. However, a handful of House reforms took hold in 1993, including reducing the number of subcommittees, eliminating four of the five select committees, restricting members to five subcommittee assignments, and allowing the names of discharge petition signers to be made public (Davidson 1995a: 33; Donovan 1992).[6] These changes, though noteworthy at the time, pale in comparison with what Newt Gingrich and his fellow Republicans wrought two years later.

Rolodexes around Capitol Hill had to be changed in early 1995 as House committee names and domains were shuffled. The Senate emerged largely unchanged, but three House committees disappeared overnight: Post Office and Civil Service, Merchant Marines and Fisheries, and the District of Columbia. Meanwhile, a number of subcommittees were abolished and some committee jurisdictions were realigned. Current House and Senate committees are shown in Table 6.1, and panels undergoing recent name and jurisdiction changes are noted.

Resentment had been building over aspects of the committee system for some time, and several committee changes were even promised in

---

6 Exceptions were made for Appropriations and Foreign Affairs. The total number of House subcommittees dropped from 135 in 1992 to 115 by the end of 1994. This was further reduced in 1995 to 84 subcommittees (see Ornstein, Mann, and Malbin 1996: 119). Publicizing the names of those signing discharge petitions was not widely discussed nor supported by the Joint Committee on the Organization of Congress. However, a movement among backbench Republicans brought the issue to light. Minority party members assumed that publicizing discharge petitions would undermine the powers of entrenched committee chairs – all of whom were Democrats at the time. The unintended result, however, is that committee chairs now know exactly which members are trying to undermine them, making it easier to focus retaliation on the few signers willing to go public. On discharge petitions generally, see Beth (1994).

Table 6.1. *Standing Committees of the House and Senate, 104th Congress*
(1995–6)

Committees	Members	Subcommittees
House – 19 Committees		
Agriculture (minor jurisdiction change)	49	5
Appropriations	56	13
Banking and Financial Services (name and minor jurisdiction change)	50	5
Budget	42	0
Commerce (name and jurisdiction change)	48	5
Economic and Educational Opportunities (name change)	43	5
Government Reform and Oversight (name and jurisdiction change)	52	7
House Oversight (name change)	12	0
International Relations (name change)	43	5
Judiciary	35	5
National Security (name and minor jurisdiction change)	55	5
Resources (name and minor jurisdiction change)	49	5
Rules	13	2
Science (name and jurisdiction change)	50	4
Small Business	43	4
Standards of Official Conduct	10	0
Transportation and Infrastructure (name and jurisdiction change)	61	6
Veterans' Affairs	33	3
Ways and Means	37	5
Senate – 16 Committees		
Agriculture, Nutrition, and Forestry	18	4
Appropriations	28	13
Armed Services	21	6
Banking, Housing, and Urban Affairs	16	5
Budget	22	0
Commerce, Science, and Transportation	19	6
Energy and Natural Resources	20	5
Environment and Public Works	16	4
Finance	20	6

Table 6.1. *(continued)*

Committees	Members	Subcommittees
Foreign Relations	18	7
Government Affairs	15	3
Judiciary	18	6
Labor and Human Resources	16	4
Rules and Administration	16	0
Small Business	19	0
Veterans' Affairs	12	0

Source: Davidson and Oleszek (1996: 200).

the Republicans' Contract with America.[7] Once the new Congress arrived in Washington, the House made several changes. Besides eliminating some committees and shuffling jurisdictions of others, it made many institutional reforms. It banned proxy voting in committees, cut committee staffs by one-third, abolished the practice of sending one bill to multiple committees, and set a six-year term limit for committee chairs. Some of these changes, such as the ban on proxy voting and their own internal term limits, promised to weaken committee chairs. However, chairs enhanced their powers to hire and fire subcommittee staffs and retained the ability to determine the jurisdictions of their own subcommittees. Recent committee reforms are highlighted in Table 6.2, along with a comment on the likely impact of these changes on committee deliberations. Political scientist James Thurber worries that the recent reforms amount to "efficiency at the price of deliberation and representation" (quoted in Wolf 1996: 13a). While this has proved true of the Speaker's new reliance on task forces, some of the changes have the potential to enhance deliberation.

At first blush, the House committee reforms listed in Table 6.2 seem impressive indeed, at least by their sheer number and variety. Of course, committees are always adapting, but the volume of change – all at once – is exceptional (Rieselbach 1994). The only recent precedents for these kinds and number of reforms are 1978 (in the Senate), 1974 (in the House), and 1947 (in both the chambers). Beyond what we have listed in Table 6.2, the once-pervasive reliance on seniority for establishing power within committees has waned. Next, while the Democrats handed

7 There were promises to "cut the number of House committees and cut committee staff by one-third," "limit the terms of all committee chairs," "ban the casting of proxy votes in committee," and "require committee meetings to be open to the public."

Table 6.2. *House Committee Reforms and the Impact on Deliberation*

Reform	Impact
Committees Eliminated. District of Columbia, Merchant Marine, and Post Office were eliminated. Jurisdictions were given to existing committees.	*Unknown*. Depends on whether these issues are really taken up by the committee gaining jurisdiction.
Committee Jurisdictions Shuffled. Several issues in the Commerce Committee's turf were divided among other committees.	*Unknown*. Helps if a less-fragmented jurisdiction leads to "better" policy. Hurts if established expertise on related issues loses importance.
Reliance on Speaker-Lead "Task Forces" Grows. Bypassing committees, Speaker Gingrich announces the emergence of new task forces to vet legislation.	*Impedes* deliberation to the extent that the minority party is excluded from the task forces and to the extent that established expertise on the standing committees is not tapped.
Proxy Voting Banned. Chairpersons or other designees are prohibited from casting votes for absent members.	*Improves* deliberation by making it more likely that legislators will show up for committee meetings. Gives the minority party a better chance of shaping legislation in committees.
Terms Limited. Committee and subcommittee chairs may hold their position for no more than three consecutive terms.	*Unknown*. Hurts if expertise is undermined. Helps if it keeps chairpersons from blocking discussion of widely supported proposals.
Staffs Cut. Total number of committee staff cut by one-third, compared to the 103rd Congress. Most cuts suffered by Democratic staffers.	*Impedes* deliberation by restricting the quality and quantity of information available to committees.
Rolling Quorums Abolished. Committees can no longer hold open a vote indefinitely, allowing members to show up at their leisure to vote.	*Improves* deliberation by making it more likely that legislators will show up for committee meetings.
Number of Committee Assignments Reduced. Members may serve on no more than two standing committees and four subcommittees.	*Improves* deliberation by allowing legislators to focus on fewer issues.
Multiple Referrals Modified. The Speaker may no longer send a bill to more than one committee simultaneously for consideration.	*Unknown*. On balance probably reduces jurisdictional fragmentation, though at the price of increasing the Speaker's powers.
Committee Meetings Opened to the Public.	*Unknown*. Most were already open. On balance, may hurt deliberation in that legislators are reluctant to engage in "open" dialogues when the meetings themselves are open.
Committee Chairs Given More Authority over Hiring Subcommittee Staff.	*Unknown*. Presumably weakens the subcommittees as power bases for policy entrepreneurs.

subcommittee chairs, almost automatically, to the most senior committee members of the majority party, the Republicans (following their tradition in past years for choosing ranking minority members) allow the full committee chair more discretion in selecting subcommittee panelists. What is more, on several House committees in 1995, chairmanship went not to the most senior members, but to more junior members whom Speaker Gingrich proposed to the caucus.[8]

No doubt there were many changes, and no doubt the committee system changed more than in previous years. But were the changes really that significant? By at least two perspectives, they were not. One perspective involves the fact that the most significant reforms did not last. These experiments failed as members soon realized that they had ventured down an "out of equilibrium" path, suggesting that the revolution had fizzled. Moreover, the changes that did occur were small compared to what could have occurred, suggesting that the "reforms" were not so revolutionary after all.

We consider the failed revolution perspective first. The two most significant changes that Gingrich and congressional Republicans attempted were the increased use of task forces and plans to alter the jurisdictions of committees. Both attempts were fleeting, and their outcomes suggest that members largely desired the old system.

Ad Hoc Task Forces

In the early days of the 104th Congress, House Republicans began using ad hoc task forces at a rate unseen since the speakership of Henry Clay in the early 1800s. Gingrich is the first member since Clay to ascend to the speakership without first having served some time as a committee chair or ranking member. And his years in the minority were spent railing against the committees, not working within the traditional order. Perhaps for these reasons – and perhaps because he deemed the committee system too slow, too cumbersome, and too protective of the status quo – Gingrich expanded the use of task forces.

Traditional task forces have been bipartisan, short-lived, and not permitted to report legislation. They could only recommend legislation to the standing committees. However, Speaker Gingrich's task forces were predominantly "invitation-only" Republican gatherings, and they were used, in the first one hundred days, to circumvent the standing committees. As an example, the ill-fated 1995 Medicare reform bill was

8 Even this evidence may exaggerate the weakening of the seniority system. Out of twenty committees (including Select Intelligence), only three violated seniority. Although it may seem that three is a large number of violations in one year, this may be partly due to the Republicans having so many new chairs to fill.

Great Theatre

primarily vetted in the Medicare Preservation Task Force, a Speaker-controlled body devoid of Democrats. Task forces are not new, but Gingrich took to them with real gusto, hoping to avoid long delays and entrenched interests in the standing committees (Sinclair 1995). Reflecting on these changes, Walter Oleszek concludes:

> Speaker Gingrich created so many task forces that it is difficult to keep track of them all. Some of these entities are partisan and others bipartisan. His Task Force on Immigration Reform [was] composed of 47 Republicans and 7 Democrats and charged with producing a comprehensive report on ways to deal with the problem of illegal immigration. *Committees, in short, may be bypassed in whole or in part as informal arrangements are devised . . . to draft or redraft priority legislation.* (Oleszek 1996: 102–3; our emphasis)

If Oleszek is right, then we may be witnessing a truly historic shift in power from committees to the speaker, a transformation that Gingrich called for when he stepped up to the rostrum (Gingrich 1995; Koszcuk 1995). Task forces largely disallow input from minority party members and serve exclusively to further the agenda of the majority party. Accordingly, this could cause dramatic shifts in policy toward the majority party's preferences.

Furthermore, this change could cause a dramatic shift in scholars' views of the purpose of committees. Elsewhere we have tested major theories of committees by examining how well the institutions that they imply match actual committee institutions of the U.S. Congress (Groseclose and King 1997). For instance, one institution of Congress allows minority-party members equal representation and equal participation rights on committees. We suggest that this institution does not fit Cox and McCubbins' (1993) theory very well. Their theory asserts that committees exist to aid the goals of the majority party; therefore, it is not clear why the majority party would allow the minority party equal representation. However, task forces change all this, and the form of task forces that Gingrich put into place fits remarkably well with the committee system that would exist in the Cox and McCubbins theory. Thus, it is possible that while the Cox–McCubbins theory was only a mediocre fit with pre-104th Congresses, the fit may prove to be exceptional following the Republican revolution.

For this reason, the Republicans' experiment with task forces is tremendously important. It is a venture down what seemed before to be an unstable path. It provides a rare glimpse of the payoffs down that path, and it illuminates previously unseen threats to strong party control. If Gingrich's moves went unchallenged by the minority party and by his own committee chairs, then we would have reason to rewrite the textbooks. However, the minority party has objected and, more important, so have a significant number of Republicans. The chorus of criticisms against Speaker-controlled task forces is loud, and it is getting louder.

In interviews, members of the House leadership surrounding Gingrich have taken to calling the task forces a "failed experiment" (King 1997, ch. 3) The drubbing Republicans took on Medicare reform is a prime example of what can happen when the majority party bypasses committees and shuns deliberation with the minority party. Democrats held their own hearings (on the Capitol steps), which met with great media fanfare. The public did not seem to approve and, more important, moderate Republicans like Representatives Christopher Shays (CT), Jack Quinn (NY), and Jim Kolbe (AZ) apparently lost their stomach for excluding Democrats (Chappie 1996).

Perhaps most telling, in the second half of the 104th Congress, the pace of legislation routed through task forces slowed considerably. This happened for two reasons. First, committee chairs, having bided their time during the first one hundred days, now reasserted their authority. Second, President Clinton's newfound willingness to veto legislation in late 1995 convinced some Republican moderates that it might be better to compromise with Democrats through the committee system instead of provoking further public confrontations. As of this writing, Speaker Gingrich still contends that task forces should be used to augment, if not replace, committees. And to address the welling resentment that his task forces engendered among Democrats, Gingrich called for yet another task force to plan a retreat aimed at decreasing partisan bickering (Bradley 1996). The withering of partisan task forces will go a long way toward that end.

Committee Jurisdictions

Committee turf – fragmented, overlapping, and sometimes out-of-date – seemed ripe for reform in the early 1990s. California Republican David Dreier, a reform leader in the House, pointed out that the Commerce and Ways and Means committees handled a disproportionate share of important bills. "Rather than having two or three omnipotent committees," proposed Dreier, "we should have 10 or 11 very important committees" (Shillinger 1995: 1). House and Senate jurisdictions have been the targets of reformers before, and the typical pattern has been to embrace the status quo by writing into the formal rules a few jurisdictional changes that were already accepted in practice (King 1997). In early 1995, the House adopted a package of jurisdictional reforms that had been gutted by Republican committee chairs. For example, Dreier's original proposal, which had Newt Gingrich's backing, would have eliminated five (not three) standing committees and sought significant jurisdictional realignments in nine of the remaining seventeen committees (Hook and Cloud 1994). Such grand ideas were soon undone by Republican committee chairs, who had waited patiently for power to come their way. Roger Davidson explains:

Carving up powerhouse committees like Energy and Commerce or Ways and Means seemed an urgent priority when they were chaired by the likes of Democrats John Dingell (Mich.) or Dan Rostenkowski (Ill.); but when the chairs were Republicans Thomas Bliley (Va.) and Bill Archer (Texas), the script quickly changed. In the end, little damage was done to the former committee, and none at all to the latter. (Davidson 1995b: 4)

Although jurisdictional realignments were not nearly as extensive as had been promised, this did not stop reformers from proclaiming victory. "On balance," said Dreier, "20 percent of the jurisdiction of the Commerce [has been] shifted to other areas. I think that in itself is monumental" (Victor 1995: 1761). Soon that figure of 20 percent was being repeated like a mantra in the popular press. It was an exaggeration. If one examines how many public hearings the Commerce Committee devoted to the handful of issues removed by reformers, the committee's loss was less than 5 percent of its activities from 1991 through 1994. The Commerce Committee did not, however, escape unscathed, and the story behind two of its losses – authority over the Trans-Alaska pipeline (to the Resources Committee) and control of food inspections (to the Agriculture Committee) can be attributed to the distributive-politics instincts of other committees.[9]

DISCUSSION

Although the list of formal rules changes in the 104th Congress seems long and impressive, the most prominent ones, task forces and changes of jurisdictions, did not last. Moreover, even the changes that were not fleeting were not very revolutionary.

First, the importance of committees remained basically the same. Almost all bills, including those deemed most pressing and significant, were still routed through committees. Legislators continued to devote most of their law-making energies to their committees (Hall and McKissick 1997). Jurisdictions remain fiercely guarded and hotly pursued, as they continue to grant legitimacy to committee actions (King 1997). The total number of hours that committees are in session did not decline. Com-

9 Agriculture Committee members likely had the most to gain from relaxed inspections, creating a clear distributive incentive to raid the Commerce Committee's turf. Likewise, Commerce's loss of the Trans-Alaska Pipeline can be attributed to the distributive interests of Representative Don Young, an Alaska Republican and chair of the Resources Committee.

mittees still hold hearings, and the number of hearings has not changed significantly in either chamber.

Second, notwithstanding the claims of Smith and Lawrence (1997), the power of committees remained basically the same. Smith and Lawrence claim that committees in the 104th Congress reached their lowest level of independence since 1920 and that the independence was sacrificed in favor of more party control. However, even if this is true, we argue that the change in power really was not that significant on an absolute scale. Committees still have gatekeeping power – subject to the discharge petition. Chairs are still chosen largely according to seniority. Chairs and ranking minority members, not caucuses, hire the staff; chairs, not caucuses, appoint subcommittee chairs; and so on.

Regarding the latter two points, however, Evans and Oleszek (1997) argue that the reforms of the 104th House took significant power from the chairs and gave it to Speaker Gingrich. The argument is that Gingrich gained the power to appoint committee chairs. This power made chairs beholden to him, which in turn gave him an indirect, but large, degree of power to appoint subcommittee chairs and influence staff hires. The flaw in the argument, however, is that strictly speaking, Gingrich did not gain the power to appoint chairs. The caucus retained this power.[10] It is true that Gingrich nominated a list of committee chairs and the caucus followed this list completely. However, we doubt that many of these nominations were really Gingrich's first choice. Rather, we suspect that the list he nominated was his set of choices subject to the constraint that the caucus must approve the list. If Gingrich really had full power in naming chairs, we doubt he would have followed seniority in seventeen out of twenty cases. Furthermore, we doubt he would have nominated Henry Hyde (IL) and James Leach (IA), who have not always been the most loyal allies of Gingrich. This is especially relevant for the 105th Congress: Leach retained his chair despite voting against Gingrich as Speaker.

The one exception to committee power is that it may be slightly easier to enact a discharge petition. Because of reforms in the 103rd Congress, the secrecy rule was abolished. This meant that members no longer could claim to constituents that they had signed a petition if in fact they had not. According to conventional wisdom, this made it easier for a member to gather signatures. In practice, it has probably made successful discharge petitions less likely, because members no longer have the cover of anonymity to protect themselves from the powerful committee chairs whom they are trying to undermine. Furthermore, here again, the

---

10 More precisely, the caucus retained the next-to-final say on committee chairs, since the floor still had to ratify the caucus decisions.

changes that did occur were extremely small compared to changes that could have occurred. Namely, the House could have replaced the discharge petition with a much more simple and truly revolutionary method: allowing members to request an up-or-down vote on the floor to release a bill from committee.

Third, the structure of committees also remained basically the same. Committees remained largely separate across chambers, not joint. Minority-party rights remained basically the same. That is, minority members still received seats on committees in approximately the ratio they hold in the whole chamber; they still were allowed the same bill-writing privileges of majority members; they retained the same rights as majority members to ask questions at hearings; and so forth.

Moreover, a host of other norms, rules, and procedures were similarly unaffected by the Republican takeover of Congress. Freedoms from caucus pressure remained essentially the same. The seniority system remained in place, albeit slightly weakened. In the House, seniority continued to mean how long someone had served on a particular committee, not how long he or she served in the chamber. Conference committees continued to be comprised largely of members from the panels of jurisdiction; when voting on the House and Senate floor, legislators continued to take their strongest cues from committee members; committee positions continued to win the day on almost every vote on the House and Senate floor; and so on.

Our line of reasoning may seem curious to some, since the conventional wisdom is that recent reforms were indeed revolutionary. For instance, Larry Evans and Walter Oleszek conclude that "the procedural changes wrought by the 104th Congress have potentially profound implications for policy making on Capitol Hill. Particularly in the House, the new Republican majority has adopted reforms that may fundamentally affect the distribution of power among lawmakers" (Evans and Oleszek 1995: 28). Aldrich and Rohde (1995) reach similar conclusions about the scope and importance of the changes to committees in the 104th Congress.

How do we resolve the difference in interpretations? First, we should point out, as Hall and McKissick (1997) do, that policy changes witnessed in the 104th Congress may stem from any number of factors other than committee reforms. The Republicans gained power for the first time in forty years; the chairmanship of every committee changed hands; the House was populated by a near record number of first- and second-term lawmakers, and the country seemed to be embracing conservative policy solutions. It is precisely in this environment that we would expect major policy changes regardless of the committee structure

(Brady 1988). One should be exceedingly careful in untangling the effects of committee reforms from these other causes.

Next, interpretations of the changes are a matter of perspective. We agree with Aldrich and Rohde, Evans and Oleszek, and just about every other student of Congress that the changes were large when compared to any recent year. However, unlike these other students of Congress, we do not see these changes as great in an absolute sense. Just because a snail has traveled farther today than it ever has before, this does not mean it has traveled very far. Although committees changed more in the 104th Congress than in recent years, their fundamental qualities, including those that distinguish them from committees in other legislative systems, were hardly altered.

There seems to be a common sin among political scientists and close observers of American politics: When political systems change significantly relative to recent years, yet not significantly in an absolute sense, they are nonetheless proclaimed to herald the beginning of a new era. For instance, although the issues that separate left-wing and right-wing voters have hardly changed since the early 1950s, at least a half-dozen elections have been proclaimed a "new realignment." In Congress, we have been hearing about the new "era of subcommittee government" since the early 1970s. Although subcommittees indeed gained some independence in the early 1970s, their power was still trivial compared to those of committees. For instance, subcommittees still did not possess closed rules for the bills they introduced to the parent committee, nor were they given any gatekeeping power. Nevertheless, despite only slight increases in authority, political scientists announced the beginning of a new era.

CONCLUSION

While the theme of the book is that Congress is like theatre, we suggest that the changes to the committee system in the 104th Congress were like theatre as well. Although a play is filled with births, deaths, plagues, and revolutions, once the curtain closes, the dramatic events prove to be only that – drama. The actors take a bow and return backstage. The audience applauds and returns home. Committees in the 104th Congress were similar. Members fought and complained about changing jurisdictional lines, new and abolished committees, the more frequent use of task forces, and so forth, but in the end, the committee system was fundamentally the same: The promised revolution was more theatrical than real.

7

The Unfolding Drama: Party and Ideology in the 104th House

BARRY C. BURDEN AND AAGE R. CLAUSEN

In 1994 the Republican Party in the U.S. House of Representatives came in from forty years in the barren desert of minority status and assumed the mantle of majority party. For four decades no Republican had chaired a House committee or brought the House to order with the Speaker's gavel. Legislative victories were dependent upon an alliance with disaffected Democrats, who constituted a conservative minority in an otherwise liberal party.

Even Ronald Reagan's victory in 1980, which was heralded as a Republican revolution, did not produce a Republican majority in the House. Contrary to what the Founders would have predicted, the Republicans took the Senate instead. This was the chamber designed to resist flash mass movements, with only a third of its members chosen in any election. It appeared that the linkage of incumbency and electability would keep the Democrats in the House majority, absent a sea change in American politics (Jacobson 1990b).

It is no small wonder that center stage in the theatre of American politics should be captured by the new Republican majority in the House of Representatives. It dominated that stage, albeit with a strong supporting cast assembled by victories in a variety of elective offices including a new Republican majority in the Senate, eleven more Republican governors, and Republican ascendancy in nearly one in five state legislative chambers. House Speaker Newton Leroy Gingrich of Georgia charged the new Republican majority in 1995 to fulfill its Contract with America: increase the power of the people and diminish the role of government. This was to be done in the same amount of time (one hundred days) that it took Franklin D. Roosevelt's legislators in 1933 to enlarge government to represent the power of the people.

The election that produced the House majority created the perception of a conservative mandate and a sense of mission for the Republican Party. Republican candidates for the House received a total of 33.6 million votes, 9 million more than in the previous midterm election, while the Democrats drew almost 1 million fewer votes than in 1990. The 1994 election has been likened to the "positive landslides" of the 1930 and 1934 midterm elections, so named because of the large surge in votes for one party (*Congressional Quarterly* [CQ], April 15, 1995: 1076-81). The midterm elections of the 1930s heralded the dominance of the Democratic Party in the first half of the twentieth century. Would the next half-century belong to the Republicans?

PREVIEW

In this chapter we examine the proposition that the 104th House of Representatives, elected in 1994, reflected a systemic partisan and ideological shift in the Republican and conservative directions. We argue that this shift is incremental. Moreover, we contend that conservative progress cannot be appropriately assessed by comparing the 104th House to the immediately preceding Congresses; comparison must be made to the 97th House elected in 1980. The apparent political "revolution" at the electoral level in 1994 may be viewed as an evolutionary extension of the 1980 results. Prior to 1994, the 97th House represents the last strong wave of conservative electoral sentiment. The 44.1 percent of the House held by the Republicans in the 97th House was the highest figure since 1972 and was exceeded only when the 104th House convened.[1] If House Republicans show progress since 1980 (as opposed to 1992, for example), it will serve as additional evidence of a rising tide of conservatism in the ebb and flow of political fortunes in the modern era.

Our comparison of the 97th and 104th Houses examines roll call voting alignments in relation to changes in the partisan and ideological makeup of members' constituencies. Our evidence of the incremental conservative shift is drawn from analysis of legislators' positions on a liberal–conservative continuum. Though many Democrats were replaced in the 1994 elections, we hypothesize that the most conservative Democrats were the ones replaced by Republicans.

Other features of the 104th House bespeak evolutionary development. Levels of partisanship, for instance, appear to be in line with existing trends (see Chapter 5, by Herrnson in this volume). Party voting, which occurs when majorities of both parties vote in opposition to one another, hit lows in the late 1970s but became more frequent through the 1980s. As Rohde (1991) has documented, the rise of House partisanship was due to the unification of the Democratic party (see also Cooper and

1 The 1968, 1972, and 1980 elections each gave Republicans about 44 percent of House seats. One has to go back to 1956 to find a percentage that is much higher (46.2 percent).

Young 1997). Our study of voting in the 104th House also shows that the levels of partisan conflict and party cohesion have continued to grow. This trend is due in large part to the increasing ideological homogenization of the Democratic party. When much of the party consisted of conservative southerners, it was difficult for Democrats to remain cohesive and oppose the Republicans. However, as these conservatives have been replaced by either liberal Democrats or conservative Republicans, the Democratic party has increased in ideological homogeneity. As Democrats attain the unity level of the Republicans, partisanship in Congress has increased. In this light, the behavior of the 104th House is not an isolated phenomenon but the continuation of a long-term evolution.

THE CONSERVATIVE MANDATE: ILLUSION OR REALITY?

In the short term, the drama of the 104th Congress involved the suspense brought on by Gingrich's effort to make a revolution out of a mandate (Wilcox 1995). Just as Reagan's 1980 mandate lasted less than a year, Gingrich's mandate risked proving short-lived. We know now that the Republicans in the House made good on the Contract with America. The Republicans in the Senate did not sign on with enthusiasm, nor had they ever done so. We know now that President Bill Clinton recovered from political depression following an election widely interpreted as both a Republican revolution and a rejection of the administration. While Clinton's approval ratings improved during 1995, public opinion toward Gingrich became decidedly negative, causing him to vacate center stage, at least for a time, to work in the wings.

The perception of a conservative mandate for the 104th House may be challenged by a nonideological interpretation of the 1994 election: the traditional loss of seats by the party of the sitting president in a midterm election (Erikson 1988).[2] The size of the loss was proportionate to the negative reaction to Clinton at the time (Tufte 1975) and augmented by the national campaign of a Republican Party whose unity was symbolized by the commitment to the Contract with America. This unity enabled the Republicans to exploit a growing discontent with the government in Washington. Public opinion and voting data are consistent with this view of the election (Tuchfarber et al. 1995). In this traditional midterm interpretation of the 1994 election, there is no need to

2 The Democrats lost fifty-two House seats in the 1994 elections. Though this is above the average, other modern midterm elections – 1946, 1958, 1966, and 1974 – saw similar losses. The president's party lost seats in all but one midterm election held since 1862.

document a surge of conservatism in the electorate to explain the change in majority control of the House and Senate.

This reasoning leads us to a crucial point: *the increase in the number of Republican members does not necessarily imply a major ideological shift in the House.* The evolutionary change hypothesis holds that Republicans won seats from relatively conservative Democratic members representing conservative districts rather than wrestling seats from Democrats representing liberal strongholds. Thus, the critical change in Congress caused by the 1994 elections is more partisan than ideological. The shift from Democratic to Republican control had the effect of producing a conservative legislative majority *within* the Republican Party. The counterpart conservative majority in the 97th House was built *across* party lines and produced Reagan's early successes.

Our task is to describe the events of the first session of the 104th Congress, which we present as the second act of the conservatives' play for power. The first act was the "Reagan Revolution," whose legislative success diminished rapidly after the first year. However, it set the stage for the second act by establishing the "limited government" parameters for the political dialogue of the nation. The 1980 election also featured a Republican proclamation on the Capitol steps, though it lacked the scope of the contract. Instigated by Newt Gingrich, the promise was to enact the Kemp–Roth across-the-board tax cut (Drew 1996). The third act opens with the results of the 1996 election, which maintained the status quo in an apparent national tolerance of divided party government.

The House is center-stage in the second act because the conservatives' message is represented by what the Gingrich-led Republicans did in the first session of the 104th Congress. House activities cannot be adequately portrayed by the actions of just the star players but rather require the full cast of 230 Republicans, 204 Democrats (including 5 who became Republicans) and 1 independent.[3] Nor is it enough to stage only the big scenes, like the enactment of the contract. The play also requires the ordinary scenes of Congress doing the business of government: passing laws, authorizing programs, collecting taxes, and appropriating funds.

Our best indicator of the substance of the conservative agenda is the sum of the policy actions of the 104th House. The Senate was less able to realize the agenda given the presence of moderate Republican Senators and the ability of the Democratic minority to block legislation by threatening to filibuster. We review the legislative policy product of the first year of the 104th Houses in terms of the Contract with America and the Republicans' use of the appropriations process to affect policy.

---

3 Bernard Sanders is a Socialist member from Vermont.

Great Theatre

THE CONTRACT WITH AMERICA

Although the story of the first session of the 104th Congress is much more than the fulfillment of the Contract with America, the contract was certainly the featured attraction. The contract was a written pledge to Americans that if the voters made them a majority on Election Day, the Republicans would enact a laundry list of promises. Though only a small number of Americans knew of the document signed in September on the Capitol steps (Jacobson 1996), Gingrich and other House Republicans took their new majority status as a mandate for passing it into law. They began their work unusually early in 1995, promising to finish contract business in the first one hundred days of the first session. Many bills were crafted, amended, and debated to fulfill the contract; their passage in the House is a conservative message that cannot be appreciated through a rhetorical summary.

The first proposal (HR 1) was to require that Congress end its exemptions from eleven workplace laws.[4] HR 6 would have revised House rules, cutting committees and their staffs, imposing term limits on committee chairs, ending proxy voting in committees, and requiring a three-fifths majority for tax increases. The balanced budget amendment (House Joint Resolution [H J Res] 1) and a presidential line-item veto (HR 2) were also passed.

Crime legislation would have required restitution to victims (HR 665), modification of the exclusionary rule for evidence in trials (HR 666), more money for prison construction (HR 667), speedy deportation of criminal aliens (HR 668), block grants to give communities flexibility in using anticrime funds (HR 728), and limitations on death row appeals (HR 729). Major changes in the welfare system also took place. They involved converting federal welfare programs into block grants for the states, ending automatic eligibility for welfare checks, capping welfare spending, requiring work after two years of welfare benefits, and imposing five-year limits for most welfare benefits (HR 4 and parts of HR 2491). More specific legislation dealt with families and children involving parental consent for children participating in surveys (HR 1271), tax credits for adoptions and home care of elderly (parts of HR 1215 and HR 2491), increased penalties for sex crimes against children (HR 1240), and strengthened enforcement of child support orders (part of HR 4).

The middle-class tax cut portion of the contract included a $500 per

4 In this discussion, *HR* stands for House Resolution, and *H J Res* stands for House Joint Resolution. *S* in place of *H* indicates Senate-initiated bills. Each bill is assigned a unique number.

child tax credit, an easing of the "marriage penalty" for filers of joint tax returns, and an expansion of individual retirement account savings plans (parts of HR 1215 and HR 2491). Capital gains and regulations were addressed by cutting the capital gains tax rate and accelerating depreciation (parts of HR 1215 and HR 2491), reducing paperwork (Senate [S] 244), and requiring federal agencies to assess risks, use cost-benefit analysis, reduce paperwork, and reimburse property owners for reductions in property value due to regulations (HR 9, S 291, S 333, and S 343).

A national product liability law included limits on punitive damages (HR 956), provisions to make it harder for investors to sue companies (HR 1058 and S 240), and the application of "loser pays" rule to certain federal cases (HR 988). A final item imposed term limits on congressional terms by constitutional amendment (H J Res 73 and S J Res 21).

The scope of the contract can be characterized in terms of two major themes: budget balancing and dismantling government (Ornstein and Schenkenberg 1995). Yet even this representation of the contract is inadequate. It does not convey the effort to reduce crime and curtail criminal rights, the increase of support for the family, and the protection and support of business interests. This was to be more than a political revolution; the culture of America was at stake (Steeper 1995).

The Republicans succeeded in passing the contract in the House – failing only to reach the two-thirds majority needed for the term limits amendment – by maintaining an unusually high level of party discipline. On the sixty-six roll calls that implemented the contract (CQ, January 24, 1996: 6-52) – all but three of which fell within the promised time period – only twenty-seven Republicans voted against the contract more than four times (CQ, February 24, 1996: 501-3).

Journalists, pundits, and other observers made much of the fact that the Contract with America was a special legislative phenomenon (cf. Bader 1997). After watching activities in the House during 1995, they concluded that the behavior of the Republican 104th House was unlike the prior Democratic Houses (Drew 1996). We also concede some discontinuities. Among other things, the simple fact that the number of roll call votes exploded in 1995 is evidence for change. In the late 1980s the House voted on roughly 800 to 900 recorded roll calls per Congress. Though these numbers seem large, consider that members had to vote on 867 items in just the *first session* of the 104th House. Some of this increase was due to convening the 104th much earlier than normal (January 4) and the saturated legislative agenda defined by the Contract with America. In addition, new operating rules designed by the Republican majority to "open up" the legislative process allowed for more amendments and reconsiderations, thus increasing the number of roll calls associated with each bill. Beyond these factors, it seems that the doubling of the workload is probably due to a new majority that had not been in power since 1954. It was led by an aggressive Speaker and seventy-three Republican freshmen excited about the possible changes.

Competing with the contract for significance were the policy changes embodied in the House versions of the thirteen appropriations bills for fiscal year 1996. As never before, these bills made policy through the control of spending and via policy riders tacked on by the Republican leadership. "Gingrich considered this the real revolution," according to Tom DeLay (R-TX), majority whip and a member of the Appropriations Committee. "We've known from the beginning that appropriations would have to carry much of the load of what has to be done" (quoted in Drew 1996: 256–7). The authorization committees, the House's policy specialists, were frequently bypassed because of their potential for sidetracking the Gingrich agenda.

On appropriations bills and other items of legislation – accounting for the 801 roll calls not on the contract – members voted on scores of amendments and fought the innumerable procedural battles that punctuate the legislative process. Many of these activities understandably escaped the scrutiny of the media. Our methods of study enable us to exploit the data provided by the thousands of votes cast by individual members on this array of legislation. We use them to reveal the lines of cleavage between and among Democrats and Republicans in a voting alignment analysis. One alignment is sharp partisan division characterized by cohesive parties locked in legislative combat. The second type of alignment is ideological, dividing liberals and conservatives. In this broader perspective on the full roll call record, we demonstrate that voting patterns in the 104th Congress are a continuation of trends begun at least a decade before.

ALIGNMENT ANALYSIS

A trend in roll call voting over the last half-century has been increasingly structured voting. This is due to an ever-tighter braiding of three major strands of voting behavior: party, constituency, and ideology. These are interrelated to such a degree that separating one effect from another is now extremely difficult (Jackson and Kingdon 1992). We do not need to distill these forces here. However, it is possible to identify different, enduring, generalizable voting alignments without claiming a distinctive causal interpretation of each.

We examine voting in the 97th (1981–2) and 104th (1995) Houses using three roll call–voting measures. One measure was provided by Keith Poole and Howard Rosenthal. It places members of the House on a liberal–conservative continuum ranging from farthest left (-1) to far-thest right ($+1$). To simplify matters, we refer to the continuum as *libcon*. Libcon is based on an analysis of voting behavior on all non-unanimous (i.e., less than 2.5 percent in the minority) roll calls taken in the 97th House and in the first session of the 104th. Members' scores are based on the dominant dimension in a spatial model of roll call–voting behavior. Our interpretation of the dimension is that of a general partisan/ideological indicator with no presumption of the balance of the two.[5]

In an independent analysis we constructed two measures of voting alignments in the two Houses. Roll calls with more than 90 percent voting in the majority were excluded from our alignment analysis. The excluded roll calls, sometimes referred to as *universal votes*, were much less frequent in the 104th House (13 percent) than in the 97th (34 per-cent). Whatever interpretation is eventually given to this fact, the con-sequence is that we now have many more roll calls (774) in the first session of the 104th House than in the entire 97th (536) available for the alignment analysis. Whereas libcon is based on all roll calls, our alignments are based on mutually exclusive subsets of votes. Though several smaller alignments exist, we focus on a strong partisan alignment – *partisan* – and an ideological alignment – *ideol* – for reasons that will be made clear. Partisan orders members from strong Democratic parti-sanship (-1) to strong Republican partisanship ($+1$). Ideol provides an ordering of members from most liberal (-1) to most conservative ($+1$). A brief description of the content of the roll calls associated with par-tisan and ideol is provided. Descriptions of the measurement procedures can be found in the Appendix.

Content of Alignment Legislation

Beyond the high level of partisanship found on veterans benefits, welfare, and Medicare policy votes, much of partisan is defined by economic regulation and fiscal policy.[6] The economic policy concentration on par-tisan is seen in eighty-four roll calls on twelve appropriations bills. The emphasis of economic and government management policy on the most partisan alignment dates back to the late 1920s (Clausen 1973; Sinclair 1982).

5 The correlation of libcon and a member's political party is .90 in the 104th House.
6 Legislation with three or more roll calls found exclusively on partisan consists of welfare overhaul (10 votes), budget reconciliation (8), right of business to establish labor–management workplace groups (5), telecommunications regulations (5), Medicare revisions (5), continuing resolution appropriations (3), veterans' benefits (3), public debt limit (3), and regulation of pension plans (3).

Compared to partisan, the lesser concern with fiscal matters on ideol is shown by the smaller number (thirty-three) of appropriations roll calls. The ideological division accounts for all roll calls on the Clean Water Act, the exclusionary rule, and the Cuban embargo. Ideol also covers the majority of votes on civil rights and liberties – death penalty appeals, prison construction, private property rights, flag desecration, the exclusionary rule – and the limitation of governmental powers via the balanced budget amendment and unfunded mandates legislation.

The appropriations votes deserve further attention because of the important role they played in the Republican agenda. Consider the types of roll calls on partisan and ideol. On partisan, the Democrats are united in voting in opposition to Republican efforts to eliminate or downsize programs such as the Corporation for Public Broadcasting, foreign aid for development, and agricultural programs. In the area of regulation policy, Democrats opposed provisions to keep the Occupational Safety and Health Administration (OSHA) from developing more standards and to constrain pro-labor activities of the National Labor Relations Board (NLRB). They also opposed pay cuts for Capitol elevator workers and employees at the Bureau of Alcohol, Tobacco, and Firearms, and they contested the repeal of collective bargaining rights for mass transit employees. Democrats united in opposing funding cuts and supporting funding for drug elimination programs in public housing. They opposed the transfer of funds from local law enforcement block grants to federal anticrime programs and from the reimbursement of costs for jailing illegal aliens to drug control and law enforcement.

Ideol includes a variety of cost-cutting measures consistent with a conservative desire to reduce the size of government. These drew conservative Democratic support. Among the proposals were cuts in funds for the Government Printing Office, a Food and Drug Administration (FDA) building, operations of the Agency for International Development, Woodrow Wilson Center for scholars, and a global environment facility. Conservatives opposed increased funding for the assisted housing and the emergency food and shelter programs. Policy issues that also struck a liberal–conservative chord found conservative Democrats supporting limits on Department of Energy regulations and a provision that Housing and Urban Development (HUD) funds not be used to enforce the Fair Housing Act relative to property insurance.

The content analysis supports the legislative exploitation of the appropriations process on a large variety of important issues. It also establishes that voting divisions were not uniform, highlighting the distinction between heavily partisan voting and voting where ideology conflicts with partisanship, especially among southern Democrats.

Party and Ideology in the 104th House

Roll Call Voting Patterns

Our analysis of voting in the 97th House and the first session of the 104th House affirms the historical trend toward more highly structured voting. Evidence of this trend is the concentration of roll calls on two major alignments in the 104th House. Partisan includes 311 roll calls, and ideol is based on 219 roll calls. Of the analyzed roll calls, 71 percent are in these two alignments. In contrast, 50 percent of the roll calls are on the two largest alignments in the 97th House.

The preponderance of votes falling on the two largest alignments in each House masks a change in the content of the alignment structure. Although partisan and ideol in the 104th House were also present in the 97th, neither was the largest alignment then. A third alignment, not reappearing in the 104th, was actually the largest in the 97th House. It had the distinctive feature that the Democrats were more polarized than the Republicans and slightly more cohesive. The defection of sizable numbers of moderate Republicans representing more urban districts was a reaction against some of the social welfare curtailments pressed by the Reagan administration. This alignment had no predecessor in prior Congresses and has no counterpart in the 104th House.

Partisan in the 104th House is highly correlated with party, at .95. Ideol is less partisan due to the defection of Democrats to the Republican side, reducing the correlation with party to .84. In the 97th House, the difference was even greater, .91 for partisan versus .62 for ideol. The defection of Democrats to the Republican side on ideol resembles what has been called a Conservative Coalition vote, in which a majority of southern Democrats vote with a majority of Republicans against a majority of northern Democrats. This coalition vote has been given an ideological interpretation and correlates highly with interest group ratings of members as liberals and conservative. Thus, there is precedent for assigning an ideological interpretation to ideol. However, we will show that roll calls on this alignment reflect conservatism among northern Democrats as well as among those from the South. This fact takes on added significance in view of the characterization of the 104th House as one of the six most partisan in the last sixty-five years (Cooper and Young 1997).

Alignment Convergence

While they are not yet fused, party and ideology are converging in the House. As Poole and Rosenthal (1991, 1997) have shown, the voting patterns of the two major parties have become more polarized over the

Figure 7.1. *Party and Ideology in the 97th House*

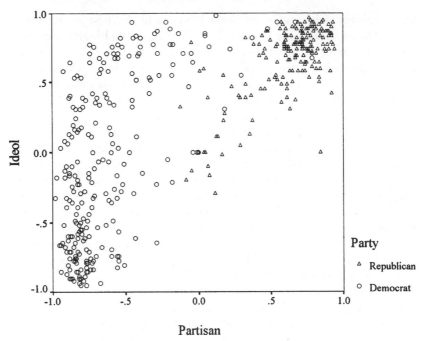

Partisan

last half century, so that they rarely overlap today. Even in the fourteen years spanning the 97th and 104th Houses, there is evidence that partisanship and ideology have converged. For example, the correlation between members' scores on the two alignments rose from .75 in the 97th House to .93 in the 104th. This is underscored by the increase in the correlation between party affiliation and members' ideol placements. In the 97th House the correlation was .62; now it has risen to .84. This is a function of the 1994 election continuing the pattern of Republican replacement of southern Democrats in the more conservative districts, which has been observed in the last two decades (Rohde 1991).

However, the large correlations between partisan and ideol overstate the similarity of their orderings of members. As a comparison, we generated scatterplots of members' positions on the two alignments for the 97th and 104th Houses (found in Figures 7.1 and 7.2). Republican members are indicated by triangles and Democrats by circles. Both of these figures also show the positive relationship between them; however, the members' locations are clearly not the same on partisan and ideol.[7] In

7 Correlations are best at detecting linear relationships between variables. Since the

Figure 7.2. *Party and Ideology in the 104th House*

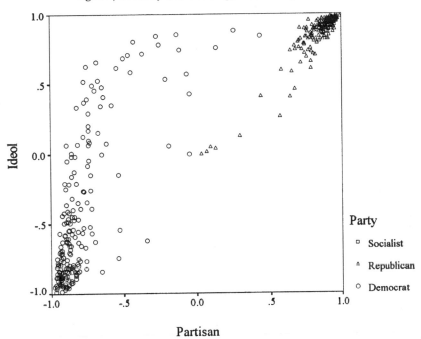

the 97th House, Democrats are distributed fairly evenly all along ideol; many are also spread across partisan. Republicans, in contrast, are fairly cohesive on both alignments. More important, the parties clearly differentiated themselves during this period. This is indicated by the tightening groupings in Figure 7.2. In the 104th House, intraparty cohesion and interparty polarization both increased. The Republicans are cohesive and polarized on both alignments; Democrats are just as polar on partisan but remain somewhat dispersed on ideol.

Though scatterplots indicate that the parties have shifted, it is helpful to have an image of where the "typical" Democrat and Republican stand in relation to one another. Using libcon, the mean Democratic position (D) in the 104th House is −.33 and the mean Republican position (R) is .40, as shown by the black triangles in Figure 7.3. Compare that pattern to the parties' locations in the 97th. The parties are more separated than in the 97th House, where the mean of the Democrats' scores was −.25 and the average Republican had a score of .31. As the arrows show, Republicans moved a small amount to the right and Democrats

scatterplots indicate curvilinear relationships, we are probably underestimating them by using Pearson's *r* as the measure of association.

Figure 7.3. *Positions on Libcon*

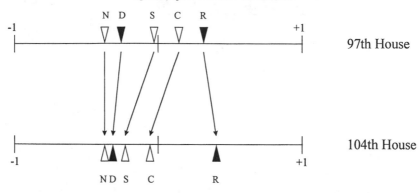

edged slightly to the left. This separation is matched by increasing cohesion within the parties, as reflected by a decrease in the spread of scores from the mean in the two parties. The Democratic and Republican scores had standard deviations of .26 and .19, respectively, in the 97th Houses, but these fell to .18 and .13, respectively, by 1995. In short, interparty differences have grown while intraparty differences have shrunk.

The changing distance between the two parties is due to the behavior of the two wings of the Democratic party. Figure 7.3 also shows that southerners (S) have moved strongly in the leftward direction, while non-southern Democrats (N) have remained in place.[8] This phenomenon is seen more vividly in the comparison of partisan and ideol voting alignments. Scores representing the positions of the parties and subgroups of the Democratic Party on partisan and ideol are produced in Figures 7.4 and 7.5. On ideol, Democrats are much closer to the center (−.47), while Republicans remain at the far end of the continuum (.89). This means that some Democrats are "defecting" to the Republican side on some of these votes. If a conservative coalition were in existence, we would expect these defectors to be mostly southern Democrats.

This is not what happens. Both northern and southern Democrats have means that are significantly closer to the center on ideol than on partisan. To verify that Democratic moderation is not an exclusively southern phenomenon, we classified Democratic members as conservative (C) if their scores were at least one standard deviation above the party mean. These conservatives are clearly to the right of their party; they are even to the right of Republicans on ideol in the 97th House. If southerners are driving Democratic defections in the 104th House, the

8 The South is defined as Alabama, Arkansas, Florida, Georgia, Kentucky, Louisiana, Mississippi, North Carolina, Oklahoma, South Carolina, and Texas.

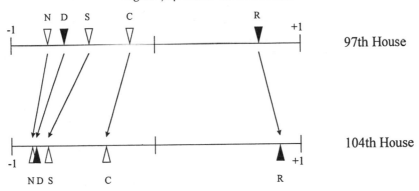

Figure 7.4. *Positions on Partisan*

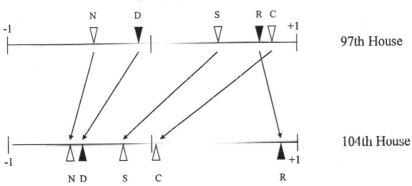

Figure 7.5. *Positions on Ideol*

conservatives should come primarily from the South, and so their locations should be similar. In reality, conservative Democrats are twice as
far from the party mean as are southerners in the 104th, and only
twenty-two of thirty-six Democrats who are conservative on ideol are
from the South. When the Democrats fail to be cohesive, the perpetrators
are no longer only from districts below the Mason–Dixon line. Northern
Democrats, once thought to be the most liberal members in Congress,
are now nearly as likely to join the Republicans on ideologically divisive
votes.

What remains of the conservative wing of the Democratic party has
become dramatically less regional. This is reflected in all three of our
voting measures. On libcon, 87 percent of conservative Democrats were
from the South in the 97th House, while in the 104th, just 55 percent
were southerners. Similarly, the percentage drops from 61 to 47 on partisan and from 89 to 63 on ideol.

LONG-TERM EVOLUTION OR REVOLUTION?

Throughout this chapter we have implied that the 1994 election is the latest in a series of elections associated with increasing partisan and ideological divergence. As part of this trend we have proposed that there has been, at most, a modest ideological shift in the conservative direction between the 97th and 104th Houses. Part of this argument rests on the claim that Republicans have replaced conservative Democrats. We provide some evidence to further the case for evolutionary change by observing shifting party fortunes at the state level in relation to the positioning of the state delegations on two measures, partisan and ideol, in the two Houses.

We use state delegations as the units of analysis out of necessity, but also in accord with preference. Necessity flows from the fact that neither individual members nor districts can be used. Individual members are not available to analyze because few of them had terms spanning the 97th and 104th Houses. Districts are also suspect because there have been two reapportionments between 1980 and 1994, not to mention the changes that can occur in fourteen years even in geographically constant districts. States are the closest approximation we have to electoral fortunes at the district level, and they add to the variation captured by the regions commonly used in longitudinal analyses. Furthermore, given the state-centricity of American politics, the state is a politically meaningful geographic entity. Political changes in the states are reflected in the ebb and flow of political fortunes across the changeable boundaries of the more artificially defined congressional districts.

Using the 97th House as a baseline recasts the apparent conservative shift in the 1994 election as part of a long-term trend in American politics. Comparing the 104th to the 103rd House, for example, there are Republican gains in 28 states, no change in 21 states, and losses in only 1. However, relative to the 97th House, Republicans gained seats in 25 state delegations, broke even in 11, and lost in 14. The delegations in which the Republicans registered gains, relative to the 97th, account for 265 members of the 104th House; 49 members are in stable delegations and 121 members are in delegations with lower proportions of Republican members.

Modest Conservative Movement

Evidence for a minimal ideological shift in the House membership between the 97th and the 104th is shown by the fact that victorious Republican candidates for the House replaced the more conservative Democrats. This occurred because the conservative Democrats represented conservative districts and were therefore most vulnerable to replacement by Republicans, who espoused the ideology preferred by these conservative constituencies.

The Republican replacement of moderate and conservative Democrats rather than liberals accords with common sense. Studies by Brady and colleagues (Brady et al. 1996) and Jacobson (1996) show that Democrats – both incumbents and open-seat candidates – fared most poorly in districts where Clinton had done worst in 1992. Making the reasonable inference that electoral support for Clinton is positively associated with the liberalism of the district, it is also reasonable to infer that the more conservative districts elect conservative and moderate Democrats who are more likely to be replaced by Republicans. We extend this inference by using the scores of House members on ideol to show that Republicans replaced the more conservative Democratic members of the House. Hence, state delegation means in the 104th House should not indicate a strong *ideological* shift compared to the 97th House. This point is underscored by a comparison with movement on partisan, where partisanship and ideology are mutually reinforcing, and the replacement of Democrats by Republicans should also produce a shift.

On partisan, 29 delegations exhibit a conservative shift and 14 show a liberal shift, whereas on ideol the number (24) of delegations showing a conservative movement barely exceeds the number (22) showing liberal movement. Moreover, on ideol the weighted mean conservative shift of .25 is slightly less than the average liberal movement of .28, hardly providing evidence of an ideological revolution.

Patterns of movement in the ideological positioning of state delegations are described by classifying state delegations into three categories. Comparing the 104th to the 97th House, did the Republican proportion of seats increase, decrease, or stay the same? State delegations should become more conservative as the proportion of Republicans increases and more liberal as Democratic strength increases. Assuming at least incremental conservative movement nationally during this period, conservative shifts should outweigh liberal movement. By the same reasoning, in the states in which the Republican proportion remains stable, conservative movement is expected. Again we compare the movements of the delegations on partisan and ideol. Because partisan registers reinforcing partisan and ideological forces, it should show the greater shift in voting behavior as the party balance changes in the state delegations. The replacement of Democrats by Republicans should have less effect on ideol since it is more sensitive to the ideological placement of members.

On partisan, the weighted mean conservative shift of the twenty-five delegations in which the Republicans gained seats (.33) exceeded the liberal shift (.20) of the fourteen delegations where Republicans lost seats.[9] In the eleven delegations without change in Republican representation, there were both liberal and conservative shifts, yielding essentially no movement (.02 more conservative). Apparently, conservative movement depends on a change in membership. On ideol we find similar results for two categories of delegations: those with fewer Republicans and those without a change in the partisan balance. The delegations with fewer Republicans show a weighted mean liberal shift of .16. Delegations without a change in Republican presence again balanced out, yielding no net ideological shift. However, for delegations in which Republicans gained seats, the findings are quite different when ideol scores are used instead of partisan scores. There is a relatively small conservative shift of .10 for the 25 delegations that elected more Republicans. Indeed, the more Republican delegations include *delegations that moved in the liberal as well as the conservative direction.* There is a conservative shift of .25 in nineteen delegations and a .19 liberal shift in five delegations.

The five state delegations in which the Republicans gained seats but conservatives lost support are all from the South: Florida, Georgia, Louisiana, North Carolina, and Texas. Summing across the five delegations, the Democrats lost 14 seats and the Republicans gained 29.[10] These states account for more than half of the Republican gain of 52 seats nationwide and play an important part in replacing conservative Democrats with conservative Republicans. This conservative-to-conservative replacement phenomenon is understandable in view of the already-conservative means (.5–.7) of these states in the 97th House.

In the search for generalization beyond these five states we tested the hypothesis that the states with the more conservative delegations would show a greater increase in the percentage of Republicans elected in 1994 relative to 1980 as shown by correlations between the two variables. This test was performed on the thirty-three state delegations with at least four members in the 97th and the 104th Houses (to minimize the impact of individual effects). We use ideol scores because of their advantage in revealing ideological leanings independent of partisan constraints. Strong support ($r = .57$) for the minimal shift hypothesis is found for the twenty-three states in which the Republicans increased their representation. We find less support ($r = .27$) when all thirty-three states are included. Indeed, if the relationship were sustained when states with Republican losses were included, it would suggest a polarization of the political system as well as a conservative shift.

9 Each delegation score is weighted by the number of congressional districts in its home state in 1995.
10 Fifteen seats were added to these five states between 1980 and 1994.

To discount the conservative shift attributed to the 1994 election when compared to the most recent elections, we compared it with the 1980 election, which is representative of the last major conservative advance. Even so, there appears to be a case for an ideological tipping of the political scales. Although phenomena more of evolution than revolution, the 1994 election and the 104th Congress represent a forward position for Republicans and conservatism. We want to temper the evidence of an evolving conservative dominance by calling attention to some indicators of a general bipolarization of American politics (McCarty, Poole, and Rosenthal 1996). For instance, we observed that some state delegations became more Democratic and more liberal despite the apparently stronger tide of conservatism leading up to the 1994 elections. There is evidence of a similar phenomenon in the behavior of voters in the 1994 election. Self-identified conservatives voted more Republican than usual, and liberals voted more Democratic (Steeper 1995); moreover, party identifiers defected less in 1994 than in other recent elections (Jacobson 1996).

CONCLUSION

The 104th House has been presented as the second act in the evolution of growing conservative influence. The first act – the early Reagan era – left no doubt that the curtain had gone down on the staging of the liberal performance that began its run in the 1930s. The closing act of the liberal play, Lyndon Johnson's Great Society of the 1960s, was the last hurrah of the New Deal. It marked the apogee of that brand of liberalism that looks to government for solutions.

Designating the 104th House as the second act of the conservative play for power has meaning only if there is indeed a rising tide of conservatism in the United States. The results of the 1996 elections neither supported a conservative staging of the third act nor ruled out the possibility. Clinton's victory, based on a centrist program, was hardly a clear repudiation of conservatism. While losing nine House seats, the Republicans still produced a historical landmark by repeating as the majority party in both houses for the first time in eighty years. Given the nonlinear movement of political forces that first favor one party and then another, the best indication that conservatism will resume its political progress may be a Democratic Party uncertain of its path.

Whatever the status of the third act, the 104th House should be long remembered as an example of the potential for change in a political system biased toward incrementalism. It is instructive that this potential arose out of a political oddity in modern U.S. politics: a united party with a strong leadership capable of delivering on a program of policy change. In contrast, in parliamentary systems with disciplined parties committed to divergent programs, such partisan performance is commonly observed. In the United States, the truly effective system of informal checks and balances embodied in the cross-cutting social, economic, ideological, and partisan cleavages is a formidable barrier to such concerted action for policy change. In this instance, radical change was supported only in the House. The Senate, the very embodiment of gradualism, did indeed serve to cool the hot cup of political passion.

Even though the 104th House exhibited a capacity for change, it was not due to the representation of constituencies that had altered their ideological inclinations and policy preferences. Nor was the ideological balance in the 104th House altered dramatically; rather, the ideological and partisan divisions came into closer alignment. It is this convergence of ideology and party in the House, combined with a Republican ascension to the majority, that made possible the second act of the Conservative Play.

APPENDIX

After removing universal votes, a modified factor analysis was used to identify the voting alignments. Factor analysis is a general statistical technique that uncovers what are thought to be the unobserved structures tying variables together. The computer produces correlations between all pairs of variables and then groups those that are most similar based on these correlations. These groups are called factors. In our setting, this means that votes that evoke the most similar voting divisions from members are loaded on a single factor. We altered the standard factor analysis to offset the procedure's tendency to account for as much variation as possible with the first factor. In the search for statistical parsimony, it may usurp some of the variance that might be explained by a hypothetical second factor correlated with the first. It is not difficult to conceive of a roll call that has its highest correlation with the second factor but also has a correlation with the first factor that is of sufficient size to be absorbed by it as it goes about maximizing explained variance. A roll call with its highest loading on the first factor was subjected to further factor analysis if its loading on another factor was greater than the loading of the roll call with the weakest loading on the first factor. This procedure was then repeated. The resulting groupings are labeled *voting alignments*.

Based on an analysis of the party means and standard deviations as well as correlations between these alignments for several Houses, we believe they are valid indicators. After reflecting roll calls to preserve polarity, scores were calculated for each member by taking the mean

value of her or his votes on each alignment. These scores range from
−1.0 to +1.0. Higher scores are more Republican/conservative and
lower scores are more Democratic/liberal.

A secondary set of data are the ideological placements produced by
Poole and Rosenthal (1991, 1997). They use a multidimensional metric-
unfolding procedure, called NOMINATE (for nominal three-step estimation), to estimate coordinates for members of Congress. When using
their data, we rely on the first dimension scores, which account for over
85 percent of the variance in roll call votes. The scores run from −1.0
(farthest left) to +1.0 (farthest right). The libcon data are first-dimension
coordinates produced by DW-NOMINATE, which is a dynamic variety
of the more generic NOMINATE (McCarty, Poole, and Rosenthal
1996).

ACKNOWLEDGMENT

The authors thank Keith Poole and Howard Rosenthal for NOMINATE coordinates and 104th House roll call data, the Interuniversity Consortium for
Political and Social Research (ICPSR) for 97th House data, Rod Anderson and
Joe McGarvey for their research assistance, and Jim Ludwig for his computing
guidance.

Congress and Other Actors

8

The Plot Thickens: Congress and the President

BARBARA SINCLAIR

The "read my lips" budget battle of 1990, the contest over the nomination of Justice Clarence Thomas, the conflict over whether to send troops to Saudi Arabia prior to the Gulf War, the struggle to enact Bill Clinton's economic program in 1993, health care warfare in 1994, the fight over the Republicans' budget in 1995 – a series of high-visibility showdowns between the president and Congress captures much of the history of the relationship between the two branches in the 1990s. Has the relationship between Congress and the president changed in a major way? Is it more conflictual and more prone to result in gridlock in the 1990s– and if so, why?

In this chapter I argue that many of the basic factors that determine the character of that relationship have not changed; however, trends with pre-1990s origins have reached a point and have combined in such a way as to alter that relationship significantly. Partisan and ideological polarization and the suffusion of the political arena by media with a negative bias and a voracious appetite for conflict lead to a more conflictual relationship between the president and the Congress and also result in that relationship, which at least since Teddy Roosevelt's time has included a considerable element of theatre, now being predominantly played out on the public stage, with audience reactions determining who wins and who loses.

Understanding what has happened and why requires first understanding the determinants of presidential–congressional relationships in general. What factors determine the mix of cooperation and conflict and who prevails when there is conflict? Once those factors are identified, the character of the relationship between the president and Congress in the 1990s can be analyzed and its consequences for policy and gover nance examined.

COOPERATION OR CONFLICT? THE DETERMINANTS

The U.S. Constitution created a national government of separate branches sharing power and, by doing so, established a relationship of mutual dependence between the president and Congress. In terms of policy making, it put the president in the weaker position (Jones 1994). The legislative power is vested in an independently elected Congress; the only specifically legislative power the Constitution gives the president is the veto. To enact legislation, the president and the Congress must cooperate or else one must be so strong it can overwhelm the other. As Madison and Hamilton made clear in the *Federalist Papers*, the system was intended to make major policy change difficult to effectuate (Hamilton, Madison, and Jay [1788] 1961).

The weak and decentralized party system that the constitutional structure fostered does not bind together the president and congressional members of his or her party in the way that a strong, centralized party system would. To be sure, even in the American system members of a party do tend to share policy preferences and have similar electoral interests. Yet, the president and his or her fellow partisans in the House of Representatives and the Senate are elected by different sets of voters at different times, and their electoral fortunes are only loosely related. Few members of Congress are likely to feel they owed their election to the president or that the president's success is the most important determinant of their future reelection. The party system does not provide the president with great leverage vis-à-vis his or her fellow partisans in Congress.

The constitutional structure and the party system have produced a powerful legislature – the most independently powerful in the world – consisting of two bodies that differ in membership and rules but are similar in their bias toward decentralization. Neither body has tolerated for long strong central leaders who can speak authoritatively for their members, and certainly, neither would tolerate a leader who claimed to speak for the Congress as a whole.

The governmental structure and the party system, in contrast, produced a president with meager constitutional powers over the legislative realm but who, by virtue of being a single executive and the head of government and of lacking a single competitor from the Congress, is by far the most visible elected official in the United States. From that, much more than from the constitutional stipulation that the president from time to time inform the Congress on the state of the union, derives the president's bully pulpit. The uses that presidents like Teddy Roosevelt, Woodrow Wilson, and, especially, Franklin Roosevelt have made of the president's position led to the expectation that he or she will function as policy leader; Americans expect the president to set the policy agenda and to engineer the passage of his or her program (Light 1983).

If the Constitution makes the president and the Congress interdependent in policy making but neither the Constitution nor the party system binds them together in common interest or gives either the capacity to command the other, what determines the character of the relationship between Congress and the president? That relationship, I contend, can be seen as a function of two sets of factors: (1) the goals of the actors (that is, the president and members of Congress) and the extent to which they coincide or conflict and (2) the actors' resources – constitutional, institutional and political.

Both the president and members of Congress have policy and electoral goals, and for the president and for members of Congress, enacting legislation is an important, though not the only, means toward the attainment of their goals; therefore, the president's and members' legislative aims – the legislation they seek to enact – are a function of both sets of goals. In other words, the president's notions of what constitutes good public policy and judgments about what will further his or her electoral interests combine to determine his or her legislative agenda. Similarly, both members' conceptions of good public policy and their reelection needs determine their support for legislation.

Members of a party share electoral goals, though not necessarily electoral priorities; both the president and his or her fellow partisans in the Congress want to hold the White House and increase the party's strength in Congress. Given their different constituencies, however, what will further the president's reelection may not further that of some of his or her fellow partisans in Congress, and vice versa. (For example, supporting free trade generally and NAFTA specifically made good electoral sense for President Clinton with his national constituency; congressional Democrats from strongly unionized, Rust Belt districts that expected to lose jobs adamantly opposed NAFTA.) Clearly, the electoral goals – though, again, not necessarily the priorities – of the president and members of the other party in Congress conflict.

Members of a party also tend to share policy goals; Republicans have, by and large, long been more conservative than Democrats. There is considerable evidence that, in recent years, the extent to which members of each of the major parties hold similar policy preferences has increased significantly (Rohde 1991; Sinclair 1995). Consequently, when members of the president's party make up the congressional majority, they and the president will often agree at least on the general thrust of policy. Conversely, when control is divided, the policy preferences of the president and the congressional majority are likely to be considerably further apart. Compromising enough to enact legislation may require real sacrifice by both sides. If, in any particular instance, either the president or the congressional majority party believe they can defeat the other and enact legislation in their preferred form, they have every reason to pursue that strategy. The differences in policy preferences also mean that sometimes no compromise exists that both sides prefer to the status quo. In sum, when the president and the congressional majorities are of the same party, cooperation is more likely than when control is divided. The extent of cooperation under either condition depends also on how homogeneous the parties are internally and the size of the ideological distance between them.

The resources that actors command affects not only who prevails but also the extent to which they are willing to compromise their policy positions. For example, a congressional majority that commanded a two-thirds vote in both chambers has no incentive to compromise; however, in the face of a determined president, a congressional majority with less will have to compromise or settle for no legislation. Resources can be classified as constitutional, institutional or political. Constitutional resources are essentially constant, though, of course, the usefulness of a given constitutional power – the veto, for example, or the Senate's power to advise and consent to presidential appointments – will vary over time and with political circumstances. Institutional resources vary more, though usually over the medium rather than the short run. Thus, the increase in staffing of both branches has enhanced their capacities. Internal changes in the House and the Senate in the 1970s and 1980s provided resources for certain actors. Political resources, however, are most variable and so most likely to account for change in the short run. For the president (and for congressional party leaders and those members who generally share the president's legislative aims), the single most useful political resource is having a large number of fellow partisans in both houses of Congress (Bond and Fleisher 1990, Light 1983). Having, or being perceived to have, public support for one's policy goals can also be a crucial resource.

If a president's programs are perceived as both salient and popular with constituents, and particularly if the president is perceived to have received an electoral mandate for the proposals, members of his or her own party will find it easy to vote in accord and opposition-party members will find it harder to oppose him. For the president to elicit support from members of the opposition party beyond that based purely upon policy agreement, such members must be persuaded that the costs of opposing the president are higher than the costs of support. The most likely basis for doing so is via a threat to the member's personal reelection chances; and the member's perception that constituents support the president's legislative aims is most likely to generate reelection-based pressure to support them. (For example, in 1981 there was a widespread perception that President Reagan had received a mandate in the 1980 election; many congressional Democrats feared that their constituents would punish them at the polls if they voted against the popular president's program.) Conversely, if the president is perceived as lacking such public support, members of his own party may feel reelection-based pressure to oppose him and members of the other party will feel no compunction about vigorous and visible opposition.

GOALS, RESOURCES AND STRATEGIES IN THE 1990S

Divided government has been commonplace during the 1990s, but that does not distinguish the decade from its post–World War II predecessors. The eight years of the Bush presidency (1989–92) and the first Clinton term (1993–6) saw only two years during which the president and both houses of Congress were controlled by the same party. From 1947 through 1988, control was divided 60 percent of the time, and from 1972 to 1988, it was 75 percent. However, because of how the political parties have changed, when control is divided in the 1990s, the policy preferences of the president and the congressional majority are further apart than in previous decades. Ideologically, American political parties at the elite level have become more homogeneous internally and have moved increasingly far apart.

A number of factors account for the changes in the political parties, but the change in the South's political landscape is most important, especially in its impact on the congressional party contingents. The civil rights revolution brought the South's black population into the voting population as committed Democrats and loosened the traditionally Democratic allegiances of conservative whites. Over time, many whites moved into the Republican camp, first as voters and later as party identifiers. As party competition increased, anyone elected as a Democrat depended on black votes. Conservative southern Democrats, once such an important component of the congressional Democratic Party, were replaced by moderate or even liberal Democrats or by Republicans (Price 1992).

As its southern wing grew, the congressional Republican Party changed as well. The party had seen its northeastern, moderate wing shrink as Democrats took their seats in the 1960s and early 1970s. The new southern Republicans tended to be very conservative and more ideological than the traditional Main Street conservatives of the Midwest. The tax revolt of the late 1970s, supply-side economics, and the tenure of Ronald Reagan all served to recruit a more ideologically conservative and more aggressive group of young Republican candidates for the

House from other regions as well. By the mid- to late 1980s, Newt Gingrich (R-GA), the epitome of the new, hard-edged southern conservative, was engaged in systematically recruiting candidates in his own image (Balz and Brownstein 1996; Connelly and Pitney 1994).

Increasing partisan polarization is evident in congressional voting. Party votes on which a majority of Democrats oppose a majority of Republicans accounted for 37 percent of all House votes, on average, in the Congresses from 1971 through 1982. From 1983 to 1988, 55 percent of all votes were party votes; during the Bush administration, 56 percent were; the percentage of party votes jumped to 64 in the 103rd Congress and to 67 in the 104th. In the Senate, the upward trend was more modest and gradual until the 103rd Congress; from 1969 to 1980, on average, 42 percent of votes were party votes, and from 1881 to 1992, 46 percent were; the percentage jumped to 60 in the 103rd and to 67 in the 104th Congresses (*Congressional Quarterly* annual figures).

The resources that key actors have available in the 1990s have been significantly affected by longer term institutional developments in both the House and the Senate, by the media environment, and by the issue context inherited from the 1980s. In the House of Representatives, the decline in the ideological heterogeneity of the parties made possible increasingly strong party leadership (Sinclair 1995). The congressional reforms of the 1970s had enhanced the leadership's resources. Using the Rules Committee, the majority-party leadership can control what legislation gets to the floor, when it is considered, and what amendments are allowed. In the 1980s, under pressure from Ronald Reagan, a conservative confrontational president who threatened their policy and election goals, Democrats became willing to allow, and even came to demand, their leadership's aggressive use of such resources. In response, the House Democratic leadership became increasingly active and central in the legislative process, often brokering intraparty agreements at the prefloor stage and then using the Rules Committee to advantageously structure members' floor choices and the party's large and increasingly effective whip system to mobilize votes.

The Republican minority followed the majority's lead in developing an active organization and giving its party leadership more powers. It also began to use the parliamentary powers available to the minority to harass the majority. With the majority party both more ideologically cohesive and more strongly led, the minority felt increasingly excluded from the legislative process, and even moderate Republicans became willing to support Newt Gingrich's aggressive tactics (Cheney 1989).

However, the House is a majority-rule chamber, where a reasonably cohesive majority can work its will. The strengthening of party leadership in the chamber during the 1980s has further empowered the party majority; it has made the majority-party leadership and the partisan majority it leads a potent actor, an invaluable ally, and a formidable foe.

The Senate, in contrast, empowers the individual. Senate rules have always given individual senators enormous power. In most cases, any senator can offer an unlimited number of amendments to a piece of legislation on the Senate floor, and those amendments need not even be germane. A senator can hold the Senate floor indefinitely unless cloture is invoked, which requires an extraordinary majority of sixty votes. Senate norms used to dictate great restraint in the use of these rules (Matthews 1960). However, changes in membership and in the political environment in the 1960s and 1970s eroded this restraint and senators became much more active on the chamber floor and in playing to a more intrusive media (Oppenheimer 1985; Sinclair 1989b).

The Senate majority leader, who has always been institutionally weaker than the House Speaker, is forced to lead by accommodation. A single senator can disrupt the work of the Senate by, for example, exercising the right of unlimited debate or objecting to the unanimous consent requests through which the Senate does most of its work. A partisan minority of any size can bring legislative activity to a standstill.

The Senate is not a majority-rule chamber. Large minorities can block action that majorities support. Even when they cannot stop legislation entirely, a determined minority can often extract substantive concessions, and sometimes even a single obdurate senator can do so. In sum, the Senate majority leadership and a Senate partisan majority are not as potent as actors or as valuable as allies as their House counterparts; a Senate minority, in contrast, is much more formidable as an actor or as an ally than is a House minority.

The media offer political actors a potentially valuable resource but one that is hard to control. During the second half of the twentieth century, the mass media, especially TV, have played an increasingly important role in American politics. In response, administrations have devoted more and more time and resources to attempting to manage their relationship with the press to the president's advantage (Grossman and Kumar 1981). Members of Congress followed suit, hiring press secretaries, for example, and also opened up much more of the congressional policy-making process to public view. Vietnam and Watergate began a trend toward a more adversarial and negative press. By the late 1980s and the 1990s, media coverage of politics had become poisonously cynical. Accelerating competition in the media business and among reporters and the advent of twenty-four-hour TV news also affected the character of news coverage. The media in the 1990s have a voracious appetite for conflict and for stories that are sensational, simple, and negative (Patterson 1993b).

Political actors who are well positioned and media savvy can use the media to further their policy and electoral goals. Presidents have always had great media access, and the skillful ones have used that as a major resource. As far back as the 1960s, senators discovered that the media could make them significant actors on the national stage, and much of the change in the Senate is a result of how senators altered their behavior in response to that new environment (Sinclair 1989b). The congressional parties became much more media aware; they set up mechanisms aimed at getting their message out most effectively and began to chose leaders with an eye toward their mediagenic qualities.

The contemporary media's predilection for conflict and for the negative and sensational is advantagous to the conveyors of such messages. Showing a sophisticated understanding of the media, Newt Gingrich, as an undistinguished backbencher, ran a highly successful, free media-based campaign to brand the Congress as corrupt and out of touch with the American people (Balz and Brownstein 1996). Selling a Congress-bashing message to the press was easy; defenders, with their complicated and boring response, could not compete. Similarly, opponents of substantial policy change usually have an advantage; the media's bias toward negativity works to the advantage of their negative message.

The issue context can be regarded as a resource or a liability because it affects an actor's chances of generating public support for particular policy proposals. The issue context the 1990s inherited from the 1980s was characterized above all by concern about enormous federal deficits and a pervasive distrust of government's capacity for doing anything right. The big deficits made policy making difficult because they made all the important choices hard ones. Thus, they worked to the disadvantage of those responsible for policy making – the president and the congressional majority. Because these actors operated within a zero-sum situation or worse, any decisions they made that had budgetary implications – and most government decisions do – were bound to be unpopular with some significant segment of the public.

More specifically, the issue context of the 1990s, like that of the 1980s, worked to the advantage of Republicans and to the disadvantage of Democrats; both the big deficits and the antigovernment sentiment make generating support for expanding government programs difficult. Democrats had lost control of the terms of the debate by the early 1980s and, except for short periods of time, never regained it. In the 1990s, as in the 1980s, Republicans framed the debate.

In combination, these factors shape the patterns of interaction between the president and Congress during the 1990s and the strategies these actors employ. Although none of the strategies are completely new, as a cluster they distinguish the 1990s from previous decades.

The character of the media environment and the ideological distance between the parties encourage actors to "go public" in an attempt to frame issues in terms favorable to their stance and thereby improve their bargaining position (Kernell 1986); bargaining between partisan opponents behind closed doors still takes place but most often in a context shaped by the actors' media strategies and sometimes by grassroots (or "astro-turf") campaigns that the actors have orchestrated as well. The appeal of going public is not that the strategy is an easy one to carry out successfully; it is not. Rather, the payoff of success can be very large, feasible alternatives for increasing one's bargaining resources are often lacking, the cost in good will is limited because party polarization has largely extinguished good will and even trust between the parties and actors know their opponents are likely to go public and are unwilling to risk yielding the public forum.

Going public is a strategy employed to some extent by all actors regardless of their goals. Other strategies are more often used either by those attempting to enact legislation or by those seeking to block policy change.

Those attempting to bring about policy change are increasingly turning to summits and to the budget process as their mechanisms. Summits – relatively formal negotiations between congressional leaders and high-ranking administration officials representing the president directly – are a recent phenomena. The president and Congress have resorted to summits when normal processes are, for one reason or another, incapable of producing legislation and the costs of failing to reach an agreement are very high (Gilmour 1990; Sinclair 1995). During the 1980s and 1990s, the deficit and the budget process, especially as revised in the mid-1980s by the Gramm–Rudman automatic spending-cut provisions, have often provided a sense of emergency and a statutory deadline that made inaction politically costly. Divided control, the sharp differences in policy preferences between presidents and congressional majorities of different parties, and the tough decisions that had to be made often stalemated normal processes.

The budget process has also become the mechanism of choice for those attempting to effect comprehensive policy change (Sinclair 1997). Packaging a myriad of legislative changes into one bill reduces the number of legislative fights that have to be won – an important consideration in a system with a strong bias for the status quo. Leaders can ask members to cast a handful of tough votes, not dozens. Critically important as well, the special rules that pertain to the budget process protect such legislation from a Senate filibuster.

Those attempting to block policy change or extract concessions from politically stronger proponents of policy change have refined a set of strategies for that purpose. The Senate filibuster has become a potent tool and is increasingly being used as a partisan weapon. Presidents facing strong opposition-party majorities in Congress now, as a matter of course, use the threat of a veto as a bargaining tool. Although going public is an all-purpose strategy, its highest development and greatest success in the 1990s has been as a blocking strategy. It was their success at going public and winning the contest for public opinion that enabled opponents to kill Clinton's stimulus plan, his health care reform, and the Republican effort to balance the budget and restructure entitlements in the 104th Congress.

The pattern of interaction between the president and Congress, the strategies these actors use, and how they are shaped by the actors' goals and resources are best illustrated by examining separately the Bush administration, Clinton's first two years, and the 104th Congress.

WITHOUT MANDATE OR MAJORITY: THE BUSH PRESIDENCY

When George Bush was elected president in 1988, many Democrats hoped for a "kinder, gentler" relationship between the branches. Ronald Reagan had been an ideological and confrontational president; Bush was thought to be less conservative and more inclined to constructive compromise. Unlike Reagan's agenda, that of Bush was modest and included items that Democrats favored. Yet, on a great many of the most important issues facing the country, the gap between the policy preferences of the congressional Democratic majorities and of President Bush proved to be very wide. In terms of personal convictions, Bush may have been significantly more moderate than Reagan, but he, more than Reagan, had to be responsive to the Republican right wing; that segment of the party had grown stronger during the Reagan years and trusted Bush considerably less than it had trusted Reagan. Democrats, for their part, were more ideologically homogeneous than they had been at the beginning of Reagan's term, with conservatives making up a smaller proportion of the membership.

Bush began his presidency resource poor; having run an issueless campaign, he was perceived as having no mandate, his party had lost a few seats in Congress, and he faced Democratic majorities in both houses. Democrats did not fear George Bush as they had feared Reagan at the beginning of his first term, having perceived Reagan to have received a mandate in the 1980 elections and feared negative electoral consequences from opposing his proposals.

Although controlling both houses by significant margins, congressional Democrats had resource problems of their own. The issue context of big deficits acted as a constraint, and Congress's already low approval ratings plummeted further in 1989 as a result of an ugly public fight over a congressional pay raise and ethics scandals involving Democratic House leaders.

Bush's modest policy agenda and the limited resources of both the president and the majority congressional Democrats made cooperation and compromise seem to be the best strategy for both. Yet, although there were some notable instances of cooperation with important policy results – notably, the Clean Air Act and the Americans with Disabilities Act – conflict and stalemate were the dominant motives. Even when compromises were reached, they were usually the end result of a highly acrimonious process, with much of the maneuvering played out on the public stage.

A measure of the extent of conflict between Bush and congressional Democrats is provided by a study of the fifty-seven pieces of major legislation on the congressional agenda during the 101st Congress.[1] Bush and the Democratically controlled House committees that considered the legislation clearly agreed on the legislation in 18 percent of the cases and clearly disagreed in 60 percent of the cases; even during the highly contentious Congress of 1981–2, Reagan and House committees agreed considerably more frequently (on 38 percent of the legislation) and disagreed less frequently (on 51 percent). In the Senate, Bush and the committees agreed on 26 percent of the legislation and disagreed on 40 percent. Of course, since Republicans controlled the Senate during Reagan's first term, he and the committees were much more likely to agree (61 percent) and less likely to disagree (9 percent).

Until late in his term, Bush was an unusually popular president. The Gulf War – short, successful and, for Americans, mostly bloodless – sent Bush's popularity through the roof to levels never attained before (Jones 1994). Yet Bush's popularity never translated into success with Congress. Members simply did not believe that the popularity represented an endorsement by the public of Bush's policy stances.

His lack of resources led Bush to rely heavily on a veto strategy; by threatening to veto legislation, he attained some bargaining leverage and thus often extracted concessions from majority Democrats. At some point during the legislative process, Bush threatened to veto 53 percent of the major measures making up the congressional agenda in the 101st Congress that were subject to a veto. During his term, he did veto thirty-

1 Data on major measures cited throughout the chapter are from a study conducted by the author. The congressional agenda of major measures is defined as *Congressional Quarterly*'s list of major legislation, augmented by those measures on which key votes occurred (again according to *Congressional Quarterly*). See Sinclair 1995.

six bills and was overridden only once. For a president with a small agenda, the veto and veto bargaining offer an effective tool for influencing outcomes.

When a president wants legislation, the weapon is less potent. On the Clean Air Act and the Americans with Disabilities Act, congressional Democrats who controlled the actual drafting of legislation maneuvered Bush into having to accept legislation considerably stronger than he preferred. Some traditionally Republican constituency groups, especially business, were unhappy but Bush could hardly veto legislation that was a prominent part of his own agenda without looking foolish.

Differences between Bush and congressional Democrats were great enough that, when legislation in the highly contentious budget domain was essential, they resorted to a summit. In 1989 Bush and congressional Democrats had held a budget summit, but they largely just papered over their differences by agreeing to a deficit reduction deal that was both modest and based to a considerable extent on "smoke and mirrors" figures. In 1990, however, Bush believed he needed to achieve real deficit reduction. Concerned about the economy and about legal provisions that were likely to force automatic spending cuts, and aware that normal processes were unlikely to bridge the big gap between the two parties' budgetary policy preferences, the president invited the congressional leaders to negotiate. Over a period of months congressional leaders and high-ranking administration officials representing the president directly negotiated a budget deal.

While the talks were taking place behind closed doors, the public campaign to define the issues and the parties' positions intensified. Since the beginning of the Reagan presidency, Republicans had painted Democrats as tax happy; Democrats had responded with a fairness argument, claiming that Republicans just wanted to cut taxes for the rich. By the late 1980s, many Republicans saw opposition to new taxes as the defining tenet of their party creed and their best election issue. During the 1988 campaign, Bush had vowed to never raise taxes, affirming his intent with the admonition, "Read my lips, no new taxes." A serious deficit reduction plan would require new taxes, but Bush wanted the Democrats to propose them. Determined not to shoulder the blame by themselves, congressional Democrats refused to do so. As the price of first, talking and, then, of a deal, they forced Bush to agree that everything, including taxes was on the table; then to issue a statement that tax revenue increases would be required; and finally to agree to a package that did include taxes. Furthermore, they used Bush's continuing insistence on a capital gains tax cut to highlight the fairness issue. The first deal reached was defeated in the House when neither party could muster a majority for it. Democrats then worked out another deal for which they could marshal a majority among Democrats. Although much less to his liking than the first agreement, Bush signed off on it. He really had little choice but to do so because the Democrats had won the media war.

The administration lost control of the issue when Democrats forced Bush to admit that the package would have to include taxes. The media played this as a huge story, placing the emphasis on Bush's reneging on his election promise. Fervent opposition among congressional Republicans to Bush's change of course made it an even bigger story. Once the question of whether taxes would be included in the package was settled, interest centered on who would be taxed, an issue on which Democrats held the upper hand. The Democrats' success in the media battle with the fairness issue convinced Republicans to drop the capital gains tax increase that Bush had so wanted. When the first package went down to defeat in the House, the president's inability to muster a majority of his members was a much bigger story than the Democratic leadership's failure, especially since Bush had made a television appeal for support. Although a significant deficit reduction package was enacted, Bush's only serious attempt at domestic policy leadership cost him and his party dearly in public perceptions.

UNITED GOVERNMENT: CLINTON AND THE 103RD CONGRESS

In 1992 Americans elected a president and congressional majorities of the same party for the first time in twelve years. Although American political parties are never perfectly homogeneous, the policy preferences of the new president and of the congressional Democratic majority were much more similar than those of Bush and the majorities he had faced. Furthermore, Bill Clinton and, to a very considerable extent, congressional Democrats believed that their future electoral success depended on breaking the gridlock and producing legislatively.

In terms of resources, Clinton and the congressional Democrats were considerably better off than Bush had been. They commanded sizable majorities in both chambers – 59 percent in the House and 57 percent in the Senate. But like Bush before him, Clinton was perceived to lack a mandate. He won only 43 percent of the popular vote, and his party actually lost a few congressional seats. The big deficit and public cynicism about government continued to present problems for Democrats. Perot's 19 percent of the popular vote in the presidential election was read as an indicator of Americans' overriding concern about the deficit.

Yet, despite these resource problems, Clinton proceeded with a big and ambitious agenda. He had proposed numerous new departures during the campaign and believed he had to deliver. Congressional Democrats whose policy goals had been largely stymied during the years of divided control were eager to move their initiatives, many of which were included in Clinton's agenda.

This constellation of goals and resources would lead us to expect co-operation between the president and the congressional majority. The minority, on the other hand, would be expected to oppose the president vigorously. Since Clinton lacked a mandate, few Republicans would fear him – and few would support him out of agreement with his policy proposals. With the election of a big and very conservative Republican freshman class, the 1992 elections had actually further increased the ideological distance between the parties.

What happened largely bears out these expectations. Clinton and congressional Democrats agreed most of the time. On the major measures on the congressional agenda, Clinton and the Democratically controlled committees of origin clearly agreed 88 percent of the time in the House and never clearly disagreed; in the Senate, the committees and Clinton clearly agreed in 81 percent of the cases and clearly disagreed in only 6 percent. The president and chamber majorities also agreed much more frequently than they had during the Bush administration. Examining those roll calls on major measures on which the president took a position, we find that in the House, Clinton and a majority agreed on 87 percent of such roll calls, while Bush and a majority agreed on only 41 percent. In the more individualistic, and less partisan, Senate, Clinton and a Senate majority agreed on 94 percent of the roll calls; for Bush the figure was 67 percent.

Republican opposition resulted in decision making being highly partisan. In the past, most major legislation passed with bipartisan support (Mayhew 1991). Minority-party members might well attempt to kill legislation in committee or water it down through amendments, but usually, the desire to grab some of the credit for legislation that was perceived as popular led an appreciable number of minority-party members to support it on final passage. The growing ideological distance between the parties has decreased that tendency. In the 103rd Congress, House floor coalitions were predominantly partisan on 60 percent of the major measures – up from 41 percent during Bush's first Congress, which itself was appreciably higher than the 26 percent during Reagan's first Congress.[2] In the Senate, where partisan coalitions seldom suffice to pass legislation, the figures are lower but the trend is the same; par-

2 Party votes are here defined as ones on which a majority of northern Democrats and a majority of southern Democrats voted against a majority of Republicans. The coalition structure on a measure is classified as predominantly partisan if all the major votes on it were party votes or if most were party votes and the re-

tisan coalitions appeared on 49 percent of major measures during Clinton's first Congress, compared to 30 percent for Bush and 25 for Reagan.

Cooperation between Clinton and congressional Democrats led to quick passage in the House of a number of measures, some of which had been stymied by presidential vetoes in the past. Parental leave legislation, a bill making voter registration easier (the "motor voter" bill), and national service legislation sped through the House. In the Senate, Republicans used the minority's power to delay and, on a number of these bills, extracted concessions before allowing them to pass.

The battle over Clinton's stimulus package exemplifies a new, highly partisan, media-dependent politics, which has become increasingly prevalent and foreshadows bigger fights to come. Although a relatively modest package, Republicans opposed it vigorously, arguing in every forum available to them that it was simply pork barrel spending and showed that the "tax and spend" Democrats had not changed their stripes. To get the 60 votes to overcome a filibuster in the Senate, Democrats needed a few Republican votes. The battle was fought in the media; to get those votes, Clinton needed to win public opinion, which he was not able to do. The Republicans were more effective in selling their definition of the package. Without public pressure to go along with Clinton, they felt no compunction about refusing to compromise and killed the president's proposal outright.

To enact his ambitious economic plan, Clinton and congressional Democrats used the budget process. In this case, too, the battle to define the package for the public was crucial. A budget package that significantly reduces the deficit will inevitably include some painful, and thus unpopular, provisions; as a result, passage will not be easy. The Clinton plan, although it raised gas taxes by 4.3 cents per gallon, limited significant tax increases to the well-off and included a number of attractive features. Yet Republicans were much more successful than Democrats at defining the package for the public. Since budget legislation of the sort that carried the Clinton plan is protected from a Senate filibuster, Republicans could not kill it as they had the stimulus package. However, by their success in the battle for public opinion, they made it much harder and more politically expensive for Democrats to enact the plan; at several critical junctures, it survived by a single vote. Not a single Republican voted for it in either house – a first for legislation of this magnitude.

mainder were votes on which a majority of all groups voted together. (See Chapter 5, by Herrnson, in this volume).

Not all the problems were caused by Republicans. The incentives toward individualism that the Senate rules provide often overwhelm those toward cooperation, even for members of the president's party and even under conditions of united control. A number of Democratic senators publicly held out and extracted concessions for their votes on the economic program.

For Clinton's health care plan, the public opinion war was decisive. Early on, the process appeared as if it were going to take a traditional course. Making policy changes of that magnitude is never easy in the American political system, so failure was always a real possibility. Yet key Republicans, most importantly Senate Minority Leader Bob Dole (R- KS), were indicating that they were open to some sort of compromise. Many Republicans, believing that health care was probably going to pass, wanted to take part in shaping the legislation and garner some of the credit. However, key Republicans on the hard right of their party, including Phil Gramm (TX) and, most important, Newt Gingrich, decided to go all out in opposing health care reform, which they believed was detrimental to their party's electoral and policy goals (Johnson and Broder 1996). They and opposition interest groups launched a campaign that completely turned around public opinion. Through about $100 million worth of media and grassroots campaigning, opponents convinced the public that the Clinton plan would lower the standard of health care available to them, decrease their choice of doctors, and raise their costs.

Opponents' success in the battle for public opinion translated into success in the legislative arena. To be sure, the Democrats' attempt to enact the sort of comprehensive policy change the health care bill represented without the protections afforded by the budget process handicapped them. However, it was the altered views of their constituents that made it impossible for Democrats to put together majorities for any significant health care bill. Members feared being blamed at election time for their failure to produce, but they feared voting for an unpopular plan even more.

To an extent unprecedented in modern American history, the filibuster became a partisan tool during the 103rd Congress. The Republicans' early and politically costless victory on the stimulus program, Clinton's mediocre-to-poor public approval ratings, and the sheer size of the president's agenda, which made it difficult for him to focus media attention, convinced Republicans that extensive use of the filibuster tool carried little risk. They wielded the weapon throughout the Congress and especially at the end, when time pressure always makes obstructionism especially effective. With members eager to get home to campaign, depriving President Clinton and congressional Democrats of victories simply required a willingness to use the available tools blatantly and often.

Republican filibusters killed campaign finance and lobbying reform bills. Although unsuccessful in the end, Republicans filibustered and tried to prevent passage of a massive crime bill, the California Desert Protection Act, and a comprehensive education bill – even though all had had considerable bipartisan support earlier in the process. Republican threats of obstructionist floor tactics were major contributors to the death of important bills revamping the Superfund environmental cleanup program, revising clean drinking water regulations, overhauling outdated telecommunications law, and applying federal labor laws to Congress. In the 103rd Congress, 47 percent of major measures encountered some sort of extended debate-related problem discernable from the public record, and most of these were partisan. In the 101st, by contrast, 28 percent of measures encountered some sort of filibuster problem, and these were not necessarily partisan in origin.

United control made the passage of a significant economic package possible, though in somewhat watered-down form; it was insufficient to make possible the enactment of the nonincremental health care program. Both attempts at significant policy change cost Democrats dearly, while obstructionism paid off handsomely for Republicans at the polls.

A "MANDATED" CONGRESS

In 1994, Republicans won control of both chambers of Congress; in the House, this was the first victory in forty years. The House Republican freshman class was huge – comprising seventy-three representatives, over 30 percent of their party's House membership – and predominantly from the right wing of the party. All but one of the eleven Republican freshmen senators were also staunch conservatives. The elections, thus, shifted the ideological center of gravity of both chambers substantially to the right and enormously increased the distance between the president's policy preferences and those of the congressional majority.

The 1994 elections left both Clinton and congressional Democrats resource poor. Their congressional majorities were gone, and with them, procedural control of the institution. Furthermore, with American voters issuing a stinging rebuke to Democrats, the elections stripped the president and his fellow partisans in the Congress of much of their representational legitimacy, at least in the eyes of the media and of Republicans.

Although their margins of control were narrow in both chambers, Republicans emerged from the elections with what they interpreted as a mandate. To a considerable extent the media agreed. Congressional Republicans in an off-year election had run a national, issue-based campaign. In an unprecedented move, House Republicans had drafted the ten-point Contract with America and most GOP candidates, incumbents and challengers, had pledged themselves to bringing all the items in the contract to a vote within the first one hundred days. Polls showed that most voters were unaware of the contract, but in the euphoria of their momentous win, the Republicans' mandate interpretation was inevitable.

Most Republicans and the media credited Newt Gingrich with the win. Gingrich had worked and schemed to build a majority for many years (see Connelly and Pitney 1994); he had recruited many of the challengers who won and had helped them with fund raising and campaign advice; moreover, the Contract with America was Gingrich's idea and he had orchestrated its realization (Koopman 1996).

Consequently, the election results gave Gingrich enormous prestige. They also provided him with a membership that was both unusually ideologically homogeneous and determined to enact major policy change. The huge freshman class consisted largely of true believers, who were deeply committed to cutting the size and scope of government and to balancing the budget; with the sophomores, who were very similar in outlook, they made up over half of the Republican House membership. For these members and a considerable number of more senior Republicans, both their policy and their electoral goals dictated enacting sweeping policy change. Even moderate Republicans strongly agreed that, for the party to maintain its majority, Republicans had to deliver on their promises.

House Republicans dominated the agenda-setting process during the first year of the 104th Congress. During the many preceding years of divided control, congressional Democrats had become less and less inclined to defer to a president of the other party in agenda setting and, as they became more cohesive during the 1980s, they had had some success in advancing their own agenda (Sinclair 1995). What Gingrich and the Republicans undertook was, however, of a different order of magnitude. They proposed a revolution in public policy that would fundamentally change the direction of government.

The combination of an extraordinarily ambitious agenda, a new majority united behind the agenda, and a leader with enormous prestige made the exercise of strong leadership both necessary and possible in the House. Without strong central direction, passing the agenda would have been impossible. Without a membership united in its commitment to swift and drastic policy change, no Speaker could have exercised centralized direction of the legislative process to the extent Gingrich did. Using tools developed by Democrats in the preceding decade, the Republican House leadership brought all of the items in the contract to a House floor vote in the first one hundred days as promised and passed all but term limits, which, as a constitutional amendment, required a two-thirds vote.

A different membership and different rules produced a different result for the contract in the Senate. Senate Republicans had not signed the contract but, because the media and Republican activists had made it a litmus test of success, they were under considerable pressure to pass it. Even with its new members, the Senate Republican party was not as conservative as its House counterpart. More important, however, the Senate, unlike the House, is not a majority-rule chamber; in the Senate, minorities can block legislation. Having had the filibuster wielded against them so effectively in the previous congress, Democrats made full use of their prerogatives under Senate rules and blocked or watered down the controversial contract items; by the end of 1995 only a few broadly supported bills had become law.

For Democrats, including Clinton, Senate rules served as an important barrier to drastic policy change sweeping through Congress during the initial months of the 104th. The administration, realizing that its resources were too meager to allow for a more aggressive role, stayed out of the limelight and played defense during that period. Rather than proposing an agenda of its own or attempting to work with a Republican Party that believed it did not need to compromise, it concentrated on working with Senate Democrats to stop provisions there or, failing that, to assure a veto override–proof minority.

The Republican majority attempted to use the congressional budget process to make comprehensive policy change. Republicans managed to get through both chambers a massive reconciliation bill that drastically curtailed the federal government's role by cutting domestic spending and restructuring a number of the biggest federal entitlement programs, including Medicare. While Republicans were legislating, Democrats concentrated on their media strategy and were increasingly successful in defining the package as extreme and a threat to Medicare.

For much of the year, Republicans had dismissed Clinton as irrelevant: They had the mandate, and he was a repudiated and, they were sure, lame duck president. True, he possessed the veto; but the Republicans were convinced that Clinton would cave in under pressure. Using a traditional congressional strategy, they had attached to appropriations bills provisions that they knew Clinton would veto if they came to him as free-standing legislation. Appropriation bills fund the government; if they do not become law by the beginning of the fiscal year, much of the government shuts down. Nonetheless, Clinton vetoed the reconciliation bill as well as several appropriations bills and threatened to veto others.

The vetoes set the stage for a high-stakes confrontation that would determine the legislative fate of the 104th Congress; key scenes of the drama, as is so often the case nowadays, were played out on the public stage, with the audience reaction determining the outcome. The actors had long been positioning themselves for the showdown – congressional Republicans by passing the legislation that balanced the budget in seven years and by threatening to shut down the government if Clinton did not go along with their policy thrust; the Democrats by attacking the Republicans for cutting Medicare to pay for tax cuts for the rich; and Clinton by agreeing that the budget should be balanced within a set number of years but contending that this could, and should, be done in a less draconian and more equitable fashion.

Given the vast distance between the policy preferences of the president and the congressional majority, only summit negotiations at the highest level offered any chance of reaching a compromise. After several weeks of negotiations failed to produce an agreement, Republicans shut down the government twice, the second time for much longer than had ever happened before. They were shocked when, not only did Clinton not cave in to their demands, the public blamed them rather than Clinton for the unseemly spectacle. Although a considerable proportion of the ideologically committed Republican House freshmen wanted to persevere, the public's negative verdict decided the outcome. The Republicans' ambitious plan to make comprehensive policy change was dead.

Months of stalemate followed. The Republicans were still not willing to compromise sufficiently to get legislation through the Senate and to the president in a form acceptable to him. Of course, as his public approval increased, Clinton's bargaining position was strengthened. He had engaged in veto bargaining throughout the 104th Congress; like Bush, another resource-poor president facing a hostile Congress, he threatened to veto almost all significant legislation. Now, however, he could demand greater concessions.

The reversal of political fortunes emboldened congressional Democrats, who began a campaign to raise the minimum wage. Through the procedural devices available to the minority – which are meager in the House but ample in the Senate – and a concerted media offensive, the Democrats made the issue highly visible. In order to counter the Democrats' strategy of offering the minimum wage increase as an amendment to every bill considered on the Senate floor, the Republican Senate leadership was forced to keep legislation off the floor, and the Senate ground to a halt.

By the summer of 1996, news stories branding the 104th Congress as the least productive in history and polls showing that Republicans might lose control of the House were eating away at the Republicans' ideological resolve. Compromises that had previously been unthinkable became acceptable, and before the August recess, several important bills were cleared. Alterations in the Medicaid and food stamps programs that were unacceptable to Clinton were stripped from the welfare overhaul bill. Mindful of the message sent by the 1994 elections and of his own unfulfilled electoral promise to "end welfare as we know it," Clinton signed the legislation. Minimum wage legislation, modest health care reform, a safe drinking water measure, and a rewrite of the pesticide law were sent to Clinton in a form acceptable to him after bipartisan deals were worked out.

In 1995, a substantial majority of House Republicans, including the leaders, believed that holding fast to their principals and refusing to compromise served both their policy and electoral goals. They were convinced that the public supported their policy departures and would pressure Clinton into caving in. However, the Democrats won the battle for public opinion. By mid-1996, the Republicans saw their electoral goals being endangered and reversed course; on the basis of electoral, if not policy, grounds, some legislation was considered better than no legislation, and that required very substantial compromise.

THE DECADE OF GOVERNING UGLY

The 1990s have been the decade of governing ugly. Even when satisfactory outcomes were achieved, the process was seldom pretty. The American governmental system has a strong status quo bias; with agreement among separate institutions with different electoral bases being necessary, ordinary policy making is often not easy, and making significant policy change is usually hard. When this system must function in a context of partisan polarization, tough decisions, and an intrusive, negatively biased media, governing becomes excruciatingly difficult. Clinton and Democratic congressional majorities in the 103rd Congress, as well as the new Republican majorities in the 104th Congress, attempted to effect nonincremental policy change; neither succeeded, at least in part because of the 1990s political context. The extent of partisan polarization meant that, in each case, the partisan majority had to go it alone. In both cases the media's predilection for conflict and negative news immensely aided opponents of change in making their case with the public; the opponents, after all, only need to raise doubts. In addition, media cynicism meant that obstructionists paid little price for their tactics; according to the press, "they all do it." The basic problem in these two cases was not simply overreaching, as some have argued; the unambitious Bush presidency was not a success either.

To be sure, ordinary policy making did continue during the 1990s. Most of the time, appropriations bills to fund the government were enacted in some form; there were occasional government shutdowns, but only the Christmas shutdown in 1995 lasted more than a few days. Furthermore, each of the Congresses of the 1990s passed at least a few significant bills. Aided by unexpectedly big growth in government revenues that made the necessary compromises much less painful, Clinton and the Republican congressional majorities even managed to agree on a balanced budget package in 1997.

Yet even when agreement was reached, the process was often marked by acrimony and strident public conflict. The spectacle of governing ugly as well as the lack of results on the problems about which voters care most further erodes public confidence in government and so makes governing still harder (Hibbing and Theiss-Morse 1995).

Perhaps most seriously, the political environment and the history of the 1990s provide few incentives for political actors to address major problems comprehensively or even seriously. The factors working against success are formidable; the political costs borne by those who have tried are sobering.

9

Congress and the Courts: A Case of Casting

ELLIOT E. SLOTNICK AND SHELDON GOLDMAN

Senate confirmation battles over presidential nominees to the federal courts often provide drama for a congressional session. This is especially true when the president has the opportunity to make appointments to the U.S. Supreme Court, the nation's highest and most prestigious tribunal. President Bill Clinton twice had this opportunity during his first term, but neither nomination supplied much drama. President Clinton chose Ruth Bader Ginsburg to replace Justice Byron White in 1993, and the Senate confirmed her appointment by a vote of 96 to 3. And President Clinton nominated Stephen Breyer to replace Justice Harry Blackmun in 1994, which was confirmed by the Senate by a vote of 87 to 9. Although Supreme Court nominations get more headlines, lower-court appointments may have a larger impact on the judicial system. These nominations rarely produce drama on the public stage, but drama often occurs behind the scenes. This was especially the case in the 104th Congress, when the Senate decided not to go along with the usual script. Many judicial nominations were stalled in the Judiciary Committee, and some never reached the Senate floor. In this chapter, we analyze that unusual play of forces.

The federal judicial selection process represents a rare interface in American politics where all three branches of government are brought, sometimes sharply, into focus at the same time. Vacancies in the federal judiciary, particularly those on the Supreme Court, have, in recent years, tended to foster more discussion and debate over the role of courts in the American polity than anything save for the most controversial and emotionally laden Supreme Court rulings. The president's role in nominating federal judges, with confirmation of his choices taking place in the Senate, places the executive and legislative branches squarely in an interactive setting where their actions can have a profound effect on the third coequal branch of American government, the federal judiciary.[1]

---

1 There has not been a great deal of analytical work done on the interactions between

Each year, of course, presidents make literally thousands of executive appointments that are subject to Senate approval, as provided for by the Constitution's Article II, Section 2, which reads, "The President . . . shall nominate, and by and with the advice and consent of the Senate . . . appoint . . . Judges of the Supreme Court, and all other officers of the United States." Most of these appointments, including those to the federal bench, are likely to be routine and raise little opposition or attention. In the context of divided government, however, a potentially ripe setting exists for partisan division to create great difficulties for presidents seeking to appoint judges and other officeholders, particularly when such nominees are labeled "controversial" because they appear to symbolize goals and motivations of the president that are at odds with the desires of the party controlling the Senate. Indeed, appointment battles between the Senate and the president may represent defining moments in the ongoing relationship between the branches as well as political opportunities and potential pitfalls for protagonists competing for the attention and support of the American public.

Many factors that help to define executive–legislative relations in domestic policy making can be found to operate in the judicial selection domain, albeit with different levels of degree and nuances of subtlety. The process of legislating often begins with an initiative spun from the president's program. Legislators reacting to that initiative, other things being equal, will often rely on partisan positions. In some respects, the president's "proposals" emerge from a stronger base in the judicial selection arena since, constitutionally, only he or she has the formal power to nominate federal judges. Further, few lower federal court judgeship nominations will rise to the level of public controversy or prominence in the Senate that will characterize debate over major facets of the president's program. Consequently, presidents ought to be successful most of the time in designating candidates for the district courts (the trial courts in the federal judicial system) and the courts of appeals (the intermediate appellate courts in the federal judicial system, situated above the district courts and below the U.S. Supreme Court). This will partic-

the executive and the Senate over judicial appointments, and most of what has been written has focused on the Supreme Court, particularly the highly controversial nomination battles. For empirical work in this genre see, for example, Cameron, Cover, and Segal (1990); Overby et al. (1992); Segal, Cameron, and Cover (1989); and Watson and Stookey (1988). Richer descriptive analyses of Supreme Court nomination processes are found in Maltese (1995), and Silverstein (1994). For treatment of the changing institutional relationships between the executive and the Senate in lower federal court judicial selection, see Slotnick (1980). For analyses of the judicial selection processes and behavior of the last four presidential administrations, see Goldman (1981, 1989, 1993, 1995). For broader treatments of lower federal court judicial recruitment, see Barrow, Zuk, and Gryski (1996); Goldman (1997); and Rowland and Carp (1996).

ularly be the case when the nominees have the support of the senators from the state where the judge will be seated, and indeed, when those senators are from the president's party, they will likely be the initial source of names for nominees to the district court bench. Logically, the smoothest sailing for the president's nominees will likely occur when the president's party has a majority in the Senate and the nomination is made for a vacancy in a state represented by two senators from the president's party.

As the judicial selection environment deviates from such partisan symmetry it can grow considerably more complex, with the president's greatest difficulties likely to arise under divided government when the opposition party controls the Senate and, in particular, when appointments are to be made in states represented by opposition-party senators and/or when a new presidential election is on the horizon. "Defeat" for a president in such circumstances, however, should not, necessarily, be measured in actual votes rejecting nominees on the Senate floor. Such a happenstance will occur rarely and, indeed, in many such settings may never occur at all. Rather, the president's difficulties may best be assessed by the extent of delay in confirmation processes once nominations have been made, the number of nominations on which confirmation votes do not take place in a legislative session, and the number of vacancies for which no nominations are forthcoming.

Whatever the partisan reality facing the president in the Senate, only he or she has the ultimate authority to start the judgeship appointment process in motion. Several factors may help to explain presidential success in seating lower-court judges even when the partisan makeup of the Senate works in opposition. First, one should consider the goals of the administration, as can be seen in its relative emphasis on professional qualifications in its judgeship candidates as compared to the pursuit of the more controversial goal of furthering an identifiable ideological agenda through its choices. Other considerations include the posture taken by the chair of the Senate Judiciary Committee, who may seek to be accommodationist or confrontational toward the administration (a choice that may be triggered in the first instance by the administration's own emphasis on alternative recruitment goals). Further, exogenous factors such as the time in a presidential term and the unfolding of presidential electoral politics may also be important ingredients in the interplay of executive–legislative relationships in lower-court appointment processes.

Critical and pivotal nomination battles over Supreme Court vacancies, such as those that occurred in 1987 and 1991 over the candidacies of Robert Bork and Clarence Thomas, illustrate divisive appointment politics at its highest dramatic pitch. In these instances, a Democratically controlled Senate made confirmation of a Republican president's nominees extremely difficult and, in the case of Bork (an outspoken conservative jurist), rejected the nomination. With occasional exceptions, however, divided government did not usually serve to foster public controversy when Presidents Reagan and Bush carried out their less-visible task of making lifetime appointments to scores of judges to fill vacancies on the nation's principal lower federal courts, the U.S. district courts and the U.S. Courts of Appeals. A clear exception was the period following the Thomas confirmation struggle (with its allegations of sexual harassment against a nominee considered by many to have received the appointment almost solely because he was ideologically conservative and black) whose bitter aftertaste resulted in the confirmation process of federal judges coming to a standstill for several months thereafter.

With the seating of a Republican majority in Congress midway through the Clinton administration's first term in 1995, the shoe was now on the other foot, and the fundamental change in the judicial selection environment was fraught with enormous potential for divisiveness. "Payback time" was anticipated for the attacks on Bork and Thomas and the sabotaging of several lower-court nominations and potential nominations by the Democrats during the Reagan–Bush era. A vindictive and mean-spirited Congress cast in the image of its leader, Speaker of the House Newt Gingrich, some argued, was in the offing for the first Democratic president to be elected since 1976. The Senate was now led by presidential candidate Bob Dole (until his resignation in June of 1996), who stood to gain a great deal by making Clinton's life difficult on the judgeship front. Further, the all-important Senate Judiciary Committee also witnessed a critical changing of the guard in the 104th Congress.

During the first half of the Clinton presidency, the committee was chaired by Delaware Democratic Senator Joseph Biden, and advice and consent to judicial nominations ran relatively smoothly once the president's judicial selection "team" was in place. The results of federal judicial selection by the middle of the Clinton term included the designation of an unprecedented proportion of women and minority judges, as well as judges receiving unusually strong endorsement from the American Bar Association's Standing Committee on Federal Judiciary, a key actor in evaluating judicial appointments since the Dwight Eisenhower administration. With the ascendancy of Utah Republican Orrin Hatch, a vocal supporter of both Bork and Thomas, to the Judiciary Committee's chairmanship in the 104th Congress, the question emerged of how judicial selection processes would be altered in both the executive and legislative realms.

Utilizing empirical data on judicial nominees, as well as interview data from sources in both the nomination and confirmation process, this chapter addresses a number of concerns. How were relations and processes between the White House and the Senate altered in the 104th Congress in the judicial selection domain? What happened to the nominees who were in the pipeline for selection when the Republicans gained control of the Senate? How do nominees chosen after the 1994 election differ from those selected prior to the Republican ascendancy to majority status in the Senate? Prior to addressing such questions, however, it is instructive to place the contemporary politicized nominations process in more recent historical perspective.

ADVICE AND CONSENT IN RECENT HISTORICAL CONTEXT

Interestingly (and somewhat ironically from the perspective of the Clinton administration's difficulties in confirming judgeship candidates during the 104th Congress), divisive politicization of lower federal judicial recruitment processes can be traced, in part, to the reforms put in place by the Jimmy Carter administration two decades earlier. Before taking office, Carter had committed himself to the concept of using judicial selection commissions for screening and recommending qualified candidates for judicial office. This would necessarily intrude upon the prerogatives of senators of the president's party who were accustomed to having a major say in who received judicial appointments from their states. Indeed, for appointments to the district courts, home-state senators of the president's party were typically the source of nominees. Carter's initiative would place a new set of players between a traditional senatorial prerogative and the president's formal nomination, and senatorial opposition to such a fundamental change was great. A compromise, however, was reached with the then Judiciary Committee chair, Democrat James Eastland (MS), whereby the Carter initiative was limited to the circuit bench. Senators were encouraged, albeit not required, to utilize commission procedures in recommendations for district court vacancies arising in their states.

Carter's commission approach was not an end in and of itself. Rather, it was a means that was expected to facilitate the pursuit of a more representative federal bench through an aggressive affirmative action program in judicial selection. Underscoring presidential incursion into what, traditionally, had been a senatorial prerogative at the district court level, Carter asserted that, "When the senators have refused to include in their list of recommended judges those who are black or other minorities or those who are women, then we are delaying any appointments, going back to the senators and asking them to enlarge their lists"

(*Congressional Quarterly Weekly Report* 1979: 190). Adding political considerations (in the policy sense of the term) to the traditional patronage concerns in the process contributed to the politicization of the process.

Presidents Reagan and Bush continued the more politicized selection process by openly recruiting conservatives for the federal bench. A potential nominee actively in favor of abortion rights would be ruled out of contention even if the candidate's Republican credentials were impeccable.

Another development in the selection process would make selection more complex. In 1979, Massachusetts Democratic Senator Edward M. Kennedy became chair of the Senate Judiciary Committee and established an independent investigatory role for the committee. No longer would it rely only on Federal Bureau of Investigation (FBI) and administration reports on the backgrounds of judicial nominees. Now, committee investigators for both the majority and minority side would independently investigate nominees.

When Republican Strom Thurmond of South Carolina became chair in 1981 following the Reagan presidential victory and the capture of the Senate by the Republicans, he continued the committee's independent investigatory role. The potential for conflict between the Senate and the new administration was thus enhanced by this new institutional mechanism, independently of whether the Senate was controlled by the same party as the president. For example, when Reagan was president and the Senate Judiciary Committee was in Republican hands, there were highly public battles over the nomination of Daniel Manion to the U.S Court of Appeals for the Seventh Circuit and Jefferson Sessions to an Alabama district court position. Committee investigators for the Democrats developed a case against these nominees and liberal groups subsequently mounted nationwide campaigns against confirmation – which were only partly successful (the Sessions nomination was defeated in the Senate Judiciary Committee, while Manion, after a prolonged and bitter struggle, was barely confirmed; but Sessions gave this drama a surprise ending when, a decade later, he was himself elected to the Senate and placed on the Judiciary Committee).

When Reagan, during his last two years in office, and Bush, for all four years, faced Democratic majorities in the Senate, there was increased partisan and ideological wrangling, not only over Supreme Court nominees, but also over some lower-court nominees. Although fights at the lower level were more subdued than the Bork and Thomas battles, politicization always lurked in the shadows, waiting for an opportunity to emerge.

While divided government ended briefly in the 103rd Congress, the prospects for divisiveness and controversy over judicial selection between a president and the Senate loomed particularly large in the relationship between the Clinton administration and the 104th Congress for a number of reasons. First, the 104th Congress, as other chapters in this volume amply demonstrate, may be characterized as an institution in which partisan and ideological lines were drawn very sharply. While Newt Gingrich's leadership of the Congress was formally confined to his position in the House of Representatives, it was hard to believe that the effects of the Gingrich revolution would not be felt in the Senate. Further, the Republican takeover of the Senate brought with it the rise of Orrin Hatch to head the Judiciary Committee. Hatch had been a major player in the previous judicial selection dramas, and many felt that he would be a prominent thorn in the side of the Clinton administrations's judicial selection efforts. Just as importantly (until June 1996), Bob Dole's position as majority leader in the Senate allowed him to confront the president as "leader of the opposition," with judicial selection simply one battleground among many to be utilized in the unfolding of the 1996 presidential campaign.

JUDICIAL SELECTION AND THE 104TH CONGRESS

While the Senate in the 104th Congress seemed uniquely positioned to "do battle" in the judicial selection arena, the Clinton administration, in many respects, emerged as a somewhat curious and unlikely adversary. Unlike with administrations dating back at least as far as Richard Nixon, judgeships did not take center stage, by most accounts, on President Clinton's domestic policy agenda. Assistant Attorney General for Policy Development Eleanor Dean Acheson, who was responsible for judicial selection within the Justice Department, explained the administration's philosophy.

The President and the people who work with him and for him . . . came to this with . . . a somewhat unspoken common consensus. . . . We all think . . . the process has been wildly disserved by this idea that this is a huge ideological battle for the courts and . . . there is no middle ground. . . . What we've done with respect to Justice Ginsburg and Justice Breyer is what we've tried to do . . . with every nomination: to find people who have exhibited either in their prior judge life or practitioner life or law professor life a non-ideological approach.

Putting the matter equally bluntly, a key member of the president's judicial selection operation who had labored in both the White House and Justice Department facets of the process added:

What we need to do is to have everybody calm down about the federal judiciary and not think that this is some kind of life or death struggle . . . to impose or correct an ideological imbalance. I think that we have done what we can . . . to

Table 9.1. *Gender, Ethnicity, and American Bar Association Ratings of Clinton's First-Term Appointees Compared to the Appointees of Bush, Reagan, and Carter*[a]

	Clinton		Bush		Reagan		Carter	
	%	(N)	%	(N)	%	(N)	%	(N)
Gender								
Female	30.3	(60)	19.5	(36)	7.6	(28)	15.5	(40)
Male	69.7	(138)	80.5	(149)	92.4	(340)	84.5	(218)
Ethnicity								
African American	18.7	(37)	6.5	(12)	1.9	(7)	14.3	(37)
Hispanic	7.1	(14)	4.3	(8)	4.1	(15)	6.2	(16)
Asian	1.5	(3)	--	--	0.5	(2)	0.8	(2)
Native American	0.5	(1)	--	--	--	--	--	--
% White Male	47.0	(93)	72.4	(134)	86.4	(318)	66.7	(172)
ABA Ratings								
Exceptionally well/ well Qualified	66.2	(131)	58.9	(109)	54.6	(201)	56.2	(145)

[a]Lifetime appointments to lower courts of general jurisdiction (district and appeals) confirmed by the U.S. Senate

get people off this feeling that we are . . . on some kind of reverse jihad. . . . This is not a do or die fight for American culture. This is an attempt to get . . . highly competent lawyers on the federal bench so they can resolve disputes.

Diversity

The administration not only aimed to select highly qualified people who were not ideologically controversial, but also those who would add to the ethnic and gender diversity of the bench. The findings reported in Table 9.1 suggest that the administration was successful in achieving these goals.

Table 9.1 compares Clinton's first-term appointees (district and appeals courts combined) to those of Bush, Reagan, and Carter. Clinton named the largest proportion of women of any president in history. In absolute numbers, Clinton far exceeded the numbers of women appointed by Bush and Carter. The proportion of African Americans (almost one in five nominees) was also the highest. In absolute numbers, with the exception of Hispanic appointees, Clinton matched Carter's record, and in every ethnic category, Clinton's proportions surpassed every other president. Women and minorities constituted a majority of the first-term appointees. Further, utilizing the American Bar Association (ABA) ratings as an approximation of legal quality reveals that Clinton's judges had the highest proportion to be given the ABA's highest rating – a fact that so distressed the Republicans and chair Orrin Hatch that they held a hearing on the ABA's role in the selection process in May 1996.

The Senate Judiciary Committee

Despite the existence of divided government, things appear to have functioned relatively smoothly, at least on the surface, in the relationship between the Clinton administration and the Judiciary Committee chaired by Orrin Hatch. Indeed, commenting on the unusual amount of consultation and, some would argue, compromise and accommodation between the administration, individual senators, the Judiciary Committee, and, most specifically, its chair, one analyst has credited the White House with "using an approach that would have been unthinkable in recent administrations" (Bendavid 1995: 1).

The collaborative relationship between the Democratic White House and Republican-led Judiciary Committee appeared to flow from a number of sources. First, Senator Hatch exhibited substantial professionalism in refusing to play the role of omnipresent gadfly and stopgap in the confirmation process. Rather, as attested to universally by administration sources as well as by both Republican and Democratic Senate staff, he pursued a commitment to work with the administration to see nominations through to confirmation. Administratively, the rhythm of judicial selection processes in the committee operated with regularity and predictability. As noted by Eleanor Acheson, "Senator Hatch . . . hoped to have a predictable schedule that would basically involve a hearing a month at which he would agree to process a circuit court nominee and anywhere between three to five and possibly more . . . district court nominees." With very few exceptions, the committee kept to this schedule. While there were extended periods during the 104th Congress when no judges were confirmed by the Senate as a whole (more than four months in 1995 and about eleven months in 1996), this did not appear to be the result of Judiciary Committee stonewalling but, rather, inaction on the Senate floor.

Regarding Hatch's handling of the committee, an aide to a Republican Judiciary committee member underscored the chair's work ethic, the communicativeness of committee staff with all participants in the confirmation process, and the good chemistry that emerged among all key judicial selection players. Belying, perhaps, the conventional wisdom about Hatch's demeanor and orientation (particularly in view of his role in the Bork and Thomas confirmation processes), this aide added that Hatch was,

very fair, very open-minded. A man of principle. . . . I'm not surprised to see him really scrutinizing the nominees and giving them a fair hearing. He's not a knee jerk kind of person. . . . If Hatch would hear that somebody is controversial he would gather all the evidence and make a decision.

For his part, Hatch has confirmed the impressions gleaned from all of our sources in both parties about relationships among key confirmation process players.

We've been together hours and hours and hours, regularly, each week. . . . They keep running them by us. I have worked with countless people on judges from various White Houses, Republicans and Democrats, and I have yet to work with anyone who is as straight up as Vicki Radd, Ab Mikva, and Eldie Acheson (quoted in Bendavid 1995: 15).

When asked whether the mean-spiritedness of the "Gingrich revolution," a term that characterized broadly the 104th Congress, had reared its head in the relationship between the administration and the Judiciary Committee, an administration source with both White House and Justice Department credentials quickly took issue with the suggestion.

There has been no Gingrichian attempt to . . . do things completely differently. . . . We have the Constitution on our side. We still have to start the process. . . . The . . . businesslike approach that Senator Hatch has taken, admittedly from a very different perspective, has resulted in less dramatic and revolutionary change . . .
[H]is [Republican] colleagues are . . . complaining about him because he has not changed the terms of the debate. He has slowed the pace, he has done other things that are matters of degree, but he has not said, "I'm going to look at this with a completely different set of eyes. I'm going to do stuff completely different from the way Joe Biden did it."

In addition to taking note of the manner in which Senator Hatch has exercised his stewardship of the Judiciary Committee as well as the goodwill that has developed in his relationships with the Clinton administration on this issue, two other factors are critical for understanding why divided government has not led to greater change in judicial confirmation processes, at least at the committee level. First, it is important to recognize that the Senate remains a fundamentally different kind of institution than the House, and that while some differences may have been muted in the Gingrich era, they have not been obliterated. As underscored by a senior aide to an even more senior Democrat on the Judiciary Committee, what we have witnessed is

not totally unexpected because the Senate is a much more collegial place. . . . Kennedy gets along with Hatch. Kennedy gets along with Simpson, Hatch gets along with Biden and everybody sort of slaps each other on the back. And it's natural that the chairman of the Judiciary Committee would develop a close working relationship with the administration . . . nominating these people.

This is not meant to suggest that the nature of the consultation is the same with Senator Hatch as it had been with Senator Biden.

There was never any sense that Biden was vetoing judges the way Hatch seems to have the ability to say, "That just won't fly." So there was always consultation with Biden about . . . "What can we do?" But with Biden the nature of the consultation was . . . in the nature of . . . ["W]e're working together. . . . We all want to get as many judges, and as progressive judges through as we can. We'll work together to figure out what we can do.["] Now with Hatch it is more of a dance, a negotiation.

The fact that ideology is not the basis for Clinton's selection process has permitted a nonconfrontational mode of operation with the Republican dominated Judiciary Committee. As an administration source underscored: "You can't consult about ideology. If we were going to appoint activist liberals it would be a waste of time to go up there and say, 'Gee, I really think you should meet this person because you'd really like her.' "

The interactions between the administration and the Judiciary Committee in the 104th Congress have clearly flowed on a two-way street. A Republican staffer on the committee described how the Senate majority's views generally were made known.

There is a good deal of cooperation and consultation before a nomination. The President is owed a certain amount of deference and Senator Hatch is trying to be accommodating. Our preferences get known in the prenomination process. . . . We'll hear something about a nominee and if it appears there will be a problem, we'll inform the White House. Or if we have a problem, we'll make it known. They may also come to us and ask us what we think. More often than not, we will point out a problem rather than being asked about one.

The value of consulting on nominations with Senator Hatch, as well as other senators from both parties, was underscored by Eleanor Acheson.

It is just a better way of doing business. . . . He gives good advice and a good sense of what's going to work and what's not going to work. And we also have lots of other people on both sides of the aisle who give us advice and we look to for advice.

Acheson stressed, however, that all such advice is just that, advisory to, not determinative of the administration's decisions.

Senator Hatch asked us early on to consult with him. . . . He didn't expect to be part of our decision making process or to be the person that said thumbs down or thumbs up. . . . He's not going to clear everybody we send up. We never expected that and it's a trade-off. . . . We have listened to him . . . but that has not uniformly or exclusively informed either our considerations or our action.

Critical to understanding the role that consultation with the Republicans and, in particular, their Judiciary Committee leadership played in the 104th Congress is the recognition that the administration pursued a similar consultative posture during the 103rd Congress with its Republican minority. As noted by Nan Aron of the Alliance for Justice, "Consensus and consultation with Republicans . . . really captures Clinton's approach to the issue of judicial selection even before the Republicans took control." Eleanor Acheson confirmed this perception in large measure.

I don't think . . . any . . . pieces of the process have been much different. We have an obligation to consult home state senators. We did that before the election in '94 and we have done that since. There are now more Republican senators and, indeed, more states from which we have two Republican senators. . . . We are very mindful that the earlier you consult the better relations you are going to have all around. . . . In certain circumstances we've known we wanted to nominate somebody almost right from the beginning. . . . And . . . there is no question that this is not going to be the person who would be at the top of a Republican senator's list. . . . But that . . . doesn't mean they're going to find a reason to . . . ding them.

A second administration source further substantiated that the transition to the 104th Congress did not bring about a sea change in the nature of consultative relationships. "I don't have the impression that either of the component parts, Senator Biden's staff or Senator Hatch's staff, are operating particularly differently than the way they used to operate." Anticipating a question about Senator Hatch's "screening" of nominees from a position of strength in the Senate's majority in the 104th Congress, the source noted that during the Democratic 103rd Congress,

We still worked with Senator Hatch's staff to satisfy them on a candidate basis. . . . This concept that Senator Hatch's staff has become a gatekeeper I don't agree with. But to the extent that they are playing a role and having a voice and saying, "We like this person more than that person," they've been playing that role all along. It's just that they're now in a better position to make their wishes enforceable, I suppose. . . . It isn't like we completely ignored them in 1993 and 1994 and then all of a sudden had to wake up and start kowtowing to them now. We're not kowtowing to them now, we didn't ignore them before.

Criticisms of the Consultative Approach

The consultative approach to judicial selection that we have described is not, of course, universally applauded. Seen in its most negative light, the administration's behavior is characterized as showing little resolve and commitment and as representing a refusal to fight for principle. Perhaps the three most obvious examples that led to such criticism involved the White House's failure to pursue two nominations (Judith McConnell and R. Samuel Paz) from the 103rd Congress and the failure to nominate Peter Edelman to the federal bench in the 104th Congress.

McConnell and Paz had both been nominated for seats on the district courts in California and had the support of the state's Democratic Senators Barbara Boxer and Diane Feinstein. McConnell generated opposition for a child custody decision that she had made favoring the surviving gay partner of the child's deceased father over a birth mother whom she deemed unfit for parenting. Paz was opposed by law-and-order interests for his role in representing plaintiffs in police brutality suits. Edelman, an administration official known for his liberalism and the spouse of noted child welfare advocate Marian Wright Edelman, had close ties to the Clintons. Reportedly, his nomination to the Washington, D.C. Court of Appeals would have resulted in a protracted recruitment battle (Rodriguez 1995: 1). It appeared, however, that Orrin Hatch "had repeatedly and publicly blessed a district court nomination for Edelman. . . . Hatch . . . had predicted Edelman could and would be confirmed" (Rodriguez 1995: 17). Whether or not he would ultimately win such a battle became a moot point because Edelman's nomination never occurred.

In unusual criticism of the president for his failure to renominate McConnell and Paz after their nominations lapsed at the end of the 103rd Congress, Ninth Circuit Judge (and Carter appointee) Stephen Reinhardt asserted: "They were two excellent nominees . . . that an administration with principles would have stood up for. There was no legitimate beef against them" (Bendavid 1995: 16). Nan Aron of the Alliance for Justice went so far as to suggest that things might not have turned out very differently even if the Republicans had not come to power in the Senate.

I don't think Hatch had much to do with it. I would like to think it's because of Hatch but . . . Sam Paz had his hearing in late Spring. . . . They could have moved him immediately. He was opposed by some law enforcement people. Well they've got people in the White House who could deal with this. They could have mustered support. . . . I just think this administration didn't want to have the fight.

If the administration can be accused of avoiding controversy in judicial selection with a Democratic majority in the Senate in the 103rd Congress, the accusations only resounded more loudly and pointedly in the Republican-controlled 104th Congress. As noted by a lobbyist unhappy with the administration's timidity:

If you look at what became controversial this year it wasn't even anyone's opinions. It was "do we remove seats from the D.C. Circuit? Do we appoint the son of a liberal judge?" It was not substantive at all. So it's not as if someone was nominated . . . who would even conceivably raise any questions. Did we have any fights over opinions? I don't think so.

An aide to a liberal Democrat on the Judiciary Committee commented similarly, albeit more sympathetically, on the implications of the new environment faced by the Clinton White House. "I think any administration has to look at the map of the Senate and calibrate its appointments in light of what is doable, especially this year, an election year." As this aide noted, the calibration process can lead to the substitution of a moderate nominee (such as Merrick Garland) for a prominent liberal (such as Peter Edelman), for a D.C. Appeals Court vacancy. Ironically, the Garland nomination, submitted in early September 1995, died at the end of the 104th Congress without even a Judiciary Committee hearing. Only after a battle on the Senate floor during the 105th Congress was Garland confirmed on March 19, 1997, by a vote of 76 to 23.

One member of the administration's judicial selection team took issue with any suggestion that the nominees differed significantly in the aggregate in the 104th Congress when compared to those in the 103rd.

You can debate forever . . . would we have nominated this person who we chose not to nominate in the 104th Congress in the 103rd Congress? Probably there is a case or two like that. But in the broad sweep . . . I really don't think it's very different. . . . In a sense that's self-evident because . . . the district court nominees are sent to us by the senators. So that cast of characters doesn't change very much.

Assistant Attorney General Acheson was somewhat more willing to recognize a change in the administration's behavior, particularly at the outset of the 104th Congress.

I think we were much more reactively cautious. . . . Right after the elections . . . I think the rule that . . . was only fair and responsible for the President to operate with was until this thing settles out and we have a better sense of where we're going we just have to be very cautious. And then I think we sort of felt out (a) the sort of environment and (b) our relationships with Senator Hatch and his staff. You know we don't agree on everything . . . but we also know, which we didn't know then, that you can have . . . absolutely candid conversations about what is going to happen with a situation.

What some would characterize as the president's unwillingness to fight for judicial nominees was assessed by the administration in cost-benefit terms. As noted by Eleanor Acheson:

There are a couple of cases in which we decided that even if we thought we had a shot at winning a fight . . . that it was not worth the time and resources . . .

because these fights go for months and months and during that period it is very difficult to concentrate. . . . We have made very realistic, hard-headed, practical, measured judgments.

In effect, the administration did not view judicial selection as a test of its strength but, rather, as a responsibility to appoint good judges and to see them seated on the federal bench. According to Acheson, "It's not that we doubt that people would be excellent if you could ever get them into the position. It's a question . . . of at what cost?" Looking back at the scenario surrounding the administration's failure to renominate McConnell and Paz, Acheson admitted that, in her view, a mistake was made, at least with respect to McConnell. "In retrospect . . . I think almost everybody who had a role in that unanimously has come around to the point where some of us were, that we absolutely should have gone forward. . . . Because you cannot have a situation . . . where judges attempting to apply the law get penalized." Basically, the timing of the McConnell and Paz controversies during the transition from the 103rd to the 104th Congresses was credited by Acheson with having a big impact on their resolutions.

Over both those two decisions there was a lot of controversy. . . . I'm pretty confident we would have done one of them differently had we been in kind of a less . . . whacked condition. I think that [after] the election, it took a while for everybody with respect to responsibilities like these, to get a sense because it took a while for it to sift out and figure what . . . the environment was going to be like.

Regarding the administration's failure to nominate Edelman, Acheson lamented that, all too often, critics focus on what was not accomplished instead of what was.

You run into situations where people are extremely disappointed that we didn't nominate Peter Edelman because . . . he's a wonderful and fine person and would make a spectacular judge, and also what he stands for. And yet, to me, one of the frustrations of this . . . [is that] people totally failed to look at Merrick Garland. . . . It was always that we didn't do Peter Edelman as opposed to looking at . . . Merrick Garland who will bring to any court a wholly different set of experience, perspective and skills than Peter but . . . not one ounce less brilliance and work ethic and commitment to public service in the courts and reasonableness and fairness.

In the final analysis, Acheson underscored the pragmatic thrust of the choices the administration made in the context of the 104th Congress.

I would be sitting here and you wouldn't believe me if I said, "Oh, good heavens, we didn't even know there had been a change in administrations or in the Judiciary Committee." We've had to be practical and we've had to be accommodating to our broad set of political circumstances. But that does not mean we've had to accommodate Senator Hatch or any set of senators or set of principles. And I don't think we've done that. I don't think we've compromised in any real

Great Theatre

way. We have not picked some people that there was a tremendous amount of home team popular sentiment for, and that's been extremely disappointing. But I don't think we've compromised in the quality and sort of commitment to the kinds of things that we really value in our nominees.

The administration's choices in the 103rd and 104th Congresses have, of course, had consequences, and most analysts agree that the end result has been beneficial for the American judiciary. Elliot Mincberg, legal director of People for the American Way, noted: "You have to give the Administration credit. . . . They have substantially reduced the number of vacancies. They have improved diversity. They have kept the quality high. And they have de-politicized the process" (quoted in Bendavid 1995: 15). Praise, however, has not been universal, and one of the discontent groups has been the Alliance for Justice and its chief spokesperson, Nan Aron, who characterized the Clinton performance as "a missed opportunity."

JUDICIAL SELECTION OUTCOMES IN THE CONTEXT OF CONGRESSIONAL CHANGE

Can we detect a difference in the profile of those confirmed by the 103rd Congress as compared to those nominated during the 104th? Table 9.2 sheds some light on this question. Most notably, there was a marked decrease in the percentage of blacks nominated to the lower federal bench in the 104th Congress. While there was a slight increase in the proportion of women nominated during the 104th Congress, overall the percentage of white male candidates jumped from 40.8% confirmed during the 103rd Congress to a clear majority (53.0%) nominated in the 104th Congress.

Such an outcome was not surprising in a congressional setting with a Republican majority that was openly hostile to any governmental initiatives that can have the nominal label of "affirmative action" affixed to them. Coupled with an increase in the proportion of nominees who are millionaires, the data clearly suggest that nominations in the 104th Congress took on a greater "establishment orientation" than the appointments made in the 103rd Congress.

Equally telling as the kinds of people nominated to judgeships during the 104th Congress when compared to the 103rd are the graphic differences (revealed in Tables 9.3 and 9.4) in both the pace of appointment processes and the ultimate success rate of the president's nominations across the two Congresses. Further revealed when the 102nd Congress is examined as well are more general differences in the pace and outcome of appointment processes during presidential election years and in divided governmental settings when compared to congressional sessions

212

Table 9.2. *Some Background Characteristics of Clinton Appointees to the Lower Courts Confirmed during the 103rd Congress Compared to His Nominees during the 104th Congress*[a]

	Confirmed 103rd Congress		Nominated 104th Congress	
Occupation				
Politics/government	9.6%	(12)	10.0%	(10)
Judiciary	47.2%	(59)	43.0%	(43)
Large law firm (25+ members)	20.8%	(26)	14.0%	(14)
Moderate size firm (5-24)	10.4%	(13)	21.0%	(21)
Small law firm (2-4)	6.4%	(8)	1.0%	(1)
Solo practice	0.8%	(1)	6.0%	(6)
Professor of law	4.0%	(5)	4.0%	(4)
Other	0.8%	(1)	1.0%	(1)
Experience				
Judicial	52.0%	(65)	49.0%	(49)
Prosecutorial	37.6%	(47)	34.0%	(34)
Neither	29.6%	(37)	34.0%	(34)
Gender				
Male	68.8%	(86)	67.0%	(67)
Female	31.2%	(39)	33.0%	(33)
Ethnicity/Race				
White	65.6%	(82)	79.0%	(79)
African American	24.0%	(30)	11.0%	(11)
Hispanic	8.8%	(11)	6.0%	(6)
Asian	0.8%	(1)	4.0%	(4)
Native American	0.8%	(1)	--	--
Percentage White Male	40.8%	(51)	53.0%	(53)
ABA Rating				
Well Qualified	64.0%	(80)	68.0%	(68)
Qualified	33.6%	(42)	32.0%	(32)
Not Qualified	2.4%	(3)	--	--
Party				
Democrat	88.8%	(11)	94.0%	(94)
Republican	3.2%	(4)	1.0%	(1)
Other	0.8%	(1)	--	--
None	7.2%	(9)	5.0%	(5)
Past Party Activism	52.0%	(65)	63.0%	(63)
Net Worth				
Less than $200,000	15.2%	(19)	14.0%	(14)
$200,000-499,999	24.0%	(30)	20.0%	(20)
$500,000-999,999	29.6%	(37)	28.0%	(28)
$1 million +	31.2%	(39)	38.0%	(38)
Average Age at Nomination	49.2 years old		48.3 years old	
Total Number of Appointees/ Nominees	125		100	

[a] Appointees to lifetime judgeships on courts of general jurisdiction (U.S. district courts and U.S. courts of appeals) confirmed by the Senate during the 103rd Congress and all nominees to those courts nominated during the life of the 104th Congress.

Table 9.3. *Congressional Change and the Processing of Judicial Nominations to the District Courts*

Congress: President: Senate:	102nd Republican Democratic	103rd Democratic Democratic	104th Democratic Republican
Average Number of Days from Nomination Received to Date of Hearing:			
1st Session	96.8 days (N = 76)	62.8 days (N = 42)	77.0 days (N = 58)
2nd Session	77.3* (N = 24)	56.3 (N = 67)	71.8* (N = 11)
Average Number of Days from Date of Hearing to Date Nomination Reported:			
1st Session	16.9 (N = 76)	10.6 (N = 41)	13.9 (N = 56)
2nd Session	14.8* (N = 24)	15.1 (N = 66)	9.0* (N = 9)
Average Number of Days from Date Nomination Reported to Date of Confirmation:			
1st Session	1.4 (N = 76)	3.2 (N = 41)	34.1 (N = 55)
2nd Session	9.1* (N = 24)	5.0 (N = 66)	44.6* (N = 7)
Percentage of Nominations Reported That Were Confirmed:			
1st Session	100.0% (N = 76)	100.0% (N = 41)	98.2% (N = 56)
2nd Session	100.0%* (N = 24)	100.0% (N = 66)	77.8%* (N = 9)
Percentage of Nominations Received That Were Confirmed:			
1st Session	90.5% (N = 84)	97.6% (N = 42)	80.9% (N = 68)
2nd Session	40.7%* (N = 59)	86.8% (N = 76)	41.2%* (N = 17)

*Presidential election year.

Table 9.4. *Congressional Change and the Processing of Judicial Nominations to the Appeals Courts*

Congress: President: Senate:	102nd Republican Democratic	103rd Democratic Democratic	104th Democratic Republican
Average Number of Days from Nomination Received to Date of Hearing:			
1st Session	91.8 days (N = 13)	76.8 days (N = 5)	74.8 days (N = 12)
2nd Session	62.9* (N = 8)	77.6 (N = 14)	104.5* (N = 2)
Average Number of Days from Date of Hearing to Date Nomination Reported:			
1st Session	22.8 (N = 12)	25.2 (N = 5)	37.7 (N = 12)
2nd Session	14.8* (N = 8)	13.9 (N = 13)	29.0* (N = 1)
Average Number of Days from Date Nomination Reported to Date of Confirmation:			
1st Session	5.6 (N = 11)	1.4 (N = 5)	33.5 (N = 11)
2nd Session	6.5* (N = 8)	8.8 (N = 13)	--.-* (N = 0)
Percentage of Nominations Reported That Were Confirmed:			
1st Session	100.0% (N = 11)	100.0% (N = 5)	91.7% (N = 12)
2nd Session	100.0%* (N = 8)	100.0% (N = 13)	0.0%* (N = 1)
Percentage of Nominations Received That Were Confirmed:			
1st Session	64.7% (N = 17)	100.0% (N = 5)	68.8% (N = 16)
2nd Session	61.5%* (N = 13)	81.2% (N = 16)	0.0%* (N = 3)

*Presidential election year.

held in nonelection years and/or when the Senate and the presidency are held by the same party. Clearly, nomination hearings are scheduled at a much slower pace under divided government. The length of time from committee reporting of a nomination to actual Senate confirmation also tends to be greater, particularly in the 104th Congress under divided government. Most important, the percentage of nominations received by the Senate that are ultimately confirmed is greatly diminished in divided governmental settings and, in particular, during a presidential election year (Allison 1996: 11–12).[2]

In analyzing the operation of the advice-and-consent process in the Clinton administration during a period of substantial congressional change, particular note must be taken of the activity during the second session of the 104th Congress in 1996, a presidential election year, which seems to belie much of our narrative's discussion about the relative lack of controversy and smooth sailing for judicial appointments in this divided governmental context. Indeed, only on January 2 (at the end of the first session), July 10–12, 16–18, 22, 24, 25, 30, and 31, and August 2, 1996, were judicial appointments confirmed on the Senate floor, and only in small numbers (a total of eighteen district and two appeals judges), despite the fact that nominees were being processed and sent forward for confirmation by the Judiciary Committee. The logjam on the Senate floor broke temporarily the month after Senator Dole relinquished his position as Senate majority leader and resigned from his Senate seat to pursue his presidential ambitions on a full time basis.

While it is natural for the pace of judicial confirmations to slow down as a presidential election approaches, it is not typical for them to stop completely. The culprit, it appeared, was not divided government per se. Rather, the confirmation of federal judges was held hostage by presidential electoral politics and the power of the majority leader/presidential candidate to control the flow of Senate business in the interest of his campaign. Quite clearly, Dole attempted to make judgeships a major theme of his presidential campaign. In a prominent speech on April 19, 1996, he charged that Clinton was promoting "an all star team of liberal leniency" and that the president's reelection "could lock in liberal judicial activism for the next generation" (quoted in Seelye 1996, 1). Dole also charged that "many of the judges Mr. Clinton has appointed . . .

2 Means were utilized in Tables 9.3 and 9.4 to maintain consistency with existing literature, particularly Allison (1996), that examines the phenomenon of delay in confirmation processes. Since means are subject to distortion caused by outlying cases, particularly when the number of cases analyzed is small, we also calculated medians for the data reported in Tables 9.3 and 9.4. Examination of those medians results in no alteration of our textual discussion of the data in Tables 9.3 and 9.4.

are precisely the ones who are dismantling those guardrails that protect society from the predatory, the violent, and the anti-social elements in our midst" (*New York Times*, April 20, 1996: 8).

This is not to suggest that confirming judges in a divided governmental setting in an election year is generally easy (see Tables 9.3 and 9.4). George Bush appointed sixty-six judges in 1992, (many of whom were first nominated in 1991), a record for an election year. But it should also be recognized that there was no Judiciary Committee action on fifty-two nominees in 1992, also a record number (Goldman 1993: 284). The sixty-six confirmations in 1992 did, however, remain an important benchmark in the eyes of Eleanor Acheson.

We are . . . trying to be realistic here but . . . I don't want to lose sight of the little mantra that we are all going around here saying, "66, 66." I think it is quite unlikely that we'll get 66 judges. . . . I am extremely hopeful . . . that we will be in a position to do something on the order of 25 to 35 judges this year.

Twenty was actually the number confirmed in 1996.

The argument that is always made to a slow-moving Senate in an election year setting is that the judges are desperately needed to help clear backlogged dockets and give the public the judicial "service" it is entitled to receive. In March 1996, at least in the eyes of one high-ranking aide to a majority senator on the Judiciary Committee, this traditional argument was not seen as compelling.

Unlike Reagan in his last two years and the Bush administration this is not a situation where there are a lot of vacancies. Consequently, you can't say to the Republican Senate that they have to move everyone through anymore in a setting resembling "full employment." The majority today has the power and the leverage to not move people through without being open to attacks about staffing needs and criminals being left on the streets.

Eleanor Acheson rejected this argument outright.

No matter whether your party or the opposing party is in control of the Congress. . . . In order to get this Committee to really feel the pressure to act on nominees you really . . . need to keep impressing them that there are vacancies and they need to be filled. It's just like that . . . full employment thing. Yes, it's a really low number, but there are actually real Districts that are suffering those vacancies and while you can pat yourself on the back there are, in fact, real people who are unemployed. There are real vacancies that we do need to fill, there is nothing wrong with actually having no vacancy in the Federal courts.

Whether or not a "full employment" argument could justify going slow on confirmations in the winter and early spring of 1996, the argument had surely lost its force by the summer of 1996 following a half-year of total inaction on the Senate Floor. As Attorney General Janet Reno remarked weeks prior to the temporary breaking of the confirmation logjam in mid-July, "Zero judicial confirmations in this session of Congress is an extremely discouraging record. . . . Vacancies cause delays and, as victims, as prosecutors, defendants and civil litigants will all confirm, justice delayed is, indeed, justice denied" (*USA Today*, June 28, 1996: 8A).

Even after the logjam broke momentarily, confirmations occurred at a snail's pace leading to a thinly veiled threat from Democratic Senator Dorgan of North Dakota published in the *Congressional Record*.

One point about federal judges. We are nearing the end of this congressional session. Some of us believe this Congress ought not to adjourn until the majority party does for us what we did for them – yes, even in election years – and that is clear off the calendar and clear through the committee judges, federal judges that have been appointed by this President. The fact is, the record is not good. We have seen stutter-stepping and stalling. Some of us are going to decide, one of these days, nothing more is going to happen in this Senate until those many judges out there waiting for confirmation by this Senate are brought before this Senate for a vote. (June 18, 1996: S10736)

It is important to reiterate that, in the first half of 1996, Orrin Hatch and the Judiciary Committee did not appear to be the problem. As predicted by Nan Aron in March 1996: "I think they're going to pick and choose, as they've always done. . . . I think that anyone who's labeled 'controversial' will remain at the Committee. But I do think Hatch will allow some of the more conservative nominees to go through. He'll rant and rave and talk about all these liberal judges" – but, ultimately, confirmations would go forward. An aide to a liberal Democrat on the Judiciary Committee noted in March 1996 that Hatch even sent Dole a letter expressing his belief that it was necessary to move judicial nominations to the Senate floor for confirmation votes. A member of the administration's judicial selection team confirmed these characterizations of Hatch.

I think the remarkable thing about Senator Hatch is . . . that in the very speech . . . he gave . . . complaining about one nominee and two appointees he said he was going to continue to confirm judges. . . . He's willing to move people who are highly qualified. But a lot of his colleagues . . . have kind of a visceral feeling that they don't want to do Clinton judges. . . . It's an ahistorical attitude when you compare what Democratic Senates have done for Republican presidents. It's an irrational attitude because it doesn't reflect . . . what we believe to be an accurate assessment of who our people are.

If Orrin Hatch's public statements about the confirmation process as well as those of our sources in the administration and on both sides of the congressional aisle are to be taken at face value, the conclusion is inescapable that Hatch was unusually ineffectual in his inability to translate committee processing of nominees to Senate floor action on their confirmations. At bottom, the normal functioning of Senate processes whereby committee actions are legitimated on the Senate floor may have been trumped in 1996 by presidential politics. The only alternative explanation of Hatch's failure to gain floor votes rapidly on committee-approved nominees – one for which we have found no evidence – is that he played the role of a "double agent," taking one position publicly and another with the Senate leadership.

The portrait of Senate floor action on judgeships in 1996 reveals an institution that, initially, was rendered immobile by the politically driven choice of the majority leader/presidential candidate to make judgeships a prime campaign issue while holding the president's nominees (even those endorsed by the Republican-led Judiciary Committee) hostage on the Senate floor. By the time Senator Dole resigned from the Senate, summer had arrived and with it had come the traditional election year slowdown that normally brings the curtain down on judgeship nominations. (A Judiciary committee aide noted that the Committee would operate until it was told not to. "The Republican caucus and the majority leader will make the decision regarding when things will slow down. The chairman will abide by that. We will schedule hearings until we're told not to." An administration spokesperson confirmed that Hatch "said that the curtain will come down at some point but ... he has indicated in a very open and above board way that he's not going to be the one pulling the plug." Eleanor Acheson referred to the phenomenon of a "Leader's Letter": "[A]llegedly there is a point in time when the majority leader cuts things off and says we're shutting down.")

Nevertheless, the administration continued to send names to the Senate. Eleanor Acheson characterized the continuing work of the administration in nominating judges as necessary to keep the pressure on and to prepare for the future. "Certainly if the President is reelected ... we don't want to create for ourselves a situation where we slip behind. We want to be as ready to go as possible in the 105th Congress."

If judicial selection in the context of a changing Congress made for "good theatre," when the curtain came down on the 104th Congress in the summer of 1996 it is critical to underscore that what we witnessed was not, necessarily, the final act of the play. Indeed, that act had not only not yet been played, it had not yet been written. It awaited the presidential election of 1996 from which to take its cue. With President Clinton's reelection, judicial nominations are occuring on a stage vacated by one key actor, Bob Dole. The politics of the presidential election appear to have been responsible for the stalling of confirmations and, in the wake of the election, it could be argued that confirmation processes would again move forward. Perhaps no greater evidence can be brought to bear on that point than to take note that, in the waning months of the 104th Senate, it was the unlikely duo of conservative Republicans

Orrin Hatch and new Majority Leader Trent Lott who took center stage in trying to facilitate the confirmation of several Clinton judges. (It should be noted, however, that no judges were confirmed on the circuit courts where nominations are tied more closely to the president than to identifiable senators, and the district court confirmations went to nominees who were acceptable to home state Republican Senators, a circumstance that is not unusual under divided government as a presidential election approaches.)

As with most dramas where the final act remains unwritten, another scenario can be suggested. The relative calm of the President's first term, with its Trojan Horse slate of nominees, will be replaced by an openly ideological selection process. As a high-ranking aide on the Judiciary Committee put it, "Second term appointees will likely be more liberal. They will be less concerned about a fight because there would be no political or reelection downsides to a confrontation." Such a denouement seems highly unlikely to us, given what appears to have been a deep seated and purposeful choice to downplay ideology in judgeship appointments in the president's first term. Nevertheless, good drama often requires a surprise ending and, as Nan Aron commented: "By and large that balance that is so very much needed I don't think has been made during this, his first term. I think there may be an opportunity for the second."

CODA: JUDICIAL SELECTION IN THE 105TH CONGRESS

At the time of this writing, nearly nine months into the second Clinton administration, some of our predictions for the 105th Congress have clearly not come to pass. Indeed, the possibility must be considered that what appeared to be a slowdown in the confirmation process in 1996, brought about largely by presidential electoral politics, may actually have been the opening round of an audacious and bold plan by Senate Republicans to bring judicial confirmations to a virtual halt in an effort to play a greater and unprecedented role in determining who, at bottom, would be seated on the federal bench. Some data seem to bear this perspective out.

While at the adjournment of the 104th Congress there were 64 vacancies on the federal bench, by the beginning of the 105th Congress the number of vacancies had grown to 74. By the end of September 1997, that number swelled to 94. Eighteen judges were confirmed through September 1997 in the 105th Congress, approximately half as many as were confirmed in the 104th Congress, and about a third as many as were confirmed during George Bush's last year in office (with a Democratic Senate) during similar time periods. As Democratic Senator Patrick Leahy of Vermont noted with great sarcasm upon the confirmation of two judicial nominees, "I am delighted to see two more hostages released by the Republican majority to serve the American people as Federal judges" (Executive Calendar, U.S. Senate, September 26, 1997).

If what we are witnessing is the Republican majority's pursuit of a court-*blocking* strategy, such behavior can be viewed as a congressional analogue of President Franklin Roosevelt's ill-fated court-*packing* plan of 1937. Both Roosevelt's scheme and the current obstructionist tactics of Senate Republicans had their genesis in displeasure with judicial rulings, and both politically motivated efforts to alter the contours of the "normal" operation of judicial recruitment processes were justified publicly, in part, by deceptive utilization of court workload statistics. Roosevelt claimed that the Supreme Court was behind in its work, while Senate Republicans charge today that judicial workloads do not justify the filling of certain judgeships, particularly some on the circuit courts.[3]

For their part, Republicans indignantly deny any such court-blocking strategy. Senator Hatch, for example, stated that: "The fact of the matter is that we have not had a White House processing these people very fast. And there are some who have problems" (*Congressional Record*, September 11, 1997: p. S9164). Weeks later, on September 29, Hatch decried the "myths and distortions that the Clinton administration has engaged in" regarding the existence of a "vacancy crisis" and a "Republican slowdown." According to Hatch, many more vacancies existed at various times during the Bush years and, in the final analysis, delay was not the Senate's fault.

[T]he picture the President paints is less than complete. Of the 68 judicial nominees submitted to the Judiciary Committee this year, nearly half of them . . . have been nominated since July 1 of this year. So, factoring in the Senate's August recess, when we were gone for better than 30 days, the Judiciary Committee has had scarcely 2 months to consider virtually one half of the President's nominees this year.

Going beyond his recitation and interpretation of the numbers game, however, Hatch admitted, "If and when the administration sends us . . . noncontroversial qualified nominees, they will be processed fairly and promptly. In the last 6 weeks or so, the administration has finally begun sending us nominees which I have, for the most part, found to be quite acceptable" (*Congressional Record*, September 29, 1997: p. S10181).

Interestingly, through much of 1997 the snail's pace at which judgeship candidates moved through the 105th Congress did not attract great

3 See, for example, the debate in the Senate over the confirmation of Merrick B. Garland to be U.S. Circuit Judge for the District of Columbia (*Congressional Record*, March 19, 1997: pp. S2515–S2541).

public scrutiny. In late September, however, a series of reports on the confirmation logjam was aired on National Public Radio newscasts and, on September 27, President Clinton "went public," underscoring his dismay about the pace of confirmations in his weekly radio address to the nation. In this context one cannot fail to notice that, while nine judges were confirmed from January 1997 through August 1997, nine more were confirmed in a 23-day period in September. While Senator Hatch attributed this to "better" nominees, Senator Leahy had a different explanation.

Anticipation of the President's radio address on the judicial vacancy crisis has obviously reached the Senate. I expect even those who have spent so much time this year holding up the confirmations of Federal judges were uncomfortable defending this Senate's record of having proceeded on only 9 of the 61 nominees received through August of this year. As rumors of the President's impending address have circulated around Capitol Hill, this Senate has literally doubled its confirmations. (Executive Calendar, U.S. Senate, September 26, 1997)

It remains to be seen whether the late September flurry of confirmation activity will continue or, alternatively, if the Republican senatorial leadership will reinstate its seeming "end-run" around the Constitution (in terms of denying the president his right to name federal judges) and whether a constitutional confrontation of greater magnitude between Clinton and Senate Republicans is in the offing.

The battle lines for such a confrontation continue to form and, important to the unfolding drama, will be the lines delivered by Orrin Hatch. In early Spring of 1997, Hatch pushed publicly for moving confirmations forward. Addressing claims that workloads did not justify filling a particular seat on the Appeals Court bench, Hatch proclaimed in apparent exasperation with his Republican colleagues, "[P]laying politics with judges is unfair, and I am sick of it. . . . [T]he statistics that have been cited . . . are not a fair or accurate characterization of the D.C. circuits's caseload" (*Congressional Record*, March 19, 1997: p. S2536). Yet, like many key actors in good drama, the Judiciary Committee chair's character seemed to change somewhat as the play progressed and, in September, he took on a more confrontational, strident tone with the administration. For his part, Joe Biden, Hatch's Democratic predecessor as Judiciary Committee chair, was quite blunt in his assessment of what has transpired. "This is about trying to keep the President of the United States of America from being able to appoint judges" (*Congressional Record*, March 19, 1997: p. S2538). The effort, Biden charged, "is not in line with the last 200 years of tradition" (*Congressional Record*, March 19, 1997: p. S2541).

If Republican court-blocking continues, it surely will test the Clinton administration's aversion to expending political capital on judicial confirmation fights. At the same time, however, "going public" appears to have had some payoffs in confirmations and the administration seemed, by the end of 1997, unable to avoid a confrontation in an effort to pursue its constitutional mandate. The stakes are high for the administration in terms of its judicial legacy and high for the judiciary in terms of its institutional integrity and independence. The stage is set and the actors have all spoken their opening lines. Let the drama continue!

IO

Behind the Scenes: The Supreme Court and Congress in Statutory Interpretation

LORI HAUSEGGER AND LAWRENCE BAUM

Interaction between the Supreme Court and Congress often involves high drama – occasionally melodrama. Indeed, the Court's constitutional decisions have served as a catalyst for some of the most compelling theatre in Congress. The Court's decisions on issues such as abortion and flag burning have led to long and emotional legislative debates. The Senate hearings on the Court nominations of Robert Bork and Clarence Thomas, both of whom garnered ardent support and intense opposition because of their views on constitutional issues, challenged the "soaps" for popular viewing interest.

But the relationship between Court and Congress sometimes takes place behind the scenes. That is the case most often with statutory interpretation. A large proportion of the Supreme Court's decisions – a substantial majority in the 1990s – involve interpretation of federal statutes rather than constitutional issues. In the statutory arena, the Court addresses such matters as the rules for criminal sentencing in federal court and the scope of federal laws that prohibit monopolistic practices. These statutory decisions seldom attract widespread attention, but this part of the Court's work has far-reaching implications. The Court's resolution of disputes over the meaning of statutory provisions has a major impact on federal policy and national life in such important areas as civil rights, environmental protection, and labor–management relations.

Once the Supreme Court interprets a statutory provision, its interpretation is authoritative: lower courts and administrative agencies must follow the Court's lead. But Congress is free to override the Court's decision simply by enacting a new statute. If a sufficient number of members disagree with the Court's interpretation, they can write into the law new language that precludes such an interpretation. If the Court gives a narrow reading to a provision that prohibits employment discrimination, Congress can override it with a new statute that explicitly establishes a broader prohibition of discrimination. It is quite common for Congress to consider overriding the Court in that way, and overrides are frequent.[1]

If Congress simply ignored the Court's interpretations of statutes, it would effectively cede to the judicial branch considerable power over national policy. To the extent that it intervenes – scrutinizing decisions and overriding some of them – it reclaims a portion of that power. Thus oversight of the judiciary in statutory law, like oversight of the bureaucracy (see Aberbach 1990), is important for Congress as an institution. To maximize its control over policy, Congress must scrutinize and respond to the actions of both sets of policy makers.

Politically, however, the two arenas for oversight differ in important respects. Unlike bureaucratic oversight, congressional response to statutory decisions of the Supreme Court typically occurs without much drama or even sustained interest. While overrides of the Court's decisions sometimes generate considerable light and heat, most of the time Congress acts quietly, giving little sense of institutional rivalry (see Miller 1990, 1992).

One reason for this lack of drama may be the clear legal and political superiority of Congress over the Court in statutory interpretation; the Court is the weaker partner in the relationship. Indeed, the Court often acknowledges congressional power to correct its interpretations of statutes and occasionally invites Congress to do so. Also important is the general absence of the partisan rivalry that often shapes congressional oversight of the executive branch.

When the Republican Party took control of both houses of Congress in 1994, there was reason to expect sweeping changes in the relationship between Congress and the other branches of the federal government. Certainly, the character of interactions between Congress and the executive branch changed fundamentally. Even when both Congress and the White House were in Democratic hands, the relationship between Congress and President Clinton was colored by institutional rivalry. Once the party link between the two had been severed, partisan rivalry became the main ingredient of that relationship. In the 104th Congress, the new Republican majorities brought with them an ambitious agenda

---

1 Following Eskridge (1991a: 332 n. 1), we define an override as referring to "any time Congress reacts consciously to, and modifies a statutory interpretation decision." This definition encompasses both full and partial alterations of decisions. Of course, it is not always easy to determine whether a congressional action qualifies as an override under this definition. Some aspects of this difficulty will be discussed later in the chapter.

for policy change and a determination to attack the executive branch. It was a primary goal of the House and Senate leadership to weaken the president's political position, and that leadership undertook a wide array of legislative mechanisms to advance this goal.

What about the relationship between Congress and the judicial branch: how would the political upheaval of the 1994 election affect congressional reactions to the courts? The most direct effect was to create new roadblocks for Bill Clinton's nominations to federal judgeships, thereby influencing the administration's initial choices and preventing the confirmation of some (see Chapter 9, by Slotnick and Goldman, in this volume). Republican control of Congress also lessened legislative support for the Court's positions on controversial issues such as abortion, and it facilitated attacks on the decisions of Clinton appointees in the federal courts.

These effects were all predictable. But the effects of the 1994 elections on the relationship between Court and Congress in statutory interpretation were, and are, less certain. Because of the limited institutional and partisan rivalry between Congress and the Court in that field, even the most dramatic political changes in Congress may have only limited effects on its reactions to the Court's statutory decisions. Attacks on the courts from congressional Republicans have served chiefly as a weapon in partisan conflict with the president. Where the Supreme Court's work has little connection with the president, as typically is the case in statutory interpretation, the Court is likely to remain insulated from the impact of partisan conflict between the other two branches.

This does not mean that we would expect no change in responses to the Court's statutory decisions after the accession of the 104th Congress. New majorities with more conservative views, sympathetic to a different set of interest groups, may respond to particular decisions in ways that differ from their predecessors. But such changes are likely to be marginal rather than fundamental. In this arena, unlike many other areas of congressional activity, and certainly unlike legislative–executive relations, the major theme may be business as usual.

It is from this perspective that this chapter considers congressional overrides of Supreme Court decisions. Compared with the constitutional arena, little has been written on Court–Congress relations in statutory law. Thus, while we are interested in the 104th Congress, we also take a longer and broader view. Our basic premise is that, in the absence of deep institutional conflicts, congressional reaction to the Court's statutory decisions is not distinctive: members respond to the policies embodied in the Court's decisions as they respond to other policies, rather than responding to the Court itself (see Clark and McGuire 1996).

CHARACTERISTICS OF OVERRIDES

One indication that Congress does not treat overrides as dramatic and distinctive acts is the difficulty of locating them. The most comprehensive list of overrides was compiled by legal scholar William Eskridge (1991a) through a laborious search of committee reports and other sources; Eskridge listed all the decisions for which he could locate an override undertaken by Congress between 1967 and 1990. But even his count is incomplete, primarily because overrides often are added to broader bills such as appropriations after committee action and without fanfare (Melnick 1994: 331 n. 13).

Keeping in mind this difficulty and its implications, we analyze overrides through two sets of analyses. The first considers the characteristics of both congressional overrides and the decisions that are the subjects of overrides, with most analyses covering the period from 1967 through 1996. These analyses are based on our extension of Eskridge's list of overrides through 1996, using similar search methods, and on data describing the characteristics of decisions from the Supreme Court Database compiled by Harold Spaeth.[2]

The second set of analyses examines the Supreme Court's statutory decisions in its 1978-89 terms, with the aim of identifying the characteristics associated with decisions that Congress overrides. These analyses are based on an integration of the Supreme Court Database with a set of additional variables: whether a decision is overridden and some potential determinants of overrides. Throughout both sets of analyses, it should be kept in mind that they are based on a substantial, but necessarily partial, list of congressional overrides.[3]

Information on congressional scrutiny of the Supreme Court's statutory decisions is incomplete and somewhat contradictory (Bawn and Shipan 1993; Eskridge 1991a; Henschen 1983; Katzmann 1992). But it is

2 The Database, whose full title is the "United States Supreme Court Judicial Database," is archived at the Inter-university Consortium for Political and Social Research (ICPSR).

3 Eskridge's implicit criteria for defining a Supreme Court decision as statutory are slightly broader than the explicit criteria used in the Supreme Court Database, so a small number of decisions that Eskridge counts as the subject of overrides (and which we thus include in analyses of overrides in the 1967–96 period) are not included (and hence the overrides are not counted) in the analysis of the 1978–89 terms.

   Eskridge limits his consideration of overrides to those actually enacted into law; those passed by Congress but killed by a presidential veto are not counted. We follow the same rule. Of course, presidents also may influence the initial passage of legislation. Nonetheless, we treat overrides as congressional behavior in this chapter because Congress typically plays the dominant role in action to override Supreme Court decisions.

clear that at least a significant minority of decisions receive meaningful scrutiny and that, not surprisingly, most override proposals ultimately fail. The result is that Congress overrides a small proportion but a significant number of the Court's decisions. Between 1967 and 1996, Congress overrode at least 158 Supreme Court decisions that had interpreted federal statutes.[4] On average, each two-year Congress overrode at least 10.5 statutory decisions. Of all the statutory decisions issued by the Court in its 1978–89 terms, at least 5.6 percent had been overridden by 1996.

There is no limit to the length of time in which Congress can override a Supreme Court decision, but there is a qualitative difference between an override in the months after a decision and one that occurs several decades later. When a decision is negated shortly after it is handed down, that action is a sign of a clear negative reaction by Congress: the policy as defined by the Supreme Court was not acceptable. When the override comes after a lapse of many years, the quality of the Court's judgment is less directly relevant and the element of institutional conflict likely is absent altogether. In the 1967–96 period, many overrides came quickly: 12 percent in the same year as the decision, 46 percent within two calendar years, 71 percent within six years. However, 20 percent of all overrides occurred more than a dozen years after the original decision.

Overrides can be divided into those that are the primary subject of an enactment and those that are only one part of a broader bill. Both are common. In the 102nd through 104th Congresses, the thirty-four overrides that we identified came in twenty-two pieces of legislation. Nine of these bills were designed specifically to override decisions. One was the Civil Rights Act of 1991, which negated nine separate decisions. This act was the most visible override in recent years and the one involving the greatest conflict between Court and Congress.

Nearly all of the other thirteen bills stood at the other end of the spectrum, in that the overrides they contained were relatively unimportant portions of the legislation. In all likelihood their inclusion in a bill had little effect on its passage; rather, the override was successful because a bill had congressional support for other reasons (see Solimine and Walker 1992: 442). In several instances it is doubtful that most members of Congress were even aware of the override provisions; an example is what one commentary called the "dark of the night" provision of the Oceans Act of 1992, a provision that changed a rule of court venue simply by adding the word "any" to the applicable statute (Franklin and Weldy 1993). This pattern of legislating – whether innocent or strategic

4 Following Eskridge's practice, we have counted twice any decisions that were subject to two distinct overrides in different years; there were four such decisions. Thus, strictly speaking, the total should be 154 rather than 158.

– underlines the general absence of interbranch confrontation in statutory overrides and cautions against the assumption that Congress as a whole always acts systematically and deliberately when it overrides Supreme Court decisions.

Historical Trends

Our expectations about trends in congressional overrides follow from our conception of overrides as more routine than distinctive. Partisan and ideological changes in Congress should not have a substantial effect on the frequency of overrides. Potentially more powerful are institutional changes that have major effects on the legislative process.

The most likely source of change is the growth that has occurred in the size of congressional staffs and in the activity of interest groups in Congress (see Eskridge 1991a: 338–41). Increased staffs, particularly committee staffs, enhance the capacity of Congress to monitor Supreme Court decisions and to devise responses to them. Growth in committee staffs occurred over a long period of time, culminating in the early to mid-1970s and leveling off since then (Ornstein, Mann, and Malbin 1994).

Increased interest group activity since the 1960s (Loomis and Cigler 1991) could be expected to have similar effects. It also expands the capacity of groups to secure the kinds of legislative changes that they seek. In the Supreme Court, there has been an enormous increase in the proportion of cases with at least one amicus curiae brief, and increasingly the Court receives briefs on behalf of multiple groups in a case (Epstein 1993: 645). That change underlines the growing presence of interest groups in legal issues, and it also means that more cases have a participating interest group that is unhappy with the outcome and looking for redress in another institution.

Another possible source of change is a limited shift in the Court's approach to statutory interpretation since 1986. One tool that justices use to ascertain the meaning of a statute is its legislative history, reflected in sources such as committee reports and floor debates. Since his appointment in 1986, Justice Antonin Scalia has argued that these sources are unreliable guides to congressional intent and that judges instead should focus on the plain meaning of statutory language (see, e.g., *Conroy v. Aniskoff* 1993). Though most justices continue to use legislative history, Scalia has gained some support from colleagues.

This development might produce more overrides in two ways. Members of Congress have expressed some unhappiness with the challenge to legislative history (Biskupic 1990), and the House Judiciary Committee held hearings on this matter in 1990 (U.S. Congress 1990). In re-

Figure 10.1. *Congressional Overrides of Supreme Court Decisions
Interpreting Federal Statutes, 1967–96*

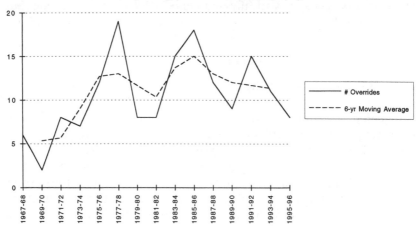

Note: Nine of the nineteen overrides in 1977–8 came in a single statute, the Bank-
ruptcy Reform Act of 1979; nine of the sixteen overrides in 1991–2 came in a single
statute, the Civil Rights Act of 1991.
Source: For 1967–90, Eskridge (1991a); for 1991–6, this chapter's authors.

sponse, Congress might scrutinize the Court's decisions more closely.
Alternatively, and more likely, refusal to take legislative history into account might increase the chances that a decision diverges from legislative
intent and thus increase the possibility of an override – as Justice John
Paul Stevens argued in a 1991 dissent (*West Virginia University Hospitals v. Casey* 1991: 112–15; see also Solimine and Walker 1992: 448).

The number of decisions that each Congress overrode in the 1967–96
period is depicted in Figure 10.1. The relatively short timespan for which
data are available and the incompleteness of the counts for each Congress counsel caution in interpreting the trends in Figure 10.1.[5]

The data suggest a general increase in the frequency of overrides during the mid-1970s, with the moving average settling at a higher plateau.
This increase is consistent with the hypothesis that growing congressional staff and interest-group activity produced more override activity,
though it does not rule out other explanations. The absence of growth
in the numbers of overrides at the end of the 1980s and in the early
1990s suggests that conflict over modes of statutory interpretation had

5 Eskridge (1991a: 338) points out that the low numbers in the first few Congresses
included in his study are consistent with the low numbers found in earlier years
by previous studies. However, the unusual thoroughness of his data collection
makes it difficult to compare his findings with those of previous studies.

no substantial effect. And if partisan and ideological changes in Congress had an impact, it was not sufficient to produce strong trends.

Issues and Parties

Federal statutes and statutory decisions cover a large number of specific legal and policy issues, and overrides reflect that diversity. We analyzed by subject matter the fifty-three decisions from the Supreme Court's 1978–89 terms that Congress overrode by 1996. The largest category, with twelve overrides, involved legal protections against discrimination; the most pronounced emphasis in override activity since the 1970s has been a series of statutes from 1978 to 1991 that reversed narrow interpretations of protections for civil rights (Eskridge 1991b). With that exception, overrides were widely scattered across policy areas and issues. This pattern is a reminder that even an active Congress leaves standing the great preponderance of the Court's rulings in most areas of statutory interpretation.

In the next section we systematically examine some effects of parties to the case on overrides; we can take a first look here by looking at distributions of overrides. What kinds of losing parties in the Supreme Court gain at least symbolic redress from Congress? Of the fifty-three overrides of the Court's 1978–89 decisions, nearly half (twenty-four) favored individuals. The federal government was vindicated by nine overrides, state and local governments by seven, businesses by nine, and other private organizations by four.

It is surprising that individuals receive congressional support so often and the federal government much less often. Of course, the figures do not take into account the total number of Supreme Court defeats for different types of parties; there is evidence that on a proportionate basis, the federal government is uniquely successful in securing overrides of unfavorable statutory decisions (Eskridge 1991a: 351–2). Still, every type of party loses a great many cases over a dozen years and thus has a multitude of opportunities to reverse Court defeats elsewhere. Eleven of the victories for individuals involved issues of discrimination, but even if these instances are set aside the congressional support for individuals is noteworthy.

The 104th Congress

Having discussed general patterns in congressional override activity, we now turn to the 104th Congress. As Figure 10.1 indicates, Congress did not stand for a high frequency of statutory overrides. Indeed, the eight overrides that we located were slightly below the average for the past three decades.[6]

However, the ideological pattern of overrides in the 104th Congress *was* distinctive. Seven of the eight overrides, or 88 percent, were aimed at liberal Supreme Court decisions; the comparable proportions in the 102nd and 103rd Congress were 13 and 36 percent, respectively. The conservative tenor of the overrides in 1995 and 1996 might in part be a product of chance, but undoubtedly it reflects the strong conservatism of both houses in the 104th Congress. The continuation of this conservatism into the 105th will allow further inquiry into the extent of the impact of partisan change in Congress.

A closer look at the overrides in 1995 and 1996 indicates that they did not constitute anything like a concerted attack on major lines of Supreme Court policy. Only two of the eight overrides were the central purposes of bills; a third was one of several major purposes in its bill. The overrides were spread widely across the various fields of statutory decisions; no two were in a single field. Among the seven overrides of liberal decisions, not all were clearly conservative in their effects. And none of the eight decisions that Congress overrode would be regarded as a major ruling.

These generalizations can be illustrated with two of the overrides in the 104th Congress. The first involved the rights of migrant farm workers. In *Adams Fruit Co. v. Barrett* (1990), the Supreme Court ruled unanimously that migrant workers who were eligible for state workers' compensation benefits for injuries suffered on the job could also bring lawsuits to recover damages for those injuries. In a bill entitled "Migrant Worker Protection," enacted in 1995, the first section overrode that decision. Thus a conservative Congress reversed a liberal decision in labor and personal injury law.

What happened, however, was more complicated than that. The *Adams* decision drew immediate opposition from some members of Congress. In 1992 the Democratic Congress enacted a nine-month moratorium on implementation of the decision, and there was an effort in 1993 to override it altogether. Democrats as well as Republicans supported both those earlier attacks on *Adams* and the override bill in 1995. But the 1995 bill developed into a partisan issue, and its passage (by

6 This small number may reflect the Supreme Court's own conservatism in recent years, in that there might be relatively few recent statutory decisions that were ideologically displeasing to the new Republican majorities of the 104th Congress. This factor might be counterbalanced, however, by the opportunity to attack a large stock of liberal statutory decisions over the years that had been "protected" by Democratic control of one or both houses but that became vulnerable to overrides once both houses had Republican majorities.

voice vote in both houses) became possible only after a compromise between groups representing farm owners and farm workers. Under that compromise, the *Adams* override was counterbalanced by some other provisions that broadened protections for workers. Thus the override bill was ideologically mixed.

The second example concerns the traditional immunity of judges from lawsuits for official acts. In *Pulliam v. Allen* (1984), the Supreme Court limited this immunity by holding that under the civil rights laws, judges could be made subject to injunctions limiting their future actions and that they could be required to pay attorneys' fees to opponents who win cases against them. *Pulliam* is best classified as a liberal decision because it favored people who seek redress for alleged violations of their rights and because the four dissenters from the decision were the Court's most conservative members.

Judges worked for years to get an override of *Pulliam*, and over time they garnered considerable support in Congress, including approval of some override proposals by Democratically controlled committees. Their efforts were finally successful with enactment of the Federal Courts Improvement Act in 1996. That legislation contained a wide range of provisions relating to the courts. Two of the provisions overrode Supreme Court decisions. One of those decisions was *Pulliam*; Congress rewrote the civil rights laws to rule out injunctions and attorneys' fee awards against judges under nearly all circumstances. Perhaps Republican control of the Senate Judiciary Committee was responsible for the addition of this provision to the bill. In all likelihood, however, the key to the override of *Pulliam* was inclusion of the override in a broad bill that enjoyed general support, one that both houses adopted by voice vote.

Thus, while it may be fair to call the 104th Congress revolutionary, that revolution did not extend to its interactions with the Supreme Court in statutory law. Rather, those interactions were relatively quiet and nonconflictual. At least in the statutory arena, the drama that characterized relations between Congress and the executive branch did not extend to the judiciary.

EXPLAINING OVERRIDES

Hypotheses

Whether or not interactions in the statutory arena change over time, we need to understand what underlies congressional response to Supreme Court decisions. Why does Congress override some Supreme Court decisions and not others? There is a body of research that probes congressional reactions to Supreme Court decisions. Included in that research are a number of empirical studies aimed to some degree at identifying the circumstances under which Congress acts against decisions (Bawn and Shipan 1993; "Congressional Reversals" 1958; Henschen 1983; Henschen and Sidlow 1989; Ignagni and Meernik 1994; Paschal 1991; Schmidhauser and Berg 1972; Stumpf 1965; Zorn 1995; Zorn and Caldeira 1995). Only a few of these studies (Eskridge 1991a; Solimine and Walker 1992) directly address the question in which we are interested: across all statutory fields, what conditions determine which decisions are the subject of overrides?[7] Other studies examine a limited set of statutory decisions; study constitutional decisions as well as, or instead of, statutory decisions; or limit their analysis to cases that provoked some congressional response.

Still, the hypotheses and findings of all these studies are relevant to our concern. Studies have tested the impact of conditions ranging from use of the "sacrosanctity argument"[8] in congressional debates over proposals to reverse Court decisions (Stumpf: 1965: 383) to the issuance of a decision in an election year (Ignagni and Meernik 1994: 360). Some variables have recurred regularly in studies, reflecting the widespread view that they are likely to influence congressional responses to decisions.

If responses to statutory decisions are not a distinctive form of legislative action, as we have argued, then the same forces that affect congressional choices in general could be expected to influence these responses. Like Ignagni and Meernik (1994: 356), then, we begin with congressional motivations. Unquestionably, reelection is central to members' goals, so central that some scholars have posited that it is the single motivation for their choices (Arnold 1990; Mayhew 1974). Most congressional scholars, however, argue that other goals also play a major role in shaping members' behavior (Clark 1996; Dodd 1977; Fenno 1973; Sinclair 1989b; Smith and Deering 1983). An interest in making good policy is among the most important of these other goals, and we see it as especially relevant to the override process. Flowing from these two motivations are three hypotheses about overrides.

First, it is hypothesized that *the greater the opposition to the Court's decision, the more likely Congress is to override it.* This hypothesis stems primarily from the interest in reelection and secondarily from the interest in good policy. Members generally are responsive to groups that are politically important to them; the greater the opposition to a decision,

---

7 These two studies provide important findings on factors associated with overrides, but neither employed multivariate analysis to test for the relative importance of these factors.

8 The "sacrosanctity argument" is basically a positive reference to a decision or to the Court (Stumpf 1965: 383–5).

the more likely it is that politically important groups are among the opponents. Further, opposition from groups with which a member identifies may signal that the Court's policy is questionable. Some studies have found a relationship between certain forms of opposition to decisions and congressional action against them (Eskridge 1991a: 351–2, 358–9; Ignagni and Meernik 1994, 358–9; Stumpf 1965: 391; Zorn and Caldeira 1995: 9). We will look broadly at possible sources of opposition to a decision by considering the interests for which a decision was a defeat.

A different type of conflict is also hypothesized to catch Congress's eye: non-unanimity of the Court. We posit that *the existence of dissent increases the likelihood that a statutory decision will be overturned.* This relationship is widely hypothesized (Henschen 1983: 447; Zorn and Caldeira 1995: 12; but compare Ignagni and Meernik 1994: 362), but with differing rationales. As some of these rationales suggest (Solimine and Walker 1992: 441; Zorn 1995: 14), dissent is important primarily because it signals to members of Congress that the Court's decision may constitute bad policy and often offers a strong rationale for that conclusion. Primarily for this reason, we would expect a lack of unanimity to encourage overrides.

Finally, we posit that *the greater the ideological distance between Congress and the Court's decision, the more likely Congress is to pass a bill overriding this decision.* The ideological positions of members reflect their responses to their constituencies as well as their own conceptions of good policy. Because of that combination of motivations, their individual and collective positions have a pervasive impact on congressional decisions. Thus, it is not surprising that some studies have found evidence of this relationship (Eskridge 1991a: 347; Zorn and Caldeira 1995: 7; but compare Ignagni and Meernik 1994: 361).[9]

The Model, Measurement, and Data

In testing these hypotheses this analysis makes use of the data described earlier in the chapter: an integration of Spaeth's Supreme Court Database, an updated version of Eskridge's (1991a) list of congressional overrides of Supreme Court statutory decisions, and a set of additional variables. All cases involving statutory interpretation by the U.S. Su-

---

9 The assumption that members of Congress respond to Supreme Court decisions in terms of the relationship between their own ideological position and that of the decisions is also central to most analyses of the Court–Congress relationship by positive political theorists (e.g., Eskridge and Frickey 1994; Schwartz, Spiller, and Urbiztondo 1994).

preme Court from the 1978 through the 1989 Court terms were selected from the Database and analyzed.

Our dependent variable is whether or not Congress passed legislation overriding decisions within six calendar years of their pronouncement. As suggested earlier, there is a qualitative difference between overrides that come relatively soon after a decision and those that Congress undertakes many years later. Because contemporaneous overrides involve more direct responses to the Court, we counted only those.[10] Since the dependent variable is treated as a dichotomous variable, a logit model of the data was estimated.

We used five independent variables to capture three different types of *opposition* to the Court's decision. First, several researchers have noted that interest groups adversely affected by a Supreme Court decision are likely to turn to Congress to alter the impact of that decision (Murphy 1962; Stumpf 1965). This analysis uses amicus curiae participation before the Supreme Court as an indicator of this opposition. Solimine and Walker support this use, arguing that amicus curiae activity before the Court should make it more likely that "such groups would return to Congress to seek relief if the decision was contrary to the groups' interest" (1992: 442).

Thus we included two variables to measure amicus activity on the losing side in the Supreme Court. The number of such briefs was used as one variable, since larger numbers tend to indicate greater opposition. A second variable is the balance of briefs submitted to the Court on the two sides, as those groups on the winning side of a decision may lobby Congress to preserve their victory. We measured this balance as the net number of amicus briefs on the losing side in the Court (i.e., the number on the losing side minus the number on the winning side).

A second type of opposition is from the federal government. Some studies have found that the U.S. government enjoys an unusually high rate of success in securing overrides of its losses in the Supreme Court (Eskridge 1991a; Zorn 1995). Such success is not surprising. The government has, after all, the resources and the access to push its claim further than most other groups.[11] We employed two dichotomous variables indicating the presence or absence of the U.S. government on the losing side of a decision, first as a party and then as amicus curiae.

The third form of opposition is from Congress itself. Congressional

10 The specific operationalization of this and other variables is described in the Appendix.
11 On the other hand, Congress is not necessarily sympathetic with the positions taken by the executive branch in litigation; particularly in periods of divided government, congressional majorities may approve of Supreme Court defeats for the federal government.

opposition is measured by a variable indicating the presence or absence of briefs from members of Congress or congressional subunits on the losing side of a decision (either as amicus or as a party to the case). The existence of such briefs should increase the likelihood of a congressional response. The investment of time and money in a brief indicates a strong commitment to a position, so that further lobbying to rectify an unfavorable outcome is likely. This issue has not been considered in the literature on overrides, and it merits attention.

The Court *unanimity* hypothesis was tested with a dichotomous variable indicating whether or not the Court was unanimous in a case. Unanimity was measured in terms of agreement on the outcome rather than agreement on doctrine, so unanimous cases may include concurring opinions by justices who disagree with the Court's doctrinal position.

We measured *ideological distance* between Congress and the Supreme Court in terms of the relationship between congressional ideology and the ideological content of Court decisions. Studies of overrides have used various measures of congressional ideology (Bawn and Shipan 1993; Henschen 1983; Ignagni and Meernik 1994), each with inevitable limitations. We chose a variable based on the Americans for Democratic Action's (ADA) mean liberalism scores for members of the two houses, modified by Groseclose, Levitt, and Snyder (1995) (and updated by Groseclose for 1995 and 1996) to take into account change over time in the ideological content of issues included in the scores.[12] The ideology of Congress had one value for each term of the Court; this value was the average ideology of the Congresses in the year in which most of the term's decisions were made (e.g., 1979 for the 1978 term) and in the six years following.[13]

We measured the ideology of the Supreme Court's decision in dichotomous terms: decisions supporting the side with the more liberal position were treated as liberal (coded as -1), those supporting the conservative side as conservative ($+1$). To gauge the impact of ideological distance, we included in the model a multiplicative term for interaction between congressional and Court ideology. That term allows us to determine

12 The ADA's scores are based on members' votes on roll calls selected by the organization, a liberal interest group. ADA scores have been regarded as problematic measures of members' ideological positions because they capture influences on votes other than members' own policy preferences – most notably, constituency influence (see Mashaw 1989: 147; Segal, Cameron and Cover 1992: 103–5). But we treat the ideological positions that members take as reflections of all their relevant goals, not just their own policy preferences; for that reason, the ADA scores as adjusted for change in ideological content of issues are appropriate.

13 To facilitate meaningful analysis of interactions between congressional and Supreme Court ideology, we subtracted the mean score for congressional ideology from the score for each year, thus centering this variable at zero.

Table 10.1. *Supreme Court Statutory Decisions, 1978–89 Terms: Timing of Congressional Overrides*

Calendar Years Between Decision and Override	Decisions		
	Number	Pct.	Cumulative Pct.
0	7	0.7	0.7
1	12	1.3	2.0
2	13	1.4	3.4
3	6	0.6	4.0
4	4	0.4	4.4
5	7	0.7	5.2
6	1	0.1	5.3
10	1	0.1	5.4
12	1	0.1	5.5
13	1	0.1	5.6
No override	893	94.4	100.0
Total	946		

whether liberal decisions are more likely to be overturned as Congress becomes increasingly conservative and whether conservative decisions are more likely to be overturned as Congress becomes increasingly liberal – in other words, whether the frequency of reversal increases with the ideological distance between Congress and the Court's decisions. Because of the ways that congressional and Court ideology were coded, a positive coefficient for the multiplicative term is consistent with the hypothesis.

Results

For the Supreme Court's statutory decisions during the 1978 through 1989 terms, Table 10.1 shows the frequency of congressional overrides and the timing of their occurrence. As the table shows, the distribution of the dependent variable is skewed: only 5.6 percent of the cases decided by the Supreme Court during this time period were overturned by Con-

Table 10.2. *Bivariate Relationships between Independent Variables and Congressional Overrides*

Independent Variables	Association with Override[a]
Losing amicus	.126**
Net losing amicus	.085**
United States as losing party	.064*
United States as losing amicus	.023
Congress as losing participant	.128***
Unanimity of Court	-.117***
Interaction of direction and ideology	.078*

[a]Point–biserial correlation used as measure of association for losing amicus, net losing amicus, and interaction of direction and ideology; Pearson's R used for other variables. All relationships are in direction posited.
*$p < .05$, one-tailed test.
**$p < .01$, one-tailed test.
***$p < .001$, one-tailed test.

gress by 1996.[14] In fact, of the 946 statutory decisions only 50 (5.3 percent) were overturned within the first six years. Thus 94.7 percent of the cases fall within one category of the dependent variable – no override of the Supreme Court decision within the first six years (or, in all but three cases, at all).

Table 10.2 summarizes the results of the bivariate analysis of the independent variables with the dependent variable. The relationships between these variables are all in the predicted direction, but none are particularly strong. However, only the variable United States as losing amicus is not statistically significant at the .05 level.

Table 10.3 presents the results of the logit analysis of all the variables

14 This skewed distribution of the dependent variable renders increases in predictive accuracy for the model as a whole virtually meaningless, but it is not problematical in other respects.

Table 10.3. *Logit Analysis of Determinants of Congressional Overrides and Statutory Decisions during the 1978–89 Terms*[a]

Independent Variables	Coefficient[b]	Standard Error
Intercept	-3.108***	0.267
Opposition		
Losing amicus	0.169*	0.080
Net losing amicus	0.081	0.075
United States as losing party	0.942**	0.386
United States as losing amicus	-0.204	0.559
Congress as losing party	1.358*	0.732
Dissent		
Unanimity of Court	-1.174***	0.370
Ideological Distance		
Direction of decision	0.004	0.166
Ideology of Congress	32.596**	12.935
Interaction: Distance (Direction x Ideology)	29.438*	13.140
Initial log likelihood function -2 log likelihood	379.285	
Log likelihood of the model -2 log likelihood	337.833	
Chi square of the model	41.451	

[a]Overrides counted if they occurred within six calendar years of the Supreme Court's decision.
[b]Significance presented for one-tailed test except for the United States as Losing Amicus, the only variable that was not related to overrides in the predicted direction.
*$p < .05$.
**$p < .01$.
***$p < .005$.

hypothesized to influence congressional overrides of Supreme Court statutory decisions; also included are the ideological direction of the Court's decision and congressional ideology, the variables on which the interaction for ideological distance is based. The log likelihood function and chi square of the model indicate that it is significantly, but only moderately, better than a null model without the independent variables.

The relationships between the independent variables and the issuance of a congressional override are all in the expected direction, with the exception of the variable measuring the United States as a losing amicus. The presence of the United States as an amicus on the losing side of a case outcome appears to make a congressional override less likely. This relationship, however, is not statistically significant.[15] Similarly, the relationship between the net number of losing amicus briefs and a congressional override is not statistically significant.

The three other variables measuring opposition to a Court decision do attain statistical significance. Amici on the losing side of a decision make an override more likely, regardless of the presence of amicus on the winning side. The more amicus briefs on the losing side of the decision, the more likely a congressional override is to occur ($p < .05$). This result fits with the general hypothesis and findings of the literature, in that groups participating at the Supreme Court are not likely to disappear when decisions adversely affect their interests but instead can be expected to seek relief from Congress. Members of Congress will take note of the lobbying of such groups and may attempt to pursue action to alleviate their concerns. Appearance of the United States as a party on the losing side of a decision also makes overrides more likely ($p < .01$) – in keeping with the predictions in the literature on the success of government in achieving reversals of its losses (see Eskridge 1991a; Zorn and Caldeira 1995). In addition, congressional briefs on the losing side of a decision are significant predictors of congressional overrides ($p < .05$). The presence of a congressional party or amicus increases the likelihood that a congressional override will occur. However, caution should probably be used in interpreting this result due to the small number of congressional briefs (these briefs existed in only 14 of the 946 cases of interest).

The presence of non-unanimity on the Court was found to be statistically very significant ($p < .005$). Unanimous decisions are less likely to be overturned by Congress. This result is consistent with our view that dissents provide a signal to Congress that the Court may have reached a bad result. However, we should reiterate that this relationship might have other sources. It is even possible that unanimity deters congres-

---

15 This finding might be explained by the complication discussed in note 11: Congressional majorities do not necessarily support the positions taken by the executive branch. This may be particularly true of positions taken in amicus briefs, which tend to reflect the ideological tenor of an administration more than the positions taken when the federal government is a party to a case.

Table 10.4. *Probabilities of Overrides for Different Values of Selected Independent Variables*[a]

Variable	Probability/Low	Probability/High
Losing amicus	2.91	5.56
United States as losing party	3.16	7.73
Unanimity of Court	5.93	1.91
Congress as losing participant	3.54	12.48

[a]These variables are all those having a statistically significant relationship with overrides in the logit model, except for the multiplicative term for direction of decision and congressional ideology (ideological distance).
[b]All the variables except the variable of interest were set at their mean. The probability was computed for this variable once at a low value and once at a high value. For losing amicus, the low value was 0 and the high value, 4; for United States as losing party and Congress as losing participant, the low value was the absence of this condition and the high value, its presence; for unanimity, the low value was unanimity and the high value, non-unanimity.

sional action by suggesting that the Court will be reluctant to give full effect to legislation that runs counter to its position.

We posited that the ideological distance between decision and Congress would affect the likelihood of overrides. The multiplicative term is consistent with that hypothesis: the more liberal the Congress, the more likely it is to override conservative rather than liberal decisions. This term, too, is statistically significant at the .05 level.

The effect of amicus briefs on the losing side of a decision, the United States as a losing party, Congress as a losing participant, and unanimity of the Court can be assessed more precisely in terms of changes in the probabilities of an override.[16] Table 10.4 includes the probabilities for different values of these independent variables, in each instance holding the other independent variables at their mean values. Overrides were nearly twice as likely when there were four losing amicus briefs than when there were none, and such congressional action was more than twice as likely when the United States was a party on the losing side. Overrides were over three times as likely when Congress was a losing participant or when a decision featured dissent than when those conditions were absent.

16 Changes in the multiplicative term are not susceptible to meaningful substantive interpretations, so probabilities for that variable are not presented.

Discussion

Based on the motivations to win reelection and make good policy, it was posited that opposition to the Court's decision, dissent on the Court, and an ideological gulf between Congress and the Court would make overrides more likely. These expectations were supported for the most part. On the whole, the variables measuring different kinds of potential opposition to the Court's decision were related positively to the frequency of overrides, and in the multivariate analysis three of those variables (losing amicus, United States as losing party, and Congress as losing participant) had statistically significant relationships with overrides. As hypothesized, unanimous decisions were much less vulnerable to overrides than decisions with dissenting votes. And our measure of ideological distance between Court decision and Congress was significantly related to the likelihood of an override.

This study was the first multivariate analysis of its type, one concerned with the enactment of statutes in response to the full range of statutory decisions by the Supreme Court. Thus it adds to our picture of the forces that shape this form of legislative action. On the whole, our findings are consistent with those of other research on congressional response to Supreme Court decisions. However, both present and past findings should be interpreted with caution. One reason is methodological: It is impossible to identify all overrides of statutory decisions. Another is theoretical: The impact of some variables such as unanimity is susceptible to differing interpretations. Still, the patterns that we have found in overrides of Supreme Court decisions are noteworthy.

CONCLUSIONS

Congressional oversight of the judicial branch has received far less attention than its oversight of the executive. But legislative response to statutory interpretations by the Supreme Court can be quite important, because the issues involved are important. Just as Congress would forfeit power to the executive branch if it failed to monitor and respond to policy choices by that branch, ignoring judicial construction of federal statutes would allow considerable control to slip to the third branch.

Our study found that about 5 percent of the Supreme Court's statutory decisions in one period of twelve Court terms were overridden by Congress to some degree – in most cases, quite substantially. The actual frequency of overrides is probably somewhat higher, but in any case, it is evident that Congress exercises significant oversight in the arena of statutory interpretation.

We have argued that this oversight tends to be undramatic, without strong institutional and partisan rivalries. Rather, it is a fairly routine activity in which Congress reacts to decisions chiefly on the basis of members' perceptions of political forces and their own policy preferences. Our findings on the characteristics and determinants of overrides are consistent with that argument.

Of particular interest in the context of this book are the historical trends in overrides. There is some evidence that increased congressional capacity and interest-group activity led to a growth in the incidence of overrides. But partisan and ideological changes in Congress, even the dramatic changes of the 104th Congress, apparently have not – at least yet – had a substantial impact on the frequency with which overrides take place. The 105th Congress – with its continuation of Republican control of both Houses – will provide an opportunity to further evaluate this finding. However, to date this finding suggests that not all congressional activities are necessarily carried along by changes in Congress, even changes that seem revolutionary.

APPENDIX: CODING RULES AND DATA SOURCES
FOR VARIABLES

Dependent Variable

Congressional Override

Coding: Presence or absence of a congressional override.

  1 = congressional override

  0 = no congressional override

Coding Rules: Any override enacted into law within six calendar years after a decision was counted as 1. If an override did not occur or if it occurred more than six years after a decision it was counted as 0.

Data Sources: Eskridge (1991a); *United States Code Congressional and Administrative News*; other congressional documents; secondary sources.

Independent Variables

Amicus on the Losing Side of the Decision

Coding: Simple number of amici curiae briefs on the losing side of the decision.

Coding Rules: All briefs that explicitly supported the losing party or the outcome desired by that party were counted.

Data Sources: Amicus briefs and the side they supported were identified from the *United States Reports*. Where the Reports were unclear as to the side supported by the amicus the brief itself was consulted in the *Briefs and Records* (microfiche) of Supreme Court cases.

Net Amicus on the Losing Side of the Decision

Coding: Number of amici curiae briefs on the losing side of the decision minus the number of amici briefs on the winning side of the decision.

Coding Rules and Data Sources: See variable above.

Congressional Briefs on the Losing Side of the Decision

Coding: Presence or absence of congressional briefs.

  1 = congressional briefs on the losing side of the decision

  0 = no congressional briefs on the losing side

Coding Rules: Any brief submitted by a member or organization of Congress – either as a party or as amicus – in support of the losing party or the outcome desired by that party was counted.

Data Source: See amicus on the losing side.

U.S. Government as a Party on the Losing Side

Coding: Presence or absence of the U.S. government as a party on the losing side.

  1 = government was on the losing side

  0 = government was not on the losing side

Coding Rules: Any brief submitted by the United States as a party on the losing side was counted.

Data Sources: See amicus on the losing side.

U.S. Government as Amicus on the Losing Side

Coding: Presence or absence of the U.S. government as amicus supporting the losing side.

  1 = government was amicus on losing side

  0 = government was not amicus on losing side

Coding Rules: Any brief submitted by the United States as amicus supporting the losing party or the outcome desired by that party was counted.

Data Sources: See amicus on the losing side.

Unanimous Decision

Coding: Was the decision of the Court rendered unanimously or not?

  1 = Court's decision rendered unanimously

  0 = Court's decision was non-unanimous

  Coding Rules: Unanimity determined by the vote on the case outcome.

  Data Sources: Harold Spaeth's Supreme Court Database.

Ideology of Court's Decision
Coding:

  1 = conservative

  −1 = liberal

  Coding Rules: Based on the variable "direction of decision" in Spaeth's Database. In the database, 1 is coded as liberal and 2 is coded as conservative. Our measure put these values at −1 and 1, respectively, in order to improve the interpretation of congressional ideology with an interaction term.

  Data Sources: Supreme Court Database

Ideology of Congress

  Coding and Coding Rules: ADA scores for members modified to convert "nominal" to "real" scores with the method used in Groseclose, Levitt and Snyder, "An Inflation Index for ADA Scores" (1995). Groseclose updated the analyses in the paper to 1996 and provided means and medians for each house for each year. The average mean for the two houses was then computed for each year. For each term of the Supreme Court from 1978 through 1989, an average congressional ideology score was created for the six-year period following that term. Thus, for the 1988 term, the congressional ideology score was the average of the seven average means for the 1989–95 years of Congress. The mean of the ideology variable was then subtracted from all its values in order to center the score on zero. This improved the interpretation of the Court decision's ideology with an interaction variable and avoided a substantial correlation between ideology and the interaction term.

  Data Sources: *ADA Today* (newsletter of Americans for Democratic Action), selected issues, 1979–96; data analyzed and results provided by Tim Groseclose.

Interaction Term

Coding and Coding Rules: Ideology of Court's Decision multiplied by Ideology of Congress.

Data Sources: See previous two variables.

ACKNOWLEDGMENTS

We would like to thank Janet Box-Steffensmeier, David Kimball, Brian Pollins, and Chris Zorn for help on methodological matters, Tim Groseclose for calculating and providing data on congressional ideology, and Craig Church for extensive assistance with data gathering and processing. Lori Hausegger would also like to acknowledge the financial assistance of the Social Sciences and Humanities Research Council of Canada.

II

Congress and Foreign Policy: A Neglected Stage

RANDALL B. RIPLEY

A special stage for the presentation of governmental theatre involves foreign policy. However, scholars have paid only modest attention to the role that Congress plays in this continuing drama. Much of the discussion of the topic that does exist revolves around normative arguments about the "proper role" of Congress – usually as contrasted to the role of the president. General empirically-based conclusions are scarce and attention to change in behavior over time has been inadequate.[1]

This chapter examines congressional foreign policy behavior empirically. After briefly summarizing salient aspects of the general context for congressional action and the influence of Congress from 1945 to 1989, the remainder of the chapter analyzes the role Congress has played in the post–Cold War era. In paying particular attention to the 104th Congress, the chapter examines the effects of the new Republican control of Congress and also comments on the link of foreign policy behavior to the election cycle.

Many aspects of congressional–presidential disputes over the substance of foreign policy in the 104th Congress resemble other periods of divided government since World War II. However, careful examination of the 104th Congress reveals great similarity between the partisan political treatment of foreign policy and the partisan political treatment of domestic policy. Congressional Republicans used foreign policy in about the same way they used domestic policy to discredit a Democratic president seeking reelection. In 1995–6, neither Congress nor the president showed more than fleeting interest in grappling seriously with the foreign policy implications of the end of the Cold War. Both Congress and the

---

1 The most recent works that, with varying degrees of success, address major aspects of the congressional role in foreign policy, include Glennon (1990); Hinckley (1994); Koh (1990); Lindsay (1994); Mann (1990); Peterson (1994); Ripley and Lindsay (1993); and Weissman (1995). Many interesting questions remain understudied: see Lindsay and Ripley (1992).

president treated the partisan political aspects of foreign policy as much more important than any attempt to redefine the substance of American foreign policy.

THE CONTEXT FOR CONGRESSIONAL FOREIGN POLICY BEHAVIOR

Any observer of Congress's foreign policy behavior must be cognizant of the context in which foreign policy is shaped. Several central contextual factors stand out as most important.

First, constitutional structure, precedent, and the simple fact that the executive branch, in contrast to Congress, is headed by a single individual – the president – mean that Congress is always less important in the broad realm of foreign affairs than is the executive branch. Saying that, however, is a long way from supporting claims that Congress is unimportant, that it is subservient to the executive branch and president, or that its activities have no substantive impact. Those claims are untrue.

But it is worth reiterating that the single-headed executive branch is the only plausible source for framing new, broad-gauged foreign policy inititiatives on a wide array of issues simultaneously: for example, conceiving of a Cold War and responding to it in a number of ways; conceiving of an "evil empire" and responding to it in a numbers of ways; conceiving of a post Cold War world and responding to it in some coherent fashion on a variety of fronts.

The executive branch is also the only possible source of what might be labeled "foreign policy spectaculars" – discrete policies or negotiations that appear to have major importance in both the short and long runs. Examples include reopening ties with China in the Nixon administration, taking the initiative in promoting accord between Israel and Egypt in the Carter administration, reaching some important arms limitations agreements with the Soviet Union late in the Reagan administration, or putting together the anti-Iraq coalition to prosecute the Gulf War in the Bush administration. Congress could not possibly have taken the lead in these ventures or others like them.

Second, it is reasonable to look for congressional influence on an array of matters that are perhaps somewhat more routine but are also very important. The details of foreign aid, international trade, and immigration policy serve as good examples. Likewise, concentrated effort on the part of influential individuals in Congress can also push the president to exercise leadership on specific foreign policy issues even though Congress itself cannot provide such leadership. Presidents vary in their desire to engage themselves in foreign affairs. Some need to be reminded of their responsibilities and opportunities. Congressional nagging is sometimes useful in generating presidential movement (see Rockman 1997).

Third, the congressional foreign policy role is not limited to passing laws. In addition to that route for influence, Congress also uses three major indirect routes in influencing foreign policy (Lindsay 1994; Lindsay and Ripley 1993). One is to engage in behavior that will generate specific, predictable reactions in the executive branch. A second is passing procedural legislation that helps determine the identity of decision makers or the procedures by which specific foreign policy decisions are made. A third involves Congress in trying to help nudge or frame public opinion – both elite and mass – in ways that will help, eventually, move the executive branch in a desired direction.

Finally, it makes sense to conceive of congressional foreign policy behavior, whether by Congress as a whole, committees and subcommittees, or individual members, as falling into one of five broad categories.[2]

1. Congress may support a presidential initiative.

2. Congress may ignore a policy area or event because of a lack of interest or an assumption that the president/executive branch will take care of it.

3. Congress make take the initiative by itself or react to presidential activity by making what turns out to be a symbolic statement about an issue. On some occasions Congress intends to make only a symbolic statement through nonbinding resolutions. On other occasions, however, Congress would like to have a genuine impact but the impact of what it does turns out to be symbolic because it cannot force immediate presidential response.

Members of Congress have a number of different reasons for seeking – or settling for, even if unwillingly – symbolic statements. Often they genuinely want to put some policy views on the record but recognize that legislative intervention is either an inappropriate limit on presidential flexibility or simply not achievable. They may also simply want to appear virtuous. They may take a symbolic position in order to cater to interests and individuals in their constituencies. Or they may want to establish deniability in case things go wrong or there is some sort of disaster. Congress often wants to be in a position to say "I told you so" or "don't blame us; the president did it."

In short, some symbolic actions express genuinely held views that can

---

2 These categories suggest the principal observable congressional options in the foreign policy realm. As with most nominal categorical schemes there are instances that do not fit easily into a single category. And the nature of congressional behavior on any specific issue may change over time.

be supported with logic and argument, some recognize the reality of superior presidential power, some are for political purposes, and some are based on a desire to establish deniability. It would be misguided to dismiss symbolic action as unimportant or uniformly cynical.

4. Congress may try to make a statement but emerge sounding confused.

5. Congress can seek genuine independent influence by blocking presidential initiatives when congressional assent is required, a situation most common when an appropriation is necessary. Congress can also seek to push the president further than he is willing to go or in a new direction altogether, but it faces stiff odds against success in such cases.

Genuine independent congressional influence is more likely if members of the House and Senate see a firm tie between a foreign policy under consideration and one or more domestic policies. This tie is often quite visible in areas such as aid, trade, and immigration. Similarly, congressional influence is likely to be higher in policy areas that present an observable opportunity to woo votes at home.

But the dominant constitutional position of the president, especially on matters involving either a real or alleged crisis, means that Congress has very limited power, even in some areas in which there is a history of controversy between Congress and the president over who has what power. A good example is the power to make war. Congress passed a War Powers Act in 1973, but the Act has made virtually no difference in the way presidents have behaved. In addition, federal courts have consistently refused to intervene in presidential–congressional disputes over foreign policy powers.

Controversy between the two branches is enhanced by "divided government" – the situation in which different parties control the White House and at least one congressional chamber.

THE CONGRESSIONAL ROLE FROM THE END OF WORLD WAR II TO THE END OF THE COLD WAR

Before World War II, the United States played no sustained role in world affairs. Consequently, congressional involvement was also very sporadic. After World War II, when the United States became a constantly engaged, major world power, Congress was heavily involved in the major foreign policy initiatives of the United States: helping create the United Nations (UN), designing and implementing the Marshall Plan and other foreign aid, and helping design and implement the North Atlantic Treaty Organization.

For approximately ten years, from the mid-1950s to the mid-1960s, Congress withdrew into a more passive role in foreign affairs. It raised no major objections to the expansion of unchecked presidential autonomy in many instances. Critically, Congress passed several resolutions that, in effect, gave the president unilateral power to use American troops almost anywhere in the world if he judged such use to be in the national interest. The final resolution that met this description was the (later-repealed) 1964 Gulf of Tonkin Resolution, which appeared to license President Lyndon Johnson's escalation of American involvement in the Vietnam War. The 1955–65 period of self-imposed congressional subservience to the president on most foreign policy matters came to a decisive halt as controversy over that war expanded and became intense. (For considerable evidence that this ten-year period was, in fact, uncharacteristic, see Carroll 1966; Kolodziej 1975; Manley 1971; and Moe and Teel 1971.)

However, even during this ten-year period of relative congressional quiescence, Congress still played a major role on a few policies involving trade, aid, and international financial institutions. For example, it was particularly important in the creation of the Development Loan Fund in 1957 and the International Development Association in 1958 (Baldwin 1966).

Careful studies of the first several decades after the end of World War II revealed considerable congressional influence on foreign policy. To be sure, presidential influence on congressional roll call voting on foreign policy matters was strong (Clausen 1973). But Congress often made important substantive contributions. One study that generally supported the view that the president is dominant in foreign affairs (Robinson 1967), also noted that in six of twenty-two specific cases analyzed, Congress was the initiator. Another study, based on a much larger number of cases, noted vigorous congressional participation even when the executive appeared dominant. It also concluded that Congress was dominant in

many areas of foreign policy which in themselves appear to be peripheral. Collectively, however, they constitute a major portion of U.S. foreign policy. For example, Congress is generally credited with dominant influence over decisions on economic-aid policy, military assistance, agricultural-surplus disposal, and the locations of facilities, to name only a few. In addition, immigration and tariff policies are generally considered part of foreign policy and there is considerable evidence to indicate that Congress remains a major actor in these fields. (Moe and Teel 1971: 49)

Beginning in the late 1960s, Congress became consistently more aggressive and assertive in foreign policy after helping end American involvement in the war in Southeast Asia. (For treatments of the revival of congressional activity in the foreign policy field after the mid-1960s to the early 1980s, see Crabb and Holt 1984; Destler 1985; Franck and Weisband 1979; Pastor 1980; Rourke 1983; and Sundquist 1981.) Congress displayed special interest and aggressiveness in the broad policy areas of foreign aid, foreign economic policy, arms sales, support for rebels in other countries, and U.S. intelligence-gathering in foreign countries.

In the Reagan administration, for example, Congress was significantly involved in the sale of airborne warning and control systems (AWACS) aircraft to Saudi Arabia (a foreign policy issue based on a military hardware question), in controversy over U.S. aid to countries with dubious to miserable records on human rights (e.g., Pakistan, Chile, Argentina, El Salvador), and in controversy over aid to rebel movements (e.g., Nicaragua, Angola). It also got engaged in continuing oversight of the Central Intelligence Agency. It was heavily involved in shaping foreign economic policy and was the initiating force in producing a major immigration bill in 1986.

THE POST–COLD WAR CONGRESSIONAL ROLE: 1989–1994

In the period between 1989 and 1991, the East European nations freed themselves from Soviet dominance and established genuinely independent regimes. Then the Soviet Union itself collapsed and vanished from the world stage with incredible speed. Suddenly, international politics looked massively different from the configuration to which everyone – including the U.S. Congress – had become accustomed since shortly after World War II. These dramatic changes in world affairs presumably created opportunities for policy innovations on the part of the United States. Did Congress participate in generating such innovations? Did congressional foreign policy behavior begin to change, or did it hew largely to previous patterns?

In general, the evidence suggests that innovation was not foremost on the congressional agenda and that previous patterns prevailed. This is not surprising given that the engine for major change almost surely has to be the president. Neither George Bush nor Bill Clinton had a compelling vision of the post–Cold War world that drove them to make specific proposals. Bush spoke of the "New World Order" but seemed unable to specify what that meant for American policy even though he was both experienced and very interested in foreign affairs. Clinton had neither such experience nor such interest and managed foreign affairs primarily to avoid trouble if he could while he focused on domestic matters and on reelection in 1996. (For a number of analyses of Bush's and Clinton's performances, see Ripley and Lindsay 1997.)

The evidence on the degree of change over time in congressional behavior on foreign policy – or on virtually all substantive issues for that matter – is qualitative.[3] Inevitably, this means that the evidence is subject to differing interpretations. The interpretation offered here asserts that the mix of congressional activity in the 1989–94 period did not vary considerably from the mix that characterized the immediately preceding administrations of Carter and Reagan. Congress was not likely to produce the impetus for refashioning American foreign policy on any grand scale following the end of the Cold War. Congress did, however, remain active in the foreign policy realm. Its general reaction was to keep involved in individual foreign policy issues, but not to seek a new paradigm for understanding or assessing those policies.

Congressional support for presidential initiatives was concentrated in the 1993–4 period, the only two of these six years during which the White House and both houses of Congress were controlled by the same political party. On issues as diverse as the North American Free Trade Agreement (NAFTA), aid to Russia, U.S. military deployment in Iraq in response to an Iraqi buildup in the southern part of the country, foreign aid appropriations, and U.S. ratification of changes in the General Agreement on Trade and Tariffs (GATT), the majority of Congress basically supported the initiatives and positions of the Clinton administration. The evidence suggests that the congressional leaders of the Democratic majority were willing to support the new president of their party, Bill Clinton, who had restored the White House to Democratic hands after twelve years in exile.

The NAFTA debate in 1993 provides a partial exception in that the president was in disagreement with some of the Democratic congressional leaders – notably the majority leader and majority whip in the House, the chamber in which the president faced the stiffest fight. Many Democrats, including the two defecting leaders, were responding to labor unions, most of whose leaders were longtime Democratic allies. The administration, therefore, had to engage in considerable dealmaking

---

3 To assess the 1989–96 period on the basis of actual events and congressional activity I relied on accounts contained primarily in *Congressional Quarterly* – both weekly reports and annual almanacs – often supplemented and/or cued by accounts in other sources. Eric Herberlig and Lisa Campoli put together the basic summaries and we discussed the most accurate interpretations to put on them. I don't claim that the accounts cover *all* congressional foreign policy activity in these years. However, we sought – and I think succeeded – in identifying all *major* areas of congressional activity during this period, even though the text itself does not refer to all of the cases we considered. The illustrations in the text are offered as suggestive, not comprehensive.

with an unusual coalition of members from both parties to achieve passage of the bill that changed U.S. law to conform to the treaty with Canada and Mexico.

Fortunately for the White House, the bill came to Congress under "fast-track" procedures, which precluded amendments. The other aspect of these procedures that made bargaining for votes easier was that the legislative proposal actually submitted by the administration could be negotiated ahead of time. The deals that would generate the necessary votes could be embedded in the presidential legislative proposal at the outset. Thus, the administration could avoid the always-perilous process of trying to craft a series of winning bargains through the amending process on the floor of one or both chambers. Pre-submission agreements on issues such as limiting Mexican exports of sugar, vegetables, and fruits to the United States; creating a North American Development Bank; altering worker retraining provisions; and environmental cleanup brought crucial votes into the fold. Ultimately, the administration prevailed in both houses: 234–200 in the House (with the Republicans 132–43 in favor and Democrats 102–156 against) and 61–28 in the Senate (with the Republicans 34–10 in favor and Democrats 27–28 against).

Support for substantial, expanded aid to Russia sought in 1993 – a total of $4.5 billion from a variety of sources and for a variety of purposes – was bipartisan and widespread. Additional aid proposals in 1994 also were supported. Congress did add a few conditions (e.g., that Russia must remove its remaining armed forces from the Baltic states in order to receive the aid), but also gave the president the power to waive the conditions if he felt it necessary.

Ratification of changes in GATT came in a lame duck session after the Democrats had already suffered an electoral debacle in November 1994. The anti-GATT coalition failed to gain the kind of momentum that had put the 1993 House NAFTA outcome in doubt, in part because many major corporate interests strongly supported GATT's extension.

Congress also engaged in symbolic behavior during both the Bush administration and the first two years of the Clinton administration. A good example of a situation in which Congress had both symbolic and real impact followed the Chinese crackdown on dissidents in early June 1989. The House twice passed bills to withdraw most-favored nation trading status for China, but the Senate did not concur. This most severe sanction symbolized outrage in the House. However, some genuine, milder sanctions were enacted.

In 1994 Congress engaged in symbolic efforts to restrict and reform the Central Intelligence Agency (CIA), which had been recently shaken badly by the case in which a blatant spy, Aldrich Ames, went undetected for many years while causing the death of a number of Russians working covertly for the United States. Ultimately, however, Congress continued funding for intelligence agencies at an unchanged level (about $28 billion, of which about $3 billion goes to the CIA) and exhorted better behavior without really producing any change through legislation.

Also in 1994, Congress produced a State Department authorization bill that included a number of policy statements that were primarily symbolic rather than designed to cause change directly. Exhortations involved a grab-bag of concerns held by different groups of members: arming the Bosnian Muslims, ending economic sanctions against Vietnam, reaffirming the necessity of arming Taiwan despite Chinese objections, providing sanctions for U.S. firms engaged in some aspects of international weapons trade, and objecting to the continuing boycott by some Arab countries of companies doing business with Israel.

In each of these cases, many of the members of Congress who took the lead held genuine views. Engaging in symbolic action is not always cynical. But they also recognized the reality of presidential power and did not push forward to institute legislative change that would result in immediate policy or bureaucratic change. Symbolic action, no doubt, had some effect on subsequent administration behavior in many of the cases, although precisely what that effect was is very hard to document. In short, calling action symbolic does not mean it is not real. But it is not likely to result in immediate major change in the desired direction.

On a number of issues during this period, Congress sought influence but could not reach internal agreement. Attempts to state a congressional position on Bosnia in 1992 fell in this category. The different views of individuals could not be reconciled. The only resolution that could be passed – and it was not binding – supported a UN statement that it was willing to use force if necessary. More detailed or specific agreement was beyond congressional reach. Similar diversity of opinion in the same year on the U.S. response to the famine in Somalia made Congress equally unable to take a single position.

In 1993 Congress discussed a foreign aid authorization bill. In recent years such bills almost never pass. Instead Congress focuses on appropriations so that money is provided for ongoing programs. The 1993 outcome was the same. The House passed a bill, but it never came to the floor of the Senate. The lack of agreement was based on partisan differences. With a new Democratic president, the Republicans now sought to restrict presidential discretion. Democrats stuck with the administration's positions.

In 1994, simple lack of agreement on the part of enough members about what to do led to lack of congressional impact on the evolving policy of the administration toward Bosnia. The administration itself, of course, did not have clearly articulated policies or preferences. This was a case in which the morass was so confusing that, without clear presidential preferences, to expect anything more of Congress was almost surely in vain. Similar confusion resulting from competing views and priorities occurred the same year with regard to preferences about the U.S. role in Haiti. The degree of genuine congressional concern for the welfare of that country was minimal.

Finally, there are many instances in which Congress directly and unambiguously sought *and achieved* some substantive influence. Examples of such contributions during the Bush administration are provided by efforts to aid Poland and Hungary, a revamping of the Food for Peace (Public Law 480) program, applying modest sanctions to post–Tiananmen Square China, and providing aid to Russia as the Soviet world collapsed. The amount of aid to Poland and Hungary was dramatically increased over the amount proposed by Bush as a result of congressional efforts. Congress found the administration to be too timid in its efforts to aid these countries as they emerged from Soviet satellite status. No doubt the concerns of some members of Congress were heightened by large numbers of voters of Polish – and, to a much lesser extent, Hungarian – ancestry in their districts.

In revising Public Law (PL) 480 Congress insisted on focusing the program strictly on providing food aid rather than leaving it as part of the presidential foreign policy arsenal to dispense or withhold on political grounds. Pressure from farm groups to make the purchase of U.S.-produced food the highest priority goes a long way to explain the congressional stance. International relief organizations also appealed to the idealistically inclined members to remove politics from the program. President Bush was not happy with this congressional intervention but did not veto the bill.

In dealing with China after Tiananmen Square, Congress – especially the Democrats – pressed Bush to be more stern. Republicans tended to support presidential flexibility. The administration avoided the restrictions most distasteful to it through vetoes, but also used the threat of congressional action to put a bit of extra pressure on the Chinese.

Congress was unsuccessful in 1990 in passing an aid bill for the Soviet Union. Democrats attacked Bush for his lack of willingness to exploit changes in the USSR; Republicans generally stuck with the president. In 1991, after a failed coup attempt in August, congressional support for aid to the Soviet Union (which itself disintegrated in December of that year) resurged. The most ambitious proposals failed because of opposition from the Bush administration. But late in November Congress still passed a $500 million package with bipartisan support. The administration was not pleased, but kept quiet, and Bush signed the bill.

In 1993–4, a Democratic Congress, now working with a Democratic president, also exercised significant influence in shaping the final versions of various foreign policies. The bargaining process that led to the final version of NAFTA legislation in 1993 has already been summarized. It resulted in substantive policy changes requested by various groups of members in exchange for their votes. In 1994 congressional leaders of both parties marshalled pressure that hastened President Clinton's actions to extract the United States from Somalia. Congressional action in 1994 with regard to the U.S. intervention in Haiti helped force the administration to spell out its plans more fully than it had initially. Also in 1994 Congress attached conditions to future use of U.S. troops in international peacekeeping operations.

As always, Congress used the confirmation process for presidential foreign policy nominations to make policy points. Even though Democrats controlled the Senate, a few controversial nominations failed because of determined Republicans. A Republican filibuster prevented the confirmation of Sam Brown as ambassador to head the U.S. delegation to the Conference on Security and Cooperation in Europe (although he attended anyway, but without that official rank) because he had been an outspoken leader in protests against the Vietnam War several decades earlier. The nomination of Robert Pastor as U.S. ambassador to Panama failed because Democratic leaders in the Senate realized that a certain Republican filibuster would be successful if the nomination came to the floor. Conservative Republicans were upset with Pastor especially because of his role in the Carter administration in negotiating the return of the Panama Canal to Panama in 1999.

Are broader patterns of congressional activity discernible during these six years? Several specific questions can guide us. First, as the magnitude of the 1989–91 changes in the world became evident, did congressional behavior change? Congressional critics of the Bush administration did, in general, view the responses of the administration to the dramatic changes in Eastern Europe and the Soviet Union as inadequate. The congressional role in pushing aid to Poland and the Soviet Union in 1989–91 can fairly be characterized as helping create U.S. policy. Congressional interest in looking for innovative policies after the Cold War tailed off after this initial burst of activity. On the other hand, both the Bush and Clinton administrations were even more reluctant to innovate in this arena. It would not have been reasonable to expect sustained congressional activity without an aggressive president.

Second, did the period of divided government (1989–92) – with a Democratically controlled Congress facing a Republican president, George Bush – differ from the 103rd Congress (1993–4), when Democratic President Bill Clinton also had to deal with a Democratically controlled House and Senate? The most dramatic change afforded by the move from divided government to one of unified party control was the fact that in the latter period, there were a number of instances of eager congressional support for some presidential positions and initiatives. Prior to that, virtually every major presidential action was questioned, even if it was ultimately supported.

Third, did congressional behavior change perceptibly as the presidential election of 1992, which featured an incumbent running for reelection, got closer? Congressional Democrats did not seem to step up their attacks on and generation of controversies with President Bush in the foreign policy realm as the 1992 presidential election drew nigh. The brunt of the Democratic campaign attack on Bush was in the domestic arena; the Democrats had a candidate for president not much interested in or knowledgeable about foreign policy, and Bush's experience in foreign policy (ambassador to China, ambassador to the United Nations, Director of Central Intelligence, and incumbent president) made it hard to portray him as ignorant in this arena.

THE CONGRESSIONAL ROLE IN THE 104TH CONGRESS: PRELUDE TO A PRESIDENTIAL ELECTION

Did the simple fact that the Republicans gained control of both houses of Congress in the 1994 election lead to significantly altered congressional foreign policy behavior in 1995 and 1996? The answer to this question is, in the classic manner of social science, both yes and no. The broadly affirmative part of the answer is based on the observation of heightened tension in general between the Democratic president and the Republican Congress. The tension was no more palpable in the foreign realm than in the domestic realm, nor was it dramatically less. And, of course, this was a period during which an incumbent president was nearing his campaign for reelection. Preelection point scoring by both parties extended to the foreign policy realm. Unlike Bush, Clinton appeared particularly vulnerable with regard to foreign policy substance, clarity, and resolve.

The broadly negative part of the answer is that, substantively, the partisan and electoral motivations for increasingly public disagreement on foreign policy did not really alter the substance of that policy much. Neither the president nor Congress sought broad new directions. The disputes were primarily about discrete matters, some of them fairly marginal.

The record of the 104th Congress on foreign policy looks, in broad terms, much like the record on domestic policy. In the first session in 1995, the Republicans were in a confrontational mood and pursued their agenda with great vigor – including their (fairly limited) foreign policy agenda. By the end of the session President Clinton, through skillful use of the veto power, made it clear that Congress could not simply impose all of its substantive priorities on him, although he was willing to bend and to compromise on some details and although on appropriations his power was more limited.

For example, the authorization and appropriations bills that included the Department of State failed to pass in 1995, ultimately because the House upheld a presidential veto in each case. In the opening months of 1996 these bills passed in greatly altered form. The final products bore many congressional footprints, especially through specific deep budget cuts such as 34 percent for multilateral financial institutions. Congressional Republican leaders did not win all of the policy battles, but in cutting money they were more successful, a reflection of constitutional fact.

There were no major occasions in these two years in which President Clinton took an initiative and Congress responded unambiguously and unhesitatingly in the affirmative. Divided government – with a new congressional majority eager to recapture the White House and a president not notable for his foreign policy stature – produced a very large change from the more supportive Democratic Congress of 1993–4.

Considerable congressional energy went into generating symbolic statements. Majority Leader Bob Dole, eager to run for president in 1996, started the new 104th Congress in January 1995 with a broad array of proposals in the foreign policy realm. He no doubt favored the positions he took but also knew, from decades of congressional experience, that moving many of them into law was unlikely. He was especially critical of U.S. policy in Bosnia and U.S. relations with the United Nations. Conflict over Bosnian policy continued for a number of months. Congress pushed, hesitated, and, ultimately, realized that the president could commit American troops to Bosnia regardless of congressional doubts. By late 1995 Congress was left visibly toothless on this question. Therefore, it undertook the symbolic action of passing resolutions that did not endorse the presidential action in committing American troops to the peacekeeping effort in Bosnia but did express support for American troops who would be sent there. With these resolutions the congressional majority set itself up to say "I told you so" if the intervention went awry and simultaneously could wave the flag in support of American sons and daughters serving in Bosnia.

Congress also made symbolic statements in response to Clinton's efforts to help bail out Mexico from its financial crisis in 1995. In this case congressional activity also resulted in some substantive changes. Clinton's initial proposal for a $40 billion package ran into considerable congressional criticism. An alliance of isolationists and liberal Democrats sought to reduce the amount of the package and also to address issues involving immigration, workers' rights, economic reforms, Mexican relations with Cuba, and the provision of collateral for the loans. The administration ultimately fashioned a $20 billion package that did not require congressional approval. The House soon thereafter passed a resolution asking the administration for an array of documents on the bailout. The administration ignored this request for the most part.

The final result was that Congress forced a smaller package for Mexico and also got to cater verbally to a variety of different interests in individual districts. But, ultimately, the president could do much of what he wanted. Lawyers in the Treasury could creatively interpret a 1934 law to allow presidential action. Congress could have passed a law challenging this interpretation but could not have overridden a sure Clinton veto of such a law. Congressional appeal to the courts, which duck such issues, would have done no good. Consequently, members of Congress opposed to the bailout had no viable option but simply remaining on the record as predicting bad consequences.

The same broad pattern was repeated in 1995 with regard to the agreement between the United States and North Korea on nuclear matters. Prominent Republicans were very hostile to the agreement but, ultimately, did not want to cast a vote that might be interpreted as preventing the freezing of the development of nuclear weapons by North Korea. Considerable speech making and a nonbinding resolution were the eventual congressional contributions: symbolic but with almost no real effect.

Another instance of primarily symbolic congressional activity involved U.S. policy toward both China and Taiwan. Congress passed resolutions and made suggestions on a variety of details that perhaps helped the Clinton administration decide to permit a private visit by the president of Taiwan to the United States, a visit that enraged the Chinese government. But Congress was not disposed to force removal of most-favored nation trading status for the People's Republic of China. The majority in Congress wanted to be on the record in support of human rights and the government of Taiwan but did not have the resolve, or votes, to force major substantive policy changes.

A better case can be made for substantive congressional influence, albeit limited, in relation to the reauthorization bill for intelligence agencies in 1995. Ultimately, Congress made modest cuts in the intelligence budget, although precise figures are secret. It also put some limits on the National Reconnaissance Office and on the proposed National Imagery and Mapping Agency.

Another major congressional effort to influence the structure of the U.S. foreign policy bureaucracy provoked an ongoing fight between

Congress – especially Senator Jesse Helms (R-NC), chair of the Senate Foreign Relations Committee – and the administration. This fight began in early 1995 and did not end in the 104th Congress until April 1996.

The bill that was the vehicle for this dispute was the authorization bill for the Department of State. Senator Helms sought to eliminate the Arms Control and Disarmament Agency (ACDA), the U.S. Information Agency (USIA), and the Agency for International Development (AID) as separate organizations and collapse them into the Department of State. He claimed, inaccurately, that Secretary of State Warren Christopher supported his plan. (Christopher had, a few months before Helms's proposal, unsuccessfully suggested a more limited consolidation to Clinton.)

The administration vigorously opposed Helms's proposal. In the end the administration won. The congressional Republicans, however, were not engaged in symbolic action. They genuinely sought a reorganized foreign policy apparatus. They also sought other policy changes, such as increasing U.S.-Taiwan military linkages and limiting the funds to be used for restoring normal relations with Vietnam. However, they lost.

During 1995 Senator Helms effectively put his committee out of business for four months during this dispute, which disrupted usually routine activity such as approval of treaties and presidential nominees for foreign policy posts that required confirmation by the Senate.

When the final conference version of the bill strongly favored by the Republicans came to the House floor in mid-March 1996 it passed by a heavily partisan vote of 226–172 (Republicans split 217–6 in favor and Democrats split 9–165 against). The Senate was even more partisan in passing the conference report in late March 1996 by 52 to 44, with all aye votes cast by Republicans and all nay votes cast by Democrats. This final version mandated the elimination of only one of the three separate agencies that had initially been in Senator Helms's sights. But the administration felt this was inappropriate congressional action that interfered with presidential responsibilities and prerogatives.

President Clinton vetoed the bill in mid-April, identifying many objectionable provisions. The House Republican leaders sought to override the veto, although they knew they had no chance of success. The demise of the bill came on April 30, 1996, with that failure: 234–188 to override, 48 votes short of the necessary two-thirds. The parties inched even farther apart, with Republicans supporting the override 229–3 and Democrats opposing it 5–184.

(The entire issue resurfaced in the 105th Congress in 1997. The details are too complicated to recount here, but the Clinton administration, Senator Helms, and other congressional leaders reached a compromise that incorporated some of the changes championed by Helms in 1995 and 1996. However, a dispute over an unrelated issue prevented the compromise from being enacted in 1997. This development nicely illustrates the general principle that issues, whether foreign or domestic, are rarely settled forever.)

Another serious, but unsuccessful, effort to replace presidential preferences with those of the Republican congressional majority involved the appropriations bill for the Department of State, a bill that also provides funds for two other departments: Commerce and Justice. The most visible target of the Republicans was U.S. participation in peacekeeping missions organized by the United Nations. The Republicans did not get all of their desired cuts, but were successful in paring funding for these efforts. The president initially asked for $445 million in the fiscal year 1996 (FY96) budget. Congress first cut this to $225 million, one of many features of the bill objectionable to Clinton, who vetoed it in December 1995. The State–Commerce–Justice appropriation was added to other appropriations bills that had failed to pass in 1995 and together they constituted an omnibus appropriations bill for FY96, which finally passed and was signed in April 1996, more than halfway through the fiscal year. Overall, the State Department appropriation for FY96 was a bit more than 90 percent of its FY95 appropriation. The compromise on peacekeeping – as in other parts of the bill – did not go as far as the congressional Republicans had initially hoped, but the changes were substantial.

In 1996 Congress took the lead in seeking to punish several regimes that are anathema to the United States: Cuba, Iran, and Libya. The effort to punish Cuba and those doing business with Cuba – even though they are primarily from nations friendly to, and allied with, the United States – was contained in the Helms–Burton bill, the final version of which passed overwhelmingly in March (74–22 in the Senate with 92 percent Republican support and 60 percent Democratic support; 336–86 in the House with 98 percent Republican support and 57 percent Democratic support). President Clinton signed the bill. Although he had doubts about its wisdom, he felt that the national mood would make a veto pointless. The Cubans had, only a few days earlier, killed four refugees who belonged to an anti-Castro, U.S.-based group when they shot down two U.S.-registered aircraft in Cuban air space.

The three most controversial provisions were those that removed much existing presidential discretion in dealing with Cuba by codifying the U.S. trade embargo, that denied U.S. entry to executives of foreign companies that had acquired property formerly owned by American citizens (Cuban immigrants who had become naturalized, for the most part), and that allowed lawsuits in U.S. federal courts against foreign businesses with such property. Clinton had the power to allow such lawsuits or prevent them. He decided to allow them, but not until winter

1997 – after the presidential election. He did not want to anger the Cuban-American population in Florida, with its much-coveted twenty-five electoral votes, by forbidding such suits. And yet he hesitated to infuriate friendly nations by allowing such lawsuits immediately. (With the election safely won, Clinton again suspended this provision for another six months in early 1997.) Since the law gave it no choice, the administration began to enforce the prescribed sanctions against company executives, which angered many friendly nations such as Canada, Mexico, and those in Western Europe.

After a long and complicated legislative history the President also signed a bill in the summer of 1996 to sanction foreign companies doing business with Iran and Libya. The meaning of the law is not fully clear, it has the potential for angering U.S. allies and friends, but it also left considerable discretion to the president. The president signed it after the final version was passed unanimously by both houses.

In summary, the newly Republican 104th Congress engaged in increasingly strident partisan warfare with President Clinton on a very wide range of issues, including some in the foreign policy arena. But the substantive impact of Congress was not notably different than in preceding Congresses. If anything, the Republicans felt there was not enough political gold to be mined from foreign policy issues to be worth spending a great deal of concentrated time fighting over them. Budget questions, welfare, and a host of other domestic issues looked more promising. In addition there was no particular collective Republican foreign policy agenda to pursue. The Contract with America, which was presumably at the center of the Republican takeover of Congress in the 1994 election, had almost nothing on foreign policy except urging expansion of the North Atlantic Treaty Organization (NATO).

President Clinton seemed most interested in simply staying out of trouble with domestic constituencies by avoiding any foreign policy mistakes from their point of view. In the words of *Washington Post* columnist Jim Hoagland, he "returned to damage control as the guiding principle in foreign policy" (Hoagland 1996: C7). Clinton wanted to give no campaign openings on foreign policy to Bob Dole.

He could, therefore, risk enraging allies and friendly nations by signing Helms–Burton – although carefully delaying full implementation until after the November 1996 election – because he was not laying himself open to the charge of not being sufficiently "pro-American" or "anti-Castro." He further reinforced his "pro-American" credentials by signing related legislation punishing friendly nations that do business with Iran and Libya. Cuban voters in Florida or "patriots" who think that the United States should be able to tell friendly nations what to do were more important than the sentiments of the leaders of those friendly nations. This sort of behavior gave congressional Republicans who care about foreign policy little room to maneuver.

Oddly enough, then, even though the political conflict between Congress and the president rose across the board in the 104th Congress, the substantive impact of Congress on the content of foreign policy remained stable at a modest level or perhaps even declined. In part, this was because politics was more important than substance for both the leaders of Congress and for the president. The Republicans put less pressure on Clinton on foreign policy than the Democrats (see Rockman 1997). Liberal Democrats are the chief advocates for having human rights concerns help shape foreign policy; a Republican majority created less pressure from this perspective. Having a Republican majority also diluted congressional pressure to take protectionist trade positions because the influence of labor unions was further reduced. The most serious substantive Republican effort, which ultimately failed in the 104th Congress, was the Helms-led initiative to incorporate AID, USIA, and ACDA into the Department of State. The administration found a way to avoid outcomes not favored by the bureaucrats in these agencies, although the issue quickly returned in the next Congress.

As the election got closer and the presidential campaign began to heat up, the political incentives for paying serious attention to foreign policy on the part of either party declined. The fact that foreign policy ranked last among sixteen issues on which voters said they would make up their minds about whom to vote for for president was not lost on the politicians in both parties (Seib 1996). And if such issues were barely visible in the presidential campaign they disappeared altogether in the races for House and Senate.

CONCLUSION

Congress, as a matter of course, engages in considerable foreign policy activity that has substantive consequences. The rate and impact of the activity vary from member to member, from issue to issue, and over time. Different academic observers of this activity discern different patterns and arrive at different broad conclusions about it (see, for example, a review of four recent books in Burgin 1996). The nature of appropriate data about the activity and rules for analyzing those data are matters of even less agreement than in many other areas of political science. But the quest for supportable generalizations – which are simultaneously hypotheses – continues. Six such generalizations follow.

First, the general level of activity by Congress in 1989–96 on foreign policy questions did not change very much from the normal expectations of the post-Vietnam era. The renewed post-Vietnam activism of Congress that began in the late 1960s continues. As the years pass, the 1955–65 period of acquiescence increasingly stands out as an aberration.

Second, congressional influence is not defined completely by final binding legislation. Symbolic statements, and even confused statements, can also help set the terms of debate for an issue over time or can signal the president and foreign policy agencies in ways that alter their behavior incrementally. Less ambiguous legislative actions, ranging from supporting legislation proposed by the president to amending it or to initiating legislation within Congress itself are, of course, important. Even when Congress supports the president it is not necessarily accurate to assume that no thought goes into the process or that Congress is blindly wielding a rubber stamp.

Congressional impact can also stem from aggressive, focused individual behavior as well as from collective behavior. Recent examples of such behavior include the strong opposition of then House Speaker Jim Wright (D-TX) to U.S. support for the Nicaraguan contra rebels in the late 1980s and the vigorous activity of Senator Richard Lugar (R-IN) urging withdrawal of U.S. support for Philippine dictator Ferdinand Marcos in the mid-1980s.

Third, partisanship is a normal feature of congressional–executive relations on foreign policy as well as on domestic policy. "Bipartisanship" – the active attempt to overcome disagreement between the two parties *or* to increase the size and visibility of interparty agreement on policy issues – occurs fairly rarely. There are also instances of "nonpartisanship," where there is passive acceptance of the fact that the issue at stake does not seem to have a partisan dimension. But Congress is a partisan body and there is no empirical reason to assume that most foreign policy issues do not or will not become embroiled in partisan considerations.

Fourth, as with most congressional (and presidential) behavior, the election cycle – the supreme instance of partisanship – is a powerful influence. Members of both parties increase jockeying for political advantage as elections, especially presidential elections, draw nigh. Attempts to discredit a sitting president and replace him in the next election help explain some of the specific congressional interventions in foreign policy from 1989 to the present. Democrats looked for opportunities to discredit Bush on these grounds, although that was not an easy task because of his foreign policy credentials.

Clinton, by contrast, was a relatively inviting foreign policy target for Republicans as they looked forward to the 1996 election. This view was underscored by the 1994 election that produced a triumphalist Republican majority in the House. That majority coopted even the new, usually mild-mannered chair of the House Committee on International Relations, Benjamin Gilman of New York. The Senate is generally not as partisan as the House, although as Bob Dole ran for the Republican nomination for president he became increasingly partisan. Jesse Helms as the new chairman of the Senate Foreign Relations Committee was especially vigorous in looking for ways to attack and embarrass Clinton.

Fifth, there are built-in tensions between Congress and any president on a whole range of issues. The constitutional position of the president and the relative lack of public interest in foreign policy both help to dampen those tensions to some extent. But normal competitiveness between the two branches also affects foreign policy behavior.

Both Bush and Clinton displayed only modest imagination at best in dealing with the changed circumstances the country faced with the collapse of the Soviet Empire and related developments. This fact has eroded the comparative advantage of the president vis-à-vis Congress in relation to foreign affairs. Bush was less susceptible to congressional challenge because of his own personal experience in foreign affairs but did not really seize leadership in terms of articulating what the New World Order was, or might mean, for the United States. Therefore, aggressive members of Congress (virtually all Democrats), who had become accustomed to challenging the president on foreign affairs when Reagan was president, felt free to challenge Bush in this realm, even on the Gulf War operations, Desert Shield and, especially Desert Storm.

Clinton is even weaker and more susceptible to congressional attack, challenges, and second-guessing in the foreign policy sphere. His lack of experience prior to the 1992 election was evident. Even more disturbing to thoughtful members of his own party as well as the entire spectrum of Republicans is his relative lack of interest and lack of much growth through experience during his presidency. This perceived lack of leadership has accelerated congressional willingness to get increasingly involved in foreign policy. Republican challenges in 1995–6, although frequent, were less successful than Democratic challenges in 1993–4, in part because of Clinton's use of the veto when faced with a majority from the other party.

Sixth, except for a brief flurry of activity during the dramatic events of 1989–91, Congress has seemed as unimaginative as Presidents Bush and Clinton in trying to reshape overall American foreign policy to recognize the end of the Cold War. Even congressional rhetoric about the changed world has dwindled. Business as usual by members of the House and Senate is the order of the day: disputes over individual issues conducted by members with a variety of motivations, including the classic trio of pursuing specific policy change, enhancing reelection prospects back home, and promoting one's own status in the House or Senate.

There is, however, no earthly reason to expect that Congress would have had an independent vision of how to deal with the post–Cold War world without presidential leadership. When a president demonstrates foreign policy leadership to confront a dramatically changed world – as, for example, in the case of Harry Truman in shaping the U.S. stance on what became the Cold War – Congress is capable of playing an important role in helping shape vital details such as, in that case, Greek–Turkish aid, the Marshall Plan, and NATO. When a president does not seem interested or able to confront external change with sustained attention to the positions of the United States. – as with Bill Clinton – Congress will surely not fill the gap by itself.

Ultimately, the central theme of this chapter is that Congress continues to exercise its "normal" post–World War II importance in foreign affairs – with the period of normalcy excluding the 1955–65 period of relative congressional subservience. This definition of "normal" accords Congress an important, but not dominant, role in foreign affairs generally, with more influence in some areas (e.g., foreign aid, trade, and immigration) than others. "Normal" also means that congressional behavior in dealing with foreign policy is shaped by many of the same forces that help shape its domestic policy activity. Domestic and foreign policy are not two separate worlds as far as the way Congress behaves.

This central theme is unglamorous. But it has the virtue of being accurate. Above all, it means that ignoring the role of Congress in developing the details of American foreign policy leads both to a distorted view of that process and to an incomplete view of Congress as an institution.

ACKNOWLEDGMENT

Thanks to Herb Weisberg and Pat Patterson, who took their editorial duties seriously with good effect. Additional thoughtful critiques were provided by Jim Lindsay and Grace Franklin, to whom I am grateful. Thanks also to Eric Heberlig and Lisa Campoli, who, as able senior graduate students in Political Science at Ohio State, summarized specific instances of congressional involvement in foreign policy from 1989 through 1996 and also critiqued the final result.

Conclusion

12

"The Play's the Thing": Congress and the Future

SAMUEL C. PATTERSON AND HERBERT F. WEISBERG

Congress is, indeed, great theatre. We have sought to analyze how Congress performs as a representative and law-making institution. In this chapter, we aim to bring together the findings of our inquiry. Then, we want to consider congressional change and speculate about the future development of the institution. We know that institutions change, and we are aware that the scholar's understanding of institutional change is incomplete. The 104th Congress, with its new majority party and changed House and Senate leaderships, pressed against the edges of institutional change, demonstrating possibilities. The electoral verdict of the 1996 election foreshadows further interesting development of Congress as it crosses the proverbial bridge to the twenty-first century.

A CONFIRMING ELECTION

We have focused on the drama of change in Congress in the 1990s, but that drama continues. The chapters of this book have described the Congresses up through the 104th, but inevitably, these Congresses were just a prelude to the 105th. It was on November 5, 1996, that the public went to the polls to choose the cast of players for that new Congress. The election proved to be a "confirming election," with the public re-electing both a Democratic president and a Republican Congress.

The Elections of the 1990s

It is easier to understand the most recent national election if we view it as part of a sequence of elections. Held every second year, congressional elections supply us with a steady record of electoral trends and fluctuations. The four elections preceding 1996 provide this kind of sequence, and we portray the outcomes in Table 12.1. The 1990s began with divided government – Republican President Bush facing a Democratic Sen-

Great Theatre

Table 12.1. *Congressional Election Outcomes, 101st to 105th Congresses*

HOUSE				
Congress:	101	102	103	104
Years:	1989-90	1991-92	1993-94	1995-96
Democrats	260	267	258	204
Republicans	175	167	176	230
Independents	0	1	1	1
Dem seat margin (D% - R%)	19.6%	23.0%	18.8%	-6.0%
Election:	1988	1990	1992	1994
Retirements	23	27	65	48
Primary defeats	1	1	19	4
General election defeats	6	15	24	34
Reelected	402	390	325	349
Reelection rate	98.3%	96.1%	88.3%	90.2%
Dem/Rep incumbent defeats	2/4	6/9	16/8	34/0
Dem/Rep open seat losses	1/2	0/6	11/8	22/4
Freshmen	30	43	108	86
Dem vote margin (D% - R%)	7.8%	7.9%	5.2%	-7.0%

SENATE				
Congress:	101	102	103	104
Years:	1989-90	1991-92	1993-94	1995-96
Democrats	55	56	57	47
Republicans	45	44	43	53
Election:	1988	1990	1992	1994
Retirements	6	3	7	9
Primary defeats	0	0	1	0
General election defeats	4	1	4	2
Reelected	23	31	23	24
Reelection rate	85.2%	96.9%	82.1%	92.3%
Dem/Rep incumbent defeats	1/3	0/1	2/2	2/0
Dem/Rep open seat losses	2/1	0/0	0/0	6/0
Freshmen	10	4	12	11

Sources: First four columns are based on Ornstein, Mann, and Malbin 1996: 42, 52, 56, 58, 60–61, with 1997–8 data added by the authors.

ate and House. Not only was Congress Democratic, but it was solidly so, with a 55–45 Democratic lead in the Senate and a 260–175 lead in the House. Democratic House Speaker Jim Wright (TX) was forced to retire early in the Congress due to ethics charges. The president's party usually loses seats in midterm elections, but Republican losses in 1990 were minimal: one Senate seat and eight House seats.

There were several forces of change in the 1992 election. Not only was this the first election after redistricting, but also several southern states were redistricted to create more majority–minority districts. This was thought to have the possible side effect of packing Democrats into fewer districts, allowing Republican seat gains. Moreover, members of Congress who retired in 1992 were the last cohort who could legally convert their unused campaign funds for personal use upon leaving Congress. The incentive to retire was further increased when the House Bank scandal embarrassed several members. The White House changed from Republican to Democratic hands, but Bill Clinton's portion of the vote was so small – only 43 percent – that his presidential coattails were short. When the election campaign dust settled, the partisan composition of Congress was nearly unchanged. The Republicans gained ten House seats, with no net change in the Senate.

The 103rd Congress was hard on the Democrats. President Clinton's top priority item – health care reform – failed. Ways and Means chair Dan Rostenkowski (D-IL) was indicted. Republican House candidates nationalized the election by signing a united platform for reform across a variety of fronts, the Contract with America. The result of the 1994 election was drastic. The Democrats lost 52 seats in the House and 8 in the Senate, with the Republicans winning majorities in both chambers. The result was often described as the political equivalent of an earthquake, an electoral tsunami.

Expectations for the 1996 Congressional Election

Elections change Congress, sometimes glacially and sometimes dramatically. It is relatively easy for analysts to account for past electoral consequences; after all, hindsight is an exact science. While Congress will continue to change in the remaining years of the 1990s, forthcoming congressional permutation is difficult to gauge. At first it appeared that the new Republican majority in the 104th Congress might precipitate huge changes in Congress, especially in the House of Representatives where the new leadership seemed particularly aggressive. Although it is too early to draw firm conclusions about those changes, the 1996 elections and the subsequent organization of the new 105th Congress answered at least some of the questions. Immediately after 1994, spec-

Great Theatre

ulation was that the Republicans would hold their congressional majority in subsequent elections. For example, the authors of most of the chapters in Klinkner's (1996) book *Midterm* agreed that continued dominance of the Republicans in the House was likely. This was especially the case because they expected the new Republican seats in the South to remain Republican.

The 104th Congress began with Speaker Newt Gingrich keeping his promise to have the House consider each part of the Contract with America in its first one hundred days. However, the Senate slowed down the pace of legislative activity. The Republicans lost much of their early advantage when the public held them responsible for federal government shutdowns in November and December 1995 caused by interparty disputes over the federal budget. Even after the Republicans capitulated on the budget impasse with the White House, partisan wrangling seemed to be preventing the passage of important bills. Rather than allow President Clinton to campaign against the "do-nothing" 104th Congress as Harry Truman had campaigned against the "do-nothing" 85th Congress forty-eight years earlier, the Republican Congress finished the year by passing major welfare reform and health insurance portability laws that were acceptable to Clinton. In the end, Clinton had a 55 percent success rate with Congress in 1996, up substantially from the very low 36 percent level in 1995, but well below the 86 percent success rate accorded to him by the Democratically controlled 103rd Congress.

The high rate of congressional retirements characteristic of the 1990s continued in the 1996 election. A total of thirteen senators and thirty-six House members had decided to retire, and fifteen additional House members ran for higher office rather than for reelection. These developments meant that a large number of congressional races in 1996 would occur in open districts, without incumbents in the fray.

According to some of the early polls, a majority of the public intended to vote for Democrats for Congress. Clinton's lead over Bob Dole remained steady through the fall election campaign, prompting the Republicans to run television ads urging votes for their party's congressional candidates to prevent giving the Democrats unified control of the federal government. In the last two weeks of the campaign there were charges that foreign nationals had given campaign funds to Bill Clinton, and his poll standings fell somewhat thereafter. By the end of the campaign, the polls showed the congressional outcome too close to call.

The 1996 Election Results

The 1996 election, returning both President Bill Clinton to the White House and the Republican majority to Congress, confirmed the pattern displayed in 1994. Clinton's victory margin over Dole was lower than most preelection polls had shown, perhaps reflecting the bad publicity suffered by the Democratic camp over charges of improper campaign financing. Bill Clinton was reelected president with 49.2 percent of the popular vote, as compared to Bob Dole's 40.7 percent, and Ross Perot's 8.4 percent (the remaining 1.7 percent was split among the usual variety of minor-party candidates). Although Clinton captured a larger proportion of the popular vote in 1996 than he had won in 1992 (43 percent), historically he joins Democrats Grover Cleveland and Woodrow Wilson as the only presidents to serve two terms in office without winning a majority in either election. As usual, the electoral college magnified this majority, Clinton winning 379 electoral votes from thirty-one states and the District of Columbia, versus the 127 for Dole from the other nineteen states. Meanwhile, turnout fell below 50 percent, one of the lowest rates in history.

Patterns of voting by individual citizens in 1996 can be compared with voting behavior in 1994, relying on the Voter News Service exit poll of 14,887 voters and comparing results from this poll with similar data for the 1994 congressional election (see *New York Times*, November 7, 1996, p. B3). The national major-party vote for House candidates was 3 percent more Democratic in 1996 than in 1994 (50 percent versus 47 percent). Inevitably, this increase was echoed for most demographic groups, and notably by a three percent increase for whites. However, the Democratic vote increase masks some interesting changes, such as a 10 percent decline in Democratic voting among blacks (82 percent of whom still voted for the Democrats in 1996). This was compensated for by an important 12 percent increase in Democratic voting among Hispanics (rising to 73 percent in 1996). As theories about partisan stability increasing with age would suggest, the gain in Democratic voting was concentrated among the young (6 percent among those under thirty), with no shift among the sixty-and-older age cohort.

Regionally, Democratic voting increased by 6 percent in both the East and Midwest, and by 4 percent in the West, while falling by 2 percent in the South. Voting for House Democrats increased by 7 percent for Catholic Americans, while falling 10 percent among the white religious right. Republican capture of the House in 1994 was fueled by winning 57 percent of the votes of political independents, but independents split their votes more evenly in 1996, favoring the Republicans by a slim 51–49 percent margin. The Democratic vote fell in larger cities but increased in rural areas, small towns, and suburbs.

The president's party normally wins biggest among those voters who are satisfied with the economy. This was true in both election years. For instance, Democratic House candidates won about eight out of every ten votes of people who thought the national economy was "excellent" and six out of ten votes of those who thought the economy was "good," versus just four out of ten votes of those viewing the economy as "not so good" and three out of ten votes of those rating the economy as "poor." What changed between 1994 and 1996, though, was voters' evaluation of the economy. A majority of voters saw the economy as weak in 1994; in contrast, a majority viewed the economy as "good" in 1996. The 13 percent increase (from 40 percent in 1994 to 53 percent in 1996) in the proportion of voters who rated the economy as "good" accounts for most of the 3 percent growth in the Democratic vote from 1994 to 1996 (multiplying the 13 percent by the 20 percent higher Democratic vote among those rating the economy "good" as opposed to "not so good"). At the same time, we must emphasize that only 4 percent of voters rated the economy "excellent," despite the very low unemployment rate in 1996. The perceived improvement in the economy between 1994 and 1996 accounts for the improved Democratic share of the vote, but the economy was not strong enough to give the Democrats majority control of the House of Representatives.

Clinton's 49–41 percent margin certainly was solid, but not so large as to carry in a Democratic House. Several Republican freshmen were defeated, but the impact of this was lessened when some open seats in the South went Democratic. The result was a nine-seat shift in the House to the Democratic side, whereas a nineteen-seat shift would have been necessary to give the Democrats control of the House. The Republicans started the 105th Congress with a narrow lead in the House of Representatives – 227 Republicans, 207 Democrats, and 1 Independent. The Republicans edged the Democrats in the national congressional vote by 41,728,600 (48.9 percent) to 41,430,929 (48.6 percent), with another 2,123,875 (2.5 percent) cast for other candidates (for results, see *Congressional Quarterly Weekly Report*, November 23, 1996, p. 3319). Republicans did best in the South, where they won a majority of the vote (53 percent), while Democrats did best in the East, where they also won a majority (53 percent). Only three incumbent Democrats were defeated (one each in Kentucky, Missouri, and Utah), while eighteen Republican incumbents lost. Republicans won nineteen of their own open seats, plus ten of the Democratic open seats. Altogether, there were seventy-four freshmen representatives in the 105th House.

The 1996 election underscored the continuation of some very real changes in regional voting patterns. In Table 12.2, we present regional breakdowns for the Democratic House seat percentages for the last quarter century. The 87th Congress (elected in 1960) is shown as a baseline, with comparisons to the 97th Congress (elected in 1980), whose voting behavior is examined by Burden and Clausen in Chapter 7 of this volume.

Table 12.2. *Proportion of Democratic Seats, by Region (in percentages)*

Congress Election Year	87th 1960	97th 1980	102nd 1990	103rd 1992	104th 1994	105th 1996
South	92	65	67	62	49	43
East	50	56	60	57	53	60
Midwest	35	48	60	57	42	47
West	57	51	56	59	43	45
Total	60	56	62	59	47	48

Sources: Adapted from Ornstein, Mann, Malbin, 1996, Tables 1–2, pp. 10–11, with 1996 data added by the authors.

Then, we show results for the first four congresses of the 1990s. The West became less Democratic through this period, while the Midwest became more Democratic. The East changed from evenly divided in its House delegations to the most Democratic. However, the sharpest change is in the South (including the border states), from the most Democratic region in 1960 (with 92 percent of the seats held by Democrats) to the least Democratic by 1996. The nearly solid Democratic South had been the foundation of Democratic control of the House from 1955 to 1995, but the 1996 election confirmed that House Democrats could no longer count on enough southern seats to give them a majority (see Campbell 1996).

On the Senate side, the Republicans added two seats to their majority, moving them up to a solid 55–45 seat majority but still well below the filibuster proof sixty-vote level. Only one incumbent senator failed to be reelected: Larry Pressler (R-SD), who lost to Democrat Tim Johnson, formerly South Dakota's lone House member. Several incumbents were in tough races, but were reelected, including, notably, John Kerry (D-MA), who defeated Governor William Weld; Jesse Helms (R-NC), who again defeated Harvey Gantt, an African American; and John Warner (R-VA), who defeated the like-named Mark Warner. In other high profile races, Democrats were able to hold their open seats in New Jersey (where Bob Torricelli defeated Dick Zimmer to replace Bill Bradley), Georgia (where Max Cleland defeated Guy Millner to replace Sam Nunn), Illinois (where Richard Durbin defeated Al Salvi to replace Paul Simon), and Louisiana (where Mary Landrieu beat Woody Jenkins to succeed J. Bennett Johnston).

Republicans took Democratic open seats in two Southern states (Jeff Sessions succeeding Howell Heflin in Alabama, and Tim Hutchinson succeeding David Pryor in Arkansas), plus one in Nebraska (Chuck Hagel succeeding Jim Exon). Republicans held their open seats in Colorado (where Wayne Allard succeeded Hank Brown), Kansas (where Pat Roberts succeeded Nancy Kassebaum), Maine (where Susan Collins succeeded William Cohen), Oregon (where Gordon Smith succeeded Mark Hatfield), and Wyoming (where Mike Enzi succeeded Alan Simpson). Republicans also held Bob Dole's Senate seat in Kansas, where Sam Brownback defeated Democrat Jill Docking. In all, fifteen freshmen were elected to the Senate. The modest partisan change in the Senate masks a greater ideological divide, since several moderate Republican senators who did not run for reelection in 1996 were succeeded by conservative Republicans, while two moderate Democratic senators were succeeded by more liberal Democrats.

The popular press interpreted the 1996 election as a vote for divided government. Following Lacy's analysis in Chapter 4, we are skeptical of that interpretation without further evidence. A slight change in the 1996 campaign (if, for example, information about foreign contributors to the Clinton campaign had not become public until after the election) might have been enough to let the Democrats regain control of the House. A national vote difference for the House of .3 percent seems insufficient to view the result as a vote as a rational choice by the electorate in favor of continued divided government.

Yet in the end, we accept the view of the 1996 election as a confirming election. The country reelected a president, while still not giving him a majority of the vote. The Senate remained Republican, as did the House, albeit more narrowly. Appropriately, Congress accepted this verdict with substantial continuity in its rules in both chambers.

The Beginning of the 105th Congress

Whereas the 104th Congress got off to a dramatic start, considering the Republican's Contract with America in its first one hundred days, the beginning of the 105th Congress was mostly marked by continuity. This continuity extended even to its cast – the new Congress was about as diverse as the 104th Congress. It contained 60 women (51 in the House and 9 in the Senate), 38 blacks (37 in the House and 1 in the Senate), 19 Hispanics (all in the House), 5 Asians and Pacific Islanders (3 in the House and 2 in the Senate), and 1 American Indian (*Congressional Quarterly Weekly Report*, January 4, 1997, p. 28).

The Senate leaders continued in office, with Trent Lott (R-MS) receiving favorable press comment for his handling of the Majority Leader position. Senate Republicans made an interesting rules change by prohibiting top committee chairs from chairing any other committee or subcommittee. This act of retribution against Appropriations Committee chairman Mark Hatfield's (R-OR) crucial vote against the balanced budget amendment in the 104th Congress had the result of enabling some Senate freshmen to become chairs. Most notably, this led to Fred Thompson (R-TN) heading the Governmental Affairs Committee, which investigated Democratic party fundraising in the 1996 campaign.

House Democrats once again chose Dick Gephardt (D-MO) as their leader. There was a challenge to one committee ranking minority member – Henry Gonzalez (TX) on the House Banking Committee (*Congressional Quarterly Weekly Report*, November 23, 1996, p. 3305). After he made a moving speech to the House Democratic Caucus on November 20, Gonzalez won a plurality of the votes in a three-way contest for the lead Democratic seat on the committee, and the second place finisher conceded rather than forcing a runoff.

Seniority was also followed by House Republicans, except that Robert Livingston (LA) retained the chair of the Appropriations Committee even though more senior Joseph McDade (PA) had been acquitted on federal racketeering charges. Republicans disbanded their eight-member Speaker's Advisory Group, replacing it with a more representative leadership group of about twenty members, including representatives from the moderate and conservative wings of the party who felt they had been excluded from the Advisory Group.

The increased Republican strength in the South was echoed in their party leadership in both chambers. The top Republican leadership – Lott (MS), Nickles (OK), Gingrich (GA), Armey (TX), and DeLay (TX) – was drawn from the South and border South.

The most unusual development at the beginning of the 105th Congress had to do with the speakership. Newt Gingrich had been hounded by ethics charges since September 7, 1994 when former Representative Ben Jones (D-GA) filed a complaint alleging Gingrich had used funds donated to his political action committee – dubbed GOPAC – to support the "Renewing American Civilization" college course that he taught. Various other ethics charges were added in the next two years, with the House ethics committee (the Committee on Standards of Official Conduct) accepting some charges and not others. Gingrich's troubles were compounded in late 1994 after he signed a book contract that would give him a $4.5 million advance from a publishing company whose head had an interest in several issues facing Congress. On December 30, 1994, Gingrich gave up that contract and instead received a $1 advance for the book.

In December 1995, the ethics committee found Gingrich guilty of three offenses but recommended no punishment. It dismissed two charges and hired a special counsel to look into tax issues. In September 1996, the committee expanded its investigation to see if Gingrich had given them accurate and complete information about the college course he taught and its relationship to GOPAC. There was press speculation that the House Republicans might dump him, but two weeks after the election the Republican caucus voted by acclamation to choose him once again as their leader. Then, in December 1996, the investigating subcommittee of the ethics committee released a report that Gingrich had not given them complete and accurate information. It announced that the Speaker accepted this conclusion.

The first day of the 104th Congress was high theatre when the Republicans took over the House after forty years in a minority, proceeding to enact wholesale rules changes that day. The first day of the 105th Congress was also high theatre, but of a different type. The press had trumpeted the vote on the speakership after a few Republican members announced they would not vote for Gingrich. In the end, four Republicans voted for other Republicans rather than for Speaker Gingrich when the 105th Congress convened on January 7, 1997. The vote total was 216 for Gingrich, 205 for Democratic leader Richard Gephardt (MO).

The necessary vote was a majority of the 425 members present and voting (not counting 5 Republicans and Gephardt, who voted "present") – 213 votes. Gingrich received only 3 spare votes. Three members were ill or claimed airplane delay, and the Speaker abstained. Jim Leach (R-IA) was able to vote against Gingrich as Speaker without fearing loss of his position as chair of the Banking and Financial Services Committee. On January 17, the ethics committee decided by a vote of 7–1 to recommend a reprimand of Gingrich along with a $300,000 fine, while making the information it collected on tax issues available to the Internal Revenue Service for their investigation (*Congressional Record*, January 20, 1997, p. D34). The full House reprimanded Gingrich on January 21 by a vote of 395–28 (with 5 members voting "present" and 6 not voting), levying the $300,000 fine (*Congressional Record*, January 21, 1997, pp. H234–35).

As is common in the theatre, there was more to this episode than is apparent at first. On the face of it, the Democrats came out strongly against Gingrich's ethics problems, seemingly seeking to remove him as Speaker. In reality, House Democrats and President Clinton wanted Gingrich to remain as Speaker. After all, his very low approval ratings in the polls meant that he provided a good target for Democrats, whereas a new Republican Speaker untainted by ethics problems would take away a Democratic campaign target. Thus, the Democrats quickly accepted the committee's recommendation on punishment for the Speaker and did not push for a stronger censure motion, the passage of which might have forced Gingrich to resign as Speaker.

The early expectation was that Gingrich would survive the ethics problem, at least temporarily, but that his power as Speaker would be weakened. As political scientist John Pitney remarked, "Newt Gingrich will be more of a stage manager in this Congress than a leading actor" (quoted in *Congressional Quarterly Weekly Report*, November 9, 1996, p. 3201).

The 105th Congress started with both sides speaking about the need for bipartisan cooperation. Gingrich himself spoke directly of the need for accommodation with the president, and Clinton similarly recognized the need to work with Republicans in Congress. However, as discussed below, there were real limits to bipartisanship in the 105th Congress.

As it turned out, Republican control of the 105th Congress did not foreshadow smooth majority party policy making, harmony and bipartisanship, or cooperative relations between Republican congressional leaders and the White House. The Republicans were no longer armed with a coherent and widely-agreed upon program of action – such as their Contract with America during the 104th Congress – and their internal disagreements often became public. At the same time, the 1996 election reverberated through the 105th Congress in investigations of charges of campaign corruption, Republican cries for the appointment of special prosecutors to investigate the 1996 campaign fund-raising conducted by both President Clinton and Vice President Al Gore, and interparty conflict over the shape of campaign finance reform legislation. Sharp partisan conflicts persisted over budget issues, but there was occasionally a bipartisan tone, as when compromise bills for balancing the federal budget in five years and for cutting taxes were passed and signed into law in early August, 1997.

The party leaders did not have an easy time in the first session of the 105th Congress in either chamber. The leadership efforts of Senate Republican Majority Leader Lott were increasingly frustrated by a dogged Democratic minority with a keen instinct for the obstructive use of Senate rules. Meanwhile, House Speaker Gingrich's position was weakened by his ethical problems, as well as by the narrow size of the Republican majority. With a lead of only a few House seats, the leadership could lose whenever any faction of the party decided to vote with the Democrats. Conservative Republicans occasionally did this to demonstrate their leverage and punctuate their dissatisfaction with the leadership – especially after Republican leaders, mindful of how badly they had been burned for "closing down the government" in late 1995, conceded to White House demands for the passage of a flood relief bill without unrelated riders.

The drama became especially intense in the House. There, the tensions in Republican ranks climaxed in an act in two scenes staged behind closed curtains in the summer of 1997. The first transpired on the evening of July 10, 1997, when several Republican congressional leaders held a secret meeting with conservative compatriots who were plotting a coup against Speaker Gingrich. At this tense session, the leaders apparently discussed possible replacements as Speaker with the dissidents. When news of the meeting became public, the Speaker removed one appointed leader, William Paxon (NY), while the elected leaders minimized their roles in the coup attempt. This melodrama ended at a closed-door meeting of the House Republicans on July 23, 1997, at which the Speaker pleaded for unity, all elected leaders retained their posts, and the Republicans agreed to communicate with one another better. The Speaker's support was greater among moderates in the party than among conservatives, but he survived as speaker – at least until a later act.

Future Trends

The contest for the 1998 midterm elections began as soon as the 1996 election returns were tallied. Normally, the president's party loses congressional seats in midterm elections, and sharper losses are not uncommon in a president's second term. The extent of these loss rates for the president's party is markedly influenced by the well-being of the economy and the president's popularity level. Unemployment was very low throughout 1997, and President Clinton enjoyed higher popularity ratings than at any time during his first term. These favorable conditions raised Democrats' hopes for success in 1998. In particular, continued low unemployment and high presidential popularity would encourage strong Democrats to run for Congress and discourage some strong Republican candidates – the so-called "strategic politicians" dynamic – which could minimize Democrats losses in 1998 (Jacobson and Kernell 1983).

The role of elections in the legislative drama is to set the stage for the next round of Congress as theatre. Thus, the 1996 election provided the setting for the new Congress, offering another opportunity for the members, parties, and party leaders to play to the public. As we watch and await this continuing drama, it is appropriate to review the specific findings of the previous chapters.

A SUMMARY OF FINDINGS

As we have collectively examined the U.S. Congress at the end of this century, we appreciate its institutional properties, its strength and resilience, its stability, and the changes that have been wrought in the institution, both in the last half-century and with the switch to Republican Party majorities after the 1994 congressional election. Our enterprise yields a sequence of important substantive conclusions about the Congress of our time.

The problem of representation remains a recurring one for the congressional system. The founders of the Republic encountered the problem in the form of disputation about balancing representation of citizens (and only white males were considered then) and representation of the component states of the American union. They chose to establish a House of Representatives in which states would receive representation based upon their census population (originally counting African Americans on a three-to-five ratio to whites), and a Senate based on equal representation of the states. This "Connecticut Compromise" at the Constitutional Convention prevailed, interrupted by removal of the three-fifths formula ratio for slaves with the adoption of the Fourteenth Amendment to the Constitution (adopted in 1868), and provision of the direct popular election of senators with approval of the Seventeenth Amendment (ratified in 1913).

Then, the problem of representation was addressed in the 1960s, when attacks on legislative malapportionment led the U.S. Supreme Court to determine that, within each state, congressional districts must be drawn so that they are equal in their census population. The decisions of the Court established the doctrine of "one person, one vote" as the basis for drawing congressional district boundary lines. But equal population districting did not resolve the knotty problem of racial representation. In Chapter 2 of this volume, Kenny Whitby and Franklin Gilliam recount the creation of congressional districts after the 1990 census that reflected "affirmative gerrymandering" – drawing boundries that would create districts in which African-American congressional candidates could get elected. The problem of racial redistricting remains a continuing dilemma.

Citizens' evaluations of Congress depend, among other things, on discrepancies between expectations and perceptions. Americans' support or disapproval of Congress's performance depends importantly upon the extent of the gap in public attitudes between expectations of what Congress ought to be like, on the one hand, and perceptions of what it actually is like, on the other. Samuel Patterson and David Kimball, in Chapter 3 of this volume, show that much of public dissatisfaction with Congress is caused by the wide gap that exists today between high expectations of what Congress should be and perceptions that Congress falls short. It became clear during the 1996 election campaign that public dissatisfaction with Congress had been aroused by Congress's own behavior – by the breakdown of comity within Congress, the negativism, the petty bickering, the shrill partisanship of leaders, and the partisan confrontation between Congress and the president. If congressional politicians improve their public image, if Congress does better at living up to public expectations, congressional approval levels will rise, other things being equal. Restoring public trust in Congress is one of the guiding imperatives of the 105th Congress, which organized for business in early 1997.

Divided government remains a continuing contextual feature of our congressional politics. The American constitutional system engenders outcomes in which the president and the congressional majorities may be of different political party allegiances; and the two bodies of the bicameral Congress may be under different party majorities, as well. For much of the last half century, the president has been a member of one political party, mainly Republican, and Congress has been in the hands of the other party. For four decades after World War II, the Democrats were usually in the congressional majority, although more often than not, a Republican was elected president.

For the first time in the memory of most living Americans, the Republicans won majorities in both the House of Representatives and the Senate in the 1994 midterm election, and their majorities were confirmed in 1996 even though the electorate retained Democratic President Bill Clinton. Dean Lacy, in Chapter 4, demonstrates that voters did not intentionally bring about divided government in 1994; rather, their congressional voting behavior depended mainly on their appraisal of the president's performance. Then American voters reelected President Clinton in 1996, and also returned majorities of Republicans to both congressional houses, retaining divided government in the nation's capital.

The sea change in congressional politics has been the emergence of strong political party leadership in both houses. Stronger party leadership is symptomatic of the partisan polarization of the congressional membership since the early 1980s. Paul Herrnson, in Chapter 5 of this volume, lays out the anatomy of leadership in today's Congress, showing both the growing strength of congressional leadership and the impediments and limitations the institution imposes on its leaders. Today, the impact of leadership change can be most dramatically observed in the House of Representatives. Speaker Jim Wright (D-TX), who advocated a bold policy agenda on behalf of the Democratic caucus, was forced to resign in 1989 largely through the dogged efforts of Representative Newt Gingrich (R-GA).

Then, Speaker Tom Foley (D-WA) was defeated for reelection in 1994 after Republican attacks on his leadership and his opposition to term limits propositions popular in his own state. Finally, in January 1997 Speaker Newt Gingrich (R-GA) was reprimanded by a vote of the House, and fined $300,000, for admitted ethical violations. Although supported by the House Republican caucus, and reelected speaker for the 105th Congress, Gingrich's ethical problems weakened his leadership capacity, and shifted congressional leadership to Senate Majority Leader Trent Lott (R-MS), who was uncontaminated by ethical difficulties and free of the contumely visited upon his House counterpart.

The bulwark of congressional operations remains in its committees and subcommittees. Although there was much speculation about committee reorganization during the 104th Congress (1995–7) and some experimentation at doing without the longstanding committees of the House of Representatives, the congressional committee system has survived. In Chapter 6, Tim Groseclose and David King chart the changes made in House committees by the new Republican majority, led by Speaker Newt Gingrich (R-GA). That the internal distribution of power in the congressional houses has not fundamentally altered despite the so-called "Republican revolution" of the mid-1990s seems to be confirmed by the more conventional commencement of committee and subcommittee operations when the 105th Congress (1997–9) convened. The viscosity of the congressional institution has proved remarkable, a tribute to the stamina and resilience of political institutions.

Congressional decision making has become strikingly more polarized both in partisanship and ideology. Although this polarization emerged inexorably over the Reagan years of the 1980s, it culminated in the 104th Congress (1995–7), which was dominated by the first Republican party majorities in both houses in four decades and masterminded in the House by Speaker Newt Gingrich (R-GA) and his lieutenants. Epitomized by a determination to achieve favorable House votes on the proposals of the Contract with America, the Republican manifesto, the 104th House of Representatives showed its marked ideological conservatism in the voting behavior of its members.

Barry Burden and Aage Clausen, in Chapter 7, document this "rising tide of conservatism" in their meticulous analysis of roll call voting in the House, and sharpen their conclusions by making comparisons with members' voting in the House of the 97th Congress that convened in the 1980s. Some diminution in House Republican ranks as a result of the 1996 congressional election hardly affected the conservative tilt of that body. And the 1996 election strengthened the ranks of Senate Republicans, assuring a politically conservative upper house, as well. More fundamentally, the Congresses of the 1990s will have evolved so as to strengthen the correlation between ideology and party, pitting a conservative Republican caucus in both House and Senate against a liberal Democratic caucus.

In the vortex of divided government, the president is distinctly advantaged in the confrontation with hostile congressional majorities. A legislative tango requires both congressional majorities and the president to dance together. In Chapter 8, Barbara Sinclair explains that in the 104th Congress, the Republican leadership, especially in the House, sought to use its cohesive party majority to force President Bill Clinton to accept Republican solutions, particularly those concerning the national budget. The Republican strategy came to include "shutting down the government" – failing to provide funding for the continuation of some government programs, thus temporarily closing some federal agencies.

The resulting stalemate between the White House and Capitol Hill proved highly unpopular with the public and unraveled to President Clinton's advantage. During the autumn of the 104th Congress, Republican leaders acceded to bipartisan bargains on major legislative issues, and the president agreed to several important compromise bills. But partisan polarization in the congressional houses, and gridlock between the congressional Republican majority and the president, brought negativism, acrimony, and considerable policy paralysis. It was a time, as Sinclair puts it, for "governing ugly."

The spirit of partisan confrontation between Democratic president and Republican Congress took its toll in the judicial arena, denoted by the unwillingness of Republican-led Senate committee majorities to agree to the confirmation of federal district and appellate judges. Although no U.S. Supreme Court nominations were called for during the 104th Congress, the Clinton administration sought to fill vacancies on the benches of lower federal courts. In Chapter 9, Elliot Slotnick and Sheldon Goldman show that, requiring Senate confirmation, many judicial nominations made by President Clinton languished for lack of Senate approval.

Presidential-congressional clashes over appointments to the federal judiciary are not replicated in the wider realm of congressional responses to statutory interpretation by the United States Supreme Court. Interestingly, Lori Hausegger and Lawrence Baum (in Chapter 10) demonstrate that the reaction of the Republican dominated 104th Congress to the Court's interpretation of federal statutes did not expose the partisan polarization so notable in other regards. Rather, the drumbeats of the Court's declarations interpreting the meaning and application of congressional enactments were quite routine, showing striking continuity with contemporary practice. Hausegger and Baum argue that statutory interpretation is rather insulated from the partisan conflicts boiling up in other arenas because the president is not directly involved.

Congress has come to have an important role in foreign policy decision making, but presidential leadership prevails. Bipartisanship in foreign policy is today largely a matter of nostalgia, and the post–Cold War era has presented Congress with increasing incentive to involvement in foreign policy issues. In Chapter 11, Randall Ripley argues that the congressional role, while an important and growing one over the last half-century, showed no significant signs of alteration as a result of the Republican accession to congressional power in 1995. The congressional Republican leadership may have sought to use putative foreign policy shortcomings to attempt to discredit a Democratic president in an election year (as the Democrats had sought to do against President Bush in 1992), but on balance, congressional and presidential foreign policy roles maintained a kind of equilibrium during the 104th Congress.

THE FUTURE OF CONGRESS

Journalists and even congressional scholars have a way of exaggerating or overstating the extent of changes in Congress over time. Perhaps this tendency stems from not having anything with which to compare Congress, prone as we are to avoid investigating congressional life as part and parcel of the experiences of parliamentary institutions generally. Our proclivity to overstate congressional change may also be rooted in limited understanding of institutions themselves, and insufficient appreciation of their tenacity, their longevity, and their resilience (see Patterson 1995). Thus we often speak of Congress as a "new" Congress, just as we recently characterized a nominal change in political party majorities as a "revolution." Ralph K. Huitt put the matter in perspective when he spoke of Congress as a "durable partner": "Congress changes, as all living things must change; it changes slowly, adaptively, as institutions change" (Huitt 1990: 151).

Our analyses of congressional politics surrounding the 104th Congress underscore the paradigmatic course of change in Congress. From the 1960s onward, Congress adapted to the changing context of political representation: the House of Representatives to the new world of equal population districting, the Senate to the new urbanization. Efforts to improve House representation of racial and ethnic minorities helped to shape the 104th Congress, especially precipitating both the election of more African Americans and Republicans. The post-1994 Republican majorities in House and Senate, flexing their hard-won majority power, made various changes in organization and procedure, most notably in the House. Many of their changes were improvements, some long advocated by congressional reformers (one thinks especially of application of civil and employee rights protections to congressional staffs, streamlining committees and subcommittees, remodeling of rules of procedure in the House, or downsizing staffs). House committees, at the heart of the deliberative process there, experienced initial turbulence but, as the curtain rose on the 105th Congress they resumed their normal ways.

The party and ideological polarization of Congress, stronger than has been true for at least half a century, has taken its toll on intracongressional comity and congressional–presidential harmony. Fundamental re-alignments in the American electorate – denoted particularly by the shift of many white southern voters from Democratic to Republican party loyalty – lie behind the pattern of conflict in Congress. Unlike parliamentary systems such as the European democracies, the congressional arena is not entirely congenial to party government. The congressional parties themselves may lack determination and will and their leaders may not relish sustained party confrontation. We have demonstrated that party polarization in recent Congresses, while very real, has not been earth shattering. Party conflict is relative; in the American context, partisan differences may, on the one hand, be trivialized as "bickering" or, on the other hand, be blown out of proportion.

Party polarization may amplify policy disagreements between the congressional leadership and the president. But legislative–executive tension is nothing new. It is a venerable practice of American politics, grounded in the constitutional separation of institutions. Rivalry and discord between the institutions at each end of Pennsylvania Avenue – Capitol Hill and the White House – are time worn, and come to be noticed even when both ends of the avenue are in the hands of the same political party. "Governing ugly" is a matter of degree.

But fulsome appreciation of the presence and virtue of the stability of democratic institutions (institutions stable enough to adapt to change) cannot gainsay the reality of change. Just as it matters who is president and who are the members of the highest courts, so it makes a difference who are the members and leaders of Congress. Among other things, it matters whether the House and Senate are controlled by the Republicans or by the Democrats. This matters more today than it has for a long time because the middle ground has evanesced; the Republicans truly are a conservative party and the Democrats, a liberal party. It matters which side wins. Moreover, alternation in party majorities in the House and Senate probably is quite beneficial in an institutional sense, permitting the legislative bodies to clear out cobwebs, renew and sharpen purposes, perfect organizations and processes, define leadership, and reverse ossification when one party has retained its majority too long.

The soaring public negativism about Congress is disturbing even to the heartiest soul familiar with the historical skepticism of Americans toward their government. We understand that short-run escalations in public hostility stem from congressional performance itself, epitomized in scandals, the senseless peccadilloes of members, the arrogance of leaders, or the policy making inadequacies of the legislative bodies (see Durr, Gilmour, and Wolbrecht 1997; Hibbing and Theiss-Morse 1995). Americans' expectations about congressional performance can be unrealistic or ill-informed, and their demands for performance can be unreachable except in heaven. Americans' negativity toward Congress is not without consequences, but this negativity lies primarily in the realm of *specific* or *operational* support for Congress, Hibbing and Theiss-Morse tell us, and not in the spongier region of *diffuse* or *existential* support (1995: 158–62). In other words, Americans' hostility toward the Congress of the day, or toward the members of Congress at a particular time, does not cast much of a shadow on their more fundamental loyalty to Congress as an institutional component of the American constitutional system.

In the 1996 national election, voters retained the governing status quo, reelecting Democratic President Bill Clinton and the Republican majorities in the congressional houses. The leitmotif for postelection rhetoric was that of advancing interparty cooperation, eschewing bickering and nastiness, and flowering congressional–presidential bipartisanship. This happened despite the partisan brouhaha over the ethics charges against Republican House Speaker Newt Gingrich and allegations of moral and political wrongdoing in the White House. Ralph Huitt once prophetically said that "it is not easy for a feudal system to make national policy" (1990: 150). The renewed Republican 105th House of Representatives began its deliberations in some turmoil, its leader, Speaker Gingrich, sullied by ethics admissions and a lopsided vote for reprimand and a fine.

With Gingrich's leadership weakened, the center of gravity shifted to the Senate leadership of Majority Leader Trent Lott (R-MS), and toward the policy initiatives of President Clinton. In "American Survey," a feature of the weekly magazine the *Economist*, it was said of the early days of the 105th Congress that: "Political theatre does not come much richer. As the saga of Speaker Gingrich unfolded in Congress, and as Washington buzzed with preparations for Bill Clinton's second inauguration, observers might be forgiven for thinking that politics in that city is pure performance art" (January 11, 1997, p. 23). The unfolding congressional drama, with Republicans maintaining control of both houses at a second congressional election for the first time within the living memory of many involved, spotlights the capacity of the new leaders to manage the institution, work constructively with the president, and guide national policy making. The drama continues to unfold, a drama that bears a fascination of its own. As an uncertain Hamlet aptly said, "[T]he play's the thing wherein I'll catch the conscience of the king" (Shakespeare's *Hamlet, Prince of Denmark*, at the end of Act II, Scene 2).

References

Aberbach, Joel D. 1990. *Keeping a Watchful Eye: The Politics of Congressional Oversight.* Washington, DC: Brookings Institution.

Abramowitz, Alan. 1995. "The End of the Democratic Era? 1994 and the Future of Congressional Election Research." *Political Research Quarterly* 48:873–89.

Abramson, Paul R., John H. Aldrich, and David W. Rohde. 1994. *Change and Continuity in the 1992 Elections.* Washington, DC: Congressional Quarterly Press.

Adams Fruit Co. v. Barrett. 1990. 494 US 638.

Aldrich John, and David Rohde. 1995. "Theories of the Party in the Legislature and the Transition to Republican Rule in the House." Typescript, Duke University.

Alesina, Alberto, and Howard Rosenthal. 1995. *Partisan Politics, Divided Government, and the Economy.* New York: Cambridge University Press.

Alesina, Alberto, Howard Rosenthal, and John Londregan. 1993. "A Model of the Political Economy of the United States." *American Political Science Review* 87:12–33.

Allison, Garland. 1996. "Delay in Senate Confirmation of Federal Judicial Nominees." *Judicature* 80:8–15.

Alvarez, R. Michael, and Jonathan Nagler. 1995. "Economics, Issues, and the Perot Candidacy: Voter Choice in the 1992 Presidential Election." *American Journal of Political Science* 39:714–44.

Alvarez, R. Michael, and Matthew M. Schousen. 1993. "Policy Moderation or Conflicting Expectations? Testing the Intentional Models of Split Ticket Voting." *American Politics Quarterly* 21:410–38.

American Society of Legislative Clerks and Secretaries. 1991. *Inside the Legislative Process.* Denver, CO: National Conference of State Legislatures.

Andrain, Charles F. 1971. *Children and Civic Awareness.* Columbus, OH: Charles E. Merrill.

Ards, Sheila, and Marjorie Lewis. 1992. "Vote Dilution Research: Methods of Analysis." *Trotter Review* 6:29–31.

Armey, Dick. 1993. *Under the Clinton Big Top: Policy, Politics and Public Relations in the President's First Year.* Washington, DC: Republican Conference, US House of Representatives.

Armey, Dick, Jennifer Dunn, and Christopher Shays. 1994. *It's Long Enough: The Decline of Popular Government under Forty Years of Single Party Con-*

References

trol of the US House of Representatives. Washington, DC: Republican Conference, US House of Representatives.

Arnold, R. Douglas. 1990. *The Logic of Congressional Action*. New Haven, CT:
Yale University Press.

Asher, Herb. 1995. "The Perot Campaign." In *Democracy's Feast: Elections in
America*, ed. Herbert F. Weisberg. Chatham, NJ: Chatham House.

Asher, Herbert B., and Michael K. Barr. 1994. "Popular Support for Congress
and Its Members." In *Congress, the Press, and the Public*, ed. Thomas E.
Mann and Norman J. Ornstein. Washington, DC: American Enterprise Institute and Brookings Institution.

Babson, Jennifer. 1995. "Armey Stood Guard over Contract." *Congressional
Quarterly Weekly Report* April 8, p. 87.

Bader, John B. 1997. "The Contract with America: Origins and Prospects." In
Congress Reconsidered, ed. Lawrence C. Dodd and Bruce I. Oppenheimer.
6th ed. Washington, DC: Congressional Quarterly Press.

Baker v. Carr. 1962. 369 U.S. 186.

Baldwin, David A. 1966. "Congressional Initiative in Foreign Policy." *Journal
of Politics* 28:754–73.

Balz, Dan, and Ronald Brownstein. 1996. *Storming the Gates: Protest Politics
and the Republican Revival*. Boston: Little, Brown.

Barrow, Deborah J., Gary Zuk, and Gerald S. Gryski. 1996. *The Federal Judiciary and Institutional Change*. Ann Arbor: University of Michigan Press.

Bawn, Kathleen, and Charles R. Shipan. 1993. "Congressional Responses to
Supreme Court Decisions: An Institutional Perspective." Presented at the
annual meeting of the American Political Science Association, Washington,
DC, September 2–5.

Beer v. United States. 1976. 425 U.S. 130.

Bem, Daryl J., and H. K. McConnell. 1970. "Testing the Self-Perception Explanation of Dissonance Phenomena: On the Salience of Premanipulation Attitudes." *Journal of Personality and Social Psychology* 14:23–31.

Bendavid, Naftali. 1995. "Judicial Selection Clinton Style: Avoiding the Big
Fight." *Legal Times* September 11, p. 1.

Beth, Richard S. 1994. "Control of the House Floor Agenda: Implications from
the Use of the Discharge Rule, 1931– 1994." Presented at the annual meeting of the American Political Science Association, New York.

Biskupic, Joan. 1990. "Scalia Takes a Narrow View in Seeking Congress' Will:
The Textualist Approach Is Gaining Ground but Irking Some on the Hill."
Congressional Quarterly Weekly Report 24:523–30.

Bobo, Lawrence D., and Franklin D. Gilliam, Jr. 1990. "Race, Sociopolitical
Participation, and Black Empowerment." *American Political Science Review*
84:1–28.

Bond, Jon, and Richard Fleisher. 1990. *The President in the Legislative Arena*.
Chicago: University of Chicago Press.

Born, Richard. 1994. "Split-Ticket Voters, Divided Government, and Fiorina's
Policy-Balancing Model." *Legislative Studies Quarterly* 19:95–115.

Bradley, Jennifer. 1996. "Date, Site Picked for Bipartisan Retreat Originally Proposed during Reform Week." *Roll Call* September 16, p.1.

Brady, David W. 1988. *Critical Elections and Congressional Policy Making*.
Stanford, CA: Stanford University Press.

Brady, David W., John F. Cogan, Brian J. Gaines, and Douglas Rivers. 1996.
"The Perils of Presidential Support: How the Republicans Took the House
in the 1994 Midterm Elections." *Political Behavior* 18:345–67.

References

Bullock, Charles S., III. 1995. "The Impact of Changing the Racial Composition of Congressional Districts on Legislators' Roll Call Behavior." *American Politics Quarterly* 23:141–58.

Burgin, Eileen. 1996. "Congress and the Presidency in the Foreign Arena." *Congress and the Presidency* 23:57–64.

Burke, Kenneth. 1945. *A Grammar of Motives*. Berkeley: University of California Press.

Burns, James McGregor. 1982. *The Vineyard of Liberty*. New York: Knopf.

Bush v. Vera. 1996. 64 USLW 4452.

Cameron, Charles, Albert Cover, and Jeffrey Segal. 1990. "Senate Voting on Supreme Court Nominees: A Neo-Institutional Model." *American Political Science Review* 84:525–34.

Cameron, Kenneth M., and Theodore J. C. Hoffman. 1969. *The Theatrical Response*. London: Macmillan.

Campbell, Angus. 1960. "Surge and Decline: A Study of Electoral Change." *Public Opinion Quarterly* 24:397–418.

Campbell, James E. 1985. "Explaining Presidential Losses in Midterm Congressional Elections." *Journal of Politics* 47:1140–57.

  1993. *The Presidential Pulse of Congressional Elections*. Lexington: University Press of Kentucky.

  1996. *Cheap Seats: The Democratic Party's Advantage in US House Elections*. Columbus: Ohio State University Press.

Carroll, Holbert N. 1966. *The House of Representatives and Foreign Affairs.* 2nd ed. Boston: Little, Brown.

Cassata, Donna. 1995a. "Gingrich to End Briefings." *Congressional Quarterly Weekly Report* May 6, p. 1224.

  1995b. "GOP Leaders Walk a Fine Line to Keep Freshmen on Board." *Congressional Quarterly Weekly Report* October 14, pp. 3122-3.

Center for Responsive Politics. 1990. *Dateline Capitol Hill: Congress, the Public, and the News Media*. Washington, DC: Center for Responsive Politics.

Chappie, Damon. 1996. "If Republicans Hang On to the House . . ." *Roll Call*, September 23 p. 1.

Cheney, Richard B. 1989. "An Unruly House." *Public Opinion* 11:41–4.

Citrin, Jack. 1974. "Comment: The Political Relevance of Trust in Government." *American Political Science Review* 68:973–88.

City of Mobile v. Bolden. 1980. 446 US 55.

Clark, John A. 1996. "Congressional Salaries and the Politics of Unpopular Votes." *American Politics Quarterly* 24:150–68.

Clark, John A., and Kevin T. McGuire. 1996. "Congress, the Supreme Court, and the Flag." *Political Research Quarterly* 49:771–81.

Clausen, Aage R. 1973. *How Congressmen Decide*. New York: St. Martin's.

Cloud, David S. 1995a. "GOP, to Its Own Great Delight, Enacts House Rules Changes." *Congressional Quarterly Weekly Report*, January 7, p. 987.

  1995b. "Speaker Wants His Platform to Rival the Presidency." *Congressional Quarterly Weekly Report* February 4, pp. 331–5.

Congressional Districts in the 1990s: A Portrait of America. 1993. Washington, DC: Congressional Quarterly.

Congressional Quarterly Almanac. 1993. Washington, DC: Congressional Quarterly.

Congressional Quarterly Weekly Report. 1979–97. Washington, DC: Congressional Quarterly.

References

Congressional Record. 1995. 104th Cong., 1st sess. H3831–2.

    1997. 143. January 21. 105th Cong., 1st sess., H234–5.

"Congressional Reversals of Supreme Court Decisions: 1945–57 [Note]." 1958. *Harvard Law Review* 71:1324–37.

Connelly, William F., Jr., and John J. Pitney, Jr. 1994. *Congress' Permanent Minority? Republicans in the US House.* Lanham, MD: Rowman and Littlefield.

Conroy v. Aniskoff. 1993. 507 US 511.

Cook, Timothy E. 1989. *Making Laws and Making News: Media Strategies in the US House of Representatives.* Washington, DC: Brookings Institution.

Cooper, Joseph, and Garry Young. 1997. "Partisanship, Bipartisanship, and Crosspartisanship in Congress since the New Deal." In *Congress Reconsidered*, ed. Lawrence C. Dodd and Bruce I. Oppenheimer. 6th ed. Washington, DC: Congressional Quarterly Press.

"Court Appointments." 1996. *USA Today.* June 28 p. A-8.

Cox, Gary W., and Mathew D. McCubbins. 1993. *Legislative Leviathan: Party Government in the House.* Berkeley: University of California Press.

Crabb, Cecil V., Jr., and Pat M. Holt. 1984. *Invitation to Struggle: Congress, the President and Foreign Policy.* 2nd ed. Washington, DC: Congressional Quarterly Press.

Curran, Tim. 1995. "Seize Medicare Vote, DCCC Tells Recruits." *Roll Call*, October 16.

Czwartacki, John (Press Secretary, House Republican Conference). 1995. Presentation to the University of Maryland Capitol Hill Internship Program. October 30.

Davidson, Roger H. 1969. *The Role of the Congressman.* New York: Pegasus.

    1995a. "Congressional Committees in the New Reform Era: From Combat to the Contract." In *Remaking Congress: Change and Stability in the 1990s*, ed. James A. Thurber and Roger H. Davidson. Washington, DC: Congressional Quarterly Press.

    1995b. "The 104th Congress and Beyond." In *The 104th Congress: A Congressional Quarterly Reader*, ed. Roger H. Davidson and Walter J. Oleszek. Washington, DC: Congressional Quarterly Press.

Davidson, Roger H., and Walter J. Oleszek. 1994. *Congress and Its Members.* 4th ed. Washington, DC: Congressional Quarterly Press.

    1996. *Congress and Its Members.* 5th ed. Washington, DC: Congressional Quarterly Press.

de la Garza, Rodolfo O., Louis DeSipio, Chris Garcia, John Garcia, and Angelo Falcon. 1992. *Latino Voices: Mexican, Puerto and Cuban Perspectives on American Politics.* Boulder, CO: Westview.

Democratic Caucus. 1982. *Rebuilding the Road to Opportunity.* Washington, DC: Democratic Caucus, US House of Representatives.

Destler, I. M. 1985. "Executive-Congressional Conflict in Foreign Policy: Explaining It, Coping with It." In *Congress Reconsidered*, ed. Lawrence C. Dodd and Bruce I. Oppenheimer. 3rd ed. Washington, DC: Congressional Quarterly Press.

Dewar, Helen. 1995. "Senate Republicans Put a Lid on Seniority by Limiting Terms of Chairmen." *Washington Post* July 20.

Dimock, Michael A., and Gary C. Jacobson. 1995. "Checks and Choices: The House Bank Scandal's Impact on Voters in 1992." *Journal of Politics* 57: 1143–59.

References

Dixon, Robert G., Jr. 1968. *Democratic Representation: Reapportionment in Law and Politics.* New York: Oxford University Press.

Dodd, Lawrence C. 1977. "Congress and the Quest for Power." In *Congress Reconsidered,* ed. Lawrence C. Dodd and Bruce I. Oppenheimer. New York: Praeger.

Donovan, Beth. 1992. "Busy Democrats Skirt Fights to Get House in Order." *Congressional Quarterly Weekly Report* December 12, pp. 3777–80.

Drew, Elizabeth. 1996. *Showdown: The Struggle between the Gingrich Congress and the Clinton White House.* New York: Simon and Schuster.

Duncan, Philip D., and Christine C. Lawrence, ed. 1995. *Politics in America 1996: The 104th Congress.* Washington, DC: Congressional Quarterly Press.

Durr, Robert H., John B. Gilmour, and Christina Wolbrecht. 1997. "Explaining Congressional Approval." *American Journal of Political Science* 41:175–207.

Easton, David, and Jack Dennis. 1969. *Children in the Political System: Origins of Political Legitimacy.* New York: McGraw-Hill.

Edelman, Murray J. 1964. *Politics as Symbolic Action: Mass Arousal and Quiescence.* Chicago: Markham Publishing.

———. 1965. *The Symbolic Uses of Politics.* Urbana, IL: University of Illinois Press.

———. 1995. *From Art to Politics.* Chicago: University of Chicago Press.

Enelow, James M., and Melvin J. Hinich. 1984. *The Spatial Theory of Voting.* New York: Cambridge University Press.

Engstrom, Richard L., and Michael D. McDonald. 1988. "Definitions, Measurements, and Statistics: Weeding Wildgen's Thicket." *Urban Lawyer* 20:175–91.

Epstein, Lee. 1993. "Interest Group Litigation during the Rehnquist Court Era." *Journal of Law and Politics* 9:639–717.

Erikson, Robert S. 1988. "The Puzzle of Midterm Loss." *Journal of Politics* 50:1011–29.

———. 1990. "Economic Conditions and the Congressional Vote: A Review of the Macro Level Evidence." *American Journal of Political Science* 34:373–99.

Eskridge, William N., Jr. 1991a. "Overriding Supreme Court Statutory Interpretation Decisions." *Yale Law Journal* 101:331–455.

———. 1991b. "Reneging on History? Playing the Court/Congress/President Civil Rights Game." *California Law Review* 79:613–84.

Eskridge, William N., Jr., and Philip P. Frickey. 1994. "Foreword: Law as Equilibrium." *Harvard Law Review* 108:26–108.

Eulau, Heinz, and Paul Karps. 1977. "The Puzzle of Representation." *Legislative Studies Quarterly* 2:233–54.

Evans, C. Lawrence, and Walter Oleszek. 1995. "Congressional Tsunami? Institutional Change in the 104th Congress." Presented at the annual meeting of the American Political Science Association, Chicago, IL.

———. 1997. "Congressional Tsunami? The Politics of Committee Reform." In *Congress Reconsidered,* ed. Lawrence C. Dodd and Bruce I. Oppenheimer. 6th ed. Washington, DC: Congressional Quarterly Press.

"Excerpt from Speech on the Judiciary." 1996. *New York Times,* April 20.

Federal Election Commission. 1996. "Financial Activity of the House General Election Candidates, 1986–1996." October 31. Available at http:\\www.fec.gov.

References

1997. "National Voter Turnout in Federal Elections: 1960–1996." February 17. Available at http:\\www.fec.gov.

Federal News Service. 1996. "National Press Club Luncheon." March 8.

Fenno, Richard F., Jr. 1973. *Congressmen in Committees.* Boston: Little, Brown. 1978. *Home Style: House Members in Their Districts.* Boston: Little, Brown.

Fiorina, Morris. 1988. "The Reagan Years: Turning Toward the Right or Groping toward the Middle." In *The Resurgence of Conservatism in Anglo-American Democracies,* ed. Barry Cooper, Allan Kornberg, and William Mishler. Durham, NC: Duke University Press.
1992. *Divided Government.* New York: Macmillan.

Firebaugh, Glenn. 1993. "Are Bad Estimates Good Enough for the Courts?" *Social Science Quarterly* 74:480–95.

Fiske, Susan T., and Shelley E. Taylor. 1991. *Social Cognition.* New York: McGraw-Hill.

Foner, Eric. 1988. *Reconstruction: America's Unfinished Revolution, 1863–1877.* New York: Harper and Row.

Fowler, Linda L., and Ronald G. Shaiko. 1987. "The Grass Roots Connection: Environmental Activists and Senate Roll Calls." *American Journal of Political Science* 31:484–510.

Fraley, Colette, and Andrew Taylor. 1995. "House Republicans Poised for Medicare Showdown." *Congressional Quarterly Weekly Report* October 14, pp. 3142–46.

Francis, Wayne L. 1989. *The Legislative Committee Game: A Comparative Analysis of Fifty States.* Columbus: Ohio State University Press.

Franck, Thomas M., and Edward Weisband. 1979. *Foreign Policy by Congress.* New York: Oxford University Press.

Franklin, John Hope. 1964. *From Slavery to Freedom.* New York: Knopf.

Franklin, Kurt A., and David A. Weldy. 1993. "Dark of the Night Legislation Takes Aim at Forum Selection Clauses: Statutory Revisions in Reaction to *Carnival Cruise Lines, Inc. v. Shute.*" *U.S.F. Maritime Law Journal* 6:259–71.

Gilliam, Franklin D., Jr. 1996. "Exploring Minority Empowerment: Symbolic Politics, Governing Coalitions, and Traces of Political Style in Los Angeles." *American Journal of Political Science* 40:56–81.

Gilliam, Franklin D., Jr., and Kenny J. Whitby. 1989. "Race, Class and Attitudes toward Social Welfare Spending: An Ethclass Interpretation." *Social Science Quarterly* 7:88–100.

Gilmour, John B. 1990. *Reconcilable Differences?* Berkeley: University of California Press.

Gimpel, James G. 1996. *Fulfilling the Contract: The First 100 Days.* Boston: Allyn and Bacon.

Gingrich, Newt. 1995. "Leadership Task Forces: The 'Third Wave' Way to Consider Legislation." *Roll Call* November 16, p. 6.

Glennon, Michael J. 1990. *Constitutional Diplomacy.* Princeton, NJ: Princeton University Press.

Goffman, Erving. 1959. *The Presentation of Self in Everyday Life.* Garden City, NY: Doubleday Anchor.

Goldman, Sheldon. 1981. "Carter's Judicial Appointments: A Lasting Legacy." *Judicature* 64:344–55.
1989. "Reagan's Judicial Legacy: Completing the Puzzle and Summing Up." *Judicature* 72:318–30.

References

1993. "Bush's Judicial Legacy: The Final Imprint." *Judicature* 76:287–97.

1995. "Judicial Selection under Clinton: A Midterm Examination." *Judicature* 78:276–91.

1997. *Picking Federal Judges: Lower Court Selection from Roosevelt through Reagan.* New Haven, CT: Yale University Press.

Goodsell, Charles T. 1988. *The Social Meaning of Civic Space.* Lawrence: University Press of Kansas.

Goodwin, George, Jr. 1970. *The Little Legislatures: Committees of Congress.* Amherst: University of Massachusetts Press.

Green, Donald P., and Jonathan S. Krasno. 1988. "Salvation for the Spendthrift Incumbent: Reestimating the Effects of Campaign Spending in House Elections." *American Journal of Political Science* 32:884–907.

Grofman, Bernard, Lisa Handley, and Richard G. Niemi. 1992. *Minority Representation and the Quest for Voting Equality.* New York: Cambridge University Press.

Grofman, Bernard, Michael Migalski, and Nicholas Noviello. 1985. "The 'Totality of Circumstances Test' in Section 2 of the 1982 Extension of the Voting Rights Act: A Social Science Perspective." *Law and Policy* 7:199–223.

Groseclose, Tim. 1996. "Blame-Game Politics." Typescript, Ohio State University.

Groseclose, Tim, and David C. King. 1997. "Committee Theories and Committee Institutions." Typescript, Ohio State University.

Groseclose, Tim, Steve Levitt, and Jim Snyder. 1995. "An Inflation Index of ADA Scores." Typescript, Ohio State University.

Gross, Bertram. 1953. *The Legislative Struggle: A Study in Social Combat.* New York: McGraw-Hill.

Grossman, Michael, and Kumar, Martha Joynt. 1981. *Portraying the President.* Baltimore, MD: Johns Hopkins University Press.

Gurr, Ted R. 1970. *Why Men Rebel.* Princeton, NJ: Princeton University Press.

Hall, Richard L., and Gary McKissick. 1997. "Institutional Change and Behavioral Choice in the House Committees." In *Congress Reconsidered*, ed. Lawrence C. Dodd and Bruce I. Oppenheimer. 6th ed. Washington, DC: Congressional Quarterly Press.

Hamilton, Alexander, James Madison and John Jay. [1788] 1961. *The Federalist Papers.* Reprint, New York: New American Library.

Hardt, Jan Carol. 1993. "Congressional Leadership Campaign Strategies in a More Open US Congress, 1937–1993." PhD. dissertation. University of Maryland at College Park.

Henschen, Beth. 1983. "Statutory Interpretations of the Supreme Court: Congressional Response." *American Politics Quarterly* 11:441–58.

Henschen, Beth, and Edward I. Sidlow. 1989. "The Supreme Court and the Congressional Agenda Setting Process." *Journal of Law and Politics* 5:685–724.

Hero, Rodney E., and Caroline J. Tolbert. 1995. "Latinos and Substantive Representation in the US House of Representatives: Direct, Indirect, or Nonexistent?" *American Journal of Political Science* 39:640–52.

Herrnson, Paul S. 1988. *Party Campaigning in the 1980s.* Cambridge: Harvard University Press.

1992. "Political Parties and the Postreform Congress." In *The Postreform Congress*, ed. Roger H. Davidson. New York: St. Martin's.

References

1995. *Congressional Elections: Campaigning at Home and in Washington.* Washington, DC: Congressional Quarterly Press.

Herrnson, Paul S., and Kelly D. Patterson. 1995. "Toward a More Programmatic Democratic Party? Agenda Setting and Coalition Building in the House." *Polity* 27:607–28.

Herrnson, Paul S., Kelly D. Patterson, and John J. Pitney, Jr. 1995. "From Ward Heelers to Public Relations Experts: The Parties' Response to Mass Politics." In *Broken Contract? Changing Relationships between Citizens and Government in the United States*, ed. Stephen C. Craig. Boulder, CO: Westview.

Hibbing, John R., and Samuel C. Patterson. 1994. "Public Trust in the New Parliaments of Central and Eastern Europe." *Political Studies* 42:570–92.

Hibbing, John R., and Elizabeth Theiss-Morse. 1995. *Congress as Public Enemy.* New York: Cambridge University Press.

1997. "What the Public Dislikes about Congress." In *Congress Reconsidered*, ed. Lawrence C. Dodd and Bruce I. Oppenheimer. 6th ed. Washington, DC: Congressional Quarterly Press.

Higgins, E. Tory. 1987. "Self-discrepancy: A Theory Relating Self and Affect." *Psychological Review* 94:319–40.

Hill, Kevin A. 1995. "Does the Creation of Majority Black Districts Aid Republicans? An Analysis of the 1992 Congressional Elections in Eight Southern States." *Journal of Politics* 57:384–401.

Hinckley, Barbara. 1980. "House Reelections and Senate Defeats: The Role of the Challenger." *British Journal of Political Science* 10:441–60.

1994. *Less Than Meets the Eye: Foreign Policy Making and the Myth of the Assertive Congress.* Chicago: University of Chicago Press.

Hoagland, Jim. 1996. "Coasting Till November." *Washington Post*, June 23, p. C7.

Hook, Janet, and David S. Cloud. 1994. "A Republican-Designed House Won't Please All Occupants." *Congressional Quarterly Weekly Report* December 3, pp. 3430–5.

Hosansky, David. 1995. "Rural Republicans Threaten to Revolt Over Farm Subsidies." *Congressional Quarterly Weekly Report* October 21, p. 3195.

Huitt, Ralph K. 1990. *Working within the System.* Berkeley: IGS Press, University of California.

Huntington, Samuel P. 1981. *American Politics: The Promise of Disharmony.* Cambridge: Harvard University Press.

Hurley, Patricia A., and Brink Kerr. 1997. "The Partisanship of New Members in the 103rd and 104th Houses." Typescript.

Ignagni, Joseph, and James Meernik. 1994. "Explaining Congressional Attempts to Reverse Supreme Court Decisions." *Political Research Quarterly* 47:353–71.

Jackson, John E., and John W. Kingdon. 1992. "Ideology, Interest Group Scores, and Legislative Votes." *American Journal of Political Science* 36:805–23.

Jacobson, Gary C. 1978. "The Effects of Campaign Spending in Congressional Elections." *American Political Science Review* 72:469–91.

1981. "Congressional Election, 1978: The Case of the Vanishing Challengers." In *Congressional Elections*, ed. Louis Sandy Maisel and Joseph Cooper. Beverly Hills, CA: Sage.

1985. "Money and Votes Reconsidered: Congressional Elections, 1972–1982." *Public Choice* 47:7–62.

References

1987a. "The Marginals Never Vanished: Incumbency and Competition in Elections to the US House of Representatives, 1952–1982." *American Journal of Political Science* 31:126–41.

1987b. *The Politics of Congressional Elections* 2d. ed. Boston: Scott Foresman.

1990a. "The Effects of Campaign Spending in US House Elections: New Evidence for Old Arguments." *American Journal of Political Science* 34:334–62.

1990b. *The Electoral Origins of Divided Government. Competition in US House Elections, 1946–1988.* Boulder, CO: Westview.

1996. "The 1994 House Elections in Perspective." *Political Science Quarterly* 111:203–23. Also in *Midterm: The Elections of 1994 in Context*, ed. Phillip A. Klinkner. Boulder, CO: Westview, 1996.

Jacobson, Gary C., and Samuel Kernell. 1983. *Strategy and Choice in Congressional Elections* 2nd ed. New Haven, CT: Yale University Press.

Jacoby, Mary. 1994a. "Big States Big Losers in Gingrich's Plan for Committee on Committees." *Roll Call* December 1, p. 3.

1994b. "Conference Adopts Gingrich's Steering Panel Setup." *Roll Call* December 8, p.22.

1995. "Gramm Slot on Finance Still Delayed." *Roll Call* October 12, pp.1, 20.

Jarvis, Sonia R. 1992. "Historical Overview: African-Americans and the Evolution of Voting Rights." In *From Exclusion to Inclusion: The Long Struggle for African American Political Power*, ed. Ralph C. Gomes and Linda Faye Williams. Westport, CT: Greenwood Press.

Jaynes, Gerald David, and Robin M. Williams, ed. 1989. *A Common Destiny: Blacks and American Society.* Washington, DC: National Academy Press.

Johnson, Haynes, and David Broder. 1996. *The System.* Boston: Little, Brown.

Johnson, Samuel. 1747. Prologue at the Opening of the Theatre in Drury Lane.

Joint Committee on the Organization of Congress (JCOC). 1993. *Organization of Congress: Final Report.* H. Rept. 103-413/S.Rept. 103-215. Washington, DC: US Government Printing Office. 3 vols.

Jones, Charles O. 1968. "Joseph G. Cannon and Howard W. Smith: An Essay on the Limits of Leadership in the House of Representatives." *Journal of Politics* 30:617–46.

1994. *The Presidency in a Separated System.* Washington, DC: Brookings Institution.

Kahn, Gabriel, and Timothy J. Burger. 1994. "Solomon, Livingston Win Chairs." *Roll Call* November 17, pp. 1, 8.

Kamen, Al. 1995. "Upstaged and Upset." *Washington Post*, August 11, p. A21.

Karmin, Craig. 1994. "Gingrich Ignores Seniority in Selecting Key Chairman." *The Hill*, November 16, p. 1.

Katz, Jeffrey L. 1995. "House Revives EPA Restrictions Before Passing VA-HUD Bill." *Congressional Quarterly Weekly Report* August 5, pp. 2366–9.

Katzmann, Robert A. 1992. "Bridging the Statutory Gulf between Courts and Congress: A Challenge for Positive Political Theory." *Georgetown Law Journal* 80:653–69.

Kennedy, John F. 1956. *Profiles in Courage.* New York: Harper and Brothers.

Kerbel, Matthew R. 1995. *Remote and Controlled: Media Politics in a Cynical Age.* San Francisco: Westview.

References

Kernell, Samuel. 1986. *Going Public.* Washington, DC: Congressional Quarterly Press.

Kim, Jae-On, and Charles W. Mueller. 1978. *Factor Analysis.* Beverly Hills, CA: Sage.

Kimball, David C. 1995. "Public Approval of Congress: To What Extent Do People Respond to Cues Provided by Current Events and Elite Discourse?" Presented at the annual meeting of the Midwest Political Science Association, Chicago, IL.

   1997. "The Divided Voter in American Politics." Ph.D. Dissertation. Ohio State University.

Kimball, David C., and Samuel C. Patterson. 1997. "Living up to Expectations: Public Attitudes toward Congress." *Journal of Politics* 59: 701–28.

Kinder, Donald, and D. Roderick Kiewiet. 1980. "Sociotropic Voting: The American Case." *British Journal of Political Science* 11:129–61.

King, David C. 1997. *Turf Wars: How Committees Claim Jurisdiction on Capitol Hill.* Chicago: University of Chicago Press.

Klaaren, Kristen J., Sara D. Hodges, and Timothy D. Wilson. 1994. "The Role of Affective Expectations in Subjective Experience and Decision-Making." *Social Cognition* 12:77–101.

Klinkner, Philip A., ed. 1996. *Midterm: The Elections of 1994 in Context.* Boulder, CO: Westview.

Koh, Harold Hongju. 1990. *The National Security Constitution: Sharing Power after the Iran-Contra Affair.* New Haven CT: Yale University Press.

Kolodziej, Edward A. 1975. "Congress and Foreign Policy: The Nixon Years." In *Congress against the President*, ed. Harvey C. Mansfield, Sr. New York: Academy of Political Science.

Koopman, Douglas L. 1994. "The 1994 House Elections: A Republican View." *Extension of Remarks.* December.

   1996. *Hostile Takeover: The House Republican Party 1980–1995.* Lanham, MD: Rowan and Littlefield.

Koszcuk, Jackie. 1995. "Gingrich Puts More Power into Speaker's Hands." *Congressional Quarterly Weekly Report* October 7, pp. 3049–53.

Kramer, Gerald H. 1971. "Short-Term Fluctuations in US Voting Behavior." *American Political Science Review,* 65:131–43.

   1983. "The Ecological Fallacy Revisited: Aggregate-versus Individual-Level Findings on Economics and Elections and Sociotropic Voting." *American Political Science Review* 77:92–111.

Lacy, Dean. 1994. "Nonseparable Preferences in Politics: Implications for Social Choice, Elections, and Public Opinion." Ph.D. dissertation, Duke University.

Lacy, Dean, and Emerson M. S. Niou. 1997. "Elections in Double-Member Districts with Nonseparable Voter Preferences." *Journal of Theoretical Politics.*

Langdon, Steve. 1995. " 'Contract' Dwarfs Senate GOP's Pledge." *Congressional Quarterly Weekly Report* February 25, p. 578.

Lasswell, Harold D. 1936. *Politics: Who Gets What, When, How.* New York: McGraw-Hill.

Lawson, Steven F. 1976. *Black Ballots: Voting Rights in the South, 1944–1969.* New York: Columbia University Press.

Light, Paul. 1983. *The President's Agenda.* Baltimore, MD: Johns Hopkins University Press.

References

Lindsay, James M. 1994. *Congress and the Politics of US Foreign Policy.* Baltimore, MD: Johns Hopkins University Press.

Lindsay, James M., and Randall B. Ripley. 1992. "Foreign and Defense Policy in Congress: A Research Agenda for the 1990s." *Legislative Studies Quarterly* 17:417–49.

1993. "How Congress Influences Foreign and Defense Policy." In *Congress Resurgent: Foreign and Defense Policy on Capitol Hill*, ed. Randall B. Ripley and James M. Lindsay. Ann Arbor: University of Michigan Press.

Lipscomb, Andrew A., and Albert E. Bergh, eds. 1903. *The Writings of Thomas Jefferson*, vol XI. New York.

Lipset, Seymour Martin, and William Schneider. 1987. *The Confidence Gap: Business, Labor, and Government in the Public Mind.* Baltimore, MD: Johns Hopkins University Press.

Loewen, James W. 1990. "Racial Bloc Voting and Political Mobilization in South Carolina." *Review of Black Political Economy* 19:23–37.

Long, J. Scott. 1983. *Confirmatory Factor Analysis.* Newbury Park, CA: Sage.

Loomis, Burdett A., and Allan J. Cigler. 1991. "Introduction: The Changing Nature of Interest Group Politics." In *Interest Group Politics*, ed. Allan J. Cigler and Burdett A. Loomis. 3rd ed. Washington, DC: Congressional Quarterly Press.

Lowe, Roger K. 1996. "Senate Compromise May Allow Confirmation of Federal Judges." *Columbus Dispatch* July 14, p. B-3.

Lublin, David I. 1995. "Racial Redistricting and the New Republican Majority: A Critique of the NAACP Legal Defense Fund Report on the 1994 Congressional Elections." Unpublished manuscript.

Maltese, John Anthony. 1995. *The Selling of Supreme Court Nominees.* Baltimore, MD: Johns Hopkins University Press.

Manley, John F. 1971. "The Rise of Congress in Foreign Policy-Making." *Annals of the American Academy of Political and Social Science* 337: 60–70.

Mann, Thomas. 1978. *Unsafe at Any Margin: Interpreting Congressional Elections.* Washington, DC: American Enterprise Institute.

Mann, Thomas E., ed. 1990. *A Question of Balance: The President, the Congress, and Foreign Policy.* Washington, DC: Brookings Institution.

Mann, Thomas E., and Norman J. Ornstein, ed. 1994. *Congress, the Press, and the Public.* Washington, DC: American Enterprise Institute and Brookings Institution.

Maraniss, David, and Michael Weisskopf. 1995. "Republican Word Power . . . A Freshman's Advantage." *Washington Post* October 29.

Markus, Gregory B. 1986. "Stability and Change in Political Attitudes: Observed, Recalled, and 'Explained.'" *Political Behavior* 8:21–44.

Mashaw, Jerry L. 1989. "The Economics of Politics and the Understanding of Public Law." *Chicago–Kent Law Review* 65:123–60.

Massey, Douglas S., and Nancy A. Denton. 1993. *American Apartheid: Segregation and the Making of the Underclass.* Cambridge: Harvard University Press.

Matthews, Donald R. 1960. *US Senators and Their World.* New York: Vintage Books.

Matthews, Donald R., and James W. Prothro. 1967. "Social and Economic Factors and Negro Voter Registration in the South." In *Negro Politics in America*, ed. Henry Bailey, Jr. Columbus, OH: Charles E. Merrill Co.

References

Mayhew, David R. 1974. *Congress, OH: The Electoral Connection*. New Haven, CT: Yale University Press.

1991. *Divided We Govern*. New Haven, CT: Yale University Press.

McCarty, Nolan M., Keith T. Poole, and Howard Rosenthal. 1996. "The Realignment of American Politics: From Goldwater to Gingrich." Presented at the American Enterprise Institute.

McKelvey, Richard D. 1976. "Intransitivities in Multidimensional Voting Models and Some Implications for Agenda Control." *Journal of Economic Theory* 12:472–82.

Meier, August, Elliot Rudwick, and Francis L. Broderick. 1965. *Black Protest Thought in the Twentieth Century*. 2nd ed. New York: Bobbs-Merrill.

Melnick, R. Shep. 1994. *Between the Lines: Interpreting Welfare Rights*. Washington, DC: Brookings Institution.

Mezey, Michael L. 1979. *Comparative Legislatures*. Durham, NC: Duke University Press.

Miller, Arthur H. 1974. "Political Issues and Trust in Government: 1964–1970." *American Political Science Review* 68:951–72.

Miller, Mark C. 1990. "The View of the Courts From the Hill: How Congressional Committees Differ in Their Reactions to Court Decisions." Ph.D. dissertation, Ohio State University.

1992. "Congressional Committees and the Federal Courts: A Neo-Institutional Perspective." *Western Political Quarterly* 45:949–70.

Miller v. Johnson. 1995. 132 L ED 2d 762.

Moe, Ronald C. and Steven C. Teel. 1971. "Congress as Policy-Maker: A Necessary Reappraisal." In *Congress and the President*, ed. Ronald C. Moe. New York: Goodyear.

Moretti, Marlene M., and E. Tory Higgins. 1990. "Relating Self-discrepancy to Self-esteem: The Contributions of Discrepancy Beyond Actual Self Ratings." *Journal of Experimental Social Psychology* 26:108–23.

Morin, Richard, and Mario A. Brossard. 1996. "Looking for Rascals to Throw Out." *Washington Post National Weekly Edition* June 24–30 p. 13.

Moss, Jesse (Communications and Policy Assistant, House Democratic Caucus). 1995. Presentation to the University of Maryland Capitol Hill Internship Program, October 30.

Murphy, Walter F. 1962. *Congress and the Court*. Chicago, IL: University of Chicago Press.

Nichols, Stephen M., and Paul Allen Beck. 1995. "Reversing the Decline: Voter Turnout in the 1992 Election." In *Democracy's Feast: Elections in America*, ed. Herbert F. Weisberg. Chatham, NJ: Chatham House.

Oleszek, Walter J. 1996. *Congressional Procedures and the Policy Process*. 4th ed. Washington, DC: Congressional Quarterly Press.

Oppenheimer, Bruce. 1985. "Changing Time Constraints on Congress: Historical Perspectives on the Use of Cloture." In *Congress Reconsidered*, ed. Lawrence C. Dodd and Bruce I. Oppenheimer. 3rd ed. Washington, DC: Congressional Quarterly Press, pp. 393–413.

Ornstein, Norman J. 1995. "Congress Inside Out." *Roll Call* October 23, p. 5.

Ornstein, Norman J., Thomas E. Mann, and Michael J. Malbin. 1992. *Vital Statistics on Congress 1991–1992*. Washington, DC: Congressional Quarterly Press.

References

1994. *Vital Statistics on Congress, 1993–1994*. Washington, DC: Congressional Quarterly Press.

1996. *Vital Statistics on Congress, 1995–1996*. Washington, DC: Congressional Quarterly Press.

Ornstein, Norman J., and Amy L. Schenkenberg. 1995. "The 1995 Congress: The First Hundred Days and Beyond." *Political Science Quarterly* 110:183–206.

Overby, L. Marvin, Beth Henschen, Michael Walsh, and Julie Strauss. 1992. "Courting Constituents? An Analysis of the Senate Confirmation Vote on Justice Clarence Thomas." *American Political Science Review* 86:997–1003.

Overby, L. Marvin, and Kenneth M. Cosgrove. 1996. "Unintended Consequences? Racial Redistricting and the Representation of Minority Interests." *Journal of Politics* 58:540–50.

Paschal, Richard A. 1991. "The Continuing Colloquy: Congress and the Finality of the Supreme Court." *Journal of Law and Politics* 8:142–226.

Pastor, Robert A. 1980. *Congress and the Politics of US Foreign Economic Policy*. Berkeley: University of California Press.

Patterson, Samuel C. 1978. "The Semi-Sovereign Congress." In *The New American Political System*, ed. Anthony King. Washington, DC: American Enterprise Institute for Public Policy Research.

1992. "A Congressional Party Must Stand for Something." In *The Democrats Must Lead*, ed. James MacGregor Burns, William Crotty, Lois Lovelace Duke, and Lawrence D. Longley. Boulder, CO: Westview.

1995. "Legislative Institutions and Institutionalism in the United States." *Journal of Legislative Studies* 1:10–29.

Patterson, Samuel C., and Michael K. Barr. 1995. "Congress Bashing and the 1992 Congressional Election." In *Democracy's Feast: Elections in America*, ed. Herbert F. Weisberg. Chatham, NJ: Chatham House.

Patterson, Samuel C., G. R. Boynton, and Ronald D. Hedlund. 1969. "Perceptions and Expectations of the Legislature and Support for It." *American Journal of Sociology* 75:62–76.

Patterson, Samuel C., and Gregory A. Caldeira. 1990. "Standing Up for Congress: Variations in Public Esteem since the 1960s." *Legislative Studies Quarterly* 15:25–47.

Patterson, Samuel C., Ronald D. Hedlund, and G. Robert Boynton. 1975. *Representatives and Represented: Bases of Public Support for the American Legislatures*. New York: John Wiley and Sons.

Patterson, Samuel C., Randall B. Ripley, and Stephen V. Quinlan. 1992. "Citizens' Orientations toward Legislatures: Congress and the State Legislature." *Western Political Quarterly* 45:315–38.

Patterson, Thomas E. 1993a. *Out of Order*. New York: Random House.

1993b. "Trust Politicians, Not the Press." *New York Times* December 15, p. 34.

Peterson, Paul E., ed. 1994. *The President, the Congress, and the Making of Foreign Policy*. Norman: University of Oklahoma Press.

Petrocik, John. 1991. "Divided Government: Is It All in the Campaigns?" In *The Politics of Divided Government*, ed. Gary W. Cox and Samuel Kernell. Boulder, CO: Westview.

Petrocik, John R., and Scott W. Desposato. 1995. "The Partisan Consequence of Majority-Minority Redistricting in the South, 1992 and 1994." Presented

References

at the annual meeting of the American Political Science Association, Chicago, August 31–September 3.

Pfiffner, James P. 1996. "President Clinton and the 103rd Congress: Winning Battles and Losing Wars." In *Rivals for Power*, ed. James A. Thurber. Washington, DC: Congressional Quarterly Press.

Pitkin, Hanna. 1967. *The Concept of Representation.* Berkeley: University of California Press.

Plott, Charles. 1967. "A Notion of Equilibrium and Its Possibility under Majority Rule." *American Political Science Review* 63:787–807.

Poole, Keith T., and Howard Rosenthal. 1991. "Patterns of Congressional Voting." *American Journal of Political Science* 35:228–78.

1997. *Congress: A Political-Economic History of Roll Call Voting.* Oxford, UK: Oxford University Press.

Price, David E. 1992. *The Congressional Experience: A View from the Hill.* Boulder, CO: Westview.

Pulliam v. Allen. 1984. 466 US 522.

Quarles, Benjamin J. 1964. *The Negro in the Making of America.* New York: Macmillan.

Rich, Spencer. 1995. "Democrats Press Attack over Medicare." *Washington Post* October 3, p. 5.

Rich, Spencer, and Eric Pianin. 1995. "Democrats Stage Walkout over Medicare." *Washington Post* October 3, p. 5.

Rieselbach, Leroy N. 1994. *Congressional Reform: The Changing Modern Congress.* Washington, DC: Congressional Quarterly Press.

1995. *Congressional Politics: The Evolving Legislative System.* Boulder, CO: Westview.

Ripley, Randall. 1983. *Congress: Process and Policy* 3rd ed. New York: Norton.

Ripley, Randall B., and James M. Lindsay, ed. 1993. *Congress Resurgent: Foreign and Defense Policy on Capitol Hill.* Ann Arbor: University of Michigan Press.

1997. *U.S. Foreign Policy after the Cold War: Processes, Structures, and Policies.* Pittsburgh, PA: University of Pittsburgh Press.

Ripley, Randall B., Samuel C. Patterson, Lynn M. Maurer, and Stephen V. Quinlan. 1992. "Constituents' Evaluations of US House Members." *American Politics Quarterly* 20:442–56.

Robinson, James A. 1967. *Congress and Foreign Policy-Making.* Rev. ed. Homewood, IL: Dorsey.

Rockman, Bert A. 1997. "The Presidency and Bureaucratic Change after the Cold War." In *Change in US Foreign Policy after the Cold War: Processes, Structures, and Policies*, ed. Randall B. Ripley and James M. Lindsay. Pittsburgh, PA: University of Pittsburgh Press.

Rodriguez, Eva M. 1995. "Case in Point: Edelman." *Legal Times* September 11, p. 1.

Rohde, David W. 1991. *Parties and Leaders in the Postreform House.* Chicago, IL: University of Chicago Press.

Rosenstiel, Thomas. 1995. "Why Newt Is No Joke." *Newsweek* April 10.

Rourke, John. 1983. *Congress and the Presidency in US Foreign Policymaking: A Study of Interaction and Influence, 1945–1982.* Boulder, CO: Westview.

Rowland, C. K., and Robert A. Carp. 1996. *Politics and Judgment in Federal District Courts.* Lawrence: University Press of Kansas.

References

Sait, Edward M. 1927. *American Political Parties and Elections.* New York: Century Company.

Sammon, Rich. 1995. "Television Gets a Welcome From Senate Leaders." *Congressional Quarterly Weekly Report* January 7, p. 19.

Schmidhauser, John R., and Larry L. Berg. 1972. *The Supreme Court and Congress: Conflict and Interaction, 1945–1968.* New York: Free Press.

Schuman, Howard, Charlotte Steeh, and Lawrence Bobo. 1985. *Racial Attitudes in America.* Cambridge: Harvard University Press.

Schwartz, Edward P., Pablo T. Spiller, and Santiago Urbiztondo. 1994. "A Positive Theory of Legislative Intent." *Law and Contemporary Problems* 57: 51–74.

Sears, David. 1993. "Symbolic Politics: A Social-Psychological Theory." In *Explorations of Political Psychology*, ed. Shanto Iyengar and William J. McGuire. Durham, NC: Duke University Press.

Seelye, Katherine Q. 1996. "Dole Criticizes Court Nominees." *New York Times* April 20, p. 1.

Segal, Jeffrey A., Charles M. Cameron, and Albert D. Cover. 1992. "A Spatial Model of Roll Call Voting: Senators, Constituents, Presidents, and Interest Groups in Supreme Court Confirmations." *American Journal of Political Science* 36:96–121.

Seib, Gerald F. 1996. "Lamm Inspires a Fresh Look at Voters' Mood." *Wall Street Journal* July 10, p. A18.

Shaw v. Reno. 1993. 113 S Ct 2816.

Shillinger, Kurt. 1995. "Efficiency-Minded Reformers Hit Snag." *Christian Science Monitor* February 14, p. 1.

Silverstein, Mark. 1994. *Judicious Choices: The New Politics of Supreme Court Confirmation.* New York: Norton.

Sinclair, Barbara. 1981. "The Speaker's Task Force in the Post-Reform House of Representatives." *American Political Science Review* 75:307–410.

———. 1982. *Congressional Realignment, 1925–1978.* Austin: University of Texas Press.

———. 1983. *Majority Party Leadership in the US House.* Baltimore, MD: Johns Hopkins University Press.

———. 1989a. "Leadership Strategies in the Modern Congress." In *Congressional Politics*, ed. Christopher J. Deering. Chicago, IL: Dorsey.

———. 1989b. *The Transformation of the US Senate.* Baltimore, MD: Johns Hopkins University Press.

———. 1993. "House Majority Party Leadership under Divided Control." In *Congress Reconsidered*, ed. Lawrence C. Dodd and Bruce I. Oppenheimer. 5th ed. Washington, DC: Congressional Quarterly Press.

———. 1994. "Parties in Congress: New Roles and Leadership Trends." In *The Parties Respond*, ed. Sandy Maisel. Boulder, CO: Westview.

———. 1995. *Legislators, Leaders, and Lawmaking: The US House of Representatives in the Postreform Era.* Baltimore, MD: Johns Hopkins University Press.

———. 1997. *Unorthodox Lawmaking.* Washington, DC: Congressional Quarterly Press.

Slotnick, Elliot. 1980. "Reforms in Judicial Selection: Will They Affect the Senate's Role?" *Judicature* 64:60–73, 114–31.

Smith, Steven S. 1993. "Forces of Change in Senate Leadership and Organiza-

References

tion." In *Congress Reconsidered*, ed. Lawrence C. Dodd and Bruce I. Oppenheimer. 5th ed. Washington, DC: Congressional Quarterly Press.

1994. "The Congressional Committee System." In *Encyclopedia of the American Legislative System*, ed. Joel H. Silbey. New York: Charles Scribner's Sons.

Smith, Steven S., and Christopher J. Deering. 1983. "Changing Motives for Committee Preferences of New Members of the US House." *Legislative Studies Quarterly* 8:271–81.

1990. *Committees in Congress*. 2nd ed. Washington DC: Congressional Quarterly Press.

Smith, Steven S., and Eric C. Lawrence. 1997. "Party Control of Committees in the Republican Congress." In *Congress Reconsidered*, ed. Lawrence C. Dodd and Bruce I. Oppenheimer. 6th ed. Washington, DC: Congressional Quarterly Press.

Solimine, Michael E., and James L. Walker. 1992. "The Next Word: Congressional Response to Supreme Court Statutory Decisions." *Temple Law Review* 65:425–58.

Solomon, Gerald B. H., and Donald R. Wolfensberger. 1994. "The Decline of Deliberative Democracy in the House and Proposals for Reform." *Harvard Journal on Legislation* 31:321–90.

Starobin, Paul. 1996. "Politics as Theater." *National Journal* October 5, pp. 2102–7.

Steeper, Fred. 1995. "1994 – This Swing Is Different." Market Strategies Incorporated.

Stewart, Charles, III. 1994. "Let's Go Fly a Kite: Causes and Consequences of the House Bank Scandal." *Legislative Studies Quarterly* 19:521–35.

Stewart, Charles, III, David Canon, Greg Flemming, and Brian Kroeger. 1995. "Taking Care of Business: The Evolution of the House Committee System before the Civil War." Typescript, Massachusetts Institute of Technology.

Stiehm, Jamie. 1996. "Lott Tightens Reigns on Post-Dole Senate." *The Hill* July 3.

Stumpf, Harry P. 1965. "Congressional Response to Supreme Court Rulings: The Interaction of Law and Politics." *Journal of Public Law* 14:377–95.

Sundquist, James L. 1981. *The Decline and Resurgence of Congress*. Washington, DC: Brookings Institution.

Swain, Carol M. 1993. *Black Faces, Black Interests: The Representation of African Americans in Congress*. Cambridge: Harvard University Press.

1995. "The Future of Black Representation." *American Prospect* 23:78–83.

Theiss-Morse, Elizabeth, and John R. Hibbing. 1995. "Are the Mass Media to Blame for the Public's Negativity Toward Congress?" Presented at the annual meeting of the American Political Science Association, Chicago, IL.

Thornburg v. Gingles. 1986. 478 US 30.

Towell, Pat. 1994. "GOP's Drive for a More Open House Reflects Pragmatism and Resentment." *Congressional Quarterly Weekly Report* November 19, pp. 3320–1.

Tuchfarber Alfred J., Stephen E. Bennett, Andrew E. Smith, and Eric W. Rademacher. 1995. "The Republican Tidal Wave of 1994: Testing Hypotheses about Realignment, Restructuring, and Rebellion." *PS: Political Science and Politics* 28:689–96.

References

Tucker, R. L. 1971. "Relations of Factor Scores Estimates to Their Use." *Psychometrika* 36:427–36.

Tufte, Edward R. 1975. "Determinants of the Outcomes of Midterm Congressional Elections." *American Political Science Review* 69:812–26.

United Jewish Organizations v. Carey. 1977. 430 US 144.

U.S. Bureau of the Census 1972. *Statistical Abstract of the United States.* No. 600. Washington, DC: U.S. Government Printing Office.

  1995. *Statistical Abstract of the United States.* Washington, DC: U.S. Government Printing Office.

U.S. Congress. 1990. *Statutory Interpretation and the Uses of Legislative History.* 101st Cong., 2nd sess. Hearings before Subcommittee on Courts, Intellectual Property, and the Administration of Justice, of the House Committee on the Judiciary. Committee Serial No. 107. Washington, DC: U.S. Government Printing Office.

U.S. Senate. Committee on Government Operations, Subcommittee on Intergovernmental Relations. 1973. *Confidence and Concern: Citizens' View of American Government.* 93rd Cong., 1st sess. Washington, DC: U.S. Government Printing Office.

Victor, Kirk. 1995. "Mr. Smooth." *National Journal* July 8, p. 1761.

Wahlke, John C., Heinz Eulau, William Buchanan, and Leroy C. Ferguson. 1962. *The Legislative System: Explorations in Legislative Behavior.* New York: Wiley.

Watson, George, and John Stookey. 1988. "Supreme Court Confirmation Hearings: A View From the Senate." *Judicature* 71:186–96.

Wattenberg, Martin. 1991. "The Republican Presidential Advantage in the Age of Party Disunity." In *The Politics of Divided Government*, ed. Gary W. Cox and Samuel Kernell. Boulder, CO: Westview.

Weisberg, Herbert F. 1995. "The 1994 Midterm Elections: A Possible Reappraisal." *Votes and Opinions* October/November, pp. 10–11, 31.

Weisskopf, Michael, and David Maraniss. 1995. "Republican Leaders Win Battle by Defining Terms of Combat." *Washington Post* October 29.

Weissman, Stephen R. 1995. *A Culture of Deference: Congress's Failure of Leadership in Foreign Policy.* New York: Basic Books.

Welch, Susan, and John R. Hibbing. 1984. "Hispanic Representation in the US Congress." *Social Science Quarterly* 65:328–35.

West Virginia University Hospitals v. Casey. 1991. 499 US 83.

Whitby, Kenny J. 1997. *The Color of Representation: Congressional Behavior and Black Constituents.* Ann Arbor: University of Michigan Press.

White v. Regester 1973. 412 US 755.

Wilcox, Clyde. 1995. *The Latest American Revolution?* New York: St. Martin's.

Wildgen, John K. 1988. "Adding *Thornburg* to the Thicket: The Ecological Fallacy and Parameter Control in Vote Dilution Cases." *Urban Lawyer* 20: 155–73.

Wilshire, Bruce. 1982. *Role Playing and Identity: The Limits of Theatre as Metaphor.* Bloomington: Indiana University Press.

Wilson, Woodrow. [1885] 1973. *Congressional Government.* New York: Houghton Mifflin, Reprint, Gloucester, Mass.: Peter Smith.

Wolf, Richard. 1996. "A Lean, Some Say Mean, GOP Machine." *USA Today* September 30, p. 13A.

Wood, Floris W., ed. 1990. *An American Profile – Opinions and Behavior, 1972–1989.* New York: Gale Research.

References

Young, Stark. 1986. *The Theatre*. New York: Limelight Editions.

Zorn, Christopher. 1995. "Assessing the Determinants of Congressional Response to the Supreme Court." Typescript, Ohio State University.

Zorn, Christopher, and Gregory A. Caldeira. 1995. "Separation of Powers: Congress, the Supreme Court, and Interest Groups." Presented at the annual meeting of the Public Choice Society and Economic Science Association, Long Beach, California.

Index

Aberbach, Joel D., 225
Abramowitz, Alan, 94, 99
Abramson, Paul, 84
Acheson, Eleanor D., 203, 205, 207, 208, 210, 211, 217, 219
Adams, John Quincy, 5
Adams Fruit Co. v. Barrett (1990), 232
African-American representatives, 39–40, 44, 47, 51n, 278
agenda setting, 119–21, 140
Aldrich, John, 84, 137, 150, 151
Alesina, Alberto, 87, 92
Allard, Wayne, 278
Allison, Garland, 216
Alvarez, R. Michael, 84, 89, 101
American Bar Association (ABA), 204–5
Americans for Democratic Action (ADA), 43, 44, 237, 246
Andrain, Charles F., 59
Antigone, 7
appropriations; *see* budget process
Archer, Bill, 114, 148
Ards, Sheila, 39n
Aristotle, 6
Armey, Dick, 24, 112, 115, 129, 279
Arnold, R. Douglas, 234
Aron, Nan, 208, 209, 212, 218
Asher, Herbert B., 57, 101
Aspin, Les, 118
assault weapons ban, 50
attitudes toward Congress, 52–6, 60–2
   and voter choice, 97–9, 102–3

Babson, Jennifer, 129
Bader, John B., 157
Baker v. Carr (1962), 33
Baldwin, David A., 252
Balz, Dan, 180, 182
Barbour, Haley, 130

Barr, Michael K., 53, 57, 60, 71
Barrow, Deborah, 198n
Baum, Lawrence, 286
Bawn, Kathleen, 227, 234, 237
Beck, Paul Allen, 101
Beer v. United States (1976), 38
Bem, Daryl J., 58
Bendavid, Naftali, 205, 206, 209, 212
Berg, Larry L., 234
Bergh, Albert E., 5
Beth, Richard S., 140, 141n
Biden, Joseph, 200, 206, 207, 208, 222
Bishop, Sanford, 51
Biskupic, Joan, 229
Blackmun, Harry, 197
Bliley, Thomas, 114, 118, 148
Bobo, Lawrence D., 43
Boehner, John, 28, 131
Bond, Jon, 178
Bonier, David, 24, 112
Bork, Robert, 199, 200, 202, 206
Born, Richard, 89
Boxer, Barbara, 209
Boynton, G. Robert, 57, 59
Bradley, Bill, 277
Bradley, Jennifer, 147
Brady, David W., 14, 150–1, 167
Breyer, Stephen, 197
Broder, David, 190
Broderick, Francis L., 33
Brooke, Edward W., 40n
Brossard, Mario A., 81
Brown, Hank, 278
Brownback, Sam, 278
Brownstein, Ronald, 180, 182
Bruce, Blanche K., 40n
budget process, congressional, 15–16, 21–5, 27, 28, 29, 160, 189, 263
Bullock, Charles S., III, 49n

309

Index

Bunche, Ralph J., 33
Burden, Barry, 276, 285
Burger, Timothy J., 118
Burgin, Eileen, 265
Burke, Kenneth, 7, 8
Burns, James McGregor, 35
Bush, George, 13, 18, 19, 20, 21, 83, 88,
   179, 184
   congressional relations of, 184–7, 220,
   253, 258, 271
Bush v. Vera (1996), 37, 42
Byrd, Robert, 112

Caldeira, Gregory A., 52, 57, 60, 76, 234,
   235, 241
Calhoun, John C., 4
Cameron, Charles, 198n, 237n
Cameron, Kenneth M., 8
campaign spending; see elections
Campbell, Angus, 88
Campbell, James E., 88
candidacy factor, 68–9, 73, 75, 77
Cannon, Clarence, 137
Carp, Robert A., 198n
Carroll, Holbert N., 252
Carson, Julia, 51
Carter, Jimmy, 13, 201
Cassata, Donna, 118n, 129n
Chappie, Damon, 147
Cheney, Richard B., 180
Christian Coalition, 88
Cigler, Allan J., 229
Citrin, Jack, 59
City of Mobile v. Bolden (1980), 37, 38
Civil Rights Act of 1991, 228
Clark, John A., 226, 234
Clausen, Aage R., 159, 252, 276, 285
Clay, Henry, 4, 145
Cleland, Max, 277
Cleveland, Grover, 275
Clinton, Bill, 13, 14, 16, 21, 68, 76, 80,
   86, 88, 91, 105, 154, 175, 177, 179,
   187, 197, 222, 226, 253, 258, 260,
   262, 264, 273, 274, 289
   congressional relations of, 187–95
Cloud, David S., 119, 129, 148
Coelho, Tony, 18
Cohen, William, 278
Collins, Susan, 278
committees, congressional, 121–3, 142–3,
   285
   assignment of members to, 117–9
   changes, 104th Congress, 113–14, 136–
   7, 141–51
   functions of, 137–41
   hearings in, 122–3
   jurisdiction of, 147–8

reform of, 141–5
selection of committee chairs, 118, 149,
   278–9
staffs of, 138
subcommittees of, 139, 151
Committee on Political Education (COPE),
   43, 44
Congress, highlights, 18–30
Congress-bashing, 53, 77, 81
congressional approval, 52–6, 60–2, 68–
   81, 94, 97–8, 102–4, 185, 288–9
Congressional Black Caucus, 46, 50
congressional leadership; see party
   leadership, congressional
Connelly, William F., Jr, 113, 180, 192
Conroy v. Aniskoff (1993), 229
Conservative Opportunity Society (COS),
   113
Contract with America, 14, 15, 23, 24, 28–
   30, 80, 113, 116, 129, 143, 152, 154,
   155, 156–8, 192–3, 264, 278, 281
Conyers, John, 48n
Cook, Timothy E., 110
Cooper, James Fenimore, 11
Cooper, Joseph, 153, 161
Cosgrove, Kenneth M., 49n
court-blocking, 221–3
Cover, Albert, 198n, 237n
Cox, Gary W., 146
Crabb, Cecil V., Jr., 253
Cranston, Alan, 20
crime bill, 23, 28, 50
C-SPAN, 8
Czwartacki, John, 114, 130

Daschle, Tom, 24, 25, 111, 128, 132
Davidson, Roger H., 10, 113, 117, 118,
   123, 141, 148
Deering, Christopher J., 138n, 234
de la Garza, Rodolfo O., 43
DeLay, Tom, 24, 27, 28, 111n, 158, 279
Dellums, Ron, 48n
Dennis, Jack, 59
Denton, Nancy A., 39
Desposato, Scott, 49
Destler, I. M., 253
Dewar, Helen, 119
Dies, Martin, Jr., 11
Dimock, Michael A., 106
Dingel, John, 119, 148
Dionysus, 6
discharge petition, 140, 149–50
discrepancy theory, 58–60
districting, congressional, 33–4
   color-blindness in, 34, 37–42
   racial, 34–42, 48–9
   see majority–minority districts

Index

divided government, 177–9, 199, 258–9, 284, 285
  attitudes toward, 83, 89–90, 91–3
  causes of, 91–4
  effects on elections, 98, 104
  judicial nominations under, 216
Dixon, Robert G., Jr., 33
Docking, Jill, 278
Dodd, Christopher, 24
Dodd, Lawrence C., 234
Dole, Robert, 9, 16, 18, 26, 27, 28, 98, 103, 111, 131, 190, 200, 203, 216, 219, 260, 274, 278
Donovan, Beth, 141
Dorgan, Robert, 218
Drew, Elizabeth, 155, 157, 158
Drier, David, 147
Duncan, Philip D., 4
Dunn, Jennifer, 115
Durbin, Richard, 277
Durr, Robert H., 288

Eastland, James, 201
Easton, David, 59
economic conditions, 89, 99
Edelman, Murray J., 8, 48, 80
Edelman, Peter, 209, 210, 211
Eisenhower, Dwight D., 200
election, confirming, 271
elections, congressional
  campaign spending in, 85–6, 97, 102
  challenger quality in, 86–7
  during the 1990s, 271–3
  effects of attitudes toward Congress, 97–8, 102–3
  effects of economic conditions on, 89, 99
  forces affecting, 84–94, 102–4
  midterm loss for president's party, 87–8
  model of voting in, 94–100, 101–5
  in 1980–92, 13
  in 1994, 13–14, 83–106, 154–5, 273
  in 1996, 81, 271–8
  in 1998, 282
  outcomes of, 272
  presidential, 13, 21
  presidential midterm losses in, 87–8
Enelow, James M., 59
English, Phil, 131
Engstrom, Richard L., 39n
Enzi, Mike, 278
Epstein, Lee, 229
Erikson, Robert S., 87, 154
Ervin, Sam J., 5
Eskridge, William N., Jr., 227, 228n, 229, 230n, 231, 235, 236, 241, 244

Ethics Committee
  House of Representatives, 18, 20, 21, 27, 279–80
  Senate, 19, 20
Eulau, Heinz, 43, 47
Evans, C. Lawrence, 149, 150, 151
Exon, Jim, 277
expectations about Congress, 62–4, 71n; see also expectation–perception discrepancies
expectation–perception discrepancies, 56–60, 77, 283–4
  and attitudes toward Congress, 62–79
  dimensions of, 66–8, 71, 75
  gaps, 64–6, 72, 80
  measurement of, 71n, 72
  in model of congressional approval, 69–79
experience factor, 68–9, 73, 75, 77

factor analysis, 66–8, 170–1
Federal Courts Improvement Act of 1996, 233
Federal Election Commission, 85, 88
feeling thermometer, 59, 60–1, 71n, 76
Feinstein, Diane, 209
female representatives, 278
Fenno, Richard F., Jr., 10, 110, 234
filibuster, 183, 189, 190–1
Fiorina, Morris, 84, 86, 89–90, 91–2
Firebaugh, Glenn, 39n
Fiske, Susan T., 59
Fleisher, Richard, 178
floor debate, 123–5
Foglietta, Thomas, 41
Foley, Tom, 4, 18, 85, 113, 284
Foner, Eric, 36
foreign policy behavior, congressional, 286
  context of, 249–51
  history of, 251–9
  role in the 104th Congress, 259–65
formal models, 12
Fowler, Linda L., 126
Francis, Wayne L., 138n
Franck, Thomas M., 253
Franklin, John Hope, 35
Franklin, Kurt A., 228
Franks, Gary, 41, 51
freshmen, 114, 117, 128, 191, 194
Frickey, Philip P., 235n
Frist, Bill, 124

Garland, Merrick, 210
Gantt, Harvey, 277
Gephardt, Richard, 18, 24, 112, 128, 279, 280

311

gerrymandering, racial, 41–2
Gilliam, Franklin D., Jr., 43, 48, 283
Gilmour, John B., 183, 288
Gimpel, James G., 9, 80, 116, 121, 125
Gingrich, Newt, 4, 9, 12, 15, 16, 17, 18,
    19, 23, 24, 27, 80, 81, 112, 113,
    114, 116, 117, 118, 120, 121, 123,
    128, 129, 135, 136, 139, 145, 146,
    147, 148, 152, 154, 155, 156, 158,
    180, 182, 190, 192, 200, 203, 274,
    279, 280, 281, 282, 284, 285
  ethics problems of, 279–81, 289
Ginsburg, Ruth Bader, 197
Glenn, John, 75
Glennon, Michael J., 248n
"going public," 13, 183, 222–3
Goldman, Sheldon, 198n, 217, 226, 286
Gonzalez, Henry, 279
Goodsell, Charles T., 8, 10
Goodwin, George, Jr., 135
"governing ugly," 195–6, 288
government shutdown, 16, 25, 128, 194,
    195–6
Gramm, Phil, 190
Gray, William, 18
Greece, 6, 7
Green, Donald, 86
Green, Donna Christian, 51n
Grofman, Bernard, 39n
Groseclose, Tim, 140, 146, 237, 246, 285
Gross, Bertram, 8, 11, 12
Grossman, Michael, 181
Gryski, Gerald, 198n

Hagel, Chuck, 277
Hall, Richard L., 148, 150
Hamilton, Alexander, 176
Hamlet, 289
Hamlet, 7, 289
Handley, Lisa, 39n
Hardt, Jan Carol, 112
Hatch, Orrin, 200, 203, 205, 206, 207,
    208, 209, 218, 220, 221, 222
Hatfield, Mark, 24, 119, 120, 278
Hausegger, Lori, 286
health care legislation, 190
Hedlund, Ronald D., 57, 59
Heflin, Howell, 277
Helms, Jesse, 262, 277
Henschen, Beth, 198n, 227, 234, 235, 237
Hero, Rodney E., 43
Herrnson, Paul S., 115, 116, 120, 127,
    131, 153, 189n, 284
Hibbing, John R., 43, 52, 53, 57, 58, 59,
    62, 71, 76, 80, 288, 289
Higgins, E. Tory, 58
Hill, Kevin A., 34, 48

Hinckley, Barbara, 85, 248n
Hinich, Melvin J., 59
Hispanic representation, 39–40, 44, 47,
    51n, 278
Hoagland, Jim, 264
Hodges, Sara D., 58
Hoffman, Theodore J. C., 8
Holt, Pat M., 253
Hook, Janet, 148
Hosansky, David, 124
House Bank scandal, 13, 21, 94
House of Representatives
  African-American members of, 39–40,
      51n, 278
  agenda setting in, 120, 192
  committee assignment in, 117–19, 121
  female members in, 278
  floor debate in, 123–5
  Hispanic members of, 39–40, 278
  leadership in, 111, 113–14
  members of, 109–10
  party voting in, 127–9
  see also Ethics Committee; party
      leadership, congressional
Huitt, Ralph K., 287, 289
Huntington, Samuel P., 57
Hurley, Patricia A., 127n
Hutchinson, Tim, 277
Hyde, Henry, 118, 149

ideological distance, 237–8
ideology, 72, 77, 90–1, 96, 99, 104, 127,
    128, 278
  change in Congress, 154–5, 167–9
  correlation with party, 161–5
  indicated by NOMINATE, 171
  liberal–conservative continuum, 159
  in overriding U.S. Supreme Court
      decisions, 232, 235, 237–42, 246–7
  in voting, 160–1
  see also roll-call voting
Ignagni, Joseph, 234, 235, 237
incumbency, 76, 85, 96–7
Inouye, Daniel, 111
interest group ratings, 43–7

Jackson, Andrew, 5
Jackson, John E., 158
Jacobson, Gary C., 83, 85, 86, 89, 93,
    96n, 98–9, 106, 152, 156, 167, 169
Jacoby, Mary, 117n
Jarvis, Sonia R., 35, 36
Jay, John, 176
Jaynes, Gerald David, 43
Jefferson, Thomas, 5, 12
Jenkins, Woody, 277
Johnson, Haynes, 190

Index

Index

Wilson, Woodrow, 123, 135, 176, 275
Wirt, William, 5
Wolbrecht, Christina, 288
Wolf, Richard, 143
Wolfensberger, Donald R., 138
Wood, Floris W., 43
Wright, Jim, 18, 113, 284

Young, Don, 148n
Young, Stark, 8
Young, Garry, 154, 161

Zimmer, Dick, 277
Zorn, Christopher, 234, 235, 236, 241
Zuk, Gary, 198n